Geometry

Copyright © 2020 by JM EDU.
All rights reserved.
Printed in South Korea.
No part of this publication may be reproduced or distributed in any form or by any means, or stored in a database or retrieval system, without the prior permission of the publisher, including, but not limited to, in any network or other electronic storage or transmission, or broadcast for distance learning. All credits appearing on page or at the end of the book are considered to an extension of the copyright page.
Address all inquiries to: mhpsfc@hanmail.net.

Title:	Geometry Review and Workbook
Author:	Joseph Pak
Design:	Hyoun-Young Lee
Cover Design:	Eunjin Yang
ISBN:	979-11-970670-2-0

www.jmeducation.net

Geometry

Joseph Pak

ΙΧΘΥΣ

Joseph Pak was born and raised in South Korea and moved to the United States during his teenhood. Joseph graduated from high school in Texas, where he discovered his knack for studying mathematics. He received his Bachelor's degree in mathematics at the University of Texas at Austin. Subsequently, Joseph passed a content examination(135 Mathematics 8-12), which certified him to work as a mathematics instructor at Texas Public High School.

Joseph has been teaching U.S. mathematics to students in Seoul, South Korea, for over a decade, during which time he realized a desperate need for high-quality workbooks for his students. He has been researching and developing exquisite content for his workbooks to educate his students more effectively, and to mostly alleviate the hardships students often encounter when trying to tackle new concepts in mathematics.

After years of exhaustive research in math education methodology, Joseph has finally put out a series of comprehensive workbooks that include all of the following aspects:

1. 4-step systematic workbook
   "Concept Example Review Exercise Chapter Test"

2. Detailed explanation for each topic and easy-to-understand problem-solving methods that provide a thorough understanding of the materials.

3. Step-by-step problem structure that enables students to study on their own.

4. Problems that foster creativity and thinking skills, based on a concrete understanding of the concepts.

5. A reliable and effective reference guide to preparing for standardized exams as well as school exams.

Author's Words:

A well-structured workbook plays a critical role in student's learning experience. It serves as a very influential guide for students. I hope this book helps you realize all your inner-inquisitivity in learning mathematics, as well as contribute to the advancement of U.S. mathematics at large.

As a final note, I am thrilled that you've chosen this book to help you on this journey, and please do not hesitate to reach out to us to share your challenges, concerns, and successes. Wish you all the best of luck!

Joseph Pak
JM EDU
B.A. Mathematics —University of Texas at Austin, 2006

CONTENTS

Chapter 1. Preparation for Geometry — 9

Chapter 2. Angles — 17

    1. Introduction to Angles — 18
    2. Angles and Parallel Lines — 24
    3. Angles in a Triangle — 27
    Chapter 2 Review Exercise — 30
    Chapter 2 Practice Problems — 34

Chapter 3. Congruent Triangles — 39

    1. Classifying Triangles — 40
    2. Congruent Triangles — 42
    3. Isosceles and Equilateral Triangles — 46
    Chapter 3 Review Exercise — 48
    Chapter 3 Practice Problems — 55

Chapter 4. Similar Triangles — 61

    1. Similar Triangle — 62
    2. Problems involving Similarity — 65
    Chapter 4 Review Exercise — 71
    Chapter 4 Practice Problems — 77

Chapter 5. More about Triangles — 83

    1. Special Points of a Triangle — 84
    2. Right Triangle — 90
    3. Triangles and Inequalities — 94
    Chapter 5 Review Exercise — 96
    Chapter 5 Practice Problems — 103

Chapter 6. Quadrilaterals — 107

    1. Introduction to Quadrilaterals — 108
    2. Parallelograms — 111
    3. Trapezoids — 115
    4. Rhombi, Rectangles, and Squares — 118
    5. Quadrilaterals and its Diagrams — 120
    Chapter 6 Review Exercise — 122
    Chapter 6 Practice Problems — 129

Chapter 7. Polygons and Circles — 135

    1. Introduction to Polygons — 136
    2. Area of Triangles and Quadrilaterals — 140
    3. Parallelograms and Area — 143
    4. Regular Polygons and Area — 146
    5. Circumference and Area of a Circle — 147
    6. Geometric Probability — 149
    Chapter 7 Review Exercise — 151
    Chapter 7 Practice Problems — 162

Chapter 8. More about Circles — 167

    1. Arc — 168
    2. Circle and its Chords — 169
    3. Inscribed Angles — 172
    4. Tangents — 176
    5. More Angle Measures — 180
    6. More Segment Measures — 184
    Chapter 8 Review Exercise — 187
    Chapter 8 Practice Problems — 196

Chapter 9. Three-Dimensional Geometry — 203

    1. Prisms and Pyramids — 204
    2. Cylinders and Cones — 208
    3. Spheres — 211
    Chapter 9 Review Exercise — 213
    Chapter 9 Practice Problems — 224

Chapter 10. Coordinate Geometry — 231

    1. Lines — 232
    2. Equation of Circles and Spheres — 237
    3. Coordinate Proof — 239
    Chapter 10 Review Exercise — 241
    Chapter 10 Practice Problems — 247

Chapter 11. Introduction to Trigonometry — 253

    1. Trigonometric Ratios — 254
    2. Trigonometric Ratios of Special Angles — 256
    3. Trigonometry and Area — 258
    4. Application of Trigonometry — 261
    Chapter 11 Review Exercise — 263
    Chapter 11 Practice Problems — 273

Practice Problem Solutions — 279

    Chapter 2 Practice Problem Solutions — 280
    Chapter 3 Practice Problem Solutions — 291
    Chapter 4 Practice Problem Solutions — 303
    Chapter 5 Practice Problem Solutions — 315
    Chapter 6 Practice Problem Solutions — 329
    Chapter 7 Practice Problem Solutions — 344
    Chapter 8 Practice Problem Solutions — 361
    Chapter 9 Practice Problem Solutions — 380
    Chapter 10 Practice Problem Solutions — 396
    Chapter 11 Practice Problem Solutions — 410

CHAPTER 1

Preparation for Geometry

Preparation for Geometry

1 Coordinate Plane

Coordinate Plane: The plane containing the "*x*-axis and *y*-axis."

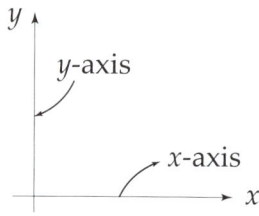

2 Point

Point: An exact location. It has no length, width or thickness. Three points *A*, *B* and *C* are on the coordinate plane as shown in the figure below. A point is usually named by a capital letter in the coordinate plane and it has 0 dimensions.

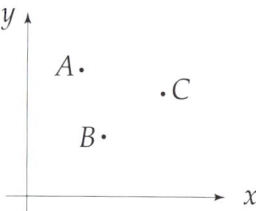

3 Line

Line: A geometrical object that is straight and infinitely long. It has no thickness or width. Line *AB*, denoted by $\overleftrightarrow{AB}$, is shown in the figure below. We sometimes use a lowercase letter to describe a line, such as line *l* in the figure.

4 Ray

Ray: A line with a start point but no endpoint. We refer to the ray as $\overrightarrow{AB}$ in the figure below where the starting point, or origin, of the ray comes first.

5 Segment(Line Segment)

Segment(Line Segment): The part of a line between two of its points, including the two points, called endpoints. In the figure below, segment AB, denoted by $\overline{AB}$, has endpoints A and B.

✓ Lines, rays, and segments are all one-dimensional figures.

6 Congruent

Congruent: Two objects are congruent if they have the same dimensions and shape. The symbol for congruence is ≅.

$\overline{AB} \cong \overline{CD}$

7 Midpoint

Midpoint: The midpoint of a segment is the point halfway between the endpoints. Because the midpoint is the same distance from both endpoints, we say it is equidistant from the endpoints.

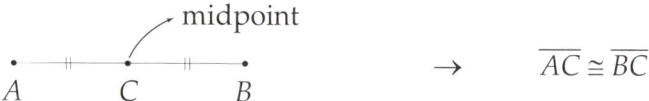

8 Segment Bisector

Segment Bisector: A line, ray, or segment which cuts another segment into two equal parts.

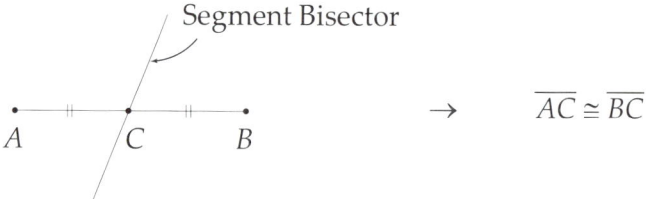

9 Collinear

Collinear: If three or more points lie on a line, as shown in the figure below, we say they are collinear.

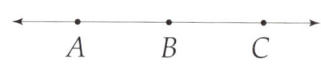

→ Three collinear points *A*, *B*, and *C*.

10 Concurrent

Concurrent: If three or more lines all pass through the same point, as shown in figure below, we say the lines are concurrent

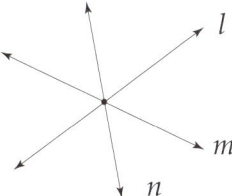

→ Three Concurrent Lines *l*, *m*, and *n*.

11 Plane

Plane: A flat surface, which extends forever, with no thickness. So, it really has no edges. Planes are two-dimensional figures and figures that exist in planes are called planar figure.

12 Coplanar

Coplanar: Objects are coplanar if they all lie in the same plane.

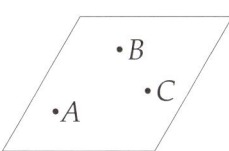

→ Three Coplanar Points *A*, *B*, and *C*.

13 Space

Space: The region in which all material objects are located and we say space is three-dimensional.

14 Postulate

Postulate: A statement that is accepted without proof. Axiom is another name for postulate.

15 Theorem

Theorem: A result that has been proved to be true using facts that were already known.

16 Two-Column Proof

Two-Column Proof: The method we use to present a logical argument using a table with two columns. The first column is used to write math statements and the second column is used to write the reasons you make those statements.

Example of two-column proof:
Prove that the sum of the measures of the angles of a triangle is 180°.

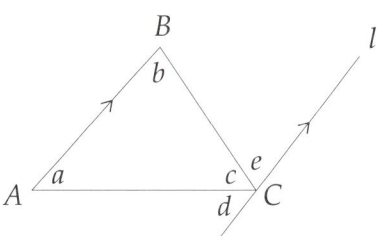

Proof:

Statements	Reasons
1. △ABC	1. Given
2. Draw parallel line l through C parallel to $\overline{AB}$.	2. Parallel line postulate
3. ∠a = ∠d	3. Alternate interior ∠s are ≅
4. ∠b = ∠e	4. Alternate interior ∠s are ≅
5. ∠c + ∠d + ∠e = 180°	5. Definition of straight ∠
6. ∠c + ∠a + ∠b = 180°	6. Substitution property

17 Paragraph Proof

Paragraph Proof: A written proof in which the statements and their corresponding reasons are written, in paragraph form, using complete sentences. Most of the time, we will write proofs in geometry either in two-column or paragraph proof.

Example of paragraph proof:
Prove that $\triangle ABC \sim \triangle ADB \sim \triangle BDC$.

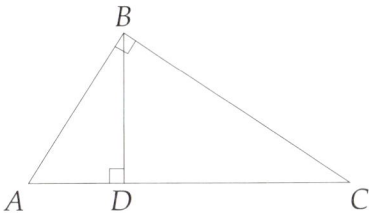

Proof:
Since $\overline{AB} \perp \overline{BC}$ and $\overline{AC} \perp \overline{BD}$, $\angle ABC \cong \angle ADB \cong \angle CDB = 90°$.
If we let $\angle A = x$, $x + 90° + \angle C = 180°$ in $\triangle ABC$ and $\angle C = 90° - x$.
Also, in $\triangle ABD$, $x + \angle ABD + 90° = 180° \rightarrow \angle ABD = 90° - x$.
In $\triangle CBD$, since $\angle C = 90° - x$, $(90° - x) + \angle CBD + 90° = 180° \rightarrow \angle CBD = x$
So, $\angle BCD + x + 90° = 180° \rightarrow \angle BCD = 90° - x$.
Therefore, since $\angle C \cong \angle ABD \cong \angle BCD$,
$\triangle ABC \sim \triangle ADB \sim \triangle BDC$ by AA Similarity.

18 Properties of Algebraic Proof

Properties of Algebraic Proof: Many of the rules of algebra are used to prove various theorems in geometry.

Suppose x, y, and z are real numbers.

(1) **Reflexive Property**	$x = x$
(2) **Commutative Property**	If $x = y$, then $y = x$.
(3) **Distributive Property**	$x(y + z) = xy + xz$
(4) **Transitive Property**	If $x = y$ and $y = z$, then $x = z$.
(5) **Addition Property**	If $x = y$, then $x + z = y + z$.
(6) **Subtraction Property**	If $x = y$, then $x - z = y - z$.
(7) **Multiplication Property**	If $x = y$, then $x \times z = y \times z$.
(8) **Division Property**	If $x = y$, then $\dfrac{x}{z} = \dfrac{y}{z}$, $z \neq 0$.
(9) **Substitution Property**	If $x = y$, then x may be replaced by y in any equation or expression.

CHAPTER 2

Angles

1. Introduction to Angles

1 Angles

Angle: The figure formed by two rays with common origin. The common origin is called **vertex** and each ray is called the **sides** of the angle. The angle in figure below is written as one of the following manner. (∠ABC, ∠CBA, or ∠B)

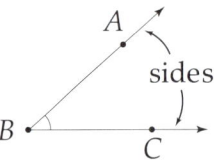

2 Interior & Exterior of the Angle

Interior & Exterior of the Angle: An angle separates a plane into three different parts, the interior of the angle, the exterior of the angle, and the angle itself.

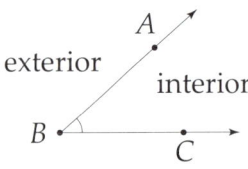

✓ Types of Angle: There are six types of angles as shown below.

3 Acute Angle

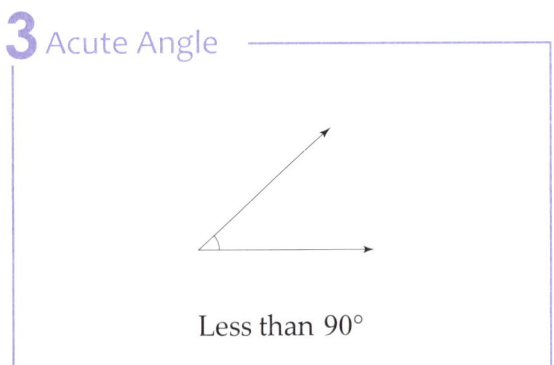

Less than 90°

4 Right Angle

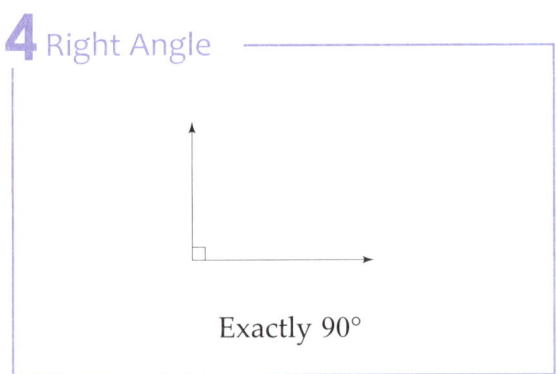

Exactly 90°

5 Obtuse Angle

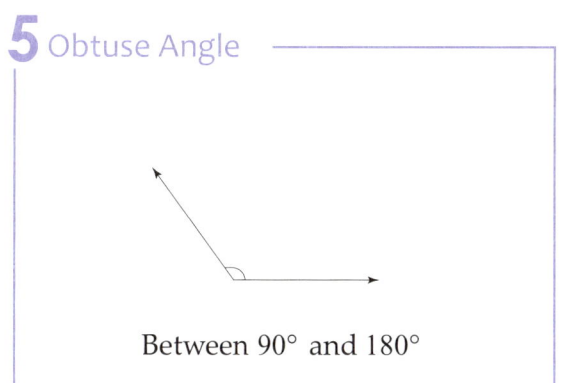

Between 90° and 180°

6 Straight Angle

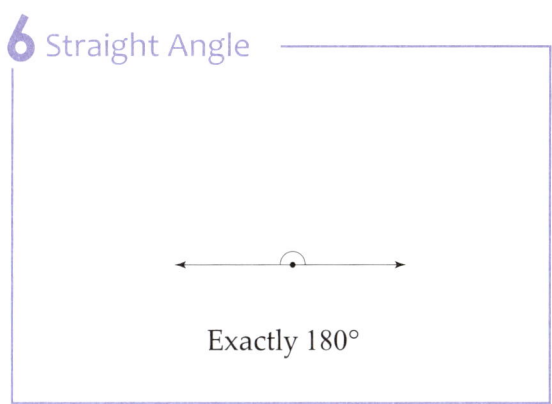

Exactly 180°

7 Reflex Angle

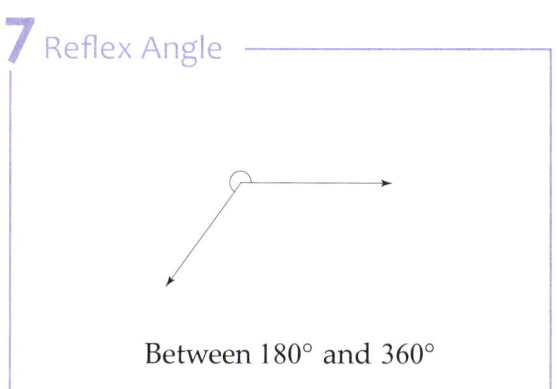

Between 180° and 360°

8 Full Angle

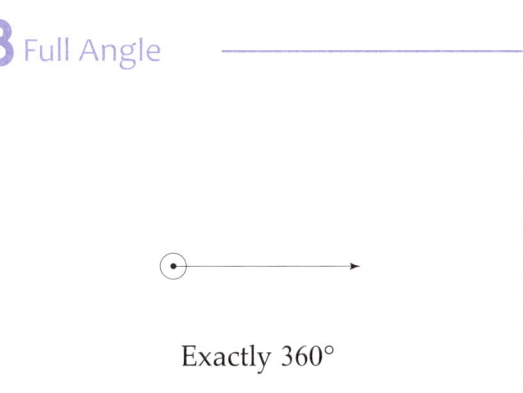

Exactly 360°

9 Adjacent Angles

Adjacent Angles: Two angles that share a common vertex and a common side but have no common interior points.

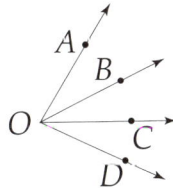

∠AOB and ∠BOC are a pair of adjacent angles, but ∠AOC and ∠BOD are not adjacent.

10 Angle Bisector

Angle Bisector: A line, ray, or segment which cuts an angle into two equal parts.

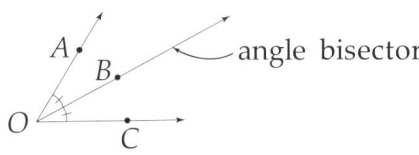

$\angle AOB \cong \angle BOC$

11 Triangle

Triangle: Figure formed by connecting three points with line segments. In the figure below, the points A, B, and C are called vertices of the triangle, and the segment $\overline{AB}, \overline{BC}$, and $\overline{AC}$ are called sides.

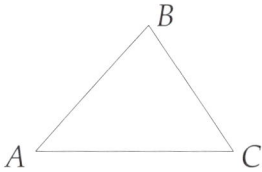

12 Complementary Angles

Complementary Angles: Two angles the sum of whose measures is 90°.

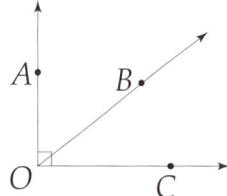

$\rightarrow \angle AOB + \angle BOC = 90°$

13 Supplementary Angles

Supplementary Angles: Two angles the sum of whose measures is 180°.

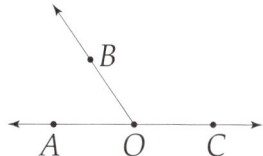 → $\angle AOB + \angle BOC = 180°$

14 Vertical Angles

Vertical Angles: Angles opposite each other when two lines intersect. They are always equal.

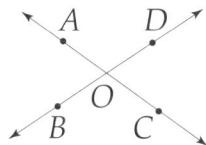

$\angle AOB$ and $\angle DOC$ are vertical angles, and $\angle AOB \cong \angle DOC$.

Proof:

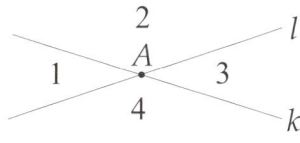

Statements	Reasons
1. Lines l and k intersect at point A	1. Given
2. $\angle 1 + \angle 2 = 180°$	2. Definition of straight $\angle$
3. $\angle 2 + \angle 3 = 180°$	3. Definition of straight $\angle$
4. $\angle 1 + \angle 2 = \angle 2 + \angle 3$	4. Substitution property
5. $\angle 1 = \angle 3$	5. Subtraction property

15 Angles and Transversal

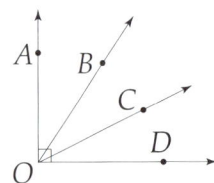

(1) **Transversal**: A line that intersects two or more lines in a plane at different points.
(2) **Corresponding Angles**: ∠1 and ∠5, ∠2 and ∠6, ∠3 and ∠7, ∠4 and ∠8
(3) **Interior Angles**: ∠3, ∠4, ∠5, ∠6
(4) **Alternate Interior Angles**: ∠3 and ∠5, ∠4 and ∠6
(5) **Consecutive Interior Angles**: ∠3 and ∠6, ∠4 and ∠5
(6) **Exterior Angles**: ∠1, ∠2, ∠7, ∠8
(7) **Alternate Exterior Angles**: ∠1 and ∠7, ∠2 and ∠8

Examples

Name two pairs of complementary angles.

Solution

∠AOB and ∠BOD, ∠AOC and ∠COD.

Examples

Name two pairs of supplementary angles.

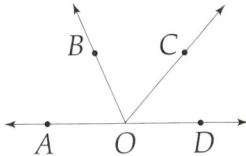

Solution

∠AOB and ∠BOD, ∠AOC and ∠COD.

Examples

In the figure below, find each of the followings.

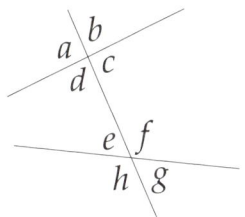

(1) Corresponding angle of ∠b.
(2) Vertical angle of ∠g.
(3) Alternate exterior angle of ∠b.
(4) Alternate interior angle of ∠e.
(5) Consecutive interior angles are ∠c and ____.

Solution

(1) Corresponding angle of ∠b → ∠f.
(2) Vertical angle of ∠g → ∠e.
(3) Alternate exterior angle of ∠b → ∠h.
(4) Alternate interior angle of ∠e → ∠c.
(5) Consecutive interior angles are ∠c and ∠f.

2. Angles and Parallel Lines

1 Parallel Lines

If two lines do not intersect, we say that they are parallel. If lines $\overleftrightarrow{AB}$ and $\overleftrightarrow{CD}$ are parallel, we write $\overleftrightarrow{AB} // \overleftrightarrow{CD}$.

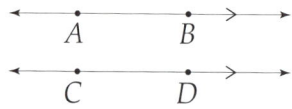

2 Perpendicular Lines

If two lines intersect at right angles to each other, we say that they are perpendicular. If lines $\overleftrightarrow{AB}$ and $\overleftrightarrow{CD}$ are perpendicular, we write $\overleftrightarrow{AB} \perp \overleftrightarrow{CD}$.

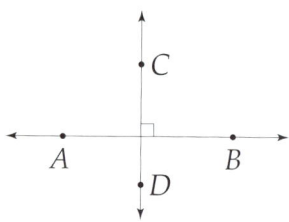

3 Relationship between Angles and Parallel Lines

Suppose two lines l and k are parallel and a line m is transversal as shown below.

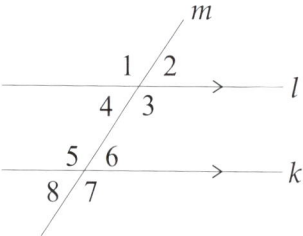

(1) Corresponding angles are equal:
∠1 ≅ ∠5, ∠2 ≅ ∠6, ∠3 ≅ ∠7, ∠4 ≅ ∠8
(2) Alternate interior angles are equal: ∠3 ≅ ∠5, ∠4 ≅ ∠6
(3) Alternate exterior angles are equal: ∠1 ≅ ∠7, ∠2 ≅ ∠8
(4) Consecutive interior angles are supplementary (Angles add up to 180°):
∠3 + ∠6 = 180°, ∠4 + ∠5 = 180°

4 Conditions for Parallel Lines

(1) If two lines in a plane are cut by a transversal so that **corresponding angles are congruent**, then the lines are parallel.
(2) If two lines in a plane are cut by a transversal so that a pair of **alternate interior angles is congruent**, then the lines are parallel.
(3) If two lines in a plane are cut by a transversal so that a pair of **alternate exterior angles is congruent**, then the lines are parallel.
(4) If two lines in a plane are cut by a transversal so that a pair of **angles is supplementary**, then the lines are parallel.

Examples

Find the value of x so that $l // k$.

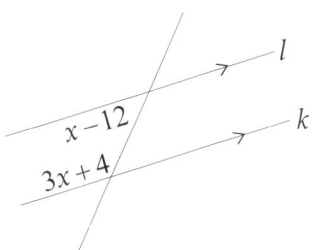

Solution

If $(3x+4)+(x-12)=180°$, then $l // k$.
$(3x+4)+(x-12)=180°$ → consecutive interior ∠s.
$4x-8=180$
$4x=188 \to x=47$
➢ $x=47$.

Examples

If two lines *l* and *k* are parallel, find *a*, *b*, *c* and *d*.

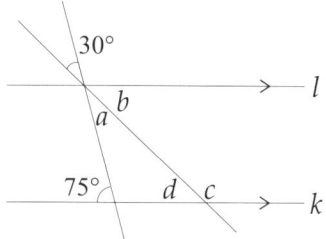

Solution

$a = 30° \rightarrow$ vertical $\angle$s

$a + b = 75° \rightarrow$ alternate interior $\angle$s

$b = 75° - a = 75° - 30° = 45°$

$d = b \rightarrow$ alternate interior $\angle$s

$d = 45°$

$d + c = 180° \rightarrow$ supplementary $\angle$s

$c = 180° - d = 180° - 45° = 135°$

➢ $a = 30°, b = 45°, c = 135°, d = 45°$.

3. Angles in a Triangle

1 Angle Sum

Angle Sum: The sum of the measures of the angles of a triangle is 180°.

Proof:

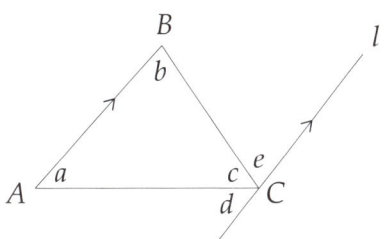

Statements	Reasons
1. △ABC	1. Given
2. Draw parallel line l through C parallel to $\overline{AB}$.	2. Parallel line postulate
3. ∠a = ∠d	3. Alternate interior ∠s are ≅
4. ∠b = ∠e	4. Alternate interior ∠s are ≅
5. ∠c + ∠d + ∠e = 180°	5. Definition of straight ∠
6. ∠c + ∠a + ∠b = 180°	6. Substitution property

2 Exterior Angles

The measure of an exterior angle of a triangle is equal to the sum of the measures of the two remote interior angles.

Proof:

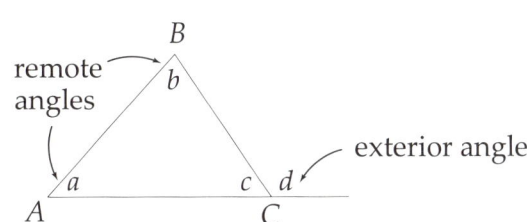

Angles 27

Statements	Reasons
1. $\triangle ABC$	1. Given
2. $\angle a + \angle b + \angle c = 180°$	2. Definition of $\angle$ sum in a $\triangle$
3. $\angle d + \angle c = 180°$	3. Definition of straight $\angle$
4. $\angle a + \angle b + \angle c = \angle d + \angle c$	4. Substitution property
5. $\angle a + \angle b = \angle d$	5. Subtraction property

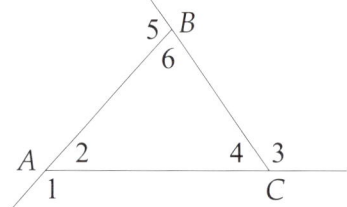

✓ $\angle 1, \angle 3,$ and $\angle 5$ are exterior angles.
   $\angle 2, \angle 4,$ and $\angle 6$ are interior angles.

Examples

If two angles of a triangle are 75° and 40°, what is the third angle?

Solution

Let the third angle be x.
$75° + 40° + x = 180°$ → sum of $\angle$s in a $\triangle$
$115° + x = 180°$, $x = 65°$
➤ $x = 65°$.

Examples

If $l // k$ and $m \perp l$ in the figure below, what is the value of a, b, c, and d?

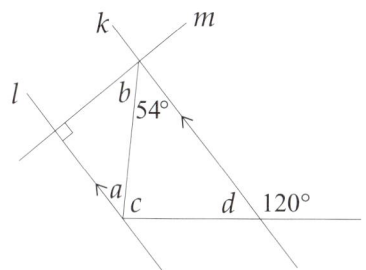

Solution

$d + 120° = 180° \rightarrow$ straight $\angle$
$d = 60°$
$c + d + 54° = 180° \rightarrow$ sum of $\angle$s in a $\triangle$
$c + 60° + 54° = 180°$, $c = 66°$
$90° + b + 54° = 180° \rightarrow$ consecutive interior $\angle$s
$b = 36°$
$90° + a + b = 180° \rightarrow$ sum of $\angle$s in a $\triangle$
$90° + a + 36° = 180° \rightarrow a = 54°$
➢ $a = 54°, b = 36°, c = 66°, d = 60°$.

Review Exercise

1. Find two angles such that

(1) The angles are adjacent and form an angle measuring 120°. The smaller angle is 31° less than the larger angle.
(2) The angles are complementary and the larger angle is 14° greater than three times the smaller angle.
(3) The angles are supplementary and the smaller angle is 24° smaller than one half of the larger angle.
(4) The angles are vertical and complementary.

Solution

(1) Let larger angle be x and smaller angle y.
$x + y = 120°$, $y = x - 31°$
$x + (x - 31°) = 120°$, $2x = 151°$, $x = 75.5°$
$y = 75.5° - 31° = 44.5°$
➢ $x = 75.5°, y = 44.5°$.

(2) Let larger angle be x and smaller angle y.
$x + y = 90°$, $x = 3y + 14°$
$(3y + 14°) + y = 90°$, $4y = 76°$, $y = 19°$
$x = 3 \cdot 19° + 14° = 71°$
➢ $x = 71°, y = 19°$.

(3) Let larger angle be x and smaller angle y.
$x + y = 180°$, $y = \dfrac{x}{2} - 24°$
$x + \left(\dfrac{x}{2} - 24°\right) = 180°$, $\dfrac{3x}{2} = 204°$, $x = 136°$
$y = \dfrac{136°}{2} - 24° = 44°$
➢ $x = 136°, y = 44°$.

(4) Let two angles be x and y.

$x = y \rightarrow$ vertical $\angle$s

$x + y = 90° \rightarrow$ complementary $\angle$s

$x + x = 90°,\ 2x = 90°,\ x = 45°,\ y = 45°$

➢ $x = 45°, y = 45°$.

2. If the ratio of $a:b:c = 3:5:4$ in the figure below, what is the value of a?

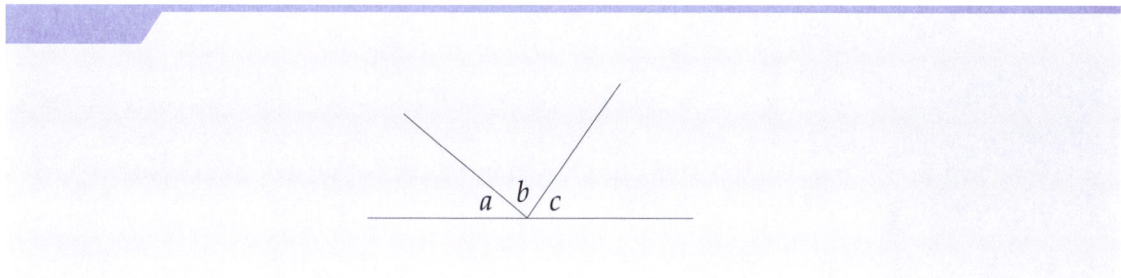

Solution

$a = 180° \times \dfrac{3}{3+5+4} = 45°$ ➢ $a = 45°$.

3. If $l // k$ in the figure below, what is the value of x and y?

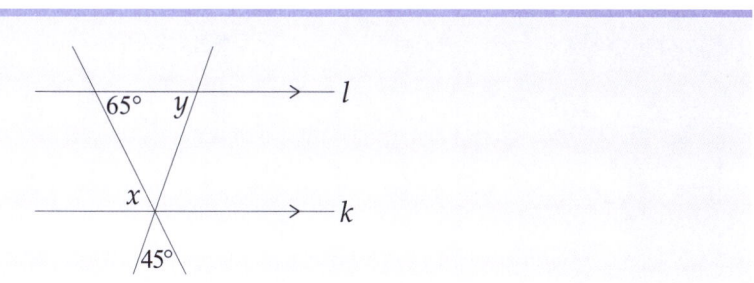

Solution

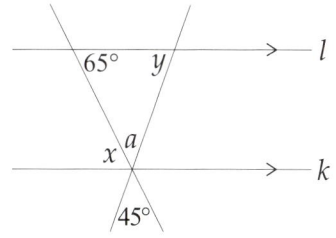

$x = 65° \rightarrow$ alternate interior $\angle$

$a = 45° \rightarrow$ vertical $\angle$

$a + 65° + y = 180°$

$45° + 65° + y = 180°,\ y = 70°$

➢ $x = 65°, y = 70°$.

4. If $l // k$ in the figure below, what is the value of x?

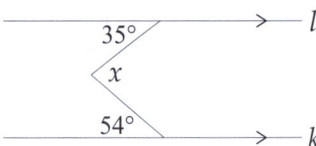

Solution

If we add line m parallel to l and k as shown in figure below, we can do some angle-chasing.

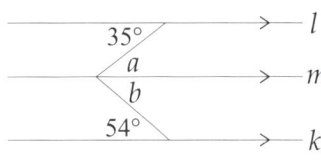

$a = 35° \rightarrow$ alternate interior $\angle$
$b = 54° \rightarrow$ alternate interior $\angle$
$x = a + b = 35° + 54° = 89°$

➢ $x = 89°$.

5. If $l // k$ in the figure below, what is the value of y?

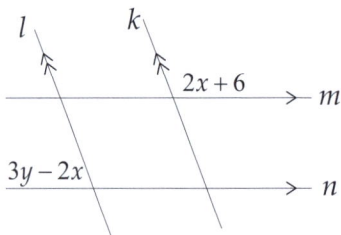

Solution

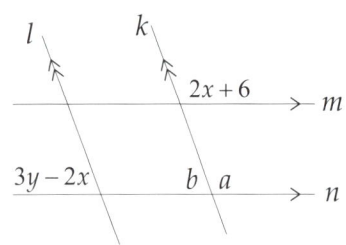

$a = 2x + 6 \rightarrow$ correponding $\angle$s
$b = 3y - 2x \rightarrow$ correponding $\angle$s
$a + b = 180° \rightarrow$ supplementary $\angle$s
$2x + 6 + 3y - 2x = 180°$
$3y = 174°, y = 58°.$

➢ $y = 58°$.

6. One angle in a triangle is three times greater than another angle, and the third angle is 48°. What is the measure of the greatest angle in the triangle?

Solution

If we let the smaller angle be x, then larger is $3x$. Since the sum of the angles of a triangle is 180°,

$x + 3x + 48° = 180°$

$4x = 132°$, $x = 33°$ and $3x = 99°$

➢ The greatest angle is 99°.

7. If $l // k$ in the figure below, what is the value of $x + y$?

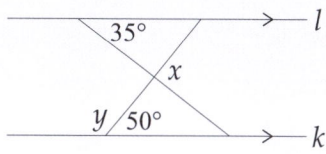

Solution

$y + 50° = 180° \rightarrow$ supplementary $\angle$s

$y = 130°$

$a = 35° \rightarrow$ alternate interior $\angle$s

$a + 50° = x \rightarrow$ exterior $\angle$ of $\triangle ABC$

$35° + 50° = x$, $x = 85°$

$x + y = 85° + 130° = 215°$.

➢ $x + y = 215°$.

Chapter 2

SOLUTION: PAGE 280

Practice Problems

01 Find the value of x.

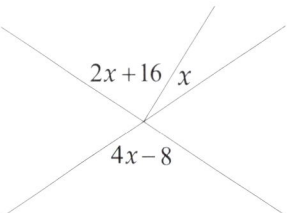

02 If $\angle EOC = 4\angle DOC$ and $\angle AOC = 2\angle BOC$ in the figure below, what is the measure of $\angle DOB$?

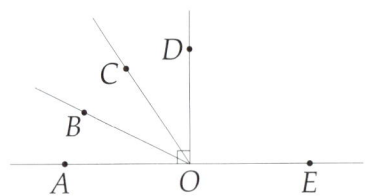

03 Find the value of a.

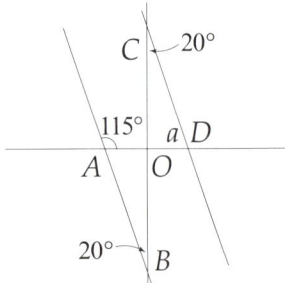

04 Let $\triangle ABC$ have interior angles in the ratio $1:2:3$. What is the measure of its largest exterior angle?

Chapter 2 *Practice Problems*

05 If $l // k$ and $m // n$ in the figure below, what is the value of x?

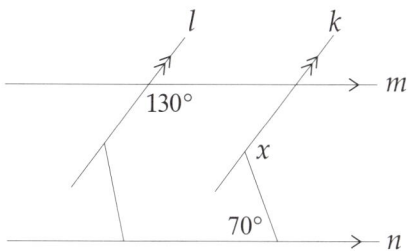

06 If $l // k$ in the figure below, what is the value of x?

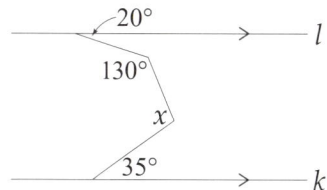

07 If $l // k$ in the figure below, what is the value of $x + y + z + m$?

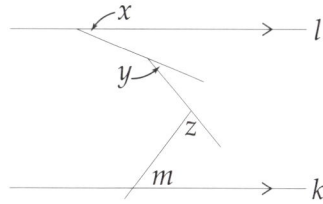

08 If $l // k$ in the figure below, what is the value of x?

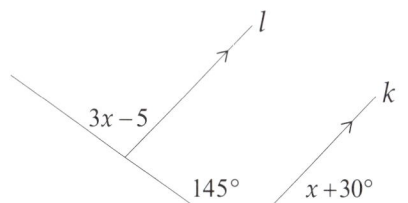

Chapter 2 *Practice Problems*

09 If $l // k$ and $m // n$ in the figure below, what is the value of $a + b$?

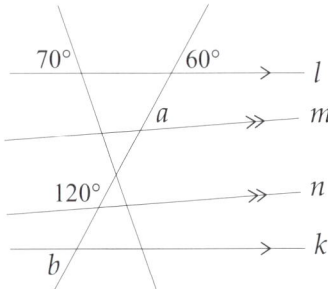

10 If $l // k$ in the figure below, what is the value of x?

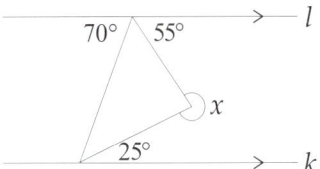

11 If $l // k$, $\angle EAD \cong \angle BAD$, and $\angle FCD \cong \angle BCD$ in the figure below, what is the value of $\angle ADC$?

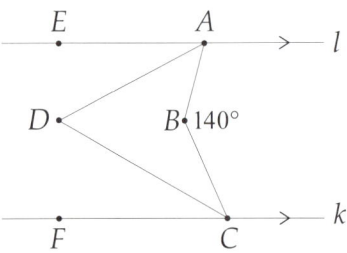

12 A piece of folded rectangular paper is shown in the figure below. If $\angle BED = 92°$, what is the measure of $\angle BFE$?

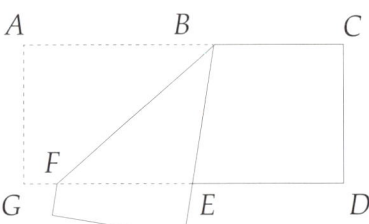

Chapter 2　　　　　　　　　　　　　　　　　　*Practice Problems*

13 Find the acute angle formed by the minute and hour hands of a clock at

(1) 7:30 A.M.　　　　　　(2) 4:35 P.M.

14 Suppose $\overline{AO} \perp \overline{CO}$ and $\overline{BO} \perp \overline{DO}$ in the figure below. If $\angle AOB + \angle COD = 100°$, what is the measure of $\angle BOC$?

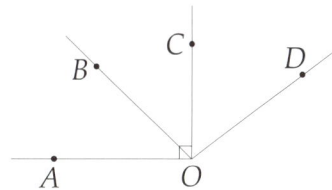

15 If $l // k$ in the figure below and $\angle ABD = 4\angle CBD$, what is the measure of $\angle CBD$?

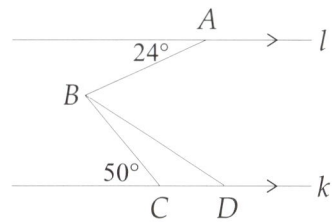

16 If $\angle BAC \cong \angle CAD$ in $\triangle ABD$, what is the value of $a + b$?

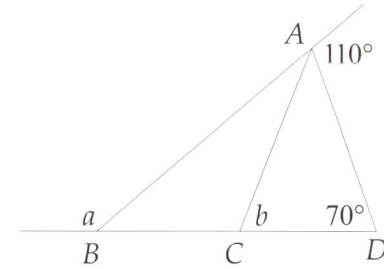

Chapter 2   *Practice Problems*

17 One angle of a triangle is equal to the sum of the other two angles. If one of the angles of the triangle is 30°, what is the measure of the other two angles?

18 If ∠FBC ≅ ∠CBD ≅ ∠DBE and ∠BAC ≅ ∠CAD ≅ ∠DAE in the figure below, what is the value of ∠BCA + ∠BDA?

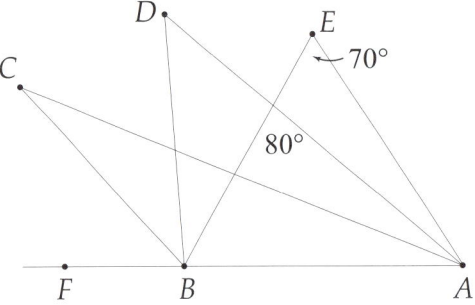

38

CHAPTER 3

Congruent Triangles

1. Classifying Triangles

1 Triangles can be classified by their angles

(1) Acute Triangle

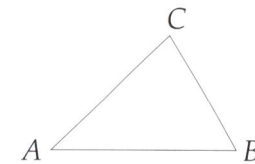

All three angles are acute.

(2) Right Triangle

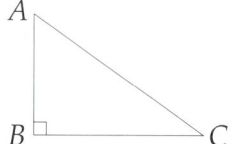

It has one right angle.

(3) Obtuse Triangle

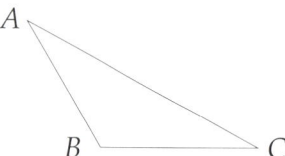

It has one obtuse angle.

2 Triangles can be classified by their sides

(1) Scalene Triangle

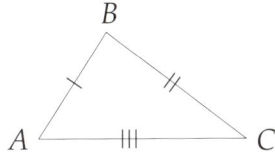

It has no equal sides.

(2) Isosceles Triangle

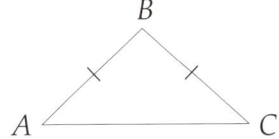

It has two equal sides.

(3) Equilateral Triangle

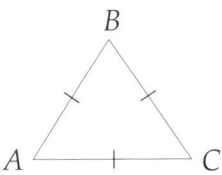

It has three equal sides.

3 Special Parts

In previous chapter, we already introduced about sides and vertices of a triangle. However, in right and isosceles triangles, some of their parts have special names.

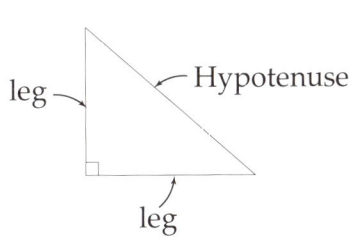

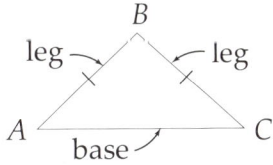

$\angle A$ and $\angle C$ are called the base angles.
$\angle B$ is called the vertex angle.

2. Congruent Triangles

1 Congruent Triangles

Congruent Triangles: If two triangles are congruent, all the corresponding pairs of sides and angles are equal. Conversely, if all pairs of corresponding sides and angles of two triangles are equal, then the triangles are congruent. In the figure below, we write $\triangle ABC \cong \triangle DEF$, which we write the vertices in the same order.

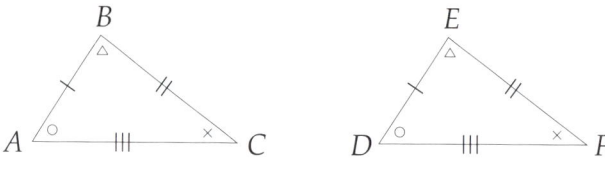

2 CPCTC

CPCTC: CPCTC is an abbreviation of the statement "Corresponding Parts of Congruent Triangles are Congruent." In figure above, $\overline{AB} \cong \overline{DE}, \overline{AC} \cong \overline{DF}, \overline{BC} \cong \overline{EF}$ and $\angle A \cong \angle D, \angle B \cong \angle E, \angle C \cong \angle F$.

3 Conditions for Congruent Triangles

(1) SSS Congruence
If three sides of one triangle are congruent to the corresponding sides of another triangle, then the triangles are congruent.

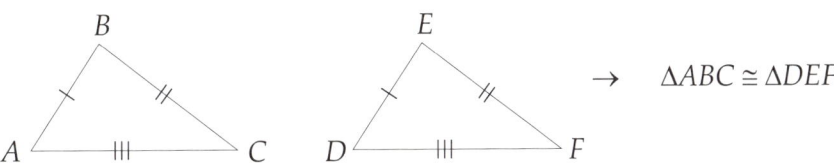

(2) SAS Congruence
If two sides and the included angle of one triangle are congruent to the corresponding sides and angle of another triangle, then the triangles are congruent.

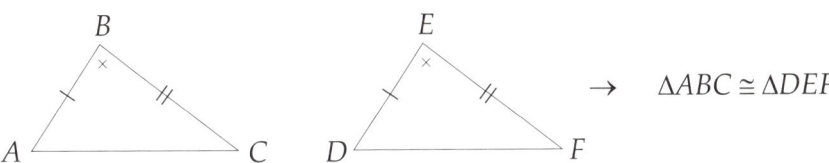

(3) ASA Congruence
If two angles and the included side of one triangle are congruent to the corresponding angles and side of another triangle, then the triangles are congruent.

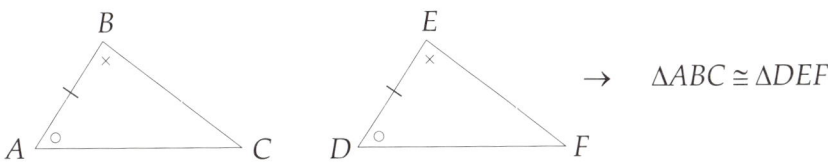

(4) **AAS Congruence**

If two angles and the non-included side of one triangle are congruent to the corresponding angles and side of another triangle, then the triangles are congruent.

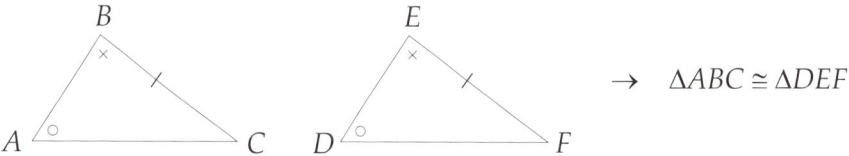

(5) **HL Congruence in a Right Triangle**

If the hypotenuse and a leg of one right triangle are congruent to the hypotenuse and corresponding leg of another right triangle, then the triangles are congruent.

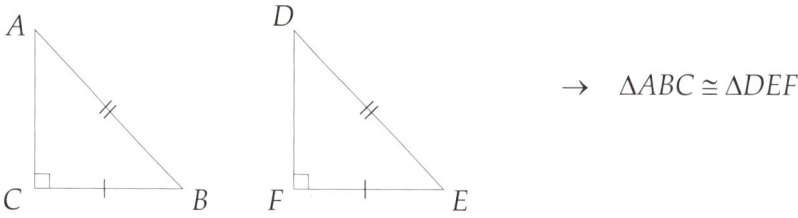

Examples

If $\triangle ABC \cong \triangle PQR$, find each of following.

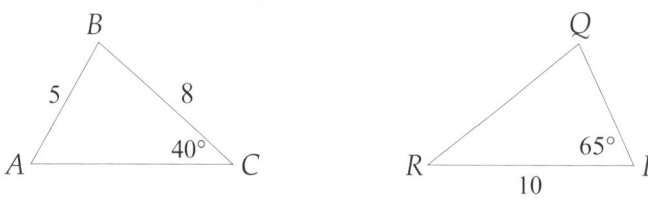

(1) $\angle A$ and $\angle Q$ (2) $\overline{AC}$ and $\overline{QR}$

Solution

(1) $\angle A \cong \angle P \to \angle A = 65°$
$\angle R \cong \angle C \to \angle R = 40°$
$\angle P + \angle Q + \angle R = 180°$
$65° + \angle Q + 40° = 180°, \angle Q = 75°$
➢ $\angle A = 65°, \angle Q = 75°$.

(2) $\overline{AC} \cong \overline{PR} \to \overline{AC} = 10$
$\overline{BC} \cong \overline{QR} \to \overline{QR} = 8$
➢ $\overline{AC} = 10, \overline{QR} = 8$.

Examples

Given $\overline{AO} \cong \overline{CO}$ and $\overline{BO} \cong \overline{DO}$, prove that $\triangle ABO \cong \triangle CDO$.

Solution

Statements	Reasons
1. $\overline{AO} \cong \overline{CO}, \overline{BO} \cong \overline{DO}$	1. Given
2. $\angle BOA \cong \angle DOC$	2. Vertical $\angle$s
3. $\triangle ABO \cong \triangle CDO$	3. SAS Congruence

3. Isosceles and Equilateral Triangles

1 Isosceles Triangle

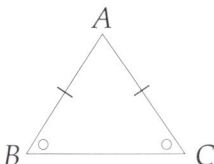

(1) If $\overline{AB} \cong \overline{AC}$ in $\triangle ABC$, then $\angle B \cong \angle C$.
(2) If $\angle B \cong \angle C$ in $\triangle ABC$, then $\overline{AB} \cong \overline{AC}$.

2 Equilateral Triangle

If all three angles of a triangle are equal, then so are all three sides. Conversely, if all three sides are equal, then all three angles are 60°.

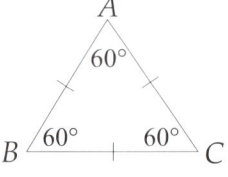

Examples

$\angle A$ is the vertex angle in an isosceles $\triangle$. If $\angle B = 2x + 6$ and $\angle C = 5x - 24$, find the measure of each angle of $\triangle ABC$.

Solution

Since ∠B = ∠C,

$2x + 6 = 5x - 24$, $3x = 30$, $x = 10$

$\angle B = 2 \cdot 10 + 6 = 26°$, $\angle C = 5 \cdot 10 - 24 = 26°$

$\angle A + \angle B + \angle C = 180°$

$\angle A + 26° + 26° = 180°$, $\angle A = 128°$

➢ $\angle A = 128°, \angle B = 26°, \angle C = 26°$.

Examples

Given $\overline{AB} \cong \overline{AC}$ in $\triangle ABC$, prove that $\angle B \cong \angle C$.

Solution

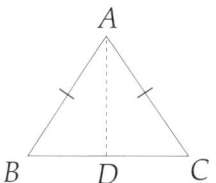

Statements	Reasons
1. $\overline{AB} \cong \overline{AC}$	1. Given
2. Let D be the midpoint of $\overline{BC}$	2. Every segment has a midpoint.
3. Draw $\overline{AD}$	3. Segment can be drawn through any 2 points.
4. $\overline{BD} \cong \overline{CD}$	4. Def. of midpoint
5. $\overline{AD} \cong \overline{AD}$	5. Reflexive property
6. $\triangle ABD \cong \triangle ACD$	6. SSS Congruence
7. $\angle B \cong \angle C$	7. CPCTC

Review Exercise

1. Find the value of x

(1)

(2)

Solution

(1) $\angle BDC \cong \angle DBC \cong \angle C = 60° \rightarrow \triangle ABC$ is equilateral $\triangle$
$\angle DBA + \angle DBC = 180° \rightarrow$ straight $\angle$
$\angle DBA + 60° = 180°$, $\angle DBA = 120°$
$\angle BAD = x \rightarrow \triangle BAD$ is isosceles $\triangle$
$\angle BAD + x + \angle DBA = 180°$
$2x + 120° = 180°$, $x = 30°$
➤ $x = 30°$.

(2) $\angle DBC = 70° \rightarrow \triangle CBD$ is isosceles $\triangle$
$\angle DBA + \angle DBC = 180° \rightarrow$ straight $\angle$
$\angle DBA + 70° = 180°$, $\angle DBA = 110°$
$\angle BDA = x \rightarrow \triangle BAD$ is isosceles $\triangle$
$\angle BDA + x + \angle DBA = 180°$
$2x + 110° = 180°$, $x = 35°$
➤ $x = 35°$.

2. Given $\overline{AB}//\overline{CD}$ and $\overline{BC}//\overline{AD}$, prove that $\triangle ABD \cong \triangle CDB$.

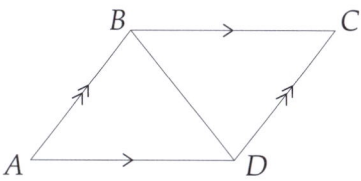

Solution

Statements	Reasons
1. $\overline{AB}//\overline{CD}, \overline{BC}//\overline{AD}$	1. Given
2. $\angle CBD \cong \angle ADB$	2. Alternate interior $\angle$s
3. $\angle CDB \cong \angle ABD$	3. Alternate interior $\angle$s
4. $\overline{BD} \cong \overline{BD}$	4. Reflexive property
5. $\triangle ABD \cong \triangle CDB$	5. ASA Congruence

3. In the figure below, choose two of the triangles that must be congruent and state the congruency principle in each case.

A.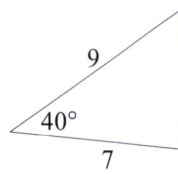

B.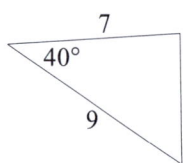

C.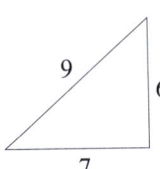

D.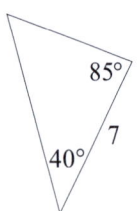

E.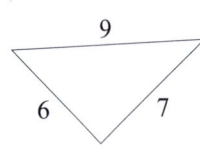

F.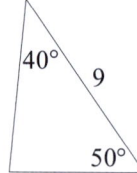

G.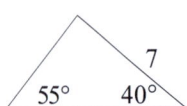

H.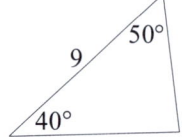

Solution

(1) F and H by ASA Congruence
(2) C and E by SSS Congruence
(3) A and B by SAS Congruence
(4) D and G by ASA Congruence

4. Find the value of x, y, and z.

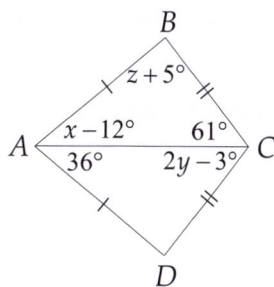

☀ **Solution**

First, it is given that $\overline{AB} \cong \overline{AD}$ and $\overline{BC} \cong \overline{DC}$. Also, $\overline{AC} \cong \overline{AC}$ by reflexive property. So, $\triangle ABC \cong \triangle ADC$ by SSS Congruence. By CPCTC,

$\angle BAC \cong \angle DAC \rightarrow x - 12° = 36°$, $x = 48°$

$\angle BCA \cong \angle DCA \rightarrow 61° = 2y - 3°$, $y = 32°$

In $\triangle ABC$, $z + 5° = 180° - (x - 12°) - 61°$, $z = 78°$

➢ $x = 48°, y = 32°, z = 78°$.

5. Given $\overline{PQ} \cong \overline{SR}$ and $\overline{PR} \cong \overline{SQ}$, prove that

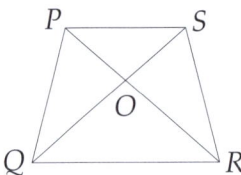

(1) $\triangle PQR \cong \triangle SRQ$ (2) $\triangle PSQ \cong \triangle SPR$ (3) $\triangle PQO \cong \triangle SRO$

Solution

(1) $\triangle PQR \cong \triangle SRQ$

Statements	Reasons
1. $\overline{PQ} \cong \overline{SR}, \overline{PR} \cong \overline{SQ}$	1. Given
2. $\overline{QR} \cong \overline{QR}$	2. Reflexive property
3. $\triangle PQR \cong \triangle SRQ$	3. SSS Congruence

(2) $\triangle PSQ \cong \triangle SPR$

Statements	Reasons
1. $\overline{PQ} \cong \overline{SR}, \overline{PR} \cong \overline{SQ}$	1. Given
2. $\overline{PS} \cong \overline{PS}$	2. Reflexive property
3. $\triangle PSQ \cong \triangle SPR$	3. SSS Congruence

(3) $\triangle PQO \cong \triangle SRO$

Statements	Reasons
1. $\overline{PQ} \cong \overline{SR}$	1. Given
2. $\triangle PQR \cong \triangle SRQ$	2. Proved from (1)
3. $\angle QPR \cong \angle RSQ$	3. CPCTC
4. $\triangle PSQ \cong \triangle SPR$	4. Proved from (2)
5. $\angle PQS \cong \angle SRP$	5. CPCTC
6. $\triangle PQO \cong \triangle SRO$	6. ASA Congruence

6. Given $\overline{AB}\parallel\overline{DE}, \overline{BC}\parallel\overline{EF}$, and $\overline{AD}$ is trisected (divided into three equal parts), prove that $\triangle ABC \cong \triangle DEF$.

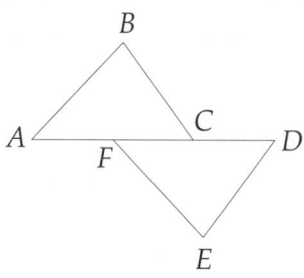

Solution

Statements	Reasons
1. $\overline{AB}\parallel\overline{DE}$	1. Given
2. $\angle BAC \cong \angle EDF$	2. Alternate interior $\angle$s
3. $\overline{BC}\parallel\overline{EF}$	3. Given
4. $\angle BCA \cong \angle EFD$	4. Alternate interior $\angle$s
5. $\overline{AF} \cong \overline{CD}$	5. Because $\overline{AD}$ is divided into three equal parts
6. $\overline{AF}+\overline{FC} \cong \overline{CD}+\overline{FC}$	6. Addition property
7. $\overline{AC} \cong \overline{FD}$	7. Substitution property
8. $\triangle ABC \cong \triangle DEF$	8. ASA Congruence

7. Given △ABC is equilateral and ∠ABD ≅ ∠BCE ≅ ∠CAF, prove that △ABD ≅ △BCE ≅ △CAF.

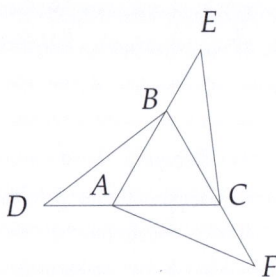

Solution

Statements	Reasons
1. △ABC is equilateral	1. Given
2. $\overline{AB} \cong \overline{BC} \cong \overline{AC}$	2. Definition of equilateral △
3. ∠BAC ≅ ∠ACB ≅ ∠CBA = 60°	3. Definition of equilateral △
4. ∠BAC + ∠DAB = 180° ∠ACB + ∠FCA = 180° ∠CBA + ∠EBC = 180°	4. Definition of straight ∠s
5. ∠DAB ≅ ∠FCA ≅ ∠EBC = 120°	5. Subtraction property
6. ∠ABD ≅ ∠BCE ≅ ∠CAF	6. Given
7. △ABD ≅ △BCE ≅ △CAF	7. ASA Congruence

Chapter 3

SOLUTION: PAGE 291

Practice Problems

01 If two angles of an equilateral triangle have measures $2a - 42°$ and $3b + 15°$, what is the value of $a + b$?

02 If two triangles are congruent in the figure below, what is the measure of $\overline{DE}$?

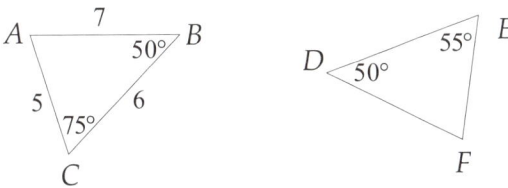

03 Given that $\overline{AB} \cong \overline{CD}$ and $\overline{BC} \cong \overline{AD}$, prove that $\angle BAC \cong \angle DCA$.

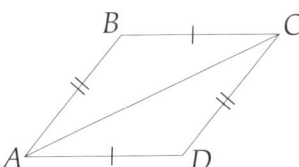

04 If O is the midpoint of $\overline{AC}$ and $\overline{BD}$ in the figure below, what is the value of x and y?

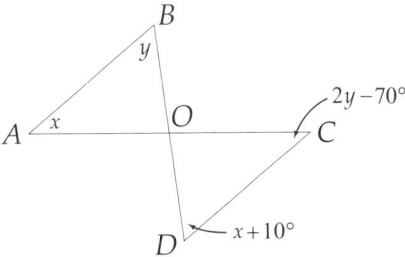

Congruent Triangles 55

Chapter 3 — Practice Problems

05 If $\overline{AB} \cong \overline{BE} \cong \overline{CE} \cong \overline{CD}$, what is the measure of $\angle ABE$?

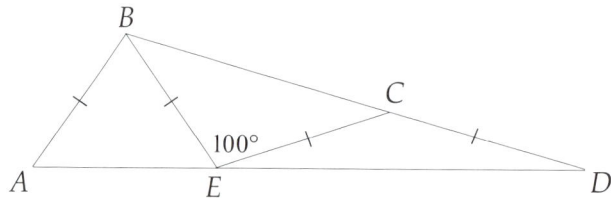

06 Given $\overline{AD} \perp \overline{DC}$, $\overline{BC} \perp \overline{CD}$, and E is the midpoint of $\overline{AB}$, prove that $\overline{AD} \cong \overline{BC}$.

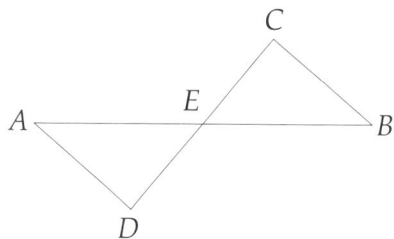

07 Given that $\triangle ABC$ is equilateral and $\overline{AD} \cong \overline{BE} \cong \overline{CF}$, prove that $\triangle DEF$ is equilateral.

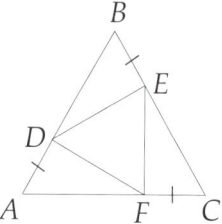

08 If $\overline{AC} \cong \overline{AB}$ and $\overline{BC} \cong \overline{BD} \cong \overline{AD}$ in the figure below, what is the measure of $\angle ABD$?

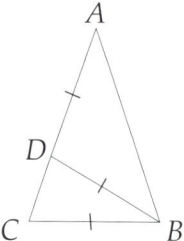

Chapter 3 *Practice Problems*

09 Given that $\overline{AB} \cong \overline{BC}$ and $\overline{AE} \cong \overline{ED} \cong \overline{DC}$, prove that $\angle BED \cong \angle BDE$.

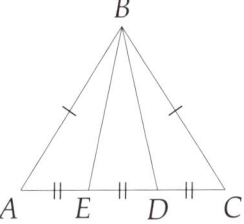

10 If $\angle BDC = 100°$ in the figure from question 9, what is the measure of $\angle EBD$?

11 If triangle ABC is equilateral and $\overline{AD} \cong \overline{BE}$ in the figure below, what is the measure of $\angle BOC$?

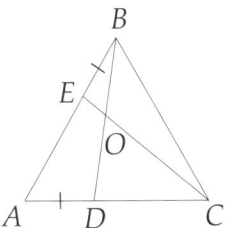

12 If B and F is the midpoint of $\overline{AC}$ and $\overline{AE}$ respectively, and $\angle ABF \cong \angle AFB$, prove that $\triangle BFC \cong \triangle FBE$.

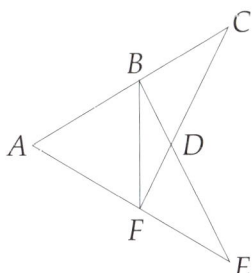

Chapter 3 *Practice Problems*

13 Given triangle *ABC* is equilateral and $\overline{AD} \cong \overline{BE} \cong \overline{CF}$, prove each of the following.

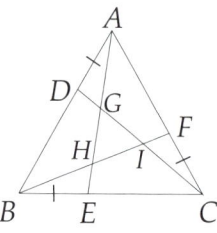

(1) $\triangle ABE \cong \triangle BCF \cong \triangle CAD$

(2) $\triangle ADG \cong \triangle BEH \cong \triangle CFI$

(3) $\triangle GHI$ is equilateral.

14 If $\overline{AE} \perp \overline{EC}$, $\overline{AC} \perp \overline{DB}$, and $\overline{AE} \cong \overline{AB}$ in the figure below, what is the measure of $\angle ADE$?

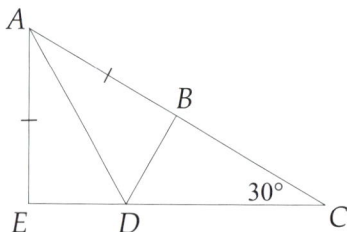

Chapter 3   *Practice Problems*

15 Given $\overline{AF} \cong \overline{AB}, \overline{FE} \cong \overline{BC}, \overline{ED} \cong \overline{CD}$, and $\angle FAD \cong \angle BAD$, prove that $\angle FED \cong \angle BCD$.

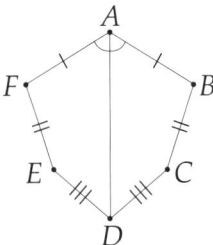

16 Given triangles ABE and BCD are equilateral, prove that $\triangle BDA \cong \triangle BCE$.

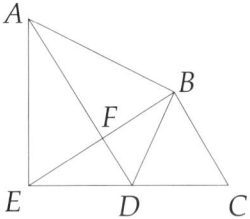

17 If $\overline{AB} \perp \overline{BD}$, $\overline{BE} \perp \overline{AD}$, and $\angle EAF \cong \angle BAF$, what is the measure of $\overline{BF}$?

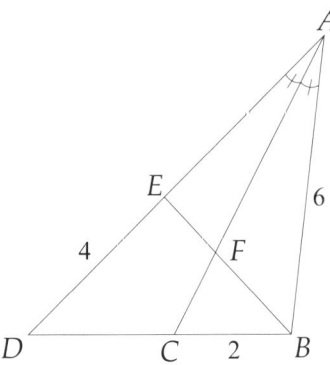

CHAPTER 4

Similar Triangles

1. Similar Triangle

1 Similar Triangles

Similar Triangles: Triangles whose corresponding angles are congruent and whose corresponding sides are in proportion. Similar triangles have the same shape although not necessarily the same size. This definition extends to all types of polygons.

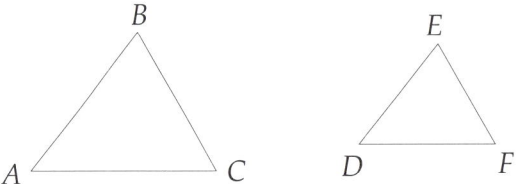

The symbol for "similar" is ~. In the figure above, we write the similar triangles as $\triangle ABC \sim \triangle DEF$ since $\angle A$ corresponds to $\angle D$, $\overline{AB}$ corresponds to $\overline{DE}$, etc. As with congruence, we care about the order of the vertices. For example, we would not write $\triangle ABC \sim \triangle EDF$ to describe the figure above.

2 Proportion

Proportion: An equality of two ratios. The corresponding lengths in similar triangles are proportional.

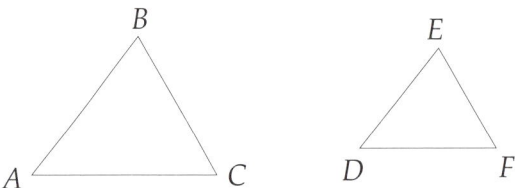

If $\triangle ABC \sim \triangle DEF$ in the figure above, we have $\dfrac{\overline{AB}}{\overline{DE}} = \dfrac{\overline{AC}}{\overline{DF}} = \dfrac{\overline{BC}}{\overline{EF}}$.

$\left(\dfrac{\overline{AB}}{\overline{DE}} = \dfrac{\overline{AC}}{\overline{DF}} \leftrightarrow \dfrac{\overline{AB}}{\overline{AC}} = \dfrac{\overline{DE}}{\overline{DF}} \text{ and } \dfrac{\overline{AC}}{\overline{DF}} = \dfrac{\overline{BC}}{\overline{EF}} \leftrightarrow \dfrac{\overline{AC}}{\overline{BC}} = \dfrac{\overline{DF}}{\overline{EF}} \text{ etc.} \right)$

3 AA Similarity

AA Similarity: If two angles of one triangle are congruent to two angles of another triangle, then the triangles are similar.

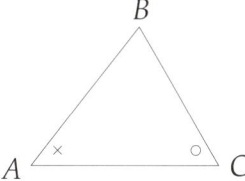 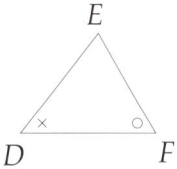

4 SSS Similarity

SSS Similarity: If the measures of the corresponding sides of two triangles are proportional, then the triangles are similar.

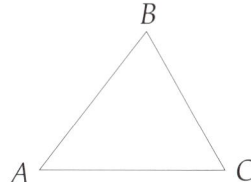 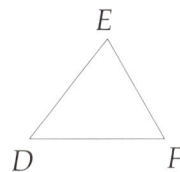 → $\dfrac{\overline{AB}}{\overline{DE}} = \dfrac{\overline{AC}}{\overline{DF}} = \dfrac{\overline{BC}}{\overline{EF}}$

5 SAS Similarity

SAS Similarity: If the measures of two sides of a triangle are proportional to the measures of two corresponding sides of another triangle and the included angles are congruent, then the triangles are similar.

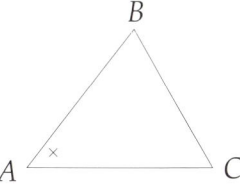 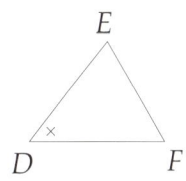 → $\dfrac{\overline{AB}}{\overline{DE}} = \dfrac{\overline{AC}}{\overline{DF}}$

◈ Examples

If $\triangle ABC \sim \triangle PQR$ in the figure below, what is the measure of $\overline{PQ}$?

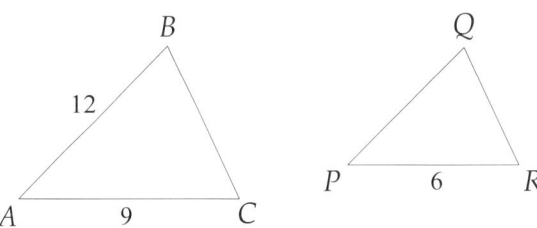

◈ Solution

Since $\triangle ABC \sim \triangle PQR$,

$\dfrac{\overline{AB}}{\overline{PQ}} = \dfrac{\overline{AC}}{\overline{PR}}$, $\dfrac{12}{\overline{PQ}} = \dfrac{9}{6}$, $\overline{PQ} = 8$

➢ $\overline{PQ} = 8$.

◈ Examples

If $\overline{AB} // \overline{EC}$ in the figure below, what is the measure of $\overline{AB}$ and $\overline{CD}$?

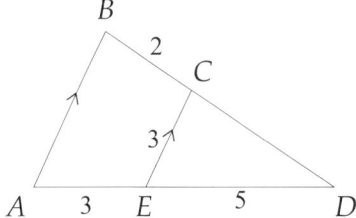

◈ Solution

Since $\overline{AB} // \overline{EC}$, $\angle ABD \cong \angle ECD$ and $\angle BAD \cong \angle CED \rightarrow$ corresponding $\angle$s
So, $\triangle ABD \sim \triangle ECD$ by AA Similarity.

$\dfrac{\overline{AB}}{\overline{EC}} = \dfrac{\overline{AD}}{\overline{ED}}$, $\dfrac{\overline{AB}}{3} = \dfrac{3+5}{5}$, $\overline{AB} = \dfrac{24}{5}$

$\dfrac{\overline{AD}}{\overline{ED}} = \dfrac{\overline{BD}}{\overline{CD}}$, $\dfrac{3+5}{5} = \dfrac{2+\overline{CD}}{\overline{CD}}$

$8\overline{CD} = 10 + 5\overline{CD}$, $\overline{CD} = \dfrac{10}{3}$

➢ $\overline{AB} = \dfrac{24}{5}, \overline{CD} = \dfrac{10}{3}$.

2. Problems involving Similarity

1 Triangle Proportionality Theorem

Triangle Proportionality: If a segment is parallel to one side of a triangle and intersects the other two sides in two distinct points, then it separates these sides into segments of proportional lengths.

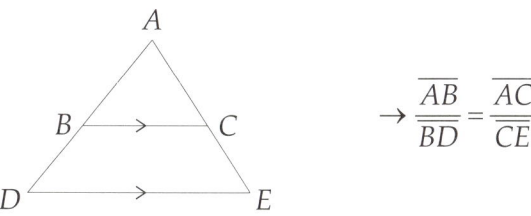

$$\rightarrow \frac{\overline{AB}}{\overline{BD}} = \frac{\overline{AC}}{\overline{CE}}$$

Proof:

Statements	Reasons
1. $\overline{BC} \parallel \overline{DE}$	1. Given
2. $\angle ABC \cong \angle ADE$ $\angle ACB \cong \angle AED$	2. Corresponding $\angle$s
3. $\triangle ABC \sim \triangle ADE$	3. AA Similarity
4. $\frac{\overline{AD}}{\overline{AB}} = \frac{\overline{AE}}{\overline{AC}}$	4. Definition of similar $\triangle$s
5. $\frac{\overline{AB}}{\overline{AB}} + \frac{\overline{BD}}{\overline{AB}} = \frac{\overline{AC}}{\overline{AC}} + \frac{\overline{CE}}{\overline{AC}}$	5. Segment addition postulate
6. $1 + \frac{\overline{BD}}{\overline{AB}} = 1 + \frac{\overline{CE}}{\overline{AC}}$	6. Simplify
7. $\frac{\overline{BD}}{\overline{AB}} = \frac{\overline{CE}}{\overline{AC}}$	7. Subtraction property

➢ Also, note that $\frac{\overline{BD}}{\overline{AB}} = \frac{\overline{CE}}{\overline{AC}} \leftrightarrow \frac{\overline{AB}}{\overline{BD}} = \frac{\overline{AC}}{\overline{CE}}$.

2 Angle Bisector Theorem

Angle Bisector Theorem: An angle bisector in a triangle separates the opposite side into segments that have the same ratio as the other two sides. To prove this, we first construct a line through point A parallel to $\overline{AC}$ and meeting $\overrightarrow{BA}$ at E as shown in figure below.

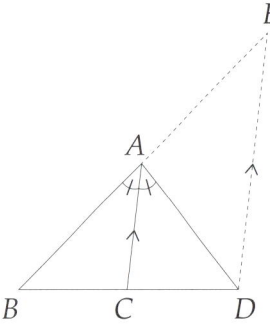

$$\rightarrow \frac{\overline{BA}}{\overline{AD}} = \frac{\overline{BC}}{\overline{CD}}$$

Proof:

Statements	Reasons
1. $\overline{AC}$ is ∠ bisector of ∠BAD	1. Given
2. ∠DAC ≅ ∠BAC	2. Definition of ∠ bisector
3. $\overline{AC} \parallel \overline{ED}$	3. Given
4. ∠BAC ≅ ∠BED	4. Corresponding ∠s
5. ∠DAC ≅ ∠EDA	5. Alternate interior ∠s
6. ∠BED ≅ ∠EDA	6. Substitution property
7. $\overline{AD} \cong \overline{AE}$	7. Because ∠BED ≅ ∠EDA
8. $\dfrac{\overline{BA}}{\overline{AE}} = \dfrac{\overline{BC}}{\overline{CD}}$	8. Triangle Proportionality
9. $\dfrac{\overline{BA}}{\overline{AD}} = \dfrac{\overline{BC}}{\overline{CD}}$	9. Substitution property

➢ Also, note that $\dfrac{\overline{BA}}{\overline{AD}} = \dfrac{\overline{BC}}{\overline{CD}} \leftrightarrow \dfrac{\overline{DA}}{\overline{AB}} = \dfrac{\overline{DC}}{\overline{CB}} \leftrightarrow \dfrac{\overline{AB}}{\overline{BC}} = \dfrac{\overline{AD}}{\overline{DC}}$.

3 Parallel Lines and Two Transversals

Parallel Lines and Two Transversals: Three or more parallel lines divide any two transversals proportionately.

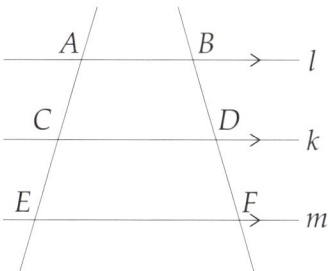

Proof:

First, draw $\overline{AH}$ parallel to $\overline{BF}$. In $\triangle AEH$, $\dfrac{\overline{AC}}{\overline{CE}} = \dfrac{\overline{AG}}{\overline{GH}}$ by Triangle Proportionality Theorem. Also, since $l // k // m$, $\overline{AG} \cong \overline{BD}$ and $\overline{GH} \cong \overline{DF}$. So, $\dfrac{\overline{AC}}{\overline{CE}} = \dfrac{\overline{AG}}{\overline{GH}} \rightarrow \dfrac{\overline{AC}}{\overline{CE}} = \dfrac{\overline{BD}}{\overline{DF}}$.

Similar Triangles

4 Similarity in Right Triangles, Part 1

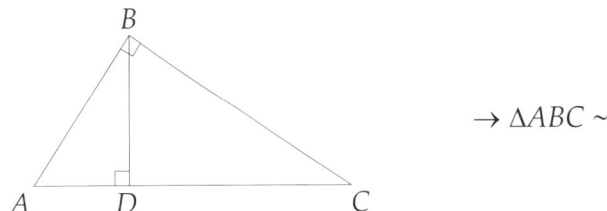

→ △ABC ~ △ADB ~ △BDC

Proof:

Since $\overline{AB} \perp \overline{BC}$ and $\overline{AC} \perp \overline{BD}$, $\angle ABC \cong \angle ADB \cong \angle CDB = 90°$.
If we let $\angle A = x$, $x + 90° + \angle C = 180°$ in △ABC and $\angle C = 90° - x$.
Also, in △ABD, $x + \angle ABD + 90° = 180° \rightarrow \angle ABD = 90° - x$.
In △CBD, since $\angle C = 90° - x$, $(90° - x) + \angle CBD + 90° = 180° \rightarrow \angle CBD = x$.
So, $\angle BCD + x + 90° = 180° \rightarrow \angle BCD = 90° - x$.
Therefore, since $\angle C \cong \angle ABD \cong \angle BCD$,
△ABC ~ △ADB ~ △BDC by AA Similarity.

5 Similarity in Right Triangles, Part 2

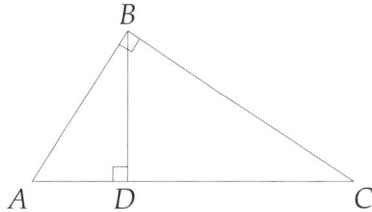

(1) $\overline{AB}^2 = \overline{AD} \cdot \overline{AC}$ (2) $\overline{BC}^2 = \overline{CD} \cdot \overline{AC}$
(3) $\overline{BD}^2 = \overline{AD} \cdot \overline{CD}$ (4) $\overline{AC}^2 = \overline{AB}^2 + \overline{BC}^2$
(5) $\overline{AC} \cdot \overline{BD} = \overline{AB} \cdot \overline{BC}$

Proof:

(1) $\triangle ABC \sim \triangle ADB \rightarrow \dfrac{\overline{AC}}{\overline{AB}} = \dfrac{\overline{AB}}{\overline{AD}}, \overline{AB}^2 = \overline{AD} \cdot \overline{AC}$

(2) $\triangle ABC \sim \triangle BDC \rightarrow \dfrac{\overline{AC}}{\overline{BC}} = \dfrac{\overline{BC}}{\overline{CD}}, \overline{BC}^2 = \overline{CD} \cdot \overline{AC}$

(3) $\triangle DBA \sim \triangle DCB \rightarrow \dfrac{\overline{AD}}{\overline{BD}} = \dfrac{\overline{BD}}{\overline{CD}}, \overline{BD}^2 = \overline{AD} \cdot \overline{CD}$

(4) From (1) and (2), we have $\overline{AB}^2 = \overline{AD} \cdot \overline{AC}$ and $\overline{BC}^2 = \overline{CD} \cdot \overline{AC}$, respectively. Then, $\overline{AB}^2 + \overline{BC}^2 = \overline{AD} \cdot \overline{AC} + \overline{CD} \cdot \overline{AC} = \overline{AC}(\overline{AD} + \overline{CD}) = \overline{AC} \cdot \overline{AC} = \overline{AC}^2$. So, $\overline{AC}^2 = \overline{AB}^2 + \overline{BC}^2$.

(5) Area of given triangle above is $\dfrac{1}{2} \cdot \overline{AC} \cdot \overline{BD} = \dfrac{1}{2} \cdot \overline{AB} \cdot \overline{BC}$. So, $\overline{AC} \cdot \overline{BD} = \overline{AB} \cdot \overline{BC}$.

Examples

If $\overline{BD}$ is an angle bisector of $\angle ABC$ in the figure below, what is the measure of $\overline{AD}$?

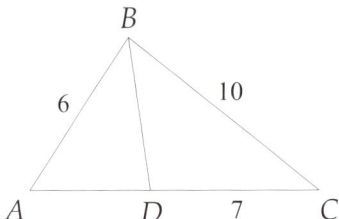

Solution

By angle bisector theorem, $\dfrac{\overline{AB}}{\overline{BC}} = \dfrac{\overline{AD}}{\overline{DC}}$, $\dfrac{6}{10} = \dfrac{\overline{AD}}{7}$, $\overline{AD} = 4.2$

Examples

If $\overline{AB} \perp \overline{BC}$ and $\overline{AC} \perp \overline{BD}$, what is the value of x?

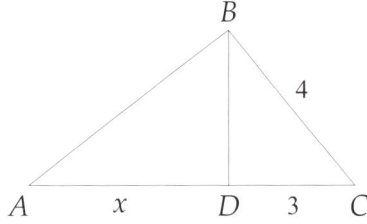

Solution

Using similarity in right triangles, $4^2 = 3(3+x)$, $16 = 9 + 3x$, $x = \dfrac{7}{3}$.

Review Exercise

1. If $\overline{AB} \parallel \overline{ED}$ in the figure below, what is the measure of $\overline{AC}$ and $\overline{ED}$?

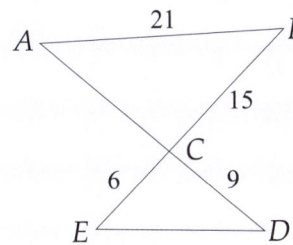

Solution

Since $\overline{AB} \parallel \overline{ED}$, $\angle ABE \cong \angle DEB, \angle BAD \cong \angle EDA \rightarrow$ alternate interior $\angle$s

So, $\triangle ABC \sim \triangle DEC$ by AA Similarity.

$$\frac{\overline{BC}}{\overline{EC}} = \frac{\overline{AC}}{\overline{DC}}, \frac{15}{6} = \frac{\overline{AC}}{9}, \overline{AC} = \frac{45}{2}$$

$$\frac{\overline{BC}}{\overline{EC}} = \frac{\overline{AB}}{\overline{ED}}, \frac{15}{6} = \frac{21}{\overline{ED}}, \overline{ED} = \frac{42}{5}$$

➤ $\overline{AC} = \frac{45}{2}, \overline{ED} = \frac{42}{5}.$

2. If the perimeter of $\triangle ABD$ is 22 in the figure below, what is the measure of $\overline{AC}$?

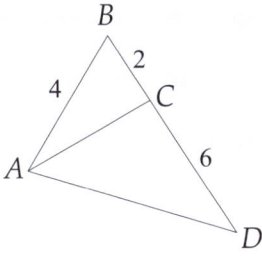

Solution

$\dfrac{\overline{AB}}{\overline{BC}} = \dfrac{4}{2} = 2$, $\dfrac{\overline{BD}}{\overline{AB}} = \dfrac{2+6}{4} = 2$, and $\angle ABC \cong \angle DBA$

$\rightarrow \triangle BAC \sim \triangle BDA$ by SAS Similarity.

Since $\overline{AB} + \overline{BD} + \overline{AD} = 22$, $\overline{AD} = 22 - 4 - 8 = 10$.

Now, $\dfrac{\overline{AB}}{\overline{BD}} = \dfrac{\overline{AC}}{\overline{AD}}$, $\dfrac{4}{8} = \dfrac{\overline{AC}}{10}$, $\overline{AC} = 5.$ ➤ $\overline{AC} = 5.$

3. Given $\overline{AB}//\overline{FC}$ and $\overline{AE}//\overline{BC}$, prove that

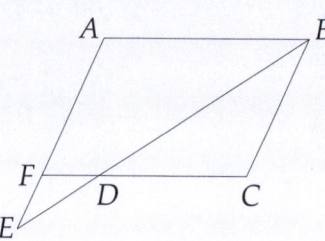

(1) $\triangle FED \sim \triangle AEB$ (2) $\triangle FED \sim \triangle CBD$

Solution

(1) $\triangle FED \sim \triangle AEB$

Statements	Reasons
1. $\overline{AB}//\overline{FC}$	1. Given
2. $\angle EDF \cong \angle EBA$	2. Corresponding $\angle$s
3. $\angle FED \cong \angle AEB$	3. A shared $\angle$
4. $\triangle FED \sim \triangle AEB$	4. AA Similarity

(2) $\triangle FED \sim \triangle CBD$

Statements	Reasons
1. $\overline{AE}//\overline{BC}$	1. Given
2. $\angle FED \cong \angle CBD$	2. Alternate interior $\angle$s
3. $\angle EDF \cong \angle BDC$	3. Vertical $\angle$s
4. $\triangle FED \sim \triangle CBD$	4. AA Similarity

4. If $\overline{AD} \perp \overline{BE}$ in $\overline{BD} \perp \overline{AC}$ the figure below, what is the measure of $\overline{AE}$?

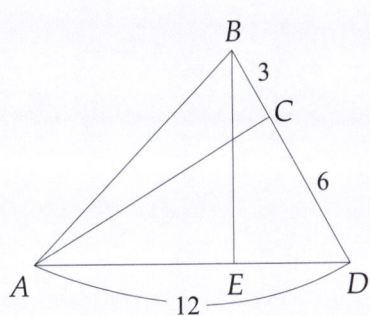

Solution

Since $\overline{AD} \perp \overline{BE}$ and $\overline{BD} \perp \overline{AC}$, $\angle DCA \cong \angle DEB = 90°$.
Also, $\angle ADC \cong \angle BDE \rightarrow$ A shared angle.
So, $\triangle ADC \sim \triangle BDE$ by AA Similarity.
Now, $\dfrac{\overline{DC}}{\overline{DE}} = \dfrac{\overline{AD}}{\overline{BD}}$, $\dfrac{6}{\overline{DE}} = \dfrac{12}{3+6}$, $\overline{DE} = \dfrac{9}{2}$.
Therefore, $\overline{AE} = \overline{AD} - \overline{DE} = 12 - \dfrac{9}{2} = \dfrac{15}{2}$.

➢ $\overline{AE} = \dfrac{15}{2}$.

5. Points D and E are points of $\overline{AB}$ and $\overline{CB}$, respectively, such that $\overline{AC} // \overline{DE}$. If $\overline{BD} = 6, \overline{DA} = 4, \overline{BE} = 4$, what is the measure of $\overline{EC}$?

Solution

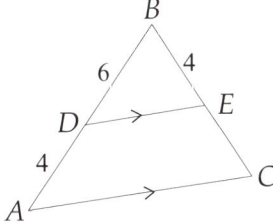

$\triangle BDE \sim \triangle BAC$ by AA Similarity $\rightarrow \dfrac{\overline{BD}}{\overline{DA}} = \dfrac{\overline{BE}}{\overline{EC}}$, $\dfrac{6}{4} = \dfrac{4}{\overline{EC}}$, $\overline{EC} = \dfrac{8}{3}$

➢ $\overline{EC} = \dfrac{8}{3}$.

6. Find the value of a and b.

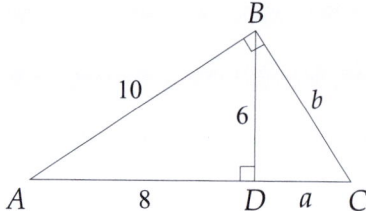

Solution

Using the formula from similarity in right triangles part 2, we have
$10^2 = 8(8+a)$, $\dfrac{25}{2} = 8+a$, $a = \dfrac{9}{2}$

$b^2 = a(a+8)$, $b^2 = \dfrac{9}{2}\left(\dfrac{9}{2}+8\right)$, $b = \dfrac{15}{2}$

➢ $a = \dfrac{9}{2}, b = \dfrac{15}{2}.$

7. If $\overline{AB}\,\|\,\overline{GC}\,\|\,\overline{ED}$ and $\overline{AB},\overline{GC},\overline{ED}$ are perpendicular to $\overline{AE}$, what is the measure of $\overline{CG}$?

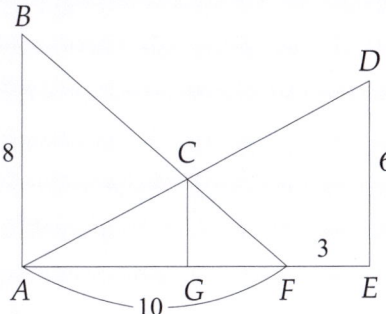

Solution

Let $\overline{CG}$ and $\overline{AG}$ be x and y, respectively.

Since $\overline{AB}\,\|\,\overline{GC}$, $\angle ABF \cong \angle GCF \rightarrow$ Corresponding $\angle$s.
So, $\triangle FCG \sim \triangle FBA$ by AA Similarity.

(1) $\dfrac{\overline{CG}}{\overline{BA}} = \dfrac{\overline{FG}}{\overline{FA}},\ \dfrac{x}{8} = \dfrac{10-y}{10},\ 10x = 8(10-y).$

Since $\overline{GC}\,\|\,\overline{ED}$, $\angle GCA \cong \angle EDA \rightarrow$ Corresponding $\angle$s.
So, $\triangle ACG \sim \triangle ADE$ by AA Similarity.

(2) $\dfrac{\overline{CG}}{\overline{DE}} = \dfrac{\overline{AG}}{\overline{AE}},\ \dfrac{x}{6} = \dfrac{y}{10+3}, 13x = 6y, y = \dfrac{13x}{6}$

By substituting (2) into (1), we have
$10x = 8\left(10 - \dfrac{13x}{6}\right),\ x = 8 - \dfrac{26x}{15}, \dfrac{41x}{15} = 10,\ x = \dfrac{120}{41}.$

➢ $\overline{CG} = \dfrac{120}{41}.$

8. Given $\overline{AD} \perp \overline{DC}$ and $\overline{BC} \perp \overline{DC}$, prove that $\triangle AED \sim \triangle CEB$.

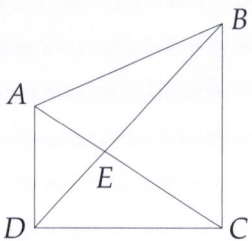

Solution

Statements	Reasons
1. $\overline{AD} \perp \overline{DC}, \overline{BC} \perp \overline{DC}$	1. Given
2. $\angle ADC \cong \angle BCD = 90°$	2. Definition of $\perp$ lines
3. $\overline{AD} \parallel \overline{BC}$	3. Because $\angle ADC \cong \angle BCD$
4. $\angle ADE \cong \angle CBE$	4. Alternate interior $\angle$s
5. $\angle AED \cong \angle CED$	5. Vertical $\angle$s
6. $\triangle AED \sim \triangle CEB$	6. AA Similarity

Chapter 4

SOLUTION: PAGE 303

Practice Problems

01 Find the value of x in each of the following.

(1)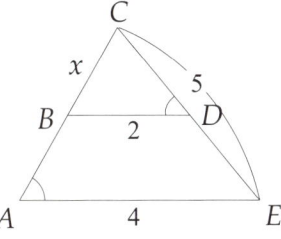

(2)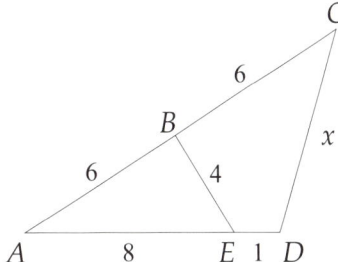

(3)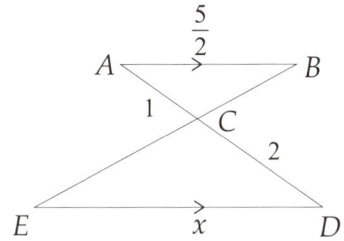

(4)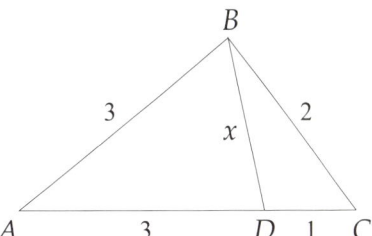

(5)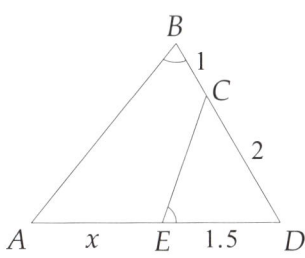

(6) 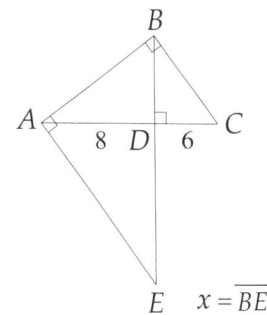 $x = \overline{BE}$

(7)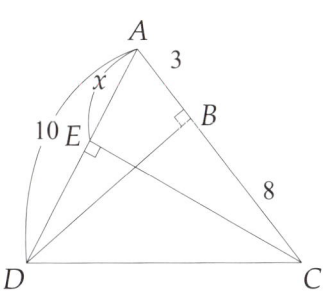

(8)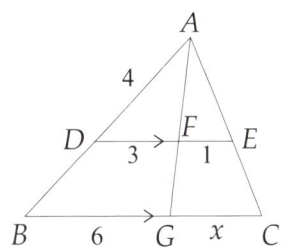

Similar Triangles 77

Chapter 4 — Practice Problems

02 If $\overline{AB} \parallel \overline{EF} \parallel \overline{CD}$ and $\dfrac{\overline{AE}}{\overline{EC}} = \dfrac{4}{3}$, what is the measure of $\overline{CD}$?

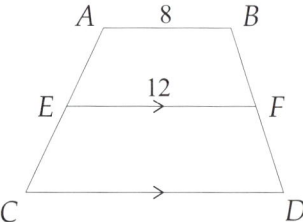

03 The triangle has side lengths of 3 inches, 4 inches, and 6 inches. If one of the side lengths of a similar triangle is 12 inches, what is the minimum number of inches possible in the perimeter of this similar triangle?

04 Points C and F are midpoints of $\overline{GD}$ and $\overline{AE}$, respectively, such that $\overline{AG} \parallel \overline{CF} \parallel \overline{DE}$. What is the measure of $\overline{DE}$?

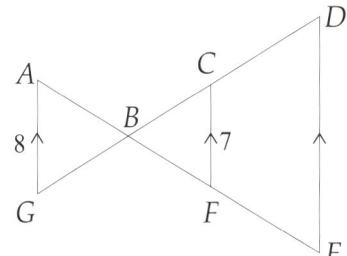

05 If $\overline{AC} \perp \overline{BD}$ and $\overline{AB} \perp \overline{BC}$, what is the measure of $\overline{BD}$?

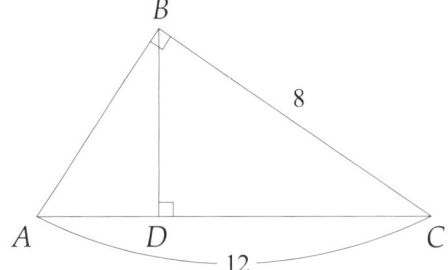

Chapter 4 *Practice Problems*

06 In the figure below, what is the measure of $\overline{CF}$?

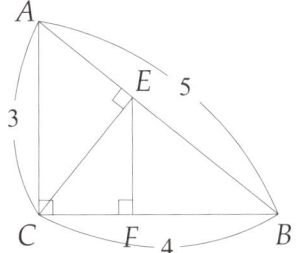

07 Given $\overline{AE} \perp \overline{CF}$ and $\overline{AC} \perp \overline{EB}$, prove that △CBD ~ △EFD ~ △CFA ~ △EBA.

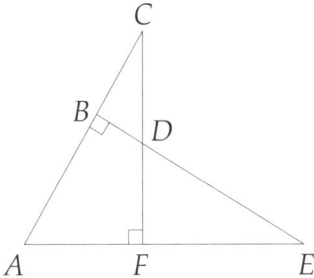

08 If $\overline{AB} \text{//} \overline{EF} \text{//} \overline{CD}$, what is the measure of $\overline{EF}$?

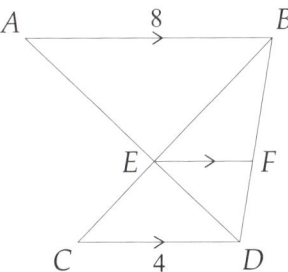

09 If a piece of rectangular paper is folded as shown in the figure below, what is the measure of $\overline{FC}$?

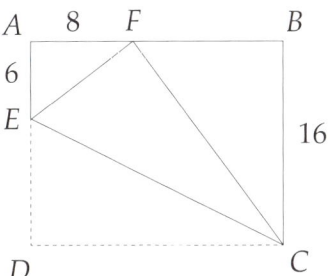

Similar Triangles 79

Chapter 4 — *Practice Problems*

10 If $\overline{AD}$ and $\overline{BE}$ are angle bisectors of ∠BAC and ∠ABC, respectively, what is the measure of $\overline{BD}$?

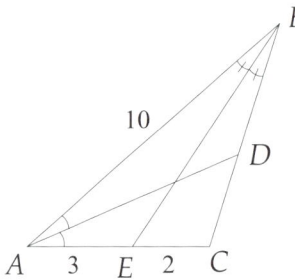

11 Given $\overline{AB} \parallel \overline{DE}$ and $\overline{BC} \parallel \overline{EF}$, prove that △ABC ~ △DEF.

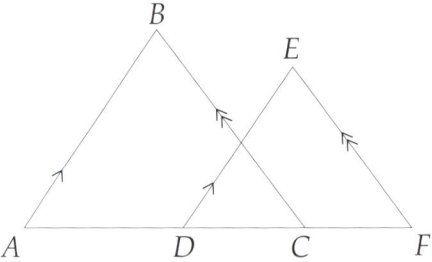

12 Given $\overline{AE} \perp \overline{AC}, \overline{AD} \perp \overline{DE}, \overline{AC} \cong \overline{AD}$, and $\overline{EB}$ is an angle bisector of ∠AED, prove that ∠ABF ≅ ∠AFB.

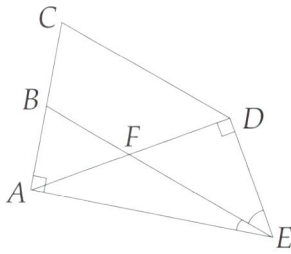

13 If △ABC ~ △CDE, what is the measure of $\overline{BF}$?

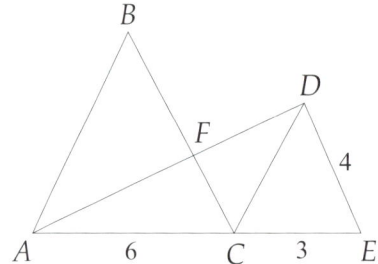

Chapter 4 — Practice Problems

14 In the figure below, a triangle *ACE* is equilateral and △*AFB* ≅ △*DFB*.

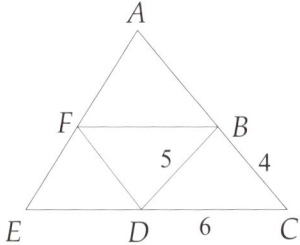

(1) Prove that △*EDF* ~ △*CBD*. (2) Find the measure of $\overline{DF}$.

15 If ∠*BAE* ≅ ∠*CBF* ≅ ∠*ACD*, what is the ratio of $\overline{DE}$ to $\overline{EF}$?

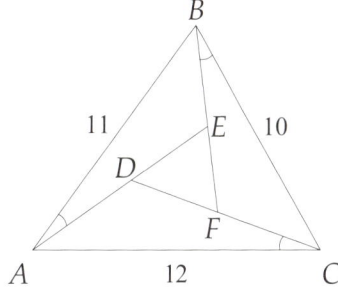

Similar Triangles 81

CHAPTER 5

More about Triangles

1. Special Points of a Triangle

1 Circumcenter

(1) Definiton: **Circumcenter** is the point where the three perpendicular bisectors of a triangle intersect. The circle centered at the circumcenter that passes through the vertices of the triangle is called the **circumcircle** of the triangle because it is **circumscribed** about the triangle. The radius of this circle is called the **circumradius**.

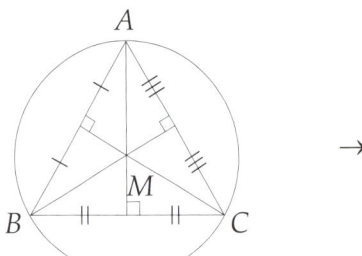

→ Point M is the circumcenter.
$\overline{AM}, \overline{AM}$, and $\overline{AM}$ are circumradius.

Proof:

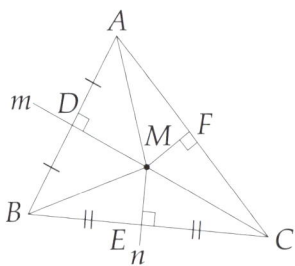

Draw two perpendicular bisector m and n that meet at M as shown in figure above. Since m is the perpendicular bisector, $\overline{AD} \cong \overline{BD}$ and $\angle ADM \cong \angle BDM = 90°$. Also, since $\overline{DM} \cong \overline{DM}$ by reflexive property, $\triangle ADM \cong \triangle BDM$ by SAS Congruence. So, $\overline{AM} \cong \overline{BM}$ by CPCTC. In the same manner, $\triangle BEM \cong \triangle CEM \rightarrow \overline{BM} \cong \overline{CM}$ and $\triangle CFM \cong \triangle AFM \rightarrow \overline{CM} \cong \overline{AM}$. Therefore, $\overline{AM} \cong \overline{BM} \cong \overline{CM}$. Now, if we draw a circle with center M and radius $\overline{AM}$, the circle will pass through all A, B, and C.

(2) **Circumcenter of a Right Triangle**: The circumcenter lies exactly at the midpoint of the hypotenuse.

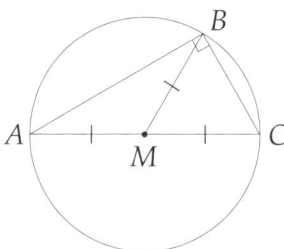

2 Incenter

(1) **Definition: Incenter** is the point where three angle bisectors of a triangle intersect. This point is equidistant from the sides of the triangle. This distance from the incenter to the sides of a triangle is called the **inradius** and the circle with **inradius** is called the **incircle**.

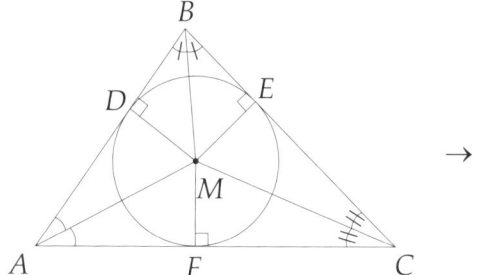

Point M is the incenter.
$\overline{DM}, \overline{EM}$, and $\overline{FM}$ are inradius.

Proof:

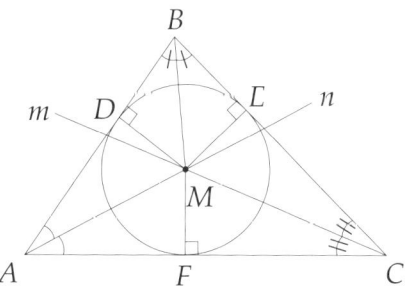

Draw two angle bisector m and n that meet at M. Also, draw three altitudes from M to each side $\overline{AB}, \overline{BC},$ and $\overline{AC}$, respectively, as shown in figure above. Since n is the angle

∠ADM ≅ ∠AFM. Finally, since $\overline{AM} \cong \overline{AM}$ by reflexive property, ∆ADM ≅ ∆AFM by AAS Congruence. So, $\overline{DM} \cong \overline{FM}$ by CPCTC. In the same manner, ∆CFM ≅ ∆CEM → $\overline{FM} \cong \overline{EM}$ and ∆BDM ≅ ∆BEM → $\overline{EM} \cong \overline{DM}$. Therefore, $\overline{DM} \cong \overline{EM} \cong \overline{FM}$. Now, if we draw a circle with center M and radius $\overline{DM}$, the circle will pass through all D, E, and F.

(2) Area: The area of a triangle equals its inradius(r) × its semiperimeter(s)

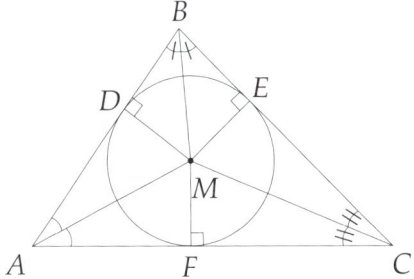

Proof:

If we let the radius of incircle be r and the semiperimeter of ∆ABC be s, where
$s = \dfrac{\overline{AB} + \overline{BC} + \overline{AC}}{2}$,

$$\text{Area of } \triangle ABC = \frac{1}{2} \cdot \overline{AB} \cdot \overline{DM} + \frac{1}{2} \cdot \overline{BC} \cdot \overline{EM} + \frac{1}{2} \cdot \overline{AC} \cdot \overline{FM}$$

$$= \frac{1}{2} \cdot \overline{AB} \cdot r + \frac{1}{2} \cdot \overline{BC} \cdot r + \frac{1}{2} \cdot \overline{AC} \cdot r$$

$$= r \left(\frac{1}{2} \cdot \overline{AB} + \frac{1}{2} \cdot \overline{BC} + \frac{1}{2} \cdot \overline{AC} \right)$$

$$= r \left(\frac{\overline{AB} + \overline{BC} + \overline{AC}}{2} \right) = rs.$$

3 Centroid

(1) Definition: **Centroid** is the point where the three medians of the triangle intersect. A **median** of a triangle is a line segment joining a vertex to the midpoint of the opposite side.

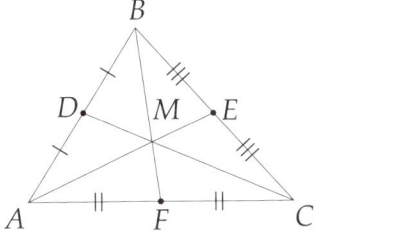

Point M is the centroid.
$\overline{AE}, \overline{BF}$, and $\overline{CD}$ are medians.

(2) **Area and Medians:** The medians of a triangle divide the triangle into six small triangles of equal area.

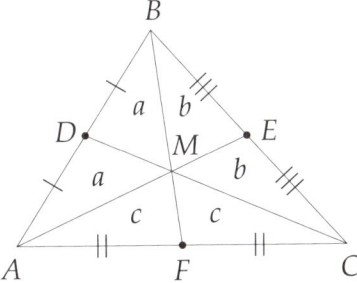

Proof:

Let the area of triangle ABC be $\triangle ABC$, the area of triangle ABF be $\triangle ABF$, and etc. First, $\triangle AFM = \triangle CFM$ because these two triangles have the same height from M to equal bases $\overline{AF}$ and $\overline{CF}$. Similarly, $\triangle ADM = \triangle BDM$ and $\triangle BEM = \triangle CEM$. Now, since $\triangle AFB$ and $\triangle CFB$ have the same height from B to equal bases $\overline{AF}$ and $\overline{CF}$, we have $\triangle AFB = \triangle CFB$. So, $2a + c = 2b + c$, $2a = 2b$, $a = b$. Similarly, $\triangle BDC = \triangle ADC$ and $2b + a = 2c + a$, $2b = 2c$, $b = c$. Therefore, we can conclude that $a = b = c$, which means all six small triangles have the equal area.

(3) **Centroid and Medians:** The centroid of a triangle cuts its medians into 2:1 ratio.

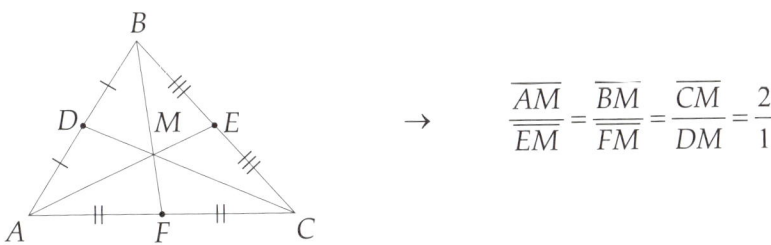

$\dfrac{\overline{AM}}{\overline{EM}} = \dfrac{\overline{BM}}{\overline{FM}} = \dfrac{\overline{CM}}{\overline{DM}} = \dfrac{2}{1}$

Proof:

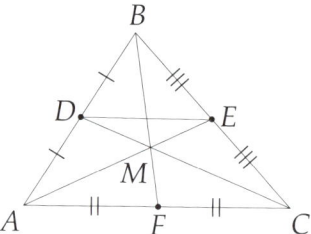

Since $\dfrac{\overline{BD}}{\overline{BA}} = \dfrac{\overline{BE}}{\overline{BC}} = \dfrac{2}{1}$, and $\angle DBE \cong \angle ABC$, we have $\triangle DBE \sim \triangle ABC$ by SAS Similarity and this concludes that $\dfrac{\overline{AC}}{\overline{DE}} = \dfrac{2}{1}$ and $\overline{DE} \parallel \overline{AC}$. So, $\angle DEM \cong \angle CAM$ and $\angle EDM \cong \angle ACM$ because they are alternate interior angles. Therefore, $\triangle MDE \cong \triangle MCA$ by AA Similarity and because $\dfrac{\overline{AC}}{\overline{ED}} = \dfrac{2}{1}, \dfrac{\overline{CM}}{\overline{DM}} = \dfrac{\overline{AM}}{\overline{EM}} = \dfrac{2}{1}$.

4

(1) Definition: **Orthocenter** is the point where the three altitudes of a triangle intersect. An **altitude** is a line that goes through a vertex and is at right angles to the opposite side.

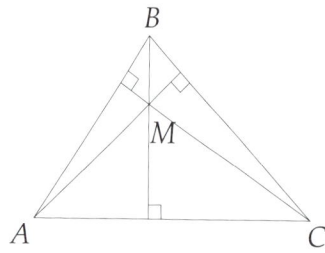   →   Point *M* is the orthocenter.

(2) Location of Orthocenter: The orthocenter can be inside, outside, or on the triangle.

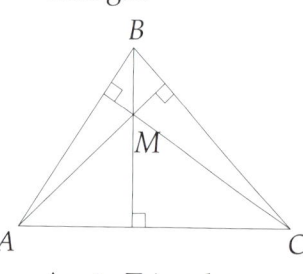 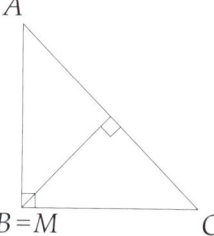 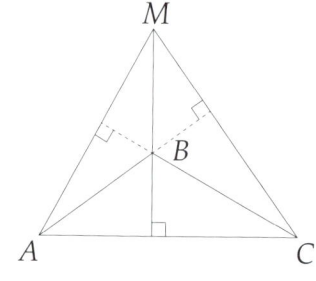

   Acute Triangle   Right Triangle   Obtuse Triangle

   ➢ Point *M* is the orthocenter.

Examples

Suppose the perpendicular bisectors of △ABC intersect at point M as shown in the figure below. Find each of the following.

(1) Find $\overline{BM}$.   (2) Find $\overline{CF}$.

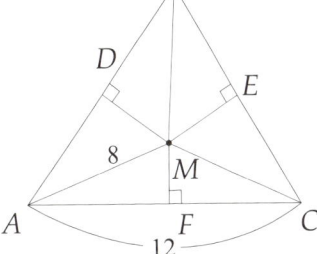

Solution

(1) Since point M is the circumcenter of △ABC, $\overline{AM} \cong \overline{BM} \cong \overline{CM}$ because they are radii of the circumcircle of △ABC. So, $\overline{BM} \cong \overline{AM} = 8$.
   ➢ $\overline{BM} = 8$.

(2) Since $\overline{FM}$ is the perpendicular bisector of $\overline{AC}$, $\overline{CF} = \dfrac{\overline{AC}}{2} = \dfrac{12}{2} = 6$.
   ➢ $\overline{CF} = 6$.

Examples

If M is the centroid of the triangle ABC and $\overline{BD} = 15$, what is the measure of $\overline{BM}$?

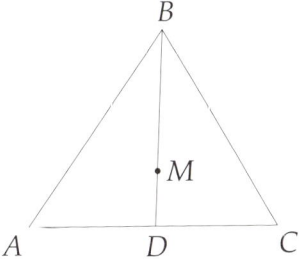

Solution

Since M is the centroid of the triangle ABC, $\overline{BM} = \dfrac{2}{3} \cdot \overline{BD} = \dfrac{2}{3} \cdot 15 = 10$.
   ➢ $\overline{BM} = 10$.

2. Right Triangle

1 Pythagorean Theorem

Pythagorean Theorem: In any right triangle, the sum of the squares of the lengths of the two legs is equal to the square of the length of the hypotenuse. In the figure below, $a^2 + b^2 = c^2$.

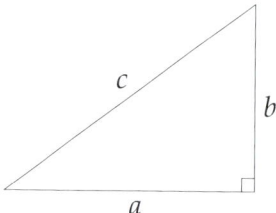

Proof:

Suppose the larger square $ACEG$ and the smaller square $BDFH$ are given as shown in the figure below.

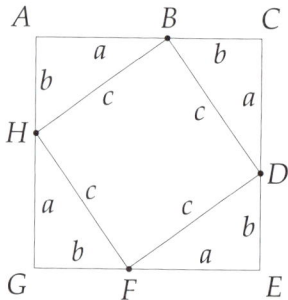

First, $\triangle ABH \cong \triangle CDB \cong \triangle EFD \cong \triangle GHF$ by SAS triangle congruence. Now, since the area of the square $ACEG$ is 4 times the area of the triangle ABH plus the area of square $BDFH$,

$$(a+b)^2 = 4 \cdot \frac{1}{2}ab + c^2 \quad \rightarrow \text{ Area}$$
$$a^2 + 2ab + b^2 = 2ab + c^2 \quad \rightarrow \text{ Expand}$$
$$a^2 + b^2 = c^2 \quad \rightarrow \text{ Simplify}$$

There are many other ways to prove the Pythagorean Theorem. We will prove some of them in practice problems.

2 Special Right Triangles

(1) **45° – 45° – 90° Triangle**: In a right triangle with acute angles of 45° and 45°, it is an isosceles right triangle and its hypotenuse is $\sqrt{2}$ times as long as either of its leg.

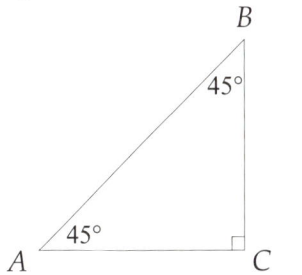 → $\overline{AC} : \overline{BC} : \overline{AB} = 1 : 1 : \sqrt{2}$

Proof:

In an isosceles right triangle, $\overline{AC} : \overline{BC} = 1 : 1$ and $\overline{AC}^2 + \overline{BC}^2 = \overline{AB}^2$ by Pythagorean Theorem. So, $1^2 + 1^2 = \overline{AB}^2$, $2 = \overline{AB}^2$, $\overline{AB} = \pm\sqrt{2}$. Since $\overline{AB} > 0$, $\overline{AB} = \sqrt{2}$. Therefore in a 45° – 45° – 90° triangle, the sides are in the ratio $1 : 1 : \sqrt{2}$.

(2) **30° – 60° – 90° Triangle**: In a right triangle with acute angles of 30° and 60°, the hypotenuse is twice as long as the shorter leg and the longer leg is $\sqrt{3}$ times as long as the shorter leg.

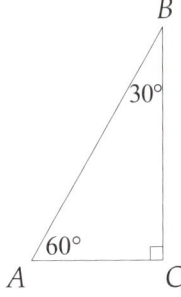 → $\overline{AC} : \overline{BC} : \overline{AB} = 1 : \sqrt{3} : 2$

Proof:

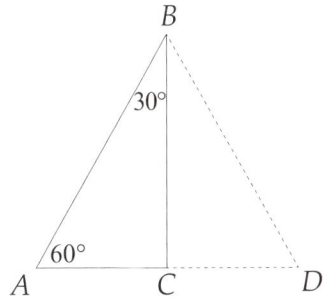

In the equilateral triangle ABD, each of its angles is 60°. If we draw $\overline{BC}$ bisecting the angle ∠ABD into two 30°s, then △ABC ≅ △DBC by ASA triangle congruence and ∠ACB ≅ ∠DCB = 90° by CPCTC. Triangle ABC therefore is a 30° – 60° – 90° triangle. Now, since $\overline{AC} \cong \overline{DC}$, $\overline{AC} = \dfrac{\overline{AD}}{2}$. This implies that $\overline{AC} = \dfrac{\overline{AB}}{2}$ because $\overline{AB} \cong \overline{AD}$. That is, $\overline{AC}:\overline{AB} = 1:2$. From Pythagorean Theorem, we have $\overline{AC}^2 + \overline{BC}^2 = \overline{AB}^2$, $1^2 + \overline{BC}^2 = 2^2$, $\overline{BC}^2 = 3$, $\overline{BC} = \pm\sqrt{3}$. Since $\overline{BC} > 0$, $\overline{BC} = \sqrt{3}$. Therefore in a 30° – 60° – 90° triangle, the sides are in the ratio $1:\sqrt{3}:2$.

Examples

Find the value of x.

(1)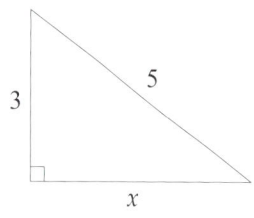

(2)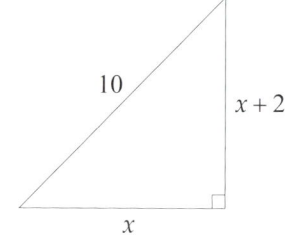

Solution

(1) $3^2 + x^2 = 5^2, x^2 = 16, x = \pm 4$
Since the length of the sides is always positive, $x = 4$.
➤ $x = 4$.

(2) $x^2 + (x+2)^2 = 10^2$
$2x^2 + 4x = 96$
$x^2 + 2x - 48 = 0$
$(x+8)(x-6) = 0, x = -8$ or $x = 6$
Since $x > 0$, $x = 6$.
➤ $x = 6$.

Examples

Find the value of *x* and *y*.

(1)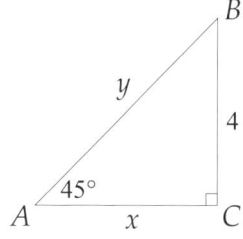

(2)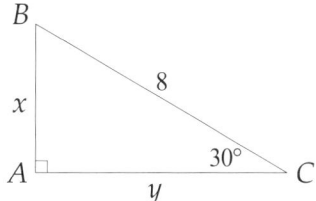

Solution

(1) $\angle B = 180° - 90° - 45° = 45°$
  $\rightarrow \triangle ABC$ is $45° - 45° - 90°$ triangle.
  $\overline{AC} : \overline{BC} = 1 : 1 \rightarrow \dfrac{1}{1} = \dfrac{x}{4},\ x = 4.$
  $\overline{AB} : \overline{BC} = \sqrt{2} : 1 \rightarrow \dfrac{\sqrt{2}}{1} = \dfrac{y}{4},\ y = 4\sqrt{2}.$
  ➤ $x = 4, y = 4\sqrt{2}.$

(2) $\angle B = 180° - 30° - 90° = 60°$
  $\rightarrow \triangle ABC$ is $30° - 60° - 90°$ triangle.
  $\overline{AB} : \overline{BC} = 1 : 2 \rightarrow \dfrac{1}{2} = \dfrac{x}{8},\ x = 4.$
  $\overline{AC} : \overline{BC} = \sqrt{3} : 2 \rightarrow \dfrac{\sqrt{3}}{2} = \dfrac{y}{8},\ y = 4\sqrt{3}.$
  ➤ $x = 4, y = 4\sqrt{3}.$

3. Triangles and Inequalities

1 Theorem 1

Theorem 1: If one side of a triangle is longer than another side, then the angle opposite the longer side is greater than the angle opposite the shorter side.

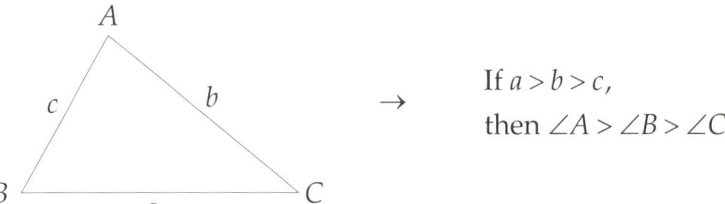

If $a > b > c$,
then $\angle A > \angle B > \angle C$

2 Theorem 2

Theorem 2: If one angle of a triangle is greater than another angle, then the side opposite the greater angle is longer than the side opposite the lesser angle.(Converse of Theorem 1)

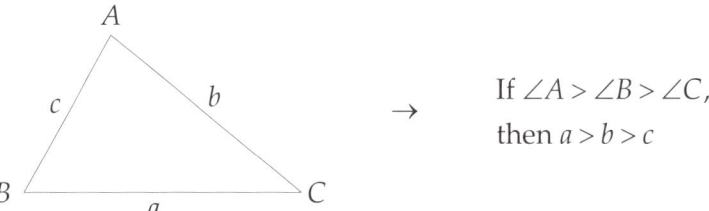

If $\angle A > \angle B > \angle C$,
then $a > b > c$

3 Triangle Inequality Theorem

Triangle Inequality Theorem: In any triangle, the sum of lengths of two sides is greater than the length of third side.

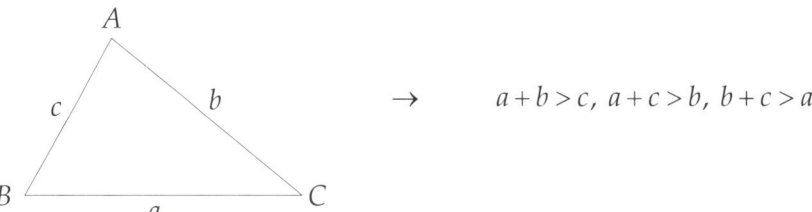

$a + b > c,\ a + c > b,\ b + c > a$

4 Pythagorean Theorem and Inequalities

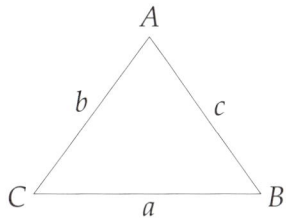

If $\angle C < 90°$,
then $c^2 < a^2 + b^2$.

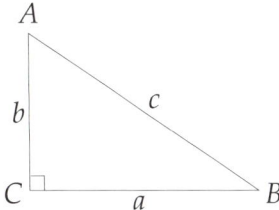

If $\angle C = 90°$,
then $c^2 = a^2 + b^2$.

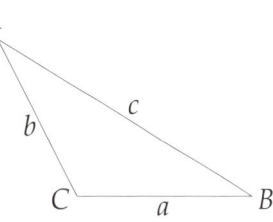

If $\angle C > 90°$,
then $c^2 > a^2 + b^2$.

Examples

The lengths of two sides of a triangle are 4 *in* and 7 *in*. What are the possible lengths for the third side of this triangle?

Solution

First, let the third side be x. By the Triangle Inequality Theorem, each of following inequalities must be true.

① If 7 is the longest side,
   $4 + x > 7$
   $x > 3$

② If x is the longest side,
   $4 + 7 > x$
   $x < 11$

➤ So, the third side must be between 3 and 11.

Review Exercise

1. If M is the circumcenter of $\triangle ABC$ and $\overline{BE}=6, \overline{AM}=8, \overline{AC}=14$, in the figure below, find each of the following sides.

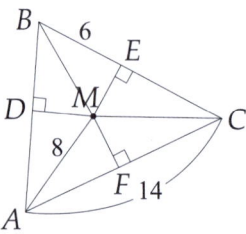

(1) $\overline{BC}$ (2) $\overline{CM}$ (3) $\overline{BM}$
(4) $\overline{CF}$ (5) $\overline{FM}$

Solution

Since M is the circumcenter of $\triangle ABC$, $\overline{AM} \cong \overline{BM} \cong \overline{CM}$ and $\overline{BE} \cong \overline{CE}$, $\overline{AF} \cong \overline{CF}, \overline{AD} \cong \overline{BD}$

(1) $\overline{BC} = 2 \cdot \overline{BE} = 2 \cdot 6 = 12$.
 ➤ $\overline{BC} = 12$.

(2) $\overline{CM} = \overline{AM} = 8$.
 ➤ $\overline{CM} = 8$.

(3) $\overline{BM} = \overline{AM} = 8$.
 ➤ $\overline{BM} = 8$.

(4) $\overline{CF} = \dfrac{\overline{AC}}{2} = \dfrac{14}{2} = 7$.
 ➤ $\overline{CF} = 7$.

(5) $\overline{FM}^2 + \overline{CF}^2 = \overline{CM}^2$
 $\overline{FM}^2 + 7^2 = 8^2, \overline{FM} = \sqrt{15}$.
 ➤ $\overline{FM} = \sqrt{15}$.

2. If $\overline{AB}=6, \overline{BC}=8$, and $\overline{AB} \perp \overline{BC}$ in the figure below, find each of the followings.

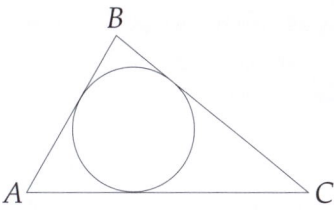

(1) Area of △ABC   (2) Circumradius   (3) Inradius

Solution

$\overline{AB}^2 + \overline{BC}^2 = \overline{AC}^2$ by Pythagorean Theorem. So, $6^2 + 8^2 = \overline{AC}^2, \overline{AC} = 10$.

(1) Since $\overline{AB} \perp \overline{BC}$, the area of $\triangle ABC = \dfrac{1}{2} \cdot 6 \cdot 8 = 24$.

   ➢ Area of △ABC = 24.

(2) Since △ABC is a right triangle, the circumcenter is the midpoint of $\overline{AC}$. So, the circumradius is $\dfrac{\overline{AC}}{2} = \dfrac{10}{2} = 5$.

   ➢ Circumradius = 5.

(3) Since the area of a triangle equals its inradius(r) times its semiperimeter(s), $24 = r \cdot s, 24 = r \cdot \dfrac{6+8+10}{2}, r = 2$.

   ➢ Inradius = 2.

3. If $\overline{BD}$ is the median of $\triangle ABC$, $\overline{AD} = 4\,in$, and the area of $\triangle ABC$ is $24\,in^2$, what is the measure of $\overline{BE}$?

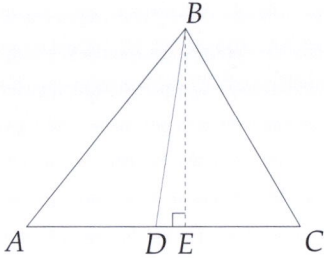

☼ **Solution**

Since $\overline{BD}$ is the median of $\triangle ABC$, $\overline{AD} \cong \overline{CD} = 4\,in$. Now,

$\frac{1}{2} \cdot \overline{AD} \cdot \overline{BE} + \frac{1}{2} \cdot \overline{CD} \cdot \overline{BE} = 24$

$\frac{1}{2} \cdot \overline{BE}(\overline{AD} + \overline{CD}) = 24$

$\frac{1}{2} \cdot \overline{BE}(4 + 4) = 24, \overline{BE} = 6.$

Alternate Solution:

Since the base $\overline{AC} = \overline{AD} + \overline{CD} = 8$,

$\frac{1}{2} \cdot \overline{BE} \cdot 8 = 24, \overline{BE} = 6.$

➢ $\overline{BE} = 6\,in.$

4. Points M and N are the centroids of $\triangle ABC$ and $\triangle AMC$, respectively, in the figure below. If $\overline{MN} = 6$, what is the measure of $\overline{BD}$?

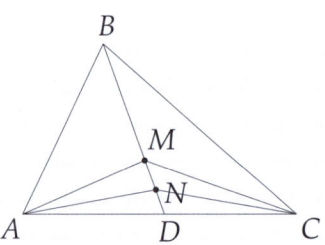

☼ **Solution**

Since $\overline{MD}$ is the median of $\triangle AMC$, $\frac{\overline{MN}}{\overline{ND}} = \frac{6}{\overline{ND}} = \frac{2}{1}, \overline{ND} = 3$. This give us that $\overline{MD} = \overline{MN} + \overline{ND} = 6 + 3 = 9$. Now, since $\overline{BD}$ is the median of $\triangle ABC$,

$\frac{\overline{BM}}{\overline{MD}} = \frac{\overline{BM}}{9} = \frac{2}{1}, \overline{BM} = 18$. So, $\overline{BD} = \overline{BM} + \overline{MD} = 18 + 9 = 27.$

➢ $\overline{BD} = 27.$

5. Point M is the incenter of $\triangle ABC$ in the figure below. If $\angle A = 60°, \angle B = 80°$, and $\angle C = 40°$, what is the measure of $\angle MBC$?

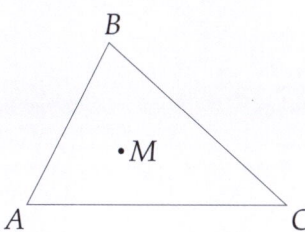

☼ Solution

Since point M is the incenter of $\triangle ABC$, $\overline{BM}$ is angle bisector of $\angle ABC$. So,
$\angle MBC = \dfrac{\angle B}{2} = \dfrac{80°}{2} = 40°$.
➤ $\angle MBC = 40°$.

6. Find the length of the inradius of a triangle with the given side lengths.

    (1) 6, 8, 10   (2) 5, 5, 8

☼ Solution

(1) Since $6^2 + 8^2 = 10^2$, it is a right triangle. So, $\dfrac{1}{2} \cdot 6 \cdot 8 = r\left(\dfrac{6+8+10}{2}\right), 24 = 12r, r = 2$.
➤ $r = 2$.

(2) Since two of sides are equal, it is an isosceles triangle.

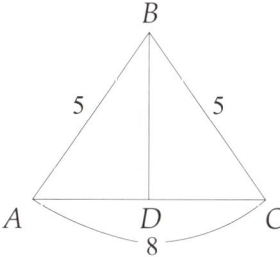

$\overline{AD} = \dfrac{\overline{AC}}{2} = \dfrac{8}{2} = 4$ and $\overline{AD}^2 + \overline{BD}^2 = \overline{AB}^2, 4^2 + \overline{BD}^2 = 5^2, \overline{BD} = 3$.
Area $= rs$, $\dfrac{1}{2} \cdot 8 \cdot 3 = r\left(\dfrac{5+5+8}{2}\right)$, $12 = 9r, r = \dfrac{4}{3}$.   ➤ $r = \dfrac{4}{3}$.

7. In right triangle ABC, D, E, and F are midpoints of $\overline{AB}$, $\overline{BC}$, and $\overline{AC}$, respectively, as shown in the figure below. If $\overline{AB} = 10$ and $\overline{AC} = 8$, find the area of the following triangles.

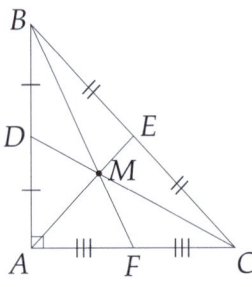

(1) $\triangle ABC$ (2) $\triangle BFC$ (3) $\triangle AEC$
(4) $\triangle BME$ (5) $\triangle DEM$ (6) $\triangle BDE$

Solution

The area of triangle ABC is $\frac{1}{2} \cdot 8 \cdot 10 = 40$, so each of small triangles has the area $\frac{40}{6} = \frac{20}{3}$.

(1) $\triangle ABC = 40$

(2) $\triangle BFC$ consists of three small triangles. So the area is $\frac{20}{3} \cdot 3 = 20$.
  ➤ $\triangle BFC = 20$.

(3) $\triangle AEC$ consists of three small triangles. So the area is $\frac{20}{3} \cdot 3 = 20$.
  ➤ $\triangle AEC = 20$.

(4) $\triangle BME$ consists of one small triangle. So the area is $\frac{20}{3}$.
  ➤ $\triangle BME = \frac{20}{3}$.

(5) $\triangle DEM \sim \triangle CAM$ by SAS Similarity and $\frac{\overline{DE}}{\overline{CA}} = \frac{2}{1}$. Since $\triangle AMC$ consists of two small triangles, its area is $\frac{20}{3} \cdot 2 = \frac{40}{3}$. So, the area of $\triangle DEM$ is $\frac{1}{4} \cdot \frac{40}{3} = \frac{10}{3}$.
  ➤ $\triangle DEM = \frac{10}{3}$.

(6) △BDE ~ △BAC by SAS Similarity and $\dfrac{\overline{DE}}{\overline{AC}} = \dfrac{2}{1}$. Since the area of △BAC is 40, the area of △BDE is $\dfrac{1}{4} \cdot 40 = 10$.

➤ △BDE = 10.

8. If $\overline{AB} = 1$ and $\overline{AB} \cong \overline{BC} \cong \overline{CD} \cong \overline{CE} \cong \overline{CF}$, what is the measure of $\overline{AF}$?

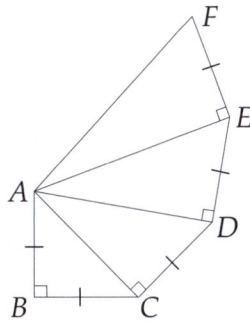

Solution

$\overline{AC} = \sqrt{\overline{AB}^2 + \overline{BC}^2} = \sqrt{1^2 + 1^2} = \sqrt{2}$.

$\overline{AD} = \sqrt{\overline{AC}^2 + \overline{CD}^2} = \sqrt{(\sqrt{2})^2 + 1^2} = \sqrt{3}$.

$\overline{AE} = \sqrt{\overline{AD}^2 + \overline{DE}^2} = \sqrt{(\sqrt{3})^2 + 1^2} = 2$.

$\overline{AF} = \sqrt{\overline{AE}^2 + \overline{EF}^2} = \sqrt{2^2 + 1^2} = \sqrt{5}$.

➤ $\overline{AF} = \sqrt{5}$.

9. In △ABC, what are the possible values of x if $\angle A > 90°$?

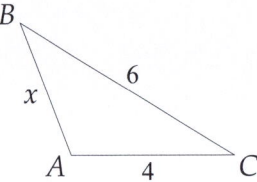

Solution

First, since $\angle A > 90°$, $\overline{BC}$ is the longest side and $x^2 + 4^2 < 6^2$, $x^2 < 20$, $0 < x < 2\sqrt{5}$. Also, by the Triangle Inequality Theorem, $x + 4 < 6$, $x < 2$. So, the possible value of x are $2 < x < 2\sqrt{5}$.

➢ $2 < x < 2\sqrt{5}$.

Chapter 5

SOLUTION: PAGE 315

Practice Problems

01 In each of the following below, if point *M* is the circumcenter of △ABC, what is the value of *x*?

(1)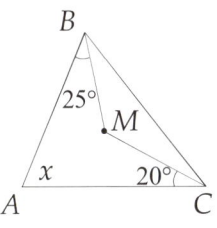

(2)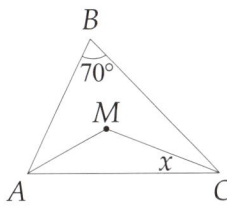

(3)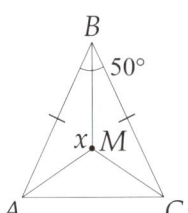

(4)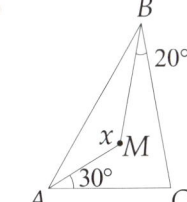

02 In each of the following below, if point *M* is the incenter of △ABC, what is the value of *x*?

(1)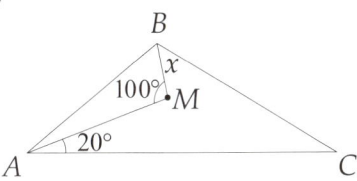

(2)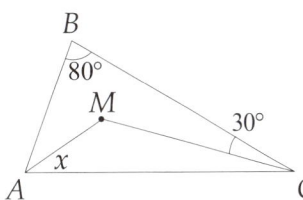

(3)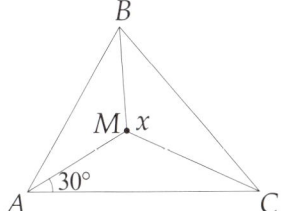

(4)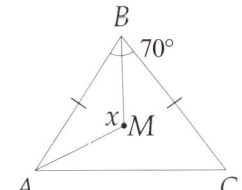

Chapter 5 *Practice Problems*

03 In each of the following below, if point M is the <u>centroid</u> of △ABC, what is the value of x?

(1)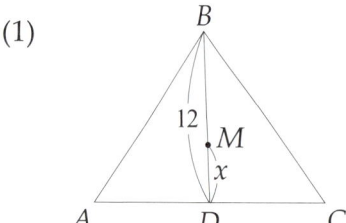

(2)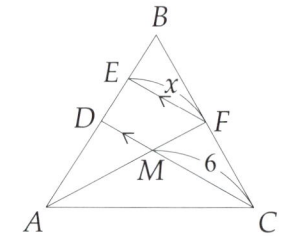

04 The area of △DME is $6 in^2$. If point M is centroid of △ABC, what is the area of △BCM?

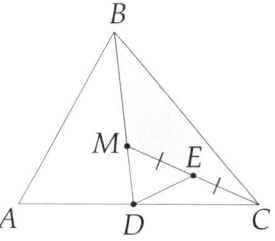

05 The area of △ABC is $72 in^2$. If points M and N are centroids of △ABC and △AMC, respectively, what is the area of △AMN?

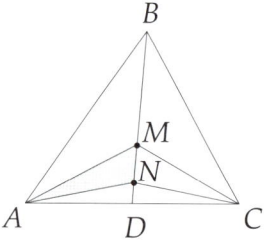

06 If points M and N are circumcenter and incenter of △ABC, respectively, what is the value of x?

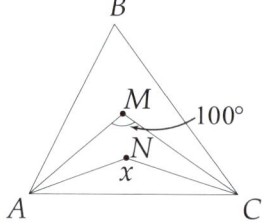

Chapter 5

Practice Problems

07 Given an isosceles triangle *ABC* in the figure below, find its circumradius and the inradius.

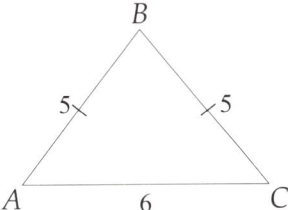

08 Find the value of *x*.

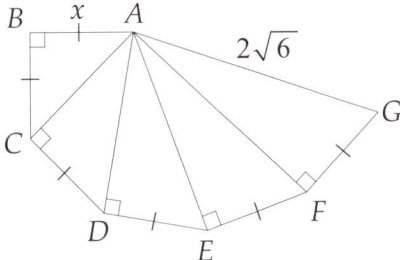

09 Find all positive integers a for which it is possible for $2a+4$, $a+7$, and $4a+7$ to be the side lengths of a triangle.

10 Given the point *M* is circumcenter of $\triangle ABC$, prove that $\angle AMC = 2\angle B$.

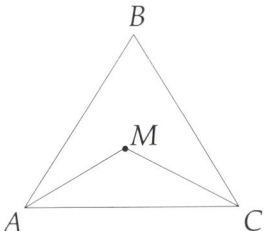

More about Triangles 105

Chapter 5 *Practice Problems*

11 Given the point M is incenter of $\triangle ABC$, prove that $\angle AMC = 90° + \dfrac{1}{2}\angle B$.

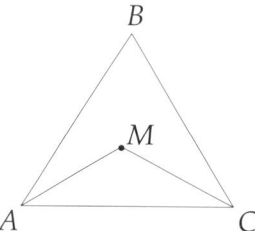

12 Given $\overline{BD}$ is a median of $\triangle ABC$, prove that $\overline{BD} > \dfrac{\overline{BA} + \overline{BC} - \overline{AC}}{2}$.

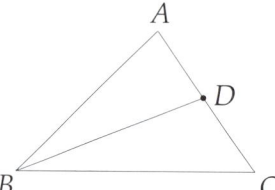

13 In each of the following figure below, prove that $c^2 = a^2 + b^2$.

(1)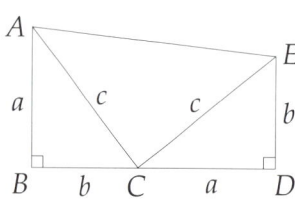

(2)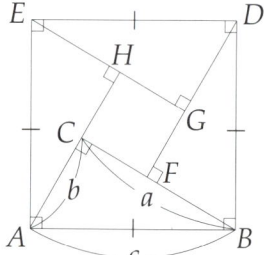

14 Given $\angle A > 90°$, prove that $\overline{BC}^2 > \overline{AB}^2 + \overline{AC}^2$.

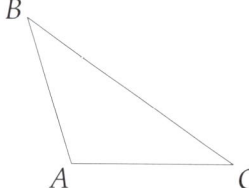

CHAPTER 6

Quadrilaterals

1. Introduction to Quadrilaterals

1 Polygon

Polygon: A closed plane figure formed by three or more line segments that meet only at their endpoints.

2 Diagonal

Diagonal: A line segment that connects two non-consecutive vertices of a polygon

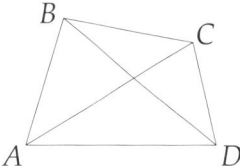 → $\overline{AC}$ and $\overline{BD}$ are diagonals.

3 Concave Polygon

Concave Polygon: A polygon that has one or more interior angles greater than 180°.

4 Convex Polygon

Convex Polygon: A polygon that has all interior angles less than 180°.

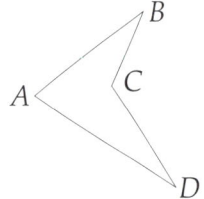
Concave Polygon

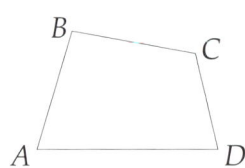
Convex Polygon

5 Quadrilateral

Quadrilateral: A polygon with four sides. The interior angles of a quadrilateral add up to 360°.

(1) **Parallelogram**: A quadrilateral with both pairs of opposite sides parallel.

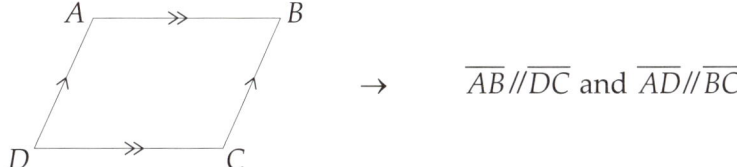

$\rightarrow$ $\overline{AB} // \overline{DC}$ and $\overline{AD} // \overline{BC}$

(2) **Trapezoid**: A quadrilateral with exactly one pair of parallel sides. The parallel sides are called **bases**, and the nonparallel sides are called **legs**.

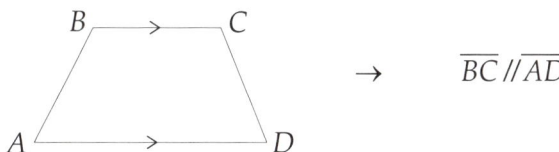

$\rightarrow$ $\overline{BC} // \overline{AD}$

In the figure above, ∠A and ∠D, ∠B and ∠C are pairs of **base angles**. A trapezoid is an **isosceles trapezoid** if its legs are congruent.

(3) **Rhombus**: A quadrilateral with four congruent sides.

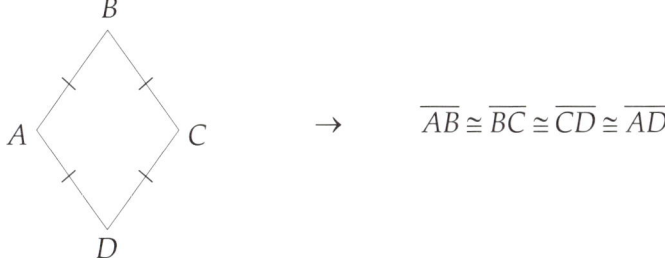

$\rightarrow$ $\overline{AB} \cong \overline{BC} \cong \overline{CD} \cong \overline{AD}$

(4) **Rectangle**: A quadrilateral with four right angles.

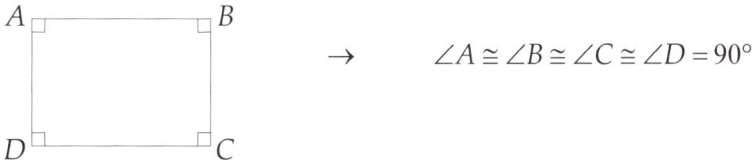

$\rightarrow$ $\angle A \cong \angle B \cong \angle C \cong \angle D = 90°$

(5) **Square**: A quadrilateral with four right angles and four congruent sides. When a quadrilateral is both a rhombus and rectangles, it is a square.

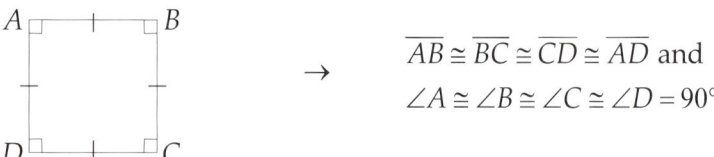

$\overline{AB} \cong \overline{BC} \cong \overline{CD} \cong \overline{AD}$ and
$\angle A \cong \angle B \cong \angle C \cong \angle D = 90°$

2. Parallelograms

1 Parallelograms

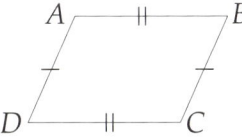 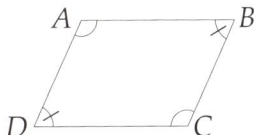 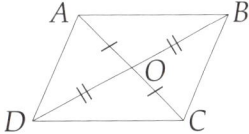

(1) $\overline{AB} \cong \overline{DC}, \overline{AD} \cong \overline{BC}$ (2) $\angle A \cong \angle C, \angle B \cong \angle D$ (3) $\overline{AO} \cong \overline{CO}, \overline{BO} \cong \overline{DO}$

Proof of (1):

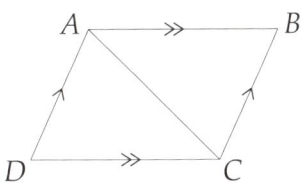

Statements	Reasons
1. $\overline{AB} // \overline{DC}$	1. Given
2. $\angle BAC \cong \angle DCA$	2. Alternate interior $\angle$s
3. $\overline{AD} // \overline{BC}$	3. Given
4. $\angle DAC \cong \angle BCA$	4. Alternate interior $\angle$s
5. $\overline{AC} \cong \overline{AC}$	5. Reflexive property
6. $\triangle ADC \cong \triangle CBA$	6. ASA Congruence
7. $\overline{AB} \cong \overline{DC}, \overline{AD} \cong \overline{BC}$	7. CPCTC

Proof of (2):

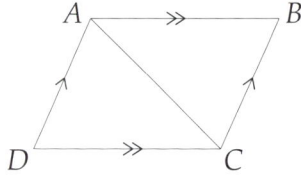

Statements	Reasons
1. △ADC ≅ △CBA	1. From proof of (1)
2. ∠B ≅ ∠D	2. CPCTC
3. ∠BAC ≅ ∠DCA	3. CPCTC
4. ∠BCA ≅ ∠DAC	4. CPCTC
5. ∠BAC + ∠DAC ≅ ∠BCA + ∠DCA	5. Addition property
6. ∠BAD ≅ ∠DCB	6. Substitution property

Proof of (3):

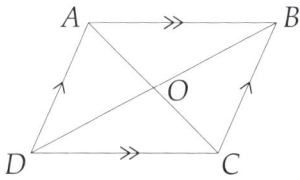

Statements	Reasons
1. $\overline{AD} \parallel \overline{BC}$	1. Given
2. ∠DAO ≅ ∠BCO	2. Alternate interior ∠s
3. ∠ADO ≅ ∠CBO	3. Alternate interior ∠s
4. $\overline{AD} \cong \overline{BC}$	4. From proof of (1)
5. △ADO ≅ △CBO	5. ASA Congruence
6. $\overline{AO} \cong \overline{CO}, \overline{BO} \cong \overline{DO}$	6. CPCTC

2 Test for Parallelograms

(1) Test 1: If both pairs of opposite sides of a quadrilateral are congruent, then the quadrilateral is a parallelogram.

Proof:

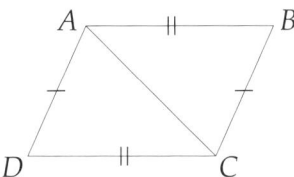

Statements	Reasons
1. $\overline{AB} \cong \overline{CD}, \overline{AD} \cong \overline{CB}$	1. Given
2. $\overline{AC} \cong \overline{CA}$	2. Reflexive property
3. $\triangle ADC \cong \triangle CBA$	3. SSS Congruence
4. $\angle DAC \cong \angle BCA, \angle DCA \cong \angle BAC$	4. CPCTC
5. $\overline{AD} // \overline{BC}$	5. $\angle DAC$ & $\angle BCA$ are alternate interior $\angle$s and $\angle DAC \cong \angle BCA$
6. $\overline{AB} // \overline{CD}$	6. $\angle DCA$ & $\angle BAC$ are alternate interior $\angle$s and $\angle DCA \cong \angle BAC$
7. ABCD is a parallelogram	7. Because both pairs of opposite sides are parallel.

(2) Test 2: If both pairs of opposite angles in a quadrilateral are congruent, then the quadrilateral is a parallelogram.

  ✓ You will be asked to prove this theorem in Review Exercises.

(3) Test 3: If the diagonals of a quadrilateral bisect each other, then the quadrilateral is a parallelogram.

  ✓ You will be asked to prove this theorem in Practice Problems.

(4) Test 4: If one pair of opposite sides of a quadrilateral is both parallel and congruent, then the quadrilateral is a parallelogram.

  ✓ You will be asked to prove this theorem in Practice Problems.

Examples

In parallelogram ABCD, $\overline{AC} = 22$, $\angle ADO = 45°$, and $\angle ABO = 30°$. Find each of the following.

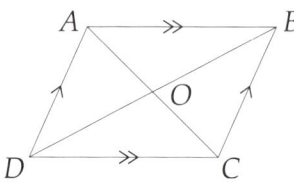

(1) $\overline{AO}$ (2) $\angle BCD$

Solution

(1) Since $\overline{AO} \cong \overline{CO}$ in parallelogram ABCD, $\overline{AO} = \dfrac{\overline{AC}}{2} = \dfrac{22}{2} = 11$.

➤ $\overline{AO} = 11$.

(2) In triangle ADB, $\angle DAB = 180° - 45° - 30° = 105°$.
Since $\angle DAB \cong \angle BCD$ in parallelogram ABCD, $\angle BCD \cong \angle DAB = 105°$.

➤ $\angle BCD = 105°$.

Examples

What values must x and y be in order for the quadrilateral below to be a parallelogram?

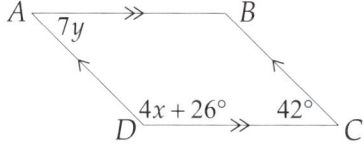

Solution

In order for the quadrilateral to be a parallelogram,
$\angle A \cong \angle C$ and $\angle D + \angle C = 180°$.

$7y = 42°, y = 6°$

$4x + 26° + 42° = 180°, x = 28°$

➤ $x = 28°, y = 6°$.

3. Trapezoids

1 Isosceles Trapezoid

(1) Theorem 1: Both pairs of base angles of an isosceles trapezoid are congruent.

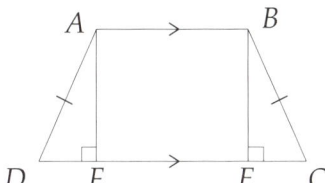

Statements	Reasons
1. $\overline{AD} \cong \overline{BC}, \overline{AB} // \overline{DC}$	1. Given
2. $\overline{AF} \perp \overline{CD}, \overline{BE} \perp \overline{CD}$	2. Draw altitudes from A and B
3. $\angle AFD \cong \angle BEC = 90°$	3. Definition of perpendicular lines
4. $\overline{AF} \cong \overline{BE}$	4. Because $\overline{AB} // \overline{DC}$
5. $\triangle AFD \cong \triangle BEC$	5. HL Congruence
6. $\angle D \cong \angle C$	6. CPCTC
7. $\angle FAD \cong \angle EBC$	7. CPCTC
8. $\angle FAB \cong \angle EBA = 90°$	8. Definition of perpendicular lines
9. $\angle FAD + \angle FAB \cong \angle EBC + \angle EBA$	9. Addition property
10. $\angle DAB \cong \angle CBA$	10. Substitution property

(2) Theorem 2: The diagonals of an isosceles trapezoid are congruent.

✓ You will be asked to prove this theorem in Review Exercises.

2 Median

Median: A line segment that connects the midpoint of the two legs of the trapezoid.

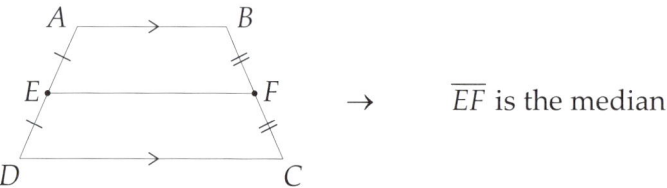
→ $\overline{EF}$ is the median

(1) Theorem 3: The median of a trapezoid is parallel to the bases.

✓ You will be asked to prove this theorem in Practice Problems.

(2) Theorem 4: The median of a trapezoid is one half the sum of the measures of the bases.

✓ You will be asked to prove this theorem in Practice Problems.

Examples

If $\overline{AB}//\overline{DC}$ in the figure below, find the value of x and y.

Solution

Since $\overline{AB}//\overline{DC}$, $(4x-15°)+(2x+15°)=180°, 6x=180°, x=30°$.
Also, $(2y-4°)+80°=180°, 2y=104°, y=52°$.
➢ $x=30°, y=52°$.

Examples

A trapezoid $ABCD$ with median $\overline{EF}$ is given in the figure below. What is the value of x?

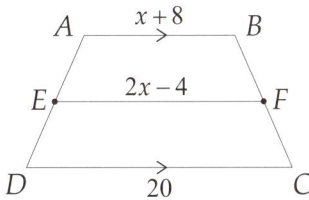

Solution

Since $\overline{AB} + \overline{DC} = 2\overline{EF}$, $(x+8) + 20 = 2(2x-4), 3x = 36, x = 12$.
➤ $x = 12$.

4. Rhombi, Rectangles and Squares

1 Rhombi (Rhombuses)

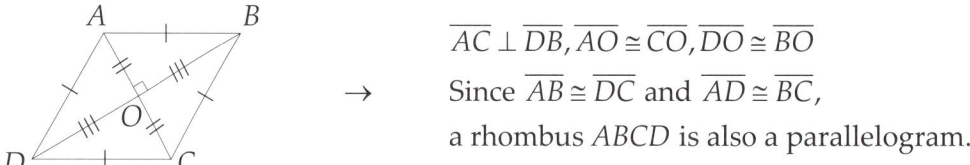

$\overline{AC} \perp \overline{DB}, \overline{AO} \cong \overline{CO}, \overline{DO} \cong \overline{BO}$

Since $\overline{AB} \cong \overline{DC}$ and $\overline{AD} \cong \overline{BC}$,

a rhombus $ABCD$ is also a parallelogram.

(1) Theorem 1: The diagonals of a rhombus are perpendicular.

Proof:

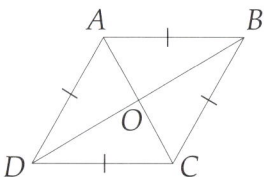

Statements	Reasons
1. $\overline{AC}$ and $\overline{DB}$ are diagonals	1. Given
2. $\overline{AB} \cong \overline{AD}$	2. Definition of rhombus
3. $\overline{BO} \cong \overline{DO}$	3. Property of parallelogram
4. $\overline{AO} \cong \overline{AO}$	4. Reflexive property
5. $\triangle ABO \cong \triangle ADO$	5. SSS Congruence
6. $\angle AOB \cong \angle AOD$	6. CPCTC
7. $\overline{AC} \perp \overline{DB}$	7. Because $\angle AOD \cong \angle AOB = 90°$

(2) Theorem 2: Each diagonal of a rhombus bisects a pair of opposite angles.

✓ You will be asked to prove this theorem in Review Exercises.

2 Rectangles

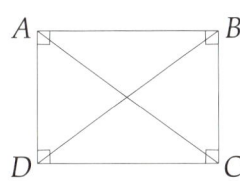 → $\overline{AC} \cong \overline{BD}$
Since $\angle A \cong \angle C$ and $\angle B \cong \angle D$,
a rectangle $ABCD$ is also a parallelogram.

(1) Theorem 1: The diagonals of a parallelogram are congruent.

Proof:

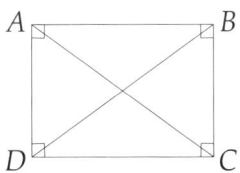

Statements	Reasons
1. $ABCD$ is a rectangle	1. Given
2. $\angle ADC \cong \angle BCD$	2. Definition of rectangle
3. $ABCD$ is a parallelogram	3. Definition of rectangle
4. $\overline{AD} \cong \overline{BC}$	4. Property of parallelogram
5. $\overline{DC} \cong \overline{CD}$	5. Reflexive property
6. $\triangle ADC \cong \triangle BCD$	6. SAS Congruence
7. $\overline{AC} \cong \overline{BD}$	7. CPCTC

3 Squares

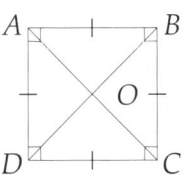 → $\overline{AC} \perp \overline{BD}, \overline{AC} \cong \overline{BD},$
$\overline{AO} \cong \overline{BO} \cong \overline{CO} \cong \overline{DO}$

5. Quadrilaterals and its Diagrams

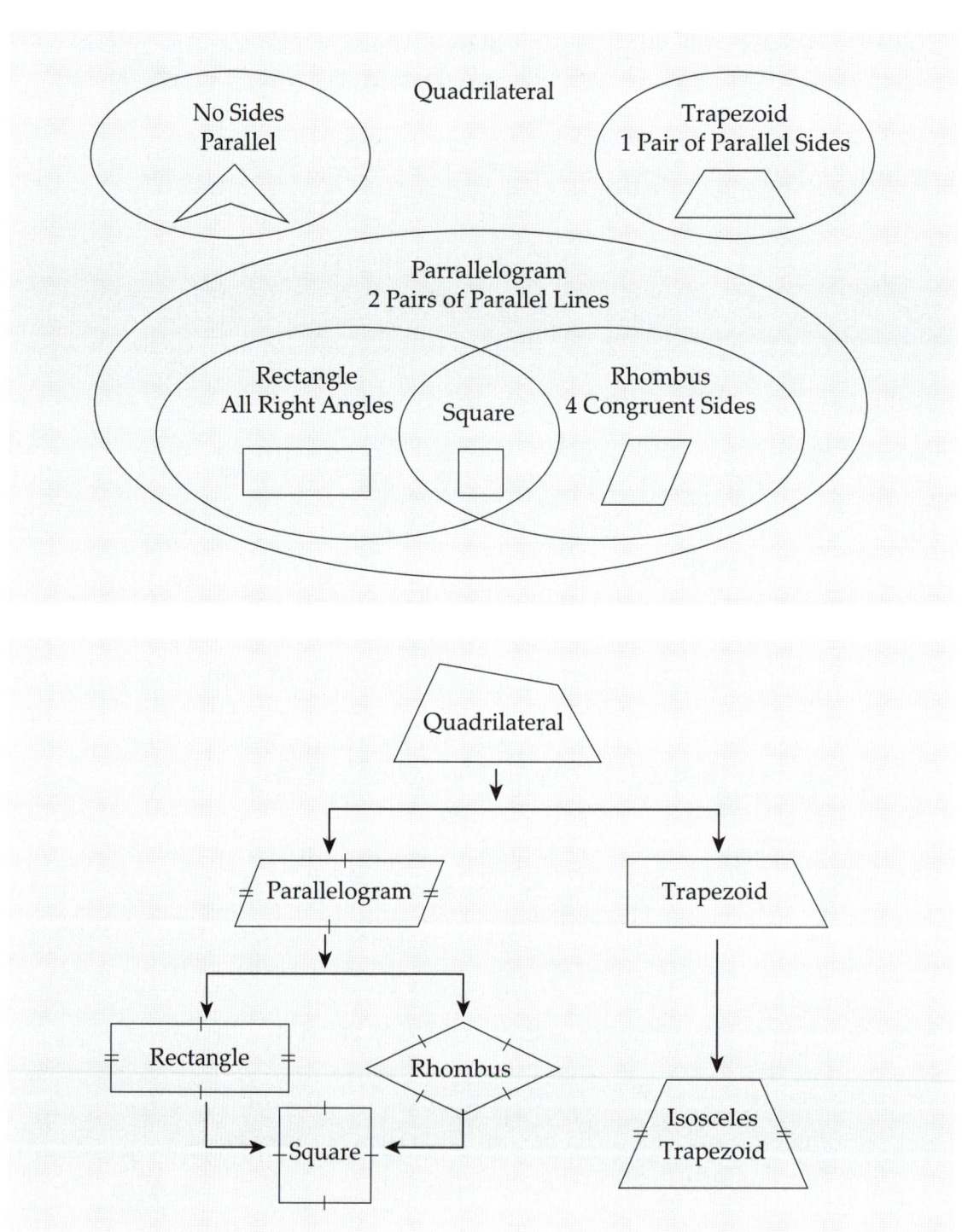

Examples

A rhombus $ABCD$ is given below. Find the value of x and y.

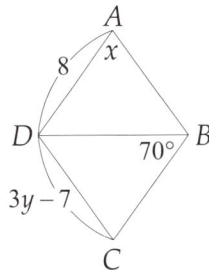

Solution

Since $\overline{BD}$ bisects $\angle ABC$, $\angle ABD = \angle CBD = 70°$.
Also, since $\overline{AD} \cong \overline{AB}$, $\angle ADB \cong \angle ABD = 70°$.
Now, in $\triangle ADB$, $x = 180° - 70° - 70° = 40°$.
Since $\overline{AD} \cong \overline{CD}$, $8 = 3y - 7$, $y = 5$.

➤ $x = 40°, y = 5$.

Review Exercise

1. A parallelogram ABCD is given below. Find the value of x.

(1)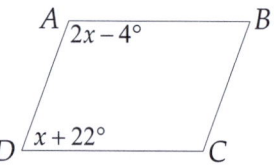

(2)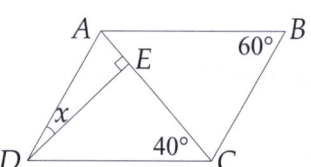

(3)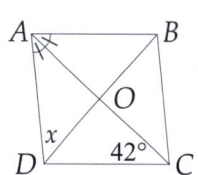

(4)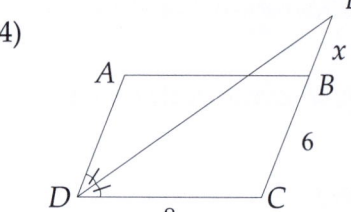

(5)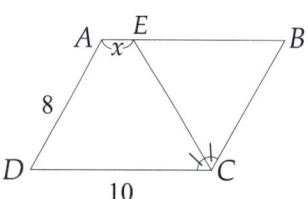

Solution

(1) Since $\angle A + \angle D = 180°$,
$(2x - 4) + (x + 22) = 180°, 3x = 162, x = 54$.
➤ $x = 54$.

(2) First, $\angle B \cong \angle D = 60°$ and $\angle CED = 90°$.
In $\triangle CDE$, $\angle CDE = 180° - 90° - 40° = 50°$.
Since $\angle D = \angle CDE + x$, $x = 60° - 50° = 10°$.
➤ $x = 10°$.

(3) Since $\overline{AC}$ bisects $\angle DAB$, a parallelogram is a rhombus.
So, $\angle DAO \cong \angle DCO = 42°$ and $\angle DOA = 90°$.
Now, in $\triangle ADO$, $x = 180° - 42° - 90° = 48°$.
➤ $x = 48°$.

(4) First, $\angle ADE \cong \angle CDE$. Since $\overline{AD} \parallel \overline{EC}$, $\angle ADE \cong \angle CED$.
So, $\angle ADE \cong \angle CDE \cong \angle CED$
and this tells us that $\triangle CDE$ is an isosceles triangle.
Now, $\overline{CD} \cong \overline{CE}, 8 = 6 + x, x = 2$.
➤ $x = 2$.

(5) First, $\angle DCE \cong \angle BCE$. Since $\overline{AB} \parallel \overline{DC}$, $\angle DCE \cong \angle BEC$.
So, $\angle DCE \cong \angle BCE \cong \angle BEC$
and this tells us that $\triangle BCE$ is an isosceles triangle.
Since, $\overline{AD} \cong \overline{BC} \cong \overline{BE} = 8$ and $\overline{AB} \cong \overline{DC} = 10$,
$\overline{AB} = x + \overline{BE}, 10 = x + 8, x = 2$.
➤ $x = 2$.

2. Given both pairs of opposite angles in a quadrilateral are congruent, prove that the quadrilateral is a parallelogram.

Solution

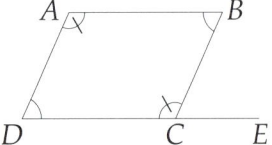

Statements	Reasons
1. $\angle A \cong \angle BCD, \angle B \cong \angle D$	1. Given
2. $\angle A + \angle B + \angle BCD + \angle D = 360°$	2. Definition of quadrilateral
3. $\angle BCD + \angle D + \angle BCD + \angle D = 360°$	3. Substitution property
4. $2\angle BCD + 2\angle D = 360°$	4. Simplify
5. $\angle BCD + \angle D = 180°$	5. Division property
6. $\angle BCD + \angle BCE = 180°$	6. Definition of straight $\angle$
7. $\angle BCD + \angle D = \angle BCD + \angle BCE$	7. Substitution property
8. $\angle D \cong \angle BCE$	8. Subtraction property
9. $\overline{AD} // \overline{BC}$	9. $\angle D$ & $\angle BCE$ are corresponding $\angle$s and $\angle D \cong \angle BCE$
10. $\angle B = \angle BCE$	10. Substitution prop.
11. $\overline{AB} // \overline{DC}$	11. $\angle B$ & $\angle BCE$ are alternate interior $\angle$s and $\angle B \cong \angle BCE$
12. $ABCD$ is a parallelogram	12. Because both pairs of opposite are parallel

3. An isosceles trapezoid ABCD is given below. Find the value of x.

(1)

(2)

(3)

(4)

$\overline{AB} \cong \overline{AD} \cong \overline{BC}$

Solution

(1)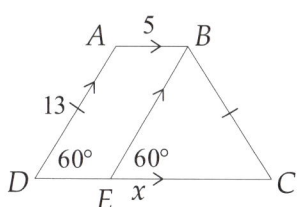

If we draw $\overline{BE}$ // to $\overline{AD}$, then $\overline{AB} \cong \overline{DE} = 5$ and $\angle ADE \cong \angle BEC = 60°$.

Since $\overline{AD} \cong \overline{BC}$, $\overline{BC} = 13$ and $\angle BCE = 60°$.

In $\triangle BEC$, $\angle EBC = 180° - 60° - 60° = 60°$.

So, $\triangle BEC$ is an equilateral triangle and $\overline{EC} \cong \overline{BC} = 13$.

Finally, $x = \overline{DE} + \overline{EC} = 5 + 13 = 18$.

➤ $x = 18$.

(2) Since $\overline{AD} \cong \overline{BC}, \angle A \cong \angle B = 110°$.

Now, since $\angle B + \angle C = 180°$, $110° + x = 180°$, $x = 70°$.

➤ $x = 70°$.

(3)
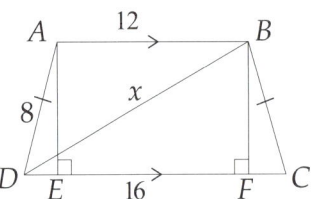

If we draw $\overline{AE}$ and $\overline{BF}$ perpendicular to $\overline{DC}$, then $\overline{DE} \cong \overline{CF}, \overline{AE} \cong \overline{BF}$.
$\overline{DE} + \overline{EF} + \overline{CF} = 2\overline{DE} + 12 = 16, \overline{DE} = 2$.
In a right triangle ADE, $2^2 + \overline{AE}^2 = 8^2, \overline{AE} = 2\sqrt{15}$.
Also, in a right triangle BDF,
$x^2 = \left(16 - \overline{CF}\right)^2 + \overline{BF}^2 = (16-2)^2 + \left(2\sqrt{15}\right)^2 = 256, x = 16$.

➢ $x = 16$.

(4) Since $\overline{AB} /\!/ \overline{DC}, \angle ABD \cong \angle CDB = 30°$.
Also, since $\overline{AB} \cong \overline{AD}$, $\angle ABD \cong \angle ADB = 30°$.
In $\triangle ABD$, $\angle A = 180° - 30° - 30° = 120°$
and $\angle A \cong \angle B = \angle ABD + x$, $120° = 30° + x$, $x = 90°$.

➢ $x = 90°$.

4. Prove that the diagonals of an isosceles trapezoid are congruent.

Solution

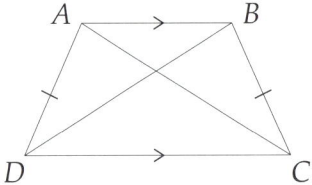

Statements	Reasons
1. $\overline{AD} \cong \overline{BC}, \overline{AB} /\!/ \overline{DC}$	1. Given
2. $\angle ADC \cong \angle BCD$	2. Proved from theorem 1 in isosceles trapezoid
3. $\overline{DC} \cong \overline{CD}$	3. Reflexive property
4. $\triangle ADC \cong \triangle BCD$	4. SAS Congruence
5. $\overline{AC} \cong \overline{BD}$	5. CPCTC

5. A rhombus ABCD is given below. Find each of the following.

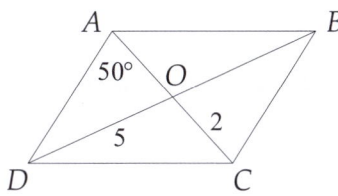

(1) $\overline{AO}$ (2) $\overline{BC}$
(3) $\angle ADO$ (4) $\angle DCB$

Solution

(1) In a rhombus $ABCD$, $\overline{AO} \cong \overline{CO} = 2$.
  - ➤ $\overline{AO} = 2$.

(2) Since $\angle COD = 90°$, $\overline{CD}^2 = 2^2 + 5^2$, $\overline{CD} = \sqrt{29}$.
   So, $\overline{BC} \cong \overline{CD} = \sqrt{29}$.
  - ➤ $\overline{BC} = \sqrt{29}$.

(3) Since $\angle AOD = 90°$ in $\triangle ADO$,
   $\angle ADO = 180° - 50° - 90° = 40°$.
  - ➤ $\angle ADO = 40°$.

(4) $\angle DCB \cong \angle DAB \cong 2\angle DAO = 2 \cdot 50 = 100°$.
  - ➤ $\angle DCB = 100°$.

6. Prove that each diagonal of a rhombus bisects a pair of opposite angles.

☀ Solution

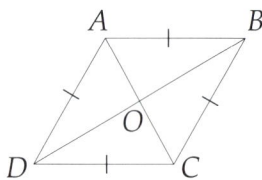

Statements	Reasons
1. ABCD is a rhombus	1. Given
2. $\overline{AB} \cong \overline{BC} \cong \overline{CD} \cong \overline{AD}$	2. Definition of rhombus
3. ABCD is a parallelogram	3. Every rhombus is a parallelogram
4. $\angle DAB \cong \angle DCB$	4. Property of parallelogram
5. $\triangle DAB \cong \triangle DCB$	5. SAS Congruence
6. $\angle ADO \cong \angle CDO, \angle ABO \cong \angle CBO$	6. CPCTC
7. $\angle ABC \cong \angle ADC$	7. Property of parallelogram
8. $\triangle ABC \cong \triangle ADC$	8. SAS Congruence
9. $\angle DAO \cong \angle BAO, \angle DCO \cong \angle BCO$	9. CPCTC

7. Find the length of a diagonal of a rectangle given that its perimeter is 36 and the length is twice as long as its width.

☀ Solution

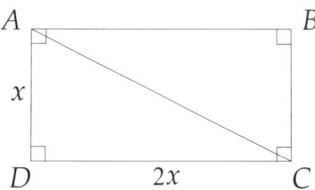

$\overline{AB} + \overline{BC} + \overline{CD} + \overline{AD} = 2x + x + 2x + x = 6x = 36, x = 6.$

$\overline{AC}^2 = x^2 + (2x)^2 = 5x^2 = 5 \cdot 6^2 = 180, \overline{AC} = 6\sqrt{5}.$

➢ $\overline{AC} = 6\sqrt{5}.$

Chapter 6

SOLUTION: PAGE 329

Practice Problems

01 Prove that sum of any two consecutive angles in the parallelogram is 180°.

02 Given one pair of opposite sides of a quadrilateral is both parallel and congruent, prove that the quadrilateral is a parallelogram.

03 A parallelogram $ABCD$ is given below. For each of the following, find the value of x

(1)

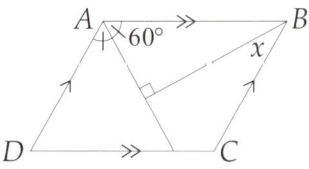

(2)

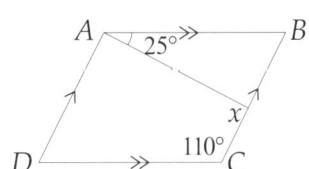

Chapter 6　　　　　　　　　　　　　　　*Practice Problems*

(3)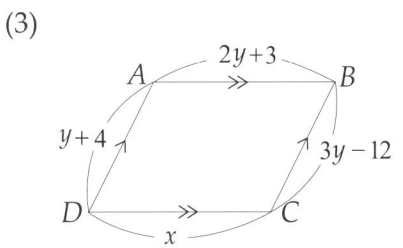

(4)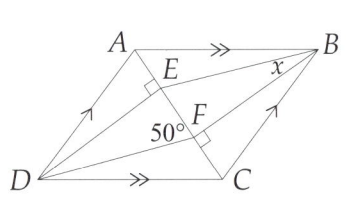

(5)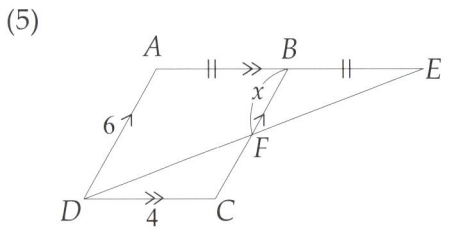

(6)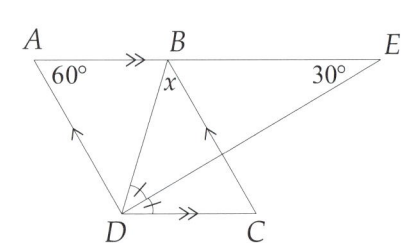

04 A trapezoid *ABCD* is given below. If $\overline{AB} \cong \overline{BC} \cong \overline{CD}$, what is the measure of $\overline{AD}$?

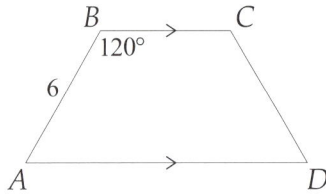

05 A trapezoid *ABCD* is given below. If $\overline{AB} \cong \overline{BC} \cong \overline{CD}$, what is the measure of $\angle ADC$?

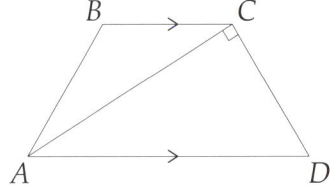

Chapter 6 — Practice Problems

06 Prove that the median of a trapezoid is parallel to the bases.

07 Prove that the median of a trapezoid is one half the sum of the measures of the bases.

08 If $ABCD$ is a trapezoid with $\overline{EG} = 3$ and $\overline{GF} = 5$, what is the measure of $\overline{AB} + \overline{CD}$?

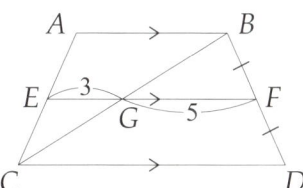

09 A rectangle $ABCD$ is given below. If $\overline{AE}$ is an angle bisector of $\angle DAC$ and $\overline{AE} \cong \overline{CE}$, what is the measure of $\angle AED$?

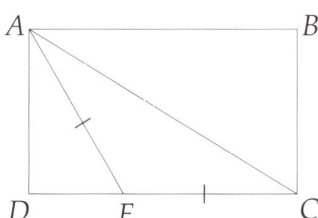

Chapter 6 — *Practice Problems*

10 A rhombus *ABCD* is given below. If △*CDE* is an equilateral triangle, what is the measure of ∠*BEC*?

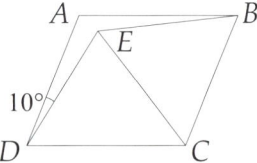

11 A square *ABCD* is given below. If $\overline{DE} \cong \overline{DF}$, what is the measure of ∠*DFE*?

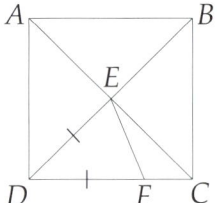

12 A square *ABCD* is given below. If $\overline{AE} \cong \overline{BG}$, what is the measure of ∠*DFG*?

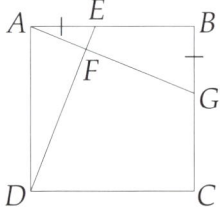

13 In quadrilateral *ABCD*, *E, F, G,* and *H* are midpoints of $\overline{AB}, \overline{BC}, \overline{CD}$, and $\overline{AD}$, respectively. Prove that *EFGH* is a parallelogram.

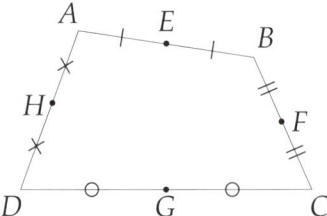

Chapter 6 — Practice Problems

14 A square $ABCD$ and an isosceles triangle AEF with $\overline{AE} \cong \overline{AF}$ is given below. What is the measure of $\angle CEF$?

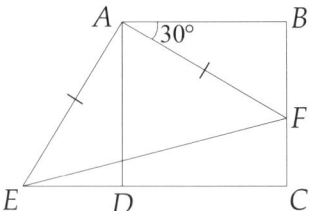

15 Given the diagonals of a quadrilateral bisect each other, prove that the quadrilateral is a parallelogram.

16 A rhombus $ABCD$ is given below. If $\overline{CE} \cong \overline{DE}$, what is the measure of $\angle BCE$?

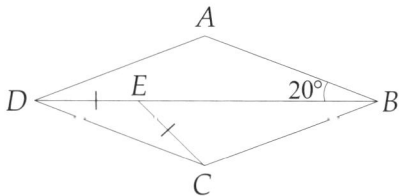

CHAPTER 7

Polygons and Circles

1. Introduction to Polygons

1 Polygon

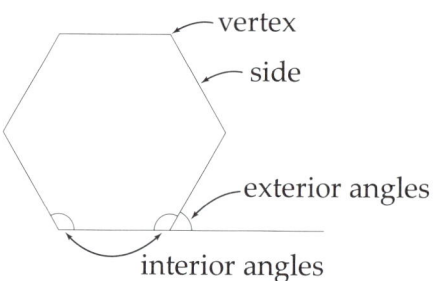

Polygons are classified by the number of sides they have. Here are some names given to different polygons.

Number of Sides	Polygon
3	Triangle
4	Quadrilateral
5	Pentagon
6	Hexagon
7	Heptagon
8	Octagon
9	Nonagon
10	Decagon
11	Undecagon
12	Dodecagon
n	n-gon

2 Regular Polygon

Regular Polygon: A polygon that is equiangular (all angles are equal in measure) and equilateral (all sides have the same length). Here are some regular polygons.

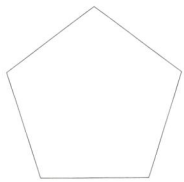 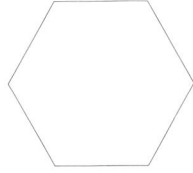 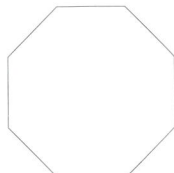

Regular Pentagon Regular Hexagon Regular Octagon

3 Interior Angle Sum Theorem

Interior Angle Sum Theorem: The sum of the measures of the angles of each polygon can be found by adding the measures of the angles of the triangles.

	Polygon	Number of Sides	Sum of Angle Measures
	Quadrilateral	4	$180° \times 2 = 360°$
	Pentagon	5	$180° \times 3 = 540°$

Polygons and Circles 137

	Polygon	Number of Sides	Sum of Angle Measures
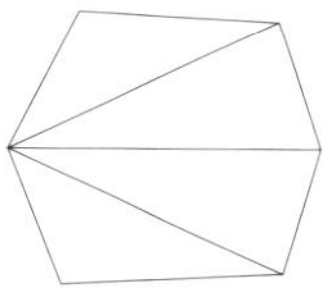	Hexagon	6	$180° \times 4 = 720°$
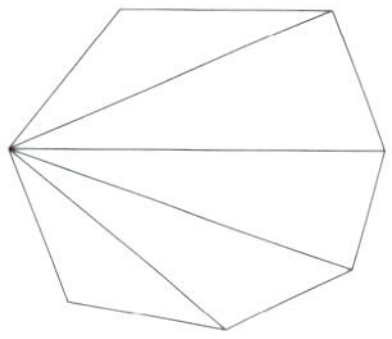	Heptagon	7	$180° \times 5 = 900°$
	n-gon	n	$180° \times (n-2)$

✓ If it is a regular polygon with n sides, the measure of each interior angle is $\dfrac{180° \times (n-2)}{n}$.

4 Exterior Angle Sum Theorem

Exterior Angle Sum Theorem: The sum of the exterior angles, one at each vertex, in a convex polygon is 360°.

Proof:

The sum of interior and exterior angles in a vertex of regular polygon is always 180°.
So, in n-gon, (Sum of interior angles) + (Sum of exterior angles) = $180° \times n$.
(Sum of interior angles) + (Sum of exterior angles) = $180° \times n$
$180° \times (n-2)$ + (Sum of exterior angles) = $180°n$
$180°n - 360°$ + (Sum of exterior angles) = $180°n$
Sum of exterior angles = $360°$.

In addition, the measure of each exterior angle in a regular n-gon is simply $\dfrac{360°}{n}$.

Examples

A regular hexagon *ABCDEF* is given below. Find each of the followings.

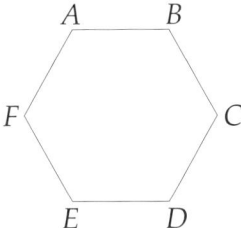

(1) Sum of interior angles
(2) Sum of exterior angles
(3) Each interior angle
(4) Each exterior angle

Solution

(1) $180° \times (n-2) = 180° \times (6-2) = 720°$.
  ➢ Sum of interior angles $= 720°$.

(2) Sum of exterior angles is always $360°$.
  ➢ Sum of exterior angles $= 360°$.

(3) $\dfrac{180° \times (n-2)}{n} = \dfrac{180° \times (6-2)}{6} = \dfrac{720°}{6} = 120°$.
  ➢ Each interior angle $= 120°$

(4) $\dfrac{360°}{6} = 60°$.
  ➢ Each exterior angle $= 60°$.

2. Area of Triangles and Quadrilaterals

1 Area of Triangles

Triangle	Equilateral Triangle
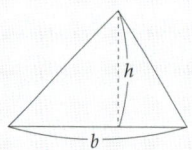	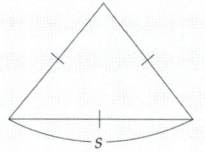
$A = \dfrac{1}{2}bh$	$A = \dfrac{\sqrt{3}}{4}s^2$

Proof: The Area of an Equilateral Triangle

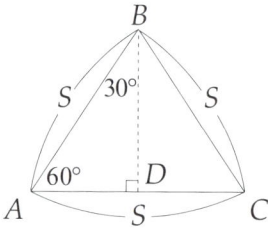

Given an equilateral triangle ABC with side S, draw $\overline{BD}$ perpendicular to $\overline{AC}$. Then, $\triangle ABD$ is $30°-60°-90°$ triangle and it has side lengths in the ratio $1:\sqrt{3}:2$. So, in terms of S, $\overline{AB} = S$, $\overline{AD} = \dfrac{1}{2}S$, and $\overline{BD} = \dfrac{\sqrt{3}}{2}S$. Now, the area of $\triangle ABC$ is

$\dfrac{1}{2} \cdot \overline{AC} \cdot \overline{BD} = \dfrac{1}{2} \cdot S \cdot \dfrac{\sqrt{3}}{2}S = \dfrac{\sqrt{3}}{4}S^2$.

2 Area of Quadrilaterals

Parallelogram

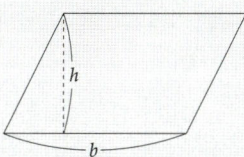

$A = bh$

Trapezoid

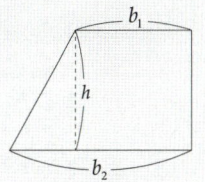

$A = \frac{1}{2}(b_1 + b_2)h$

Rhombus

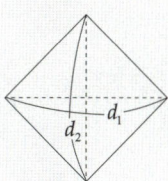

$A = \frac{1}{2}d_1 d_2$

Rectangle or Square

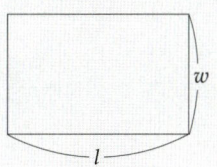

$A = lw$

Proof: The Area of a Rhombus

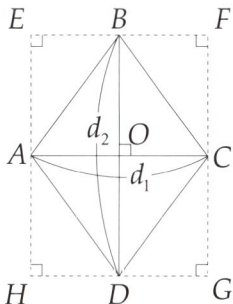

Since $\overline{AC}$ is perpendicular to $\overline{BD}$, the area of rectangle $EFGH$ is $d_1 \times d_2$. Since the area of $\triangle ABO$, $\triangle CBO$, $\triangle ADO$, and $\triangle CDO$ are each $\frac{1}{2}$ the area of $AEBO$, $\triangle CFBO$, $\triangle AHDO$, and $\triangle CGDO$, respectively, the area of rhombus $ABCD$ is $\frac{1}{2} \times$ the area of rectangle $EFGH = \frac{1}{2}d_1 d_2$.

Polygons and Circles 141

Examples

Find the area of a trapezoid $ABCD$ below.

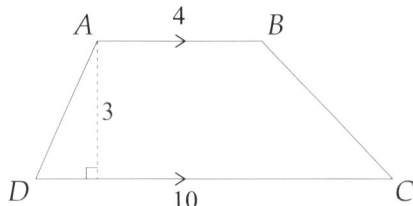

Solution

$$Area = \frac{1}{2}(b_1 + b_2)h = \frac{1}{2}(4+10) \cdot 3 = 21.$$
➢ $Area = 21.$

3. Parallelograms and Area

1 Parallelogram and Area, Part 1

A parallelogram can be divided into two triangles with equal area by a diagonal.

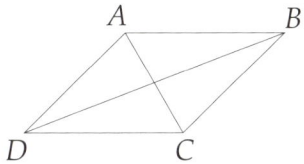

$\triangle ADC = \triangle DCB = \triangle CBA = \triangle BAD = \frac{1}{2} \times$ area of parallelogram $ABCD$.

Proof:
In $\triangle ADC$ and $\triangle CBA$, $\overline{AD} \cong \overline{CB}$ and $\overline{DC} \cong \overline{BA}$ by definition of parallelogram. Also, $\overline{AC} \cong \overline{CA}$ by reflexive property. Therefore, $\triangle ADC \cong \triangle CBA$ by SSS Congruence and this tells us that the area of $\triangle ADC$ and $\triangle CBA$ are equal. In the same manner, since $\triangle DCB \cong \triangle BAD$ by SSS Congruence, the area of $\triangle DCB$ and $\triangle BAD$ are equal. Now, since the area of $\triangle ADC, \triangle DCB, \triangle CBA,$ and $\triangle BAD$ are each equal to one half of the area of parallelogram of $ABCD$, $\triangle ADC = \triangle DCB = \triangle CBA = \triangle BAD$.

2 Parallelogram and Area, Part 2

A parallelogram can be divided into four triangles with equal area by two diagonals.

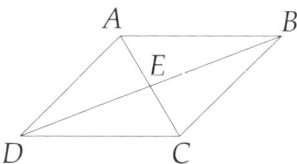

$\triangle AED = \triangle DEC = \triangle CEB = \triangle BEA = \dfrac{1}{4} \times$ area of parallelogram $ABCD$.

Proof:
In $\triangle AED$ and $\triangle CEB$, $\overline{AE} \cong \overline{CE}$ and $\overline{DE} \cong \overline{BE}$ by property of parallelogram. Also, $\angle AED \cong \angle CEB$ because they are vertical angles. Therefore, $\triangle ADE \cong \triangle CBE$ by SAS Congruence and this tells us that the area of $\triangle ADE$ and $\triangle CBE$ are equal. In the same manner, since $\triangle DCE \cong \triangle BAE$ by SAS Congruence, the area of $\triangle DCE$ and $\triangle BAE$ are equal. Now, since the area of $\triangle ADE, \triangle DCE, \triangle CBE,$ and $\triangle BAE$ are each equal to one fourth of the area of parallelogram of $ABCD$, $\triangle ADE = \triangle DCE = \triangle CBE = \triangle BAE$.

Examples

If the area of the parallelogram $ABCD$ is $48\,in^2$, what is the area of $\triangle AEB$?

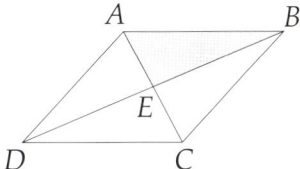

Solution

Since the area of $\triangle AEB$ is one fourth of the area of parallelogram $ABCD$, the area of $\triangle AEB$ is $\dfrac{1}{4} \times 48 = 12\,in^2$.

➢ $\triangle AEB = 12\,in^2$.

4. Regular Polygons and Area

1 Area of a Regular Polygon

Area of a Regular Polygon: If a regular polygon has an area of A square units, a perimeter of P units, and an apothem of a units, then $A = \frac{1}{2}Pa$. The **center of a regular polygon** is the center of the circle which circumscribes or inscribes a regular polygon. **Apothem** is a line segment drawn from the center of a regular polygon perpendicular to a side of the polygon.

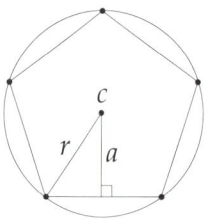

→

Center: Point C
Apothem: a
Radius: r

Examples

Find the area of a regular pentagon as shown in the figure below.

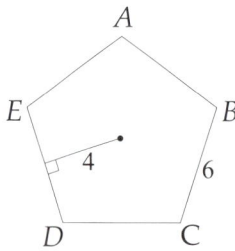

Solution

$a = 4, P = 6 \cdot 5 = 30$

$Area = \frac{1}{2}Pa = \frac{1}{2} \cdot 30 \cdot 4 = 60.$

➢ Area = 60.

5. Circumference and Area of a Circle

1 Introduction

Introduction: The length of or distance around a circle is called the **circumference** and the line segment connecting two points on a circle's circumference is called the **chord**. If the chord passes through the center of a circle, it is the **diameter** of the circle and a half of diameter is **radius**. Also, the angle subtended at the center of a circle by two given points on the circle is called the **central angle**.

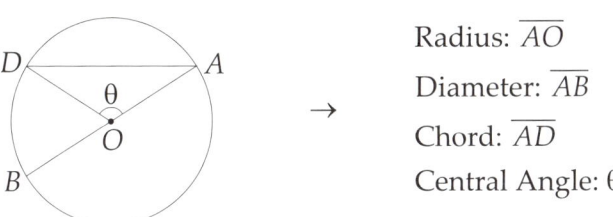

Radius: $\overline{AO}$

Diameter: $\overline{AB}$

Chord: $\overline{AD}$

Central Angle: θ

The portion of a circle connecting two points on the circle's circumference is called an **arc**. **Major arc** is any arc whose length is greater than the length of a semicircle and **minor arc** is any arc whose length is less than the length of a semicircle. Also, the **sector of a circle** is a region bounded by an arc of the circle and the two radii to the endpoints of the arc.

Major Arc: $\widehat{ACB}$

Minor Arc: $\widehat{AB}$

Sector: shaded part.

2 Circumference and Area of a Circle

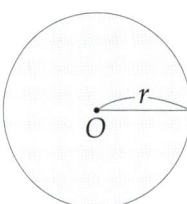

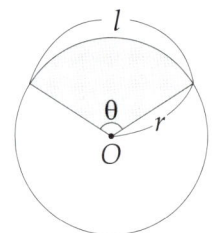

Circumference: $C = 2\pi r$

Area of a circle: $A = \pi r^2$

Arc length: $l = 2\pi r \times \dfrac{\theta°}{360°}$

Area of a sector: $A = \pi r^2 \times \dfrac{\theta°}{360°}$

Examples

A circle O with points A and B on the circumference is given below. Find each of the following.

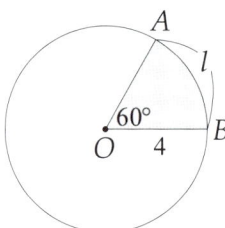

(1) The arc length l (2) The area of sector AOB

Solution

(1) $l = 2\pi r \times \dfrac{\theta°}{360°} = 2\pi(4) \times \dfrac{60°}{360°} = \dfrac{4\pi}{3}$.

➢ $l = \dfrac{4\pi}{3}$.

(2) $A = \pi r^2 \times \dfrac{\theta°}{360°} = \pi(4)^2 \times \dfrac{60°}{360°} = \dfrac{8\pi}{3}$.

➢ $A = \dfrac{8\pi}{3}$.

6. Geometric Probability

Geometric probability involves using the principles of length and area to find the probability of an event.

1 Length Probability

If a point on $\overline{AD}$ is chosen at random, then the probability that the point is on $\overline{BC}$ is $P = \dfrac{\overline{BC}}{\overline{AD}}$.

2 Area Probability

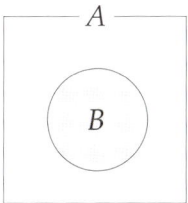

If a point in region A is chosen at random, then the probability that the point is in region B is $P = \dfrac{\text{Area of } B}{\text{Area of } A}$.

Examples

Find the probability that a point chosen at random on $\overline{AE}$ is on each segment.

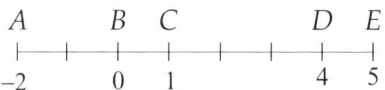

(1) $\overline{BC}$ (2) $\overline{AD}$

Solution

(1) $P = \dfrac{\overline{BC}}{\overline{AE}} = \dfrac{1-0}{5-(-2)} = \dfrac{1}{7}$.

➢ $P = \dfrac{1}{7}$.

(2) $P = \dfrac{\overline{AD}}{\overline{AE}} = \dfrac{4-(-2)}{5-(-2)} = \dfrac{6}{7}$.

➢ $P = \dfrac{6}{7}$.

Review Exercise

1. Given each polygon below, find the value of x.

(1)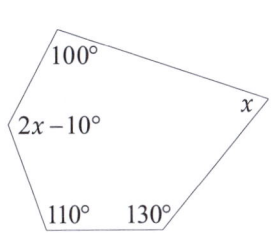

(2)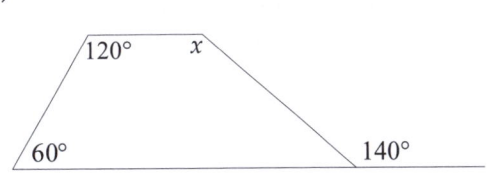

(3)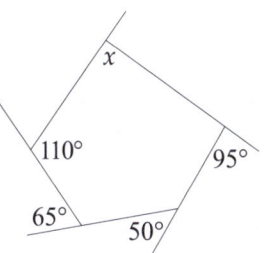

(4)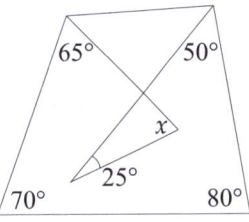

(5)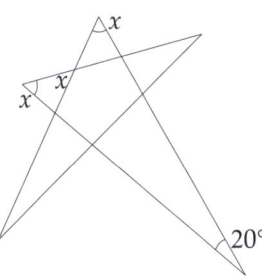

(6)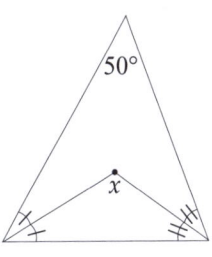

Solution

(1) Sum of interior angles of a pentagon is $180° \cdot (5-2) = 540°$.
$(2x - 10°) + x + 100° + 110° + 130° = 540°$
$3x + 330° = 540°$, $x = 70°$.
➢ $x = 70°$.

(2)

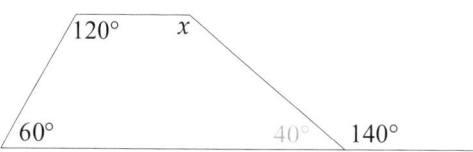

Sum of interior angles of a quadrilateral is $180° \cdot (4-2) = 360°$.
$x + 40° + 60° + 120° = 360°$, $x = 140°$.
➢ $x = 140°$.

(3)

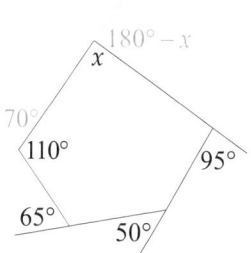

Sum of exterior angles of any polygon is always $360°$.
$(180° - x) + 95° + 50° + 65° + 70° = 360°$, $x = 100°$.
➢ $x = 100°$.

(4)

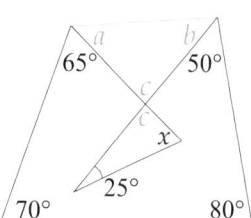

In two triangles, $a + b + c = 25° + x + c$, $a + b = 25° + x$
Since the sum of interior angles of a quadrilateral is $360°$,
$(a + 65°) + (b + 50°) + 80° + 70° = 360°$
$a + b = 95°$, $25° + x = 95°$, $x = 70°$.
➢ $x = 70°$.

(5)

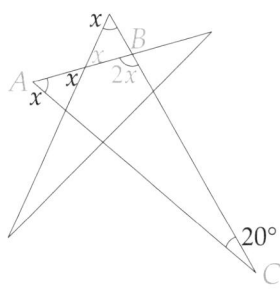

In $\triangle ABC$, $\angle ABC = 2x$ by exterior angle theorem.
Since the sum of interior angles of a triangle is 180°,
$\angle A + \angle ABC + \angle C = 180°$, $x + 2x + 20° = 180°$, $x = \dfrac{160°}{3}$.

➢ $x = \dfrac{160°}{3}$.

(6)

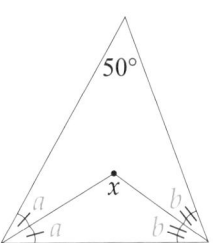

In a smaller triangle, $a + b + x = 180°$, $a + b = 180° - x \rightarrow (1)$ and
in a larger triangle, $2a + 2b + 50° = 180°$, $2(a+b) = 130° \rightarrow (2)$.
Now, if we substitute (1) into (2), then
$2(180° - x) = 130°$, $-2x = -230°$, $x = 115°$.

➢ $x = 115°$.

2. The measures of the angles of a pentagon are in the ratio of 2:3:4:5:6. What is the number of degrees in the measure of the smallest angle?

Solution

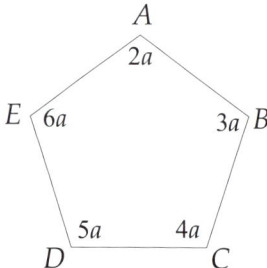

Since the ratio the angles are $2:3:4:5:6$,
we can assume the angles are $2a, 3a, 4a, 5a, 6a$.
Since the sum of interior angles of a pentagon is 540°,
$2a + 3a + 4a + 5a + 6a = 540°$, $20a = 540°$, $a = 27$.
The smallest angle $2a = 2 \cdot 27 = 54°$.

➢ The smallest angle is 54°.

3. In each of the following, find the value of x.

(1)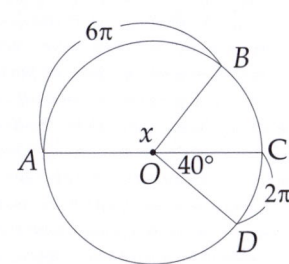

(2)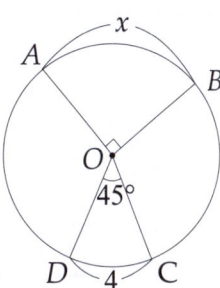

(3)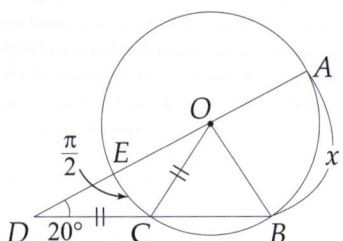

(4)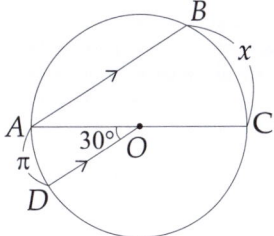

Solution

(1) $2\pi = 2\pi r \cdot \dfrac{40°}{360°}$, $r = 9$.

$6\pi = 2\pi(9) \cdot \dfrac{x°}{360°}$, $x = 120°$.

➢ $x = 120°$.

Alternate Solution:
Using the ratio,
$\dfrac{40°}{x} = \dfrac{2\pi}{6\pi}$, $x = 120°$.

(2) $4 = 2\pi r \cdot \dfrac{45°}{360°}$, $r = \dfrac{16}{\pi}$.

$x = 2\pi \left(\dfrac{16}{\pi}\right) \cdot \dfrac{90°}{360°} = 8$.

➢ $x = 8$.

Alternate Solution:

Using the ratio,
$\dfrac{x}{4} = \dfrac{90°}{45°}$, $x = 8$.

(3) In $\triangle CDO$, since $\overline{CD} \cong \overline{CO}$, $\angle COD = 20°$
and $\angle BCO = 20° + 20° = 40°$.
Also, in $\triangle COB$, since $\overline{CO} \cong \overline{BO}$, $\angle CBO = 40°$
and $\angle COB = 180° - 40° - 40° = 100°$.
So, $\angle AOB = 180° - 20° - 100° = 60°$.

Now, using the ratio, $\dfrac{x}{\frac{\pi}{2}} = \dfrac{60°}{20°}$, $x = \dfrac{3\pi}{2}$.

➢ $x = \dfrac{3\pi}{2}$.

(4)
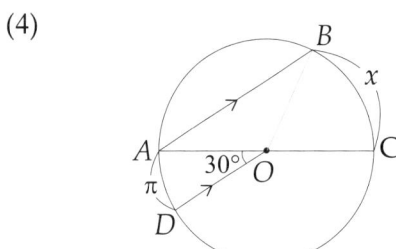

Since $\overline{AB} \parallel \overline{DO}$, $\angle DOA \cong \angle BAO = 30°$.
Also, since $\overline{AO} \cong \overline{BO}$, $\angle ABO = 30°$.
So, in $\triangle ABO$, $\angle BOC = 30° + 30° = 60°$.

Now, using the ratio, $\dfrac{x}{\pi} = \dfrac{60°}{30°}$, $x = 2\pi$.

➢ $x = 2\pi$.

4. Find the area of the shaded region.

(1)
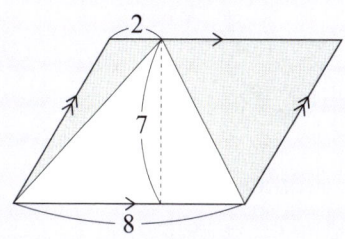

(2)
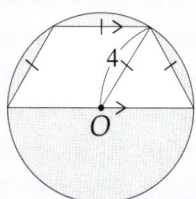

(3)
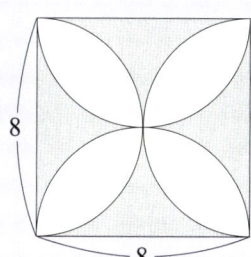

(4)
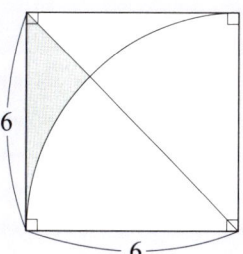

☀ Solution

(1) Area of shaded region = Area of parallelogram − Area of triangle.

$8 \cdot 7 - \frac{1}{2} \cdot 8 \cdot 7 = 28.$

➢ Area of shaded region − 28.

(2)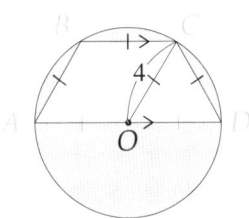

Since $\overline{AO}, \overline{BO}, \overline{CO},$ and $\overline{DO}$ are radii of the circle,
$\overline{AO} \cong \overline{BO} \cong \overline{CO} \cong \overline{DO} = 4$.
So $\triangle ABO, \triangle BCO,$ and $\triangle CDO$ and are all equilateral $\triangle$s.
Area of shaded region = Area of circle – Area of 3 equilateral $\triangle$s.

$$\pi(4)^2 - 3\cdot\left(\frac{\sqrt{3}}{4}\cdot 4^2\right) = 16\pi - 12\sqrt{3}$$

➤ Area of shaded region $= 16\pi - 12\sqrt{3}$.

(3) Area of shaded region
$= 2(\text{Area of square} - \text{Area of two semicircles with radius } 4)$.

$$2\left(8^2 - \pi(4)^2 \cdot \frac{1}{2} \cdot 2\right) = 2(64 - 16\pi) = 128 - 32\pi.$$

➤ Area of shaded region $= 128 - 32\pi$.

(4) Area of shaded region $= \frac{1}{2}(\text{Area of square} - \text{Area of sector with radius } 6)$.

$$\frac{1}{2}\left(6^2 - \pi(6)^2 \cdot \frac{1}{4}\right) = \frac{1}{2}(36 - 9\pi) = 18 - \frac{9\pi}{2}.$$

➤ Area of shaded region $= 18 - \frac{9\pi}{2}$.

5. A parallelogram ABCD with area $72 cm^2$ is given below. If E and F are midpoints of $\overline{AB}$ and $\overline{DC}$ respectively, what is the area of the shaded region?

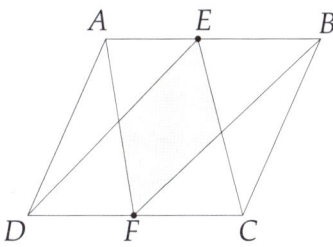

Solution

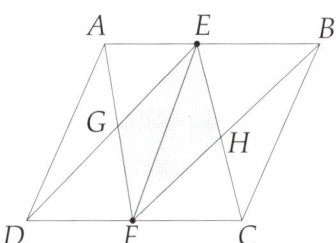

Since $\overline{EB}//\overline{DF}$ and $\overline{EB} \cong \overline{DF}$, EBFD is a parallelogram. So, $\overline{EG}//\overline{HF}$. Also, since $\overline{AE}//\overline{FC}$ and $\overline{AE} \cong \overline{FC}$, AECF is a parallelogram. So, $\overline{GF}//\overline{EH}$. Now, we know that EHFG is a parallelogram. Since the area of AEFD is one half of the area of ABCD and the area of EFG is one fourth of the area of AEFD,
$\triangle EGF = \frac{1}{4}(AEFD) = \frac{1}{4}\left(\frac{1}{2}(ABCD)\right) = \frac{1}{8}(ABCD) = \frac{1}{8} \cdot 72 = 9$. Now, since the area of shaded region is twice the area of $\triangle EFG$, the area is $2 \cdot 9 = 18$.

➢ The area is $18 cm^2$.

6. Find the area of a regular hexagon with side length 4.

Solution

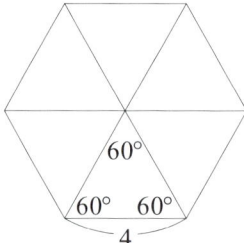

Since the angles of a regular hexagon are each $\frac{180 \cdot (6-2)}{6} = 120°$, the long diagonals split each angle into two 60° angles. Therefore, each of the little six triangles formed by drawing all three long diagonals is equilateral. So, the area of the hexagon is 6 times the area of an equilateral triangle with side length 4.

$Area = 6 \cdot \left(\frac{\sqrt{3}}{4} \cdot 4^2 \right) = 24\sqrt{3}.$

➢ $Area = 24\sqrt{3}.$

7. Find the probability that a point chosen at random in each figure is in the shaded region.

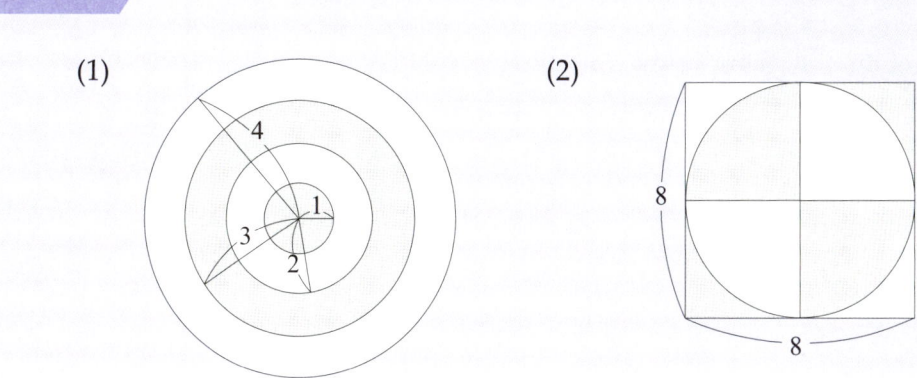

Solution

(1) $P = \dfrac{\text{Area of shaded region}}{\text{Area of whole region}} = \dfrac{\left[\pi(3)^2 - \pi(2)^2\right] + \pi(1)^2}{\pi(4)^2} = \dfrac{6\pi}{16\pi} = \dfrac{3}{8}.$

➢ $P = \dfrac{3}{8}.$

(2)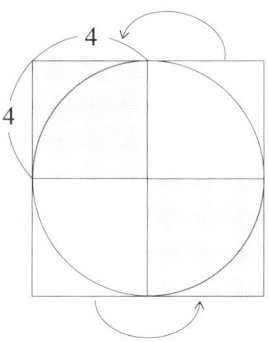

$P = \dfrac{\text{Area of shaded region}}{\text{Area of whole region}} = \dfrac{2 \cdot 4 \cdot 4}{8 \cdot 8} = \dfrac{1}{2}.$

➢ $P = \dfrac{1}{2}.$

Chapter 7

SOLUTION: PAGE 344 *Practice Problems*

01 In each of the following below, find the value of *x*.

(1)

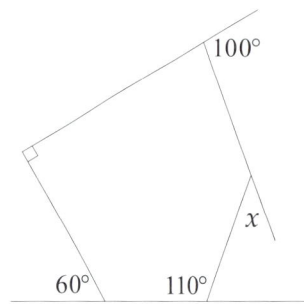

(2)

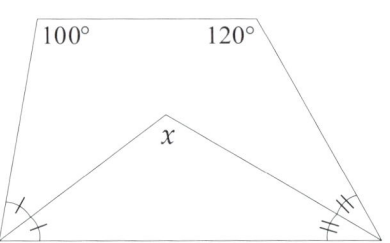

(3)

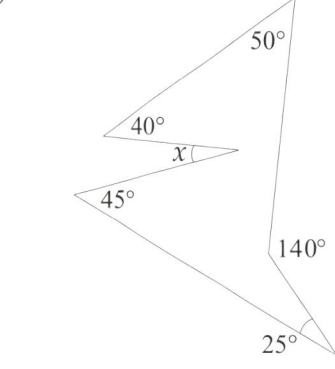

(4)

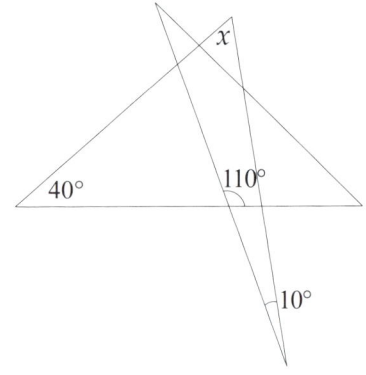

02 In the figure below, find the value of $\angle 1 + \angle 2 + \angle 3 + \angle 4 + \angle 5 + \angle 6$.

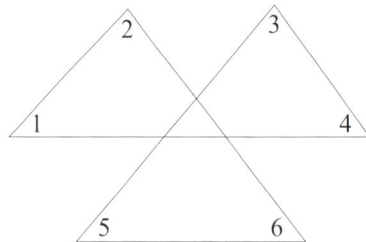

Chapter 7 *Practice Problems*

03 In the figure below, find the value of ∠1 + ∠2 + ∠3 + ∠4.

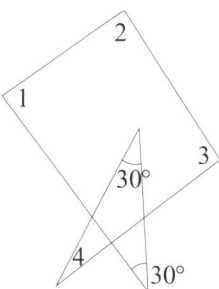

04 A regular hexagon *ABCDEF* is given below. What is the measure of ∠BGE?

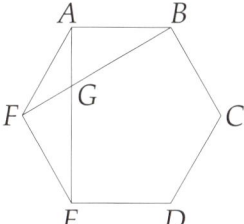

05 If the ratio of one interior angle to one exterior angle in a regular polygon is 3 to 1, then what is the measure of sum of interior angles?

06 Two rectangles *ABCD* and *EFBD* are given below. If the area of rectangle *ABCD* is $12\,m^2$, what is the area of rectangle *EFBD*?

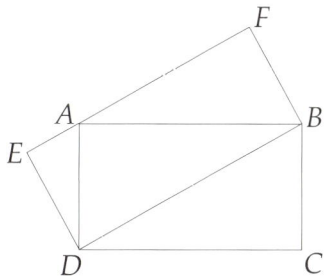

Chapter 7 *Practice Problems*

07 Find the area of trapezoid *ABCD* given below.

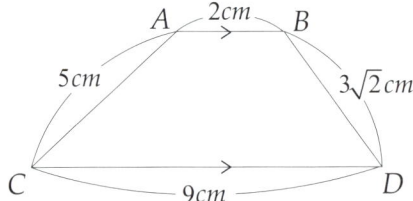

08 A parallelogram *ABCD* is given below. If the area of $\triangle AEF$ and $\triangle DEG$ are $4\,in^2$ and $8\,in^2$, what is the area of parallelogram *ABCD*?

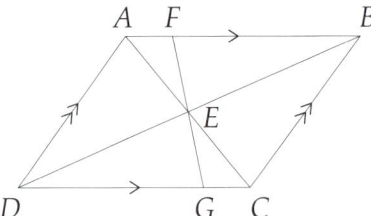

09 A rhombus *ABCD* is given below. If $\overline{AD} = 2x+5$, $\overline{CE} = 3x$, and $\overline{BE} = x+1$, what is the area of rhombus *ABCD*?

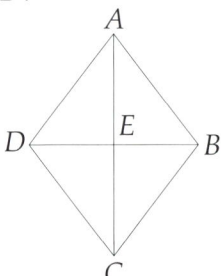

10 Two squares *ABCD* and *EFGH* are given below. Find the area of shaded region.

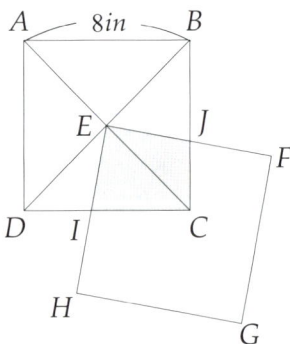

Chapter 7 *Practice Problems*

11 If the length of $\overset{\frown}{AB}$ is twice long as the length of $\overset{\frown}{BC}$, what is the measure of ∠ABO?

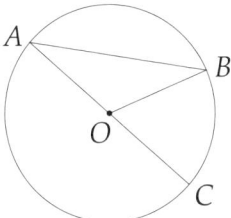

12 If ∠AOB : ∠BOC : ∠COA is 2 : 3 : 4, what is the area of sector BOC?

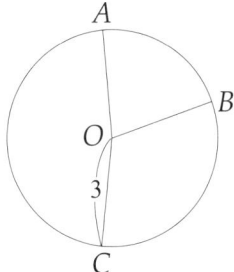

13 If $\overline{AB} \parallel \overline{OC}$ and $\overset{\frown}{CD} = 4\,in$ in the figure below, what is the measure of $\overset{\frown}{AB}$?

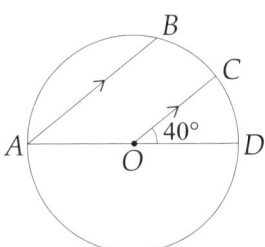

14 In each of the following, find the area of shaded region.

(1)

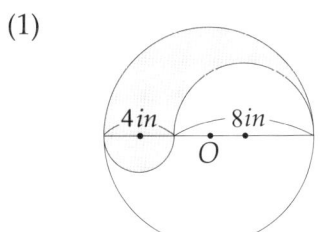

(2)

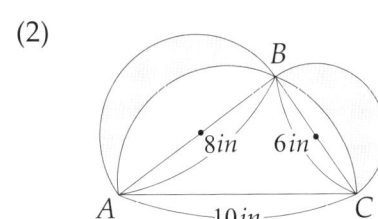

Polygons and Circles 165

Chapter 7 *Practice Problems*

(3)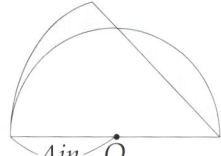

(4)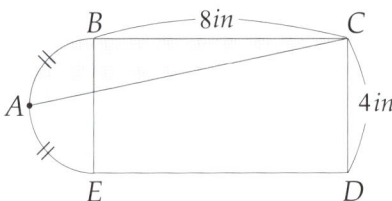

15 A regular octagon *ABCDEFGH* with side length 2 is given below. Find each of the following area.

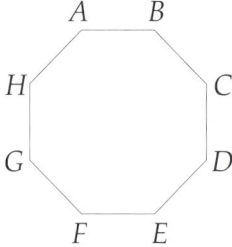

(1) *ABCDEFGH*   (2) *ABDG*

16 Find the probability that a point chosen at random in each figure is in the shaded region.

(1)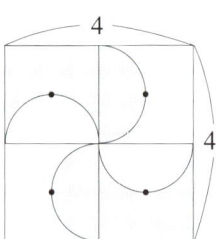

(2)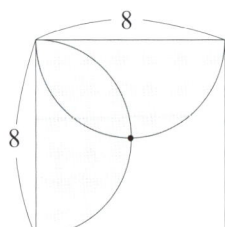

CHAPTER 8

More about Circles

1. Arc

1 Arc Measure

Arc Measure: The measure of a minor arc is the measure of its central angle. The measure of a major arc is 360° minus the measure of its central angle. The measure of a semicircle is 180°.

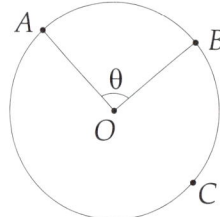
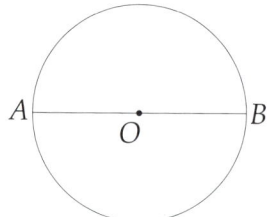

$\widehat{AB} = \theta$

$\widehat{ACB} = 360° - \theta$

$\widehat{AB} = 180°$

2 Adjacent Arcs

Adjacent Arcs: The arcs of a circle that have exactly one point in common.

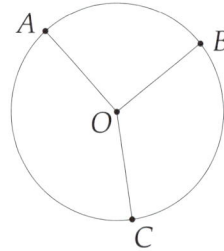

$\widehat{AB}$ and $\widehat{BC}$ are adjacent arcs.

$\widehat{ABC} = \widehat{AB} + \widehat{BC}$

2. Circle and its Chords

1 Theorem 1

Theorem 1: In a circle, if a segment from the center is perpendicular to a chord, then it bisects the chord.

If $\overline{AB} \perp \overline{OM}$,
then $\overline{AM} \cong \overline{BM}$

Proof:

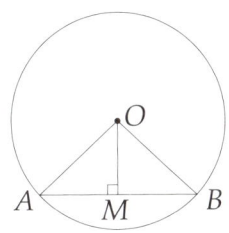

Statements	Reasons
1. $\overline{AB} \perp \overline{OM}$	1. Given
2. $\angle AMO \cong \angle BMO = 90°$	2. Because $\overline{AB} \perp \overline{OM}$
3. $\overline{AO} \cong \overline{BO}$	3. Radii of a circle are $\cong$
4. $\overline{OM} \cong \overline{OM}$	4. Reflexive property
5. $\triangle AOM \cong \triangle BOM$	5. HL Congruence
6. $\overline{AM} \cong \overline{BM}$	6. CPCTC

➤ Similarly, if a radius is perpendicular to a chord, then it bisects the arc too.

2 Theorem 2

Theorem 2: In a circle, if two arcs are congruent, their corresponding chords are congruent.

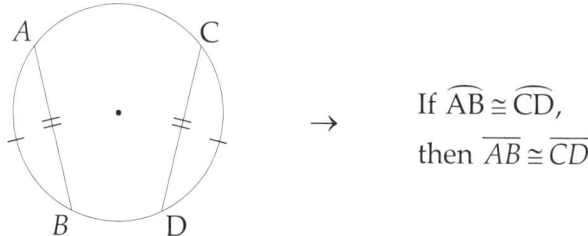

If $\widehat{AB} \cong \widehat{CD}$,
then $\overline{AB} \cong \overline{CD}$

➢ You will be asked to prove this in Practice Problems.

3 Theorem 3

Theorem 3: In a circle, if two chords are equidistant from the center, then they are congruent.

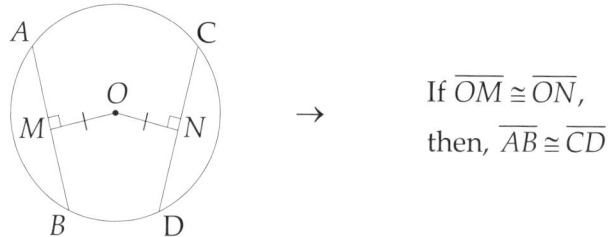

If $\overline{OM} \cong \overline{ON}$,
then, $\overline{AB} \cong \overline{CD}$

Proof:

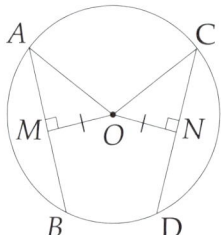

Statements	Reasons
1. $\overline{OM} \cong \overline{ON}$	1. Given
2. $\overline{AO} \cong \overline{CO}$	2. Radii of a circle are $\cong$
3. $\angle AMO \cong \angle CNO = 90°$	3. Distance between a point and segment is $\perp$
4. $\triangle AMO \cong \triangle CNO$	4. HL Congruence
5. $\overline{AM} \cong \overline{CN}$	5. CPCTC
6. $\overline{AB} = 2\overline{AM}, \overline{CD} = 2\overline{CN}$	6. Proved from theorem 1
7. $\overline{AB} \cong \overline{CD}$	7. Substitution property

Examples

Find the measure of $\overline{AB}$.

(1)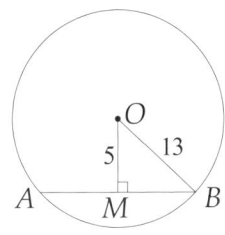

(2)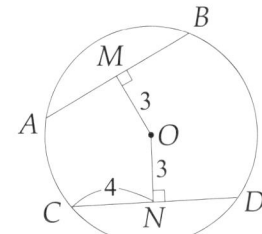

Solution

(1) In a right triangle $\triangle BOM$, $\overline{BM} = \sqrt{13^2 - 5^2} = 12$.
   Since $\overline{AM} \cong \overline{BM}$, $\overline{AB} = 2\overline{BM} = 2 \cdot 12 = 24$.
   ➤ $\overline{AB} = 24$.

(2) Since $\overline{OM} \cong \overline{ON}$, $\overline{AB} \cong \overline{CD}$.
   $\overline{AB} = 2\overline{CN} = 2 \cdot 4 = 8$.
   ➤ $\overline{AB} = 8$.

3. Inscribed Angles

1 Inscribed angle Part 1

Inscribed angle: An angle subtended at a point on the circle by two given points on the circle.

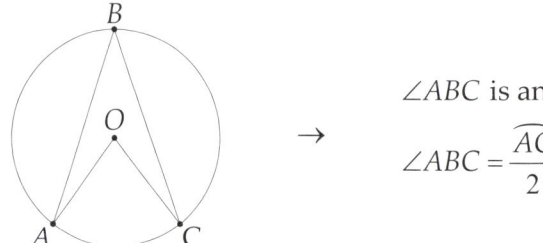

$\angle ABC$ is an inscribed angle.

$\angle ABC = \dfrac{\widehat{AC}}{2}$ or $\angle ABC = \dfrac{\angle AOC}{2}$

We say that $\angle ABC$ intercepts $\widehat{AC}$ and $\widehat{AC}$ is called the intercepted arc of $\angle ABC$. The measure of an inscribed angle is one-half the measure of the intercepted arc.

Proof:

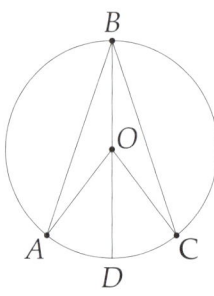

Statements	Reasons
1. $\overline{BD}$ is a diameter	1. Draw diameter $\overline{BD}$ auxiliary
2. $\overline{OA} \cong \overline{OB} \cong \overline{OC}$	2. Radii of a circle are $\cong$
3. $\angle OAB \cong \angle OBA$	3. Because $\overline{OA} \cong \overline{OB}$
4. $\angle AOD = \angle OAB + \angle OBA$	4. Exterior $\angle$ theorem
5. $\angle AOD = 2\angle OBA$	5. Substitution property
6. $\angle OCB \cong \angle OBC$	6. Because $\overline{OC} \cong \overline{OB}$
7. $\angle COD = \angle OCB + \angle OBC$	7. Exterior $\angle$ theorem
8. $\angle COD = 2\angle OBC$	8. Substitution property
9. $\angle AOD + \angle COD = \angle AOC$	9. $\angle$ addition postulate

10. $2\angle OBA + 2\angle OBC = \angle AOC$	10. Substitution property
11. $\angle OBA + \angle OBC = \dfrac{\angle AOC}{2}$	11. Division property
12. $\angle OBA + \angle OBC = \angle ABC$	12. ∠ addition postulate
13. $\angle ABC = \dfrac{\angle AOC}{2}$	13. Substitution property

2 Inscribed angle Part 2

If two or more inscribed angles of a circle intercept congruent arcs, then the angles are congruent.

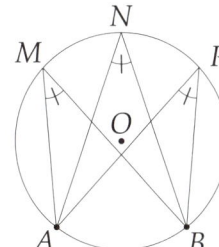   → $\angle AMB \cong \angle ANB \cong \angle APB$

3 Semicircle and Inscribed Angle

Semicircle and Inscribed Angle: If an inscribed angle of a circle intercepts a semicircle, then the angle is a right angle.

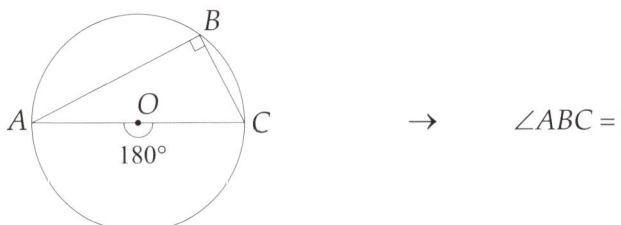   → $\angle ABC = 90°$

Proof:

Since $\angle ABC$ intercepts $\widehat{AC}$ and $\widehat{AC} = 180°$,

$\angle ABC = \dfrac{\widehat{AC}}{2} = \dfrac{180°}{2} = 90°$.

More about Circles 173

4 Cyclic Quadrilaterals

Cyclic Quadrilaterals: If a quadrilateral has all of its vertices lying on a circle, then it is called a **cyclic quadrilateral** and its opposite angles are supplementary.

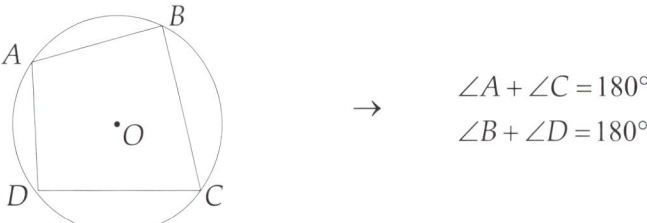

$$\rightarrow \quad \begin{array}{l} \angle A + \angle C = 180° \\ \angle B + \angle D = 180° \end{array}$$

Proof:

Since $\angle A$ and $\angle C$ intercept $\widehat{BCD}$ and $\widehat{BAD}$ respectively,

$$\angle A + \angle C = \frac{\widehat{BCD}}{2} + \frac{\widehat{BAD}}{2} = \frac{1}{2}\left(\widehat{BCD} + \widehat{BAD}\right) = \frac{1}{2}(360°) = 180°.$$

Also, since $\angle B$ and $\angle D$ intercept $\widehat{ADC}$ and $\widehat{ABC}$ respectively,

$$\angle B + \angle D = \frac{\widehat{ADC}}{2} + \frac{\widehat{ABC}}{2} = \frac{1}{2}\left(\widehat{ADC} + \widehat{ABC}\right) = \frac{1}{2}(360°) = 180°.$$

Examples

Find the value of x.

(1)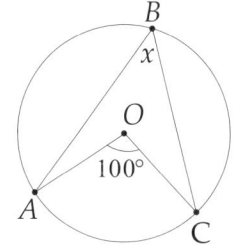

(2)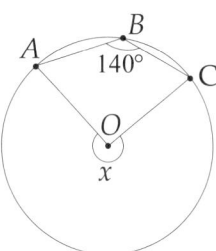

(3)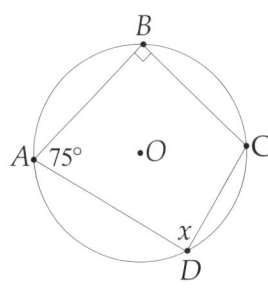

Solution

(1) $x = \dfrac{1}{2} \cdot 100° = 50°$.
   ➢ $x = 50°$.

(2) $140° = \dfrac{x}{2}$, $x = 280°$.
   ➢ $x = 280°$.

(3) Since $\angle ABC + \angle CDA = 180°$, $90° + x = 180°$, $x = 90°$.
   ➢ $x = 90°$.

4. Tangents

1 Tangent Line

Tangent Line: A line is tangent to a circle if it intersects a circle in exactly one point and this point is called a **point of tangency**. A tangent line to a circle is always perpendicular to the radius drawn to the point of tangency. If a line intersects a circle in exactly two points, it is called **a secant line**.

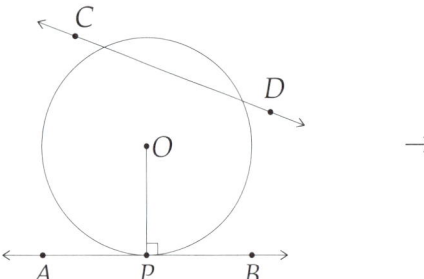

→

Tangent line : $\overleftrightarrow{AB}$

Point of tangency : P

$\overleftrightarrow{AB} \perp \overline{OP}$

Secant line : $\overleftrightarrow{CD}$

2 Tangent Line and an Exterior Point

Tangent Line and an Exterior Point: If two segments from the same exterior point are tangent to a circle, then they are congruent.

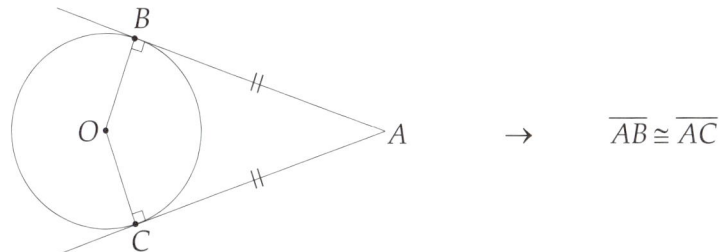

$\overline{AB} \cong \overline{AC}$

Proof:

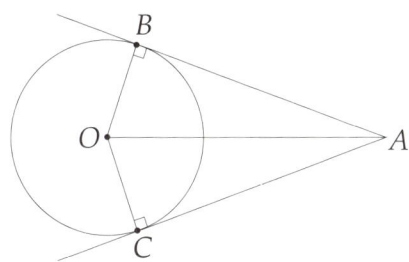

Statements	Reasons
1. $\overline{AB} \perp \overline{OB}, \overline{AC} \perp \overline{OC}$	1. Definition of a tangent line and a circle
2. $\overline{BO} \cong \overline{CO}$	2. Radii of a circle are $\cong$
3. $\overline{AO} \cong \overline{AO}$	3. Reflexive property
4. $\triangle ABO \cong \triangle ACO$	4. HL Congruence
5. $\overline{AB} \cong \overline{AC}$	5. CPCTC

3 Tangent and Chord

Tangent and Chord: If a chord and a tangent line intersect at the point of tangency, then the measure of each angle formed is one-half the measure of its intercepted arc.

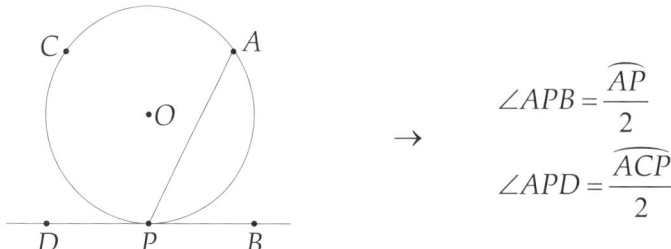

$$\angle APB = \frac{\widehat{AP}}{2}$$

$$\angle APD = \frac{\widehat{ACP}}{2}$$

Proof:

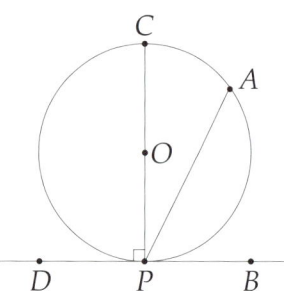

First if we draw diameter $\overline{CP}$, we have $\overline{CP} \perp \overline{DB}$ at point P and $\widehat{AC} + \widehat{AP} = 180°$.
Since $\angle APC = \frac{\widehat{AC}}{2}$, $\angle APB = 90° - \angle APC = 90° - \frac{\widehat{AC}}{2} = \frac{180° - \widehat{AC}}{2} = \frac{\widehat{AP}}{2}$.
So, $\angle APB = \frac{\widehat{AP}}{2}$. Now, since $\angle APC + \angle CPD = \frac{\widehat{AC}}{2} + \frac{\widehat{CP}}{2}$, $\angle APD = \frac{\widehat{ACP}}{2}$.

Examples

Find the value of x and y.

(1)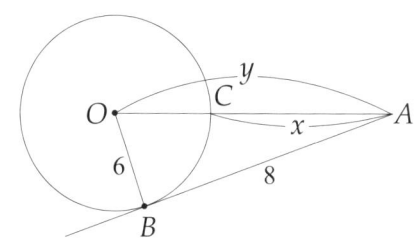

(2)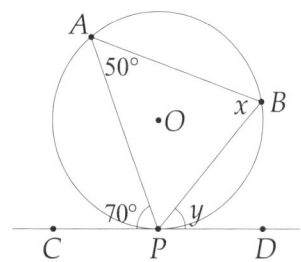

Solution

(1) Since $\overline{AB} \perp \overline{OB}$, $y = \sqrt{8^2 + 6^2} = 10$.
Also, $\overline{OB} \cong \overline{OC} = 6$, $x + \overline{OC} = y$, $x + 6 = 10$, $x = 4$.
➢ $x = 4$ and $y = 10$.

(2) Since $\angle APC = \dfrac{\widehat{AP}}{2} = \angle ABP$, $x = 70°$.
Also, since $\angle BPD = \dfrac{\widehat{BP}}{2} = \angle BAP$, $y = 50°$.
➢ $x = 70°$ and $y = 50°$.

5. More Angle Measures

1 Two Chords

Two Chords: If two chords intersect in the interior of a circle, then the measure of an angle formed is the average of the measures of the arcs intercepted by the chords.

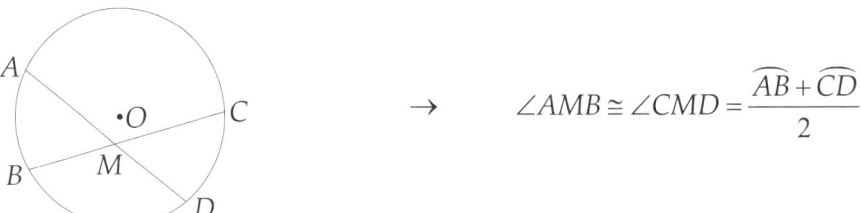

$$\angle AMB \cong \angle CMD = \frac{\widehat{AB} + \widehat{CD}}{2}$$

Proof:

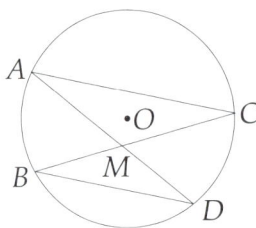

$\angle ADB = \dfrac{\widehat{AB}}{2}$ and $\angle CBD = \dfrac{\widehat{CD}}{2}$

Since $\angle CMD$ is a exterior angle of $\triangle BMD$,

$\angle CMD = \angle ADB + \angle CBD = \dfrac{\widehat{AB}}{2} + \dfrac{\widehat{CD}}{2} = \dfrac{\widehat{AB} + \widehat{CD}}{2}$.

Also, $\angle CMD \cong \angle AMB$ because they are vertical $\angle$s.

2 Tangents and Secants

Tangents and Secants: If two secants, a secant and a tangent, or two tangents intersect in the exterior of a circle, then the measure of the angle formed is one half the positive difference of the measures of the intercepted arcs.

(1) Two Secants

$$\angle CAE = \frac{\widehat{CE} - \widehat{BD}}{2}$$

Proof:

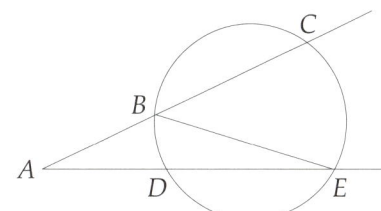

$\angle CBE \cong \dfrac{\widehat{CE}}{2}$ and $\angle BED \cong \dfrac{\widehat{BD}}{2}$

Since $\angle CBE$ is a exterior angle of $\triangle ABE$,

$\angle CBE = \angle CAE + \angle BED, \dfrac{\widehat{CE}}{2} = \angle CAE + \dfrac{\widehat{BD}}{2},$

$\angle CAE = \dfrac{\widehat{CE}}{2} - \dfrac{\widehat{BD}}{2} = \dfrac{\widehat{CE} - \widehat{BD}}{2}.$

(2) A secant and a Tangent

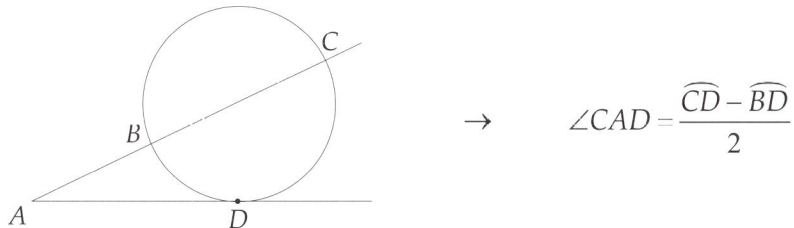

$$\angle CAD = \frac{\widehat{CD} - \widehat{BD}}{2}$$

➤ You will be asked to prove this in Practice Problems.

(3) Two Tangents

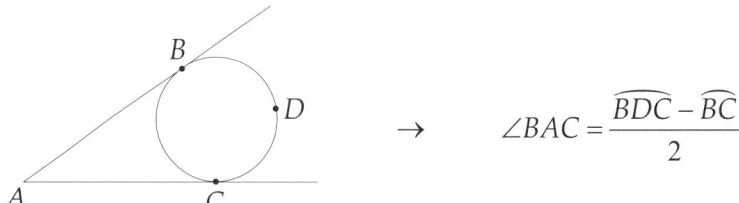

$$\angle BAC = \frac{\widehat{BDC} - \widehat{BC}}{2}$$

➢ You will be asked to prove this in Practice Problems.

Examples

Find the measure of $\angle BMD$ given that $\widehat{AB} = 100°$ and $\widehat{CD} = 60°$.

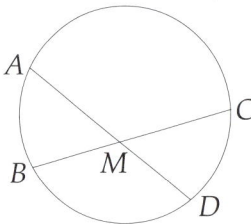

Solution

$\angle AMB = \dfrac{\widehat{AB} + \widehat{CD}}{2} = \dfrac{100° + 60°}{2} = 80°$.
$\angle BMD = 180° - \angle AMB = 180° - 80° = 100°$.
➢ $\angle BMD = 100°$.

Examples

Find the angle measure of $\widehat{CD}$ given that $\widehat{AB} = \angle DPC = 20°$.

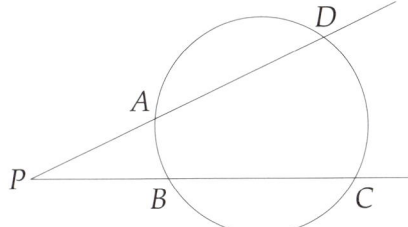

Solution

$\angle DPC = \dfrac{\widehat{CD} - \widehat{AB}}{2}, 20° = \dfrac{\widehat{CD} - 20°}{2}, \widehat{CD} = 60°.$

➢ $\widehat{CD} = 60°.$

6. More Segment Measures

Given circle O, point M not on the circle, and a line through M intersecting the circle in two points. The product of the length from M to the first point of intersection and the length from M to the second point of intersection is constant for any choice of a line through M that intersects the circle.

1 Two Chords

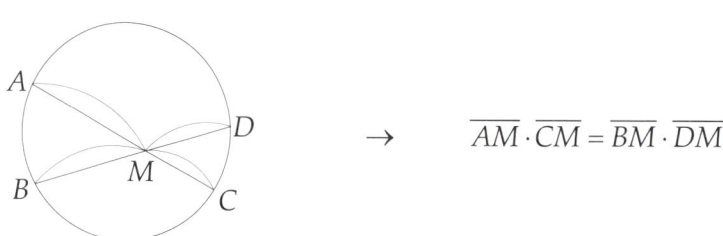

$$\overline{AM} \cdot \overline{CM} = \overline{BM} \cdot \overline{DM}$$

Proof:

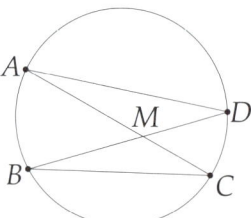

First draw $\overline{AD}$ and $\overline{BC}$. $\angle CAD \cong \angle CBD$ because they intercept the same arc $\overset{\frown}{CD}$. Also, $\angle AMD \cong \angle BMC$ since they are vertical angles. So, $\triangle AMD \sim \triangle BMC$ by AA Similarity. Therefore, $\dfrac{\overline{AM}}{\overline{BM}} = \dfrac{\overline{DM}}{\overline{CM}}$, $\overline{AM} \cdot \overline{CM} = \overline{BM} \cdot \overline{DM}$.

2 Two Secants

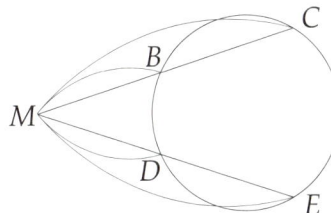 → $\overline{MB} \cdot \overline{MC} = \overline{MD} \cdot \overline{ME}$

> ➤ You will be asked to prove this in Practice Problems.

3 A Secant and a Tangent

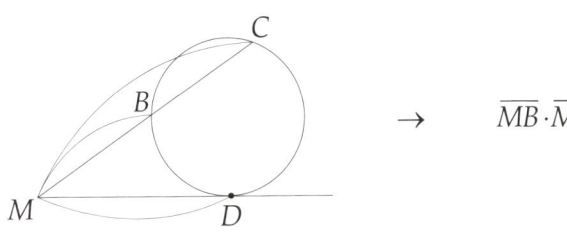 → $\overline{MB} \cdot \overline{MC} = \overline{MD}^2$

> ➤ You will be asked to prove this in Practice Problems.

Examples

Find the measure of $\overline{AM}$.

(1)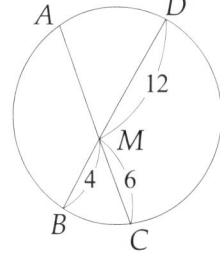

(2)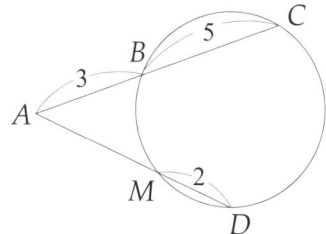

Solution

(1) $\overline{AM} \cdot \overline{CM} = \overline{BM} \cdot \overline{DM}$
$\overline{AM} \cdot 6 = 4 \cdot 12, \overline{AM} = 8.$
➢ $\overline{AM} = 8.$

(2) $\overline{AB} \cdot \overline{BC} = \overline{AM} \cdot \overline{AD}$
$3 \cdot (3+5) = \overline{AM} \cdot (\overline{AM} + 2)$
$24 = \overline{AM}^2 + 2\overline{AM}$
$\overline{AM}^2 + 2\overline{AM} - 24 = 0$
$(\overline{AM} - 4)(\overline{AM} + 6) = 0$
Since $\overline{AM} > 0$, $\overline{AM} = 4.$
➢ $\overline{AM} = 4.$

Review Exercise

1. Find x in each of the following.

(1)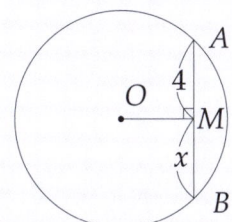

(2)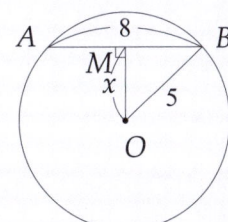

(3)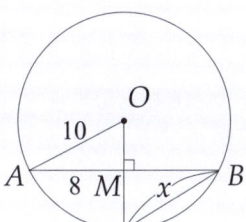

(4)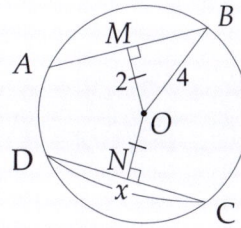

(5)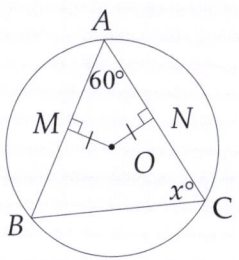

(6)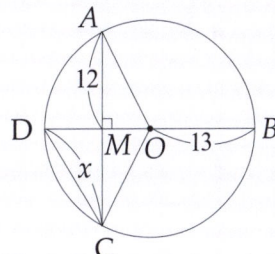

Solution

(1) Since $\overline{OM} \perp \overline{AB}$, $x = \overline{BM} \cong \overline{AM} = 4$.
➢ $x = 4$.

(2) Since $\overline{OM} \perp \overline{AB}$, $\overline{BM} = \dfrac{\overline{AB}}{2} = \dfrac{8}{2} = 4$.
In $\triangle BOM$, $x = \sqrt{5^2 - 4^2} = 3$.
➢ $x = 3$.

(3) Since $\overline{AC} \perp \overline{OB}$, $\overline{AM} \cong \overline{CM} = 8$.
Also, in $\triangle AOM$, $\overline{OM} = \sqrt{10^2 - 8^2} = 6$ and $\overline{BM} = \overline{OB} - \overline{OM} = 10 - 6 =$
Now, in $\triangle CBM$, $x = \sqrt{\overline{BM}^2 + \overline{CM}^2} = \sqrt{4^2 + 8^2} = 4\sqrt{5}$.
➢ $x = 4\sqrt{5}$.

(4) In $\triangle BOM$, $\overline{BM} = \sqrt{4^2 - 2^2} = 2\sqrt{3}$.
Since $\overline{OM} \cong \overline{ON}$, $x = \overline{AB} = 2\overline{BM} = 2 \cdot 2\sqrt{3} = 4\sqrt{3}$.
➢ $x = 4\sqrt{3}$.

(5) Since $\overline{OM} \cong \overline{ON}$, $\overline{AB} \cong \overline{AC}$.
So, $\triangle ABC$ is an isosceles $\triangle$ and $\angle B \cong \angle C = x$.
$\angle A + \angle B + \angle C = 180°$, $60° + x + x = 180°$, $2x = 120°$, $x = 60°$.
➢ $x = 60°$.

(6) First, $\overline{OC} \cong \overline{OD} \cong \overline{OB} = 13$ because they are radii same circle.
Since $\overline{AC} \perp \overline{BD}$, $\overline{CM} \cong \overline{AM} = 12$ and in $\triangle OCD$,
$\overline{OM} = \sqrt{\overline{OC}^2 - \overline{CM}^2} = \sqrt{13^2 - 12^2} = 5$. So, $\overline{DM} = \overline{OD} - \overline{OM} = 13 - 5 = 8$.
Now, in $\triangle CMD$, $x = = \sqrt{\overline{DM}^2 + \overline{CM}^2} = \sqrt{8^2 + 12^2} = 4\sqrt{13}$.
➢ $x = 4\sqrt{13}$.

2. Find x in each of the following.

(1)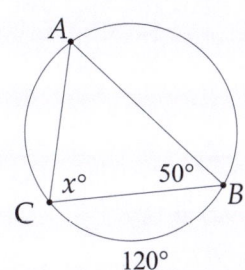

(2)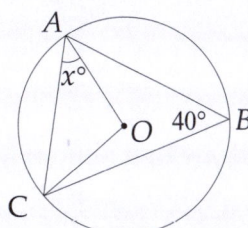

(3)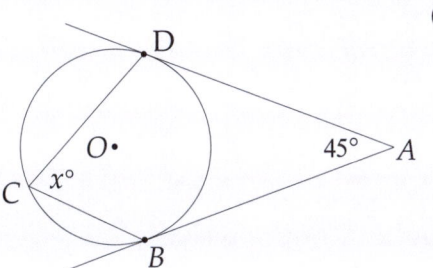

(4)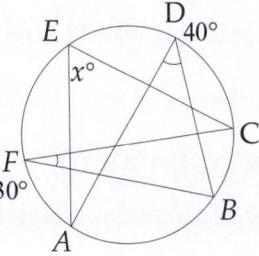

(5)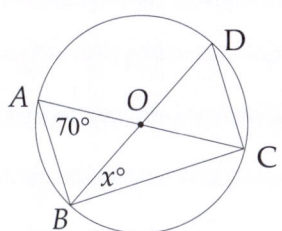

Solution

(1) Since $\angle A$ intercepts $\widehat{BC}$, $\angle A = \dfrac{\widehat{BC}}{2} = \dfrac{120°}{2} = 60°$.
So, in $\triangle ABC$, $x = 180° - 60° - 50° = 70°$.
➤ $x = 70°$.

(2) Since $\angle B$ intercepts $\widehat{AC}$, $\angle B = \dfrac{\angle AOC}{2}$, $40° = \dfrac{\angle AOC}{2}$, $\angle AOC = 80°$.
Also, since $\overline{OA} \cong \overline{OC}$, $\angle OAC \cong \angle OCA$.
Therefore, in $\triangle OAC$, $x + x + 80° = 180°$, $x = 50°$.
➤ $x = 50°$.

(3)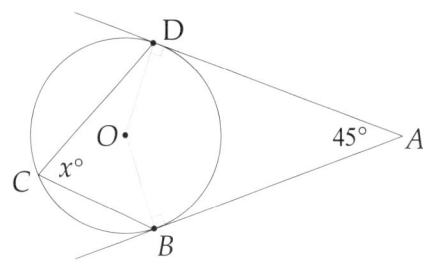

If we draw two radii $\overline{BO}$ and $\overline{DO}$ in circle O,
then $\overline{AD} \perp \overline{OD}$ and $\overline{AB} \perp \overline{OB}$.

Since $\angle C$ intercepts $\widehat{BD}$, $\angle C = \dfrac{\angle BOD}{2}$, $x = \dfrac{\angle BOD}{2}$, $\angle BOD = 2x$.

Now, in a quadrilateral $ABOD$, $45° + 90° + 2x + 90° = 360°$, $x = 67.5°$.

➢ $x = 67.5°$.

(4) First, $\widehat{ABC} = \widehat{AB} + \widehat{BC}$.

Also, $\angle D$ and $\angle F$ intercept $\widehat{AB}$ and $\widehat{BC}$, respectively.

So, $\angle D = \dfrac{\widehat{AB}}{2}$ and $\angle F = \dfrac{\widehat{BC}}{2}$.

Since $\angle E$ intercepts $\widehat{ABC}$, $x = \dfrac{\widehat{ABC}}{2} = \dfrac{\widehat{AB}}{2} + \dfrac{\widehat{BC}}{2} = \angle D + \angle F = 40° + 30° = 70°$.

➢ $x = 70°$.

(5) Since both $\angle A$ and $\angle D$ intercept $\widehat{BC}$, $\angle A \cong \angle D = 70°$.

Also, since $\angle BCD$ intercepts $\widehat{BAD}$, $\angle BCD = \dfrac{\widehat{BAD}}{2} = \dfrac{180°}{2} = 90°$.

Now, in $\triangle BCD$, $x = 180° - 90° - 70° = 20°$.

➢ $x = 20°$.

3. Find $x+y$ in each of the following.

(1)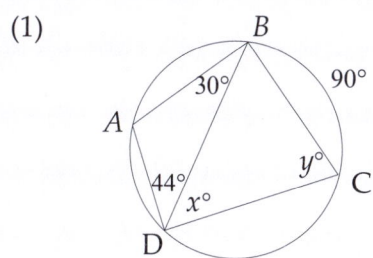

(2)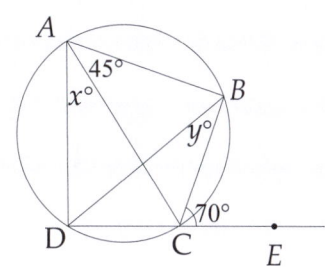

Solution

(1) Since ∠BDC intercepts $\widehat{BC}$, $x = \dfrac{90°}{2} = 45°$.

In △ABD, ∠A = 180° − 30° − 44° = 106°.
Since ∠A + ∠C = 180°, y = 180° − ∠A = 180° − 106° = 74°.
So, $x + y$ = 45° + 74° = 119°.

➢ $x + y = 119°$.

(2) First, ∠BCD = 180° − 70° = 110°.
Since ∠DAB + ∠BCD = 180°, x + 45° + 110° = 180°, x = 25°.

Also, ∠CAD ≅ ∠CBD because both ∠BCD and ∠CAD intercept $\widehat{CD}$.
So, $y = x = 25°$ and $x + y$ = 25° + 25° = 50°.

➢ $x + y$ = 25° + 25° = 50°.

4. Find x in each of the following.

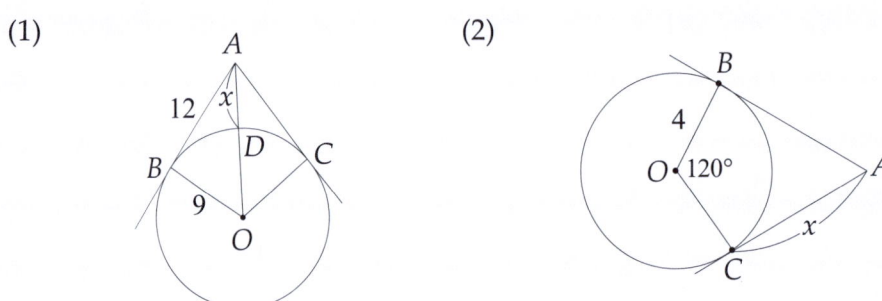

Solution

(1) First, $\overline{OB} \cong \overline{OD} = 9$ because they are radii of the same circle.
Since $\overline{AB} \perp \overline{OB}$, $\overline{AO} = \sqrt{\overline{AB}^2 + \overline{OB}^2} = \sqrt{12^2 + 9^2} = 15$.
Now, $x = \overline{AO} - \overline{DO} = 15 - 9 = 6$.
➤ $x = 6$.

(2)

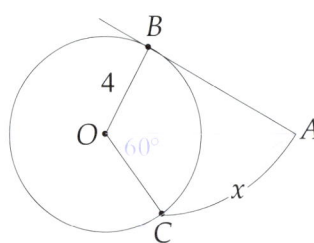

First, $\overline{OB} \cong \overline{OC} = 4$ because they are radii of the same circle.
Since $\overline{AC} \perp \overline{OC}$, $\angle ACO = 90°$ and $\angle CAO = 180° - 60° - 90° = 30°$.
Now, since $\triangle ACO$ is a $30° - 60° - 90°$ triangle,
$\dfrac{\overline{OC}}{\overline{AC}} = \dfrac{1}{\sqrt{3}} = \dfrac{4}{x}$, $x = 4\sqrt{3}$.
➤ $x = 4\sqrt{3}$.

5. Find x and y in each of the following.

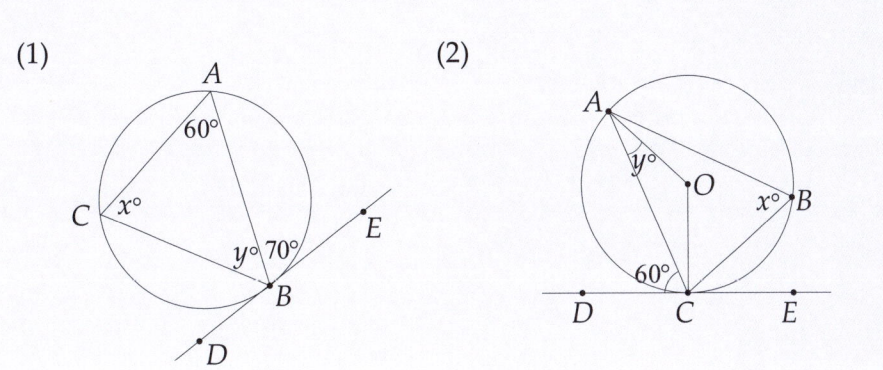

Solution

(1) First, $\angle C$ intercepts $\overset{\frown}{AB}$ so $x = \dfrac{\overset{\frown}{AB}}{2} = \angle ABE$, $x = 70°$.

In $\triangle ABD$, $y = 180° - x - 60° = 180° - 70° - 60° = 50°$.

➢ $x = 70°, y = 50°$.

(2) First, $\overline{OC} \perp \overline{DE}$ so $\angle OCD = 90°$ and $\angle OCA = 90° - 60° = 30°$.

Since $\overline{OA} \cong \overline{OC}$, $\angle OAC \cong \angle OCA \rightarrow y = 30°$.

Also, since $\angle B$ intercepts $\overset{\frown}{AC}$, $x = \dfrac{\overset{\frown}{AC}}{2} = \angle ACD \rightarrow x = 60°$.

➢ $x = 60°, y = 30°$

More about Circles 193

6. Find x, y, and z in each of the following.

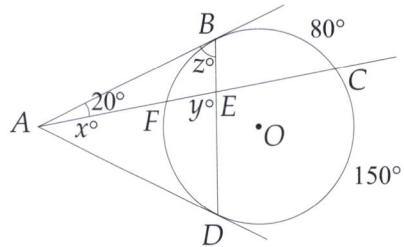

Solution

First, in $\overline{AB}$ and $\overline{AC}$, $\angle BAC = \dfrac{\widehat{BC}-\widehat{BF}}{2}$, $20° = \dfrac{80°-\widehat{BF}}{2}$, $\widehat{BF} = 40°$.

So, in a circle O, $\widehat{DF} = 360° - 150° - 80° - 40° = 90°$.

Now, in $\overline{AC}$ and $\overline{AD}$, $\angle CAD = \dfrac{\widehat{CD}-\widehat{DF}}{2}$, $x = \dfrac{150°-90°}{2} = 30°$.

Also, in $\overline{AB}$ and $\overline{BD}$, $\angle ABD = \dfrac{\widehat{BFD}}{2}$, $z = \dfrac{40°+90°}{2} = 65°$.

Finally, in $\overline{BD}$ and $\overline{CF}$, $\angle DEF = \dfrac{\widehat{BC}+\widehat{DF}}{2}$, $y = \dfrac{80°+90°}{2} = 85°$.

➤ $x = 30°, y = 85°, z = 65°$.

7. Find x in each of the following.

(1)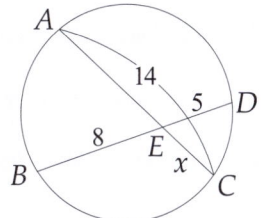
$\overline{CE} < \overline{AE}$

(2)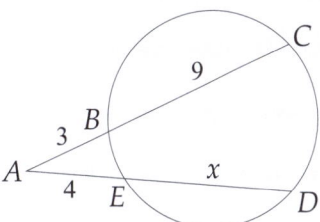

(3)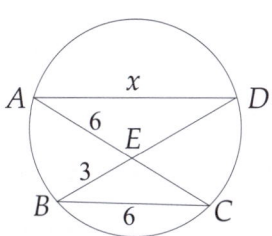

(4)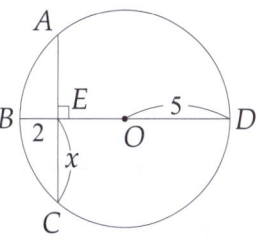

Solution

(1) $\overline{AE} \cdot \overline{CE} = \overline{BE} \cdot \overline{DE}$
$(14-x) \cdot x = 8 \cdot 5$
$14x - x^2 = 40$
$x^2 - 14x + 40 = 0$
$(x-4)(x-10) = 0$, $x = 10$ or $x = 4$
Since $\overline{CE} < \overline{AE}$, $x = 4$.
➤ $x = 4$.

(2) $\overline{AB} \cdot \overline{AC} = \overline{AE} \cdot \overline{AD}$
$3 \cdot (3+9) = 4 \cdot (4+x)$
$36 = 16 + 4x$, $x = 5$
➤ $x = 5$.

(3) Previously, we proved that $\triangle AED \sim \triangle BEC$ by AA Similarity.
So, $\dfrac{\overline{AE}}{\overline{BE}} = \dfrac{\overline{AD}}{\overline{BC}}$, $\dfrac{6}{3} = \dfrac{x}{6}$, $x = 12$.
➤ $x = 12$.

(4) Since $\overline{AC} \perp \overline{BD}$, $\overline{AE} \cong \overline{CE} = x$.
Also, $\overline{DO} \cong \overline{BO} = 5$ and $\overline{EO} = \overline{BO} - \overline{BE} = 5 - 2 = 3$.
Now, $\overline{AE} \cdot \overline{CE} = \overline{BE} \cdot \overline{DE}$,
$x \cdot x = 2 \cdot (5+3)$, $x^2 = 16$, $x = 4$. ➤ $x = 4$.

Chapter 8   SOLUTION: PAGE 361   *Practice Problems*

01 Given two arcs are congruent in a circle, prove that their corresponding chords are congruent.

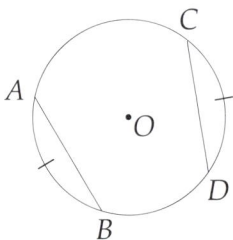

02 Find x in each of the following.

(1)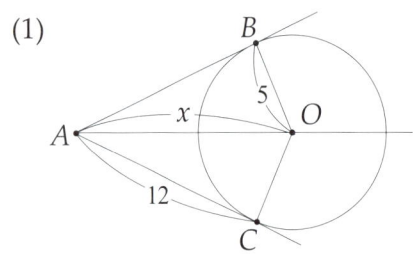

(2)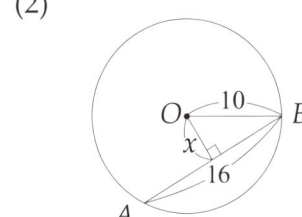

(3)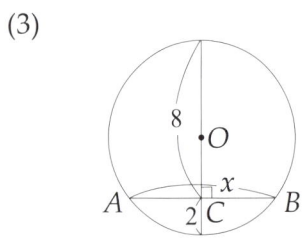

(4)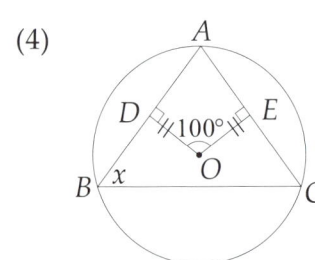

03 If $\overline{AB}$ and $\overline{AC}$ are tangent to the circle O, what is the area of shaded region?

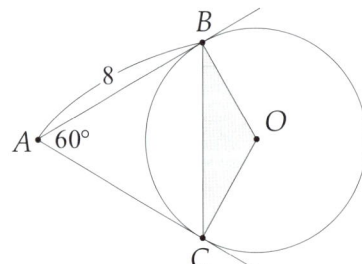

Chapter 8   *Practice Problems*

04 A portion of a circle O with radius 4 cm is folded through $\overline{AB}$ as shown in the figure below. If $\overline{CD} \cong \overline{DE}$, what is the area of $\triangle BDE$?

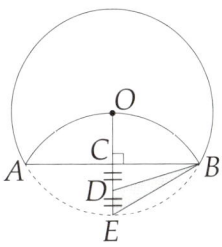

05 Find x in each of the following.

(1)

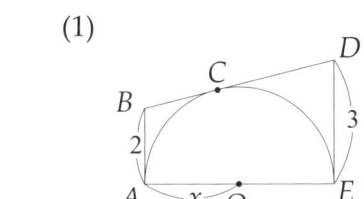

(2)

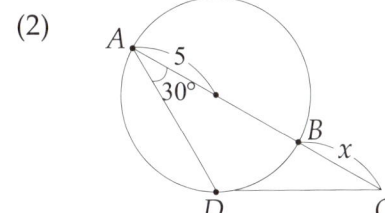

06 Find the perimeter of $\triangle BCD$ in the figure below.

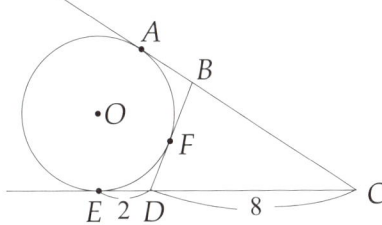

07 In the figure below, prove that $\angle CAD = \dfrac{\overarc{CD} - \overarc{BD}}{2}$.

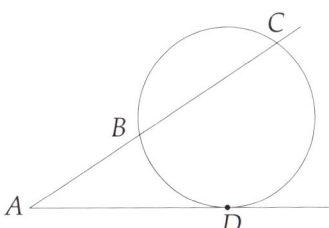

Chapter 8 — Practice Problems

08 In the figure below, prove that $\angle BAC = \dfrac{\widehat{BDC} - \widehat{BC}}{2}$.

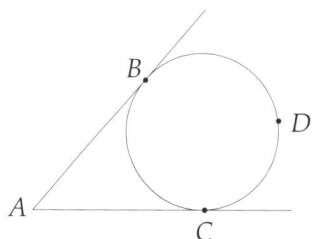

09 Find x in each of the following.

(1)

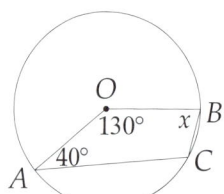

(2)

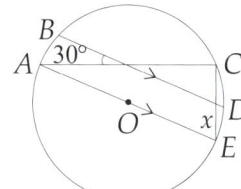

(3)

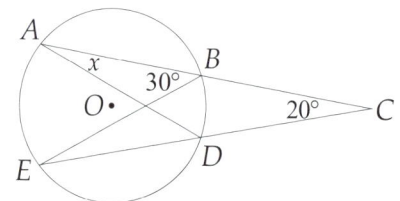

(4)

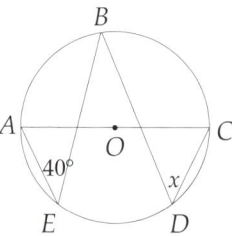

(5)

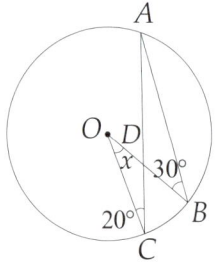

(6)

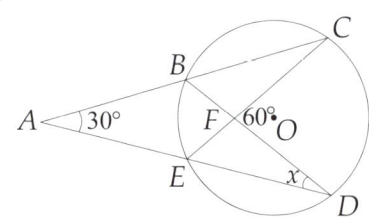

Chapter 8 — Practice Problems

10 If $\overarc{AB} : \overarc{BC} : \overarc{CA} = 1 : 2 : 3$, what is the measure of $\angle CAD$?

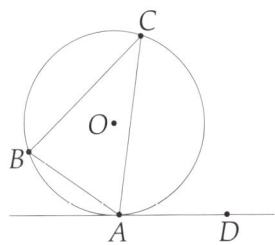

11 In the figure below, prove that $\angle EBD = \dfrac{\overarc{BD} + \overarc{BC}}{2}$.

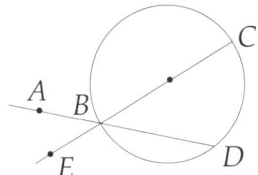

12 Find x in each of the following.

(1)

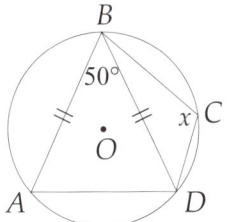

(2)

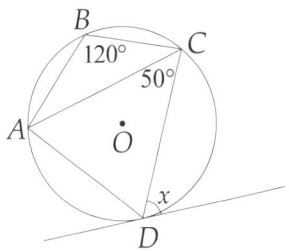

(3) (4)

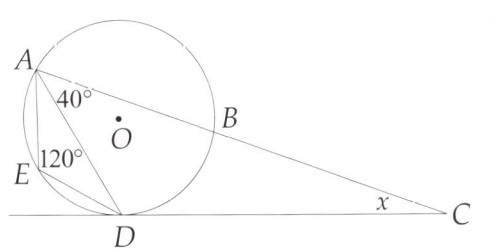

More about Circles 199

Chapter 8

Practice Problems

(5)

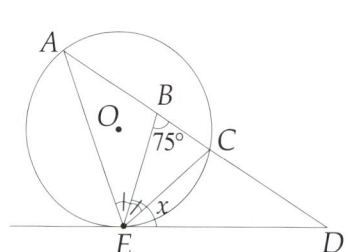

(6)

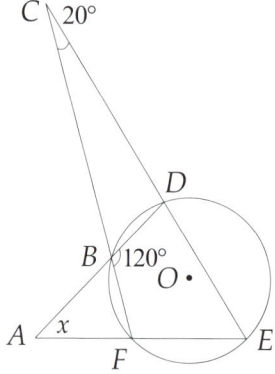

13 In the figure below, prove that $\overline{AB} \cdot \overline{AC} = \overline{AD} \cdot \overline{AE}$.

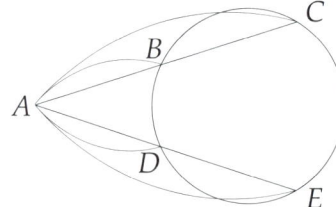

14 In the figure below, prove that $\overline{AB} \cdot \overline{AC} = \overline{AD}^2$.

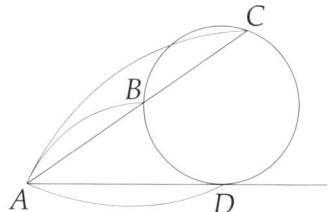

Chapter 8 — Practice Problems

15 Find *x* in each of the following.

(1)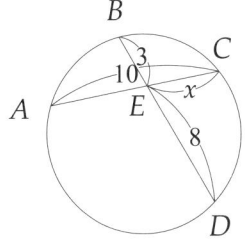

$\overline{CE} < \overline{AE}$

(2)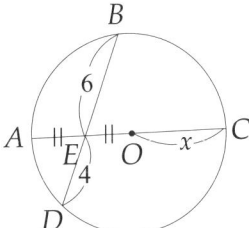

(3)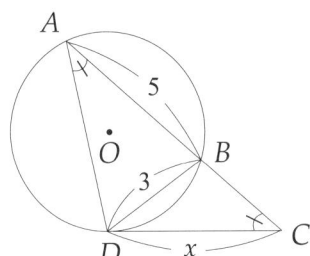

(4)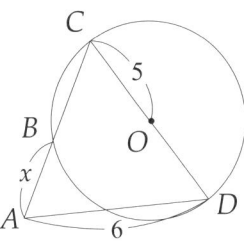

$\overline{AC} \cong \overline{CD}$

(5)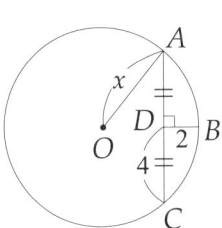

(6)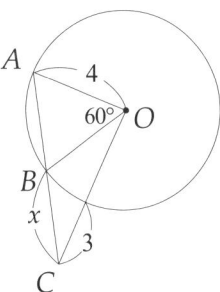

(7)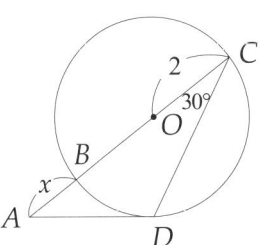

(8)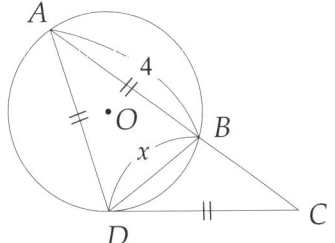

CHAPTER 9

Three-Dimensional Geometry

1. Prisms and Pyramids

1 Prisms

1. **Polyhedron**: A solid figure bounded by polygons.

2. **Prism**: A polyhedron with two congruent, parallel, polygonal bases and whose lateral faces are parallelograms. Prisms are named for the shape of the base.

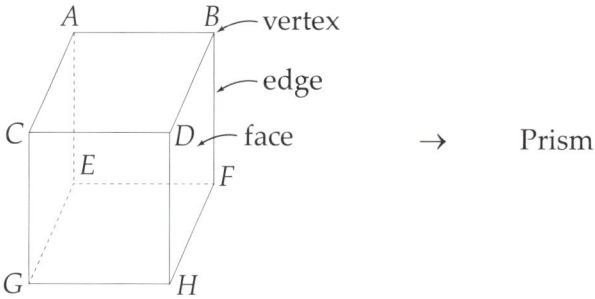 → Prism

3. **Edge**: A line that connects two consecutive vertices of a polyhedron.
   ($\overline{AB}$, $\overline{AC}$, $\overline{CD}$, and etc.)

4. **Face**: Any one of the polygons that bound a polyhedron.
   (*ABDC*, *ABFE*, and etc.)

5. **Lateral face**: A face of a polyhedron, not including its bases.
   (*ABFE*, *BDHF*, and etc.)

6. **Base**: The top and bottom face of the prism.
   (*ABDC* and *EFHG*)

7. **Face Diagonal**: A line segment linking the opposite corners of a face.
   ($\overline{AD}$, $\overline{DF}$, and etc.)

8. **Space Diagonal**: A line segment linking the opposite corners of a prims.
   ($\overline{AH}$, $\overline{BG}$, and etc.)

9. **Skew Lines**: Two non-coplanar lines that do not intersect.
   ($\overline{AE}$ & $\overline{CD}$, $\overline{BD}$ & $\overline{EF}$, etc. are skew lines.)

10. **Altitude**: A segment perpendicular to the planes containing the two bases, with an endpoints in each plane

11. **Right and Oblique Prism**: If the lateral edges of a prism are altitude, then the prism is a right prism. Otherwise, the prism is an oblique prism.

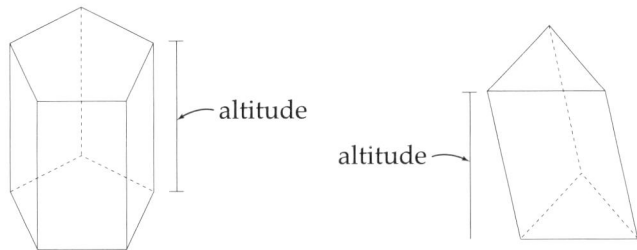

Right Pentagonal Prism   Oblique Triangular Prism

12. **(Total) Surface Area**: The area of all of the surfaces that form the borders of the polyhedron.

13. **Lateral Surface Area**: The total area of all the faces that are not considered bases.

14. **Net**: A two dimensional pattern consisting of polygons which can be folded to form a polyhedron.

Surface Area and Volume of Prisms

Surface Area: $A = 2lw + 2lh + 2wh$

Lateral Surface Area: $L.A. = 2lh + 2wh$

Volume: $V = \text{base} \times \text{height} = lwh$

2 Pyramids

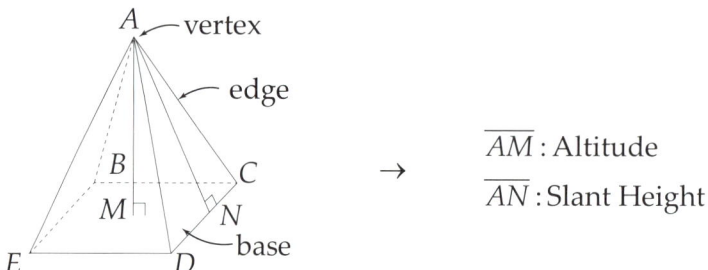

1. **Pyramid**: A polyhedron having a polygonal base and triangles as lateral faces.

2. **Slant Height**: The altitude of a lateral face of a pyramid.

Surface Area and Volume of Pyramids

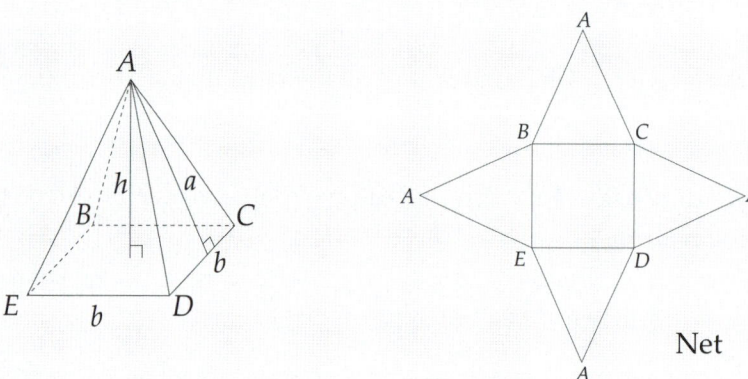

Surface Area: $A = b^2 + 4 \cdot \frac{1}{2}ba = b^2 + 2ba$

Lateral Surface Area: $L.A. = 4 \cdot \frac{1}{2}ba = 2ba$

Volume: $V = \frac{1}{3} \times \text{base} \times \text{height} = \frac{1}{3}b^2 h$

3 Regular Polyhedrons

Regular Polyhedrons: A polyhedron whose faces are identical regular polygons.

Examples

Find the lateral surface area, surface area, and volume of the triangular prism.

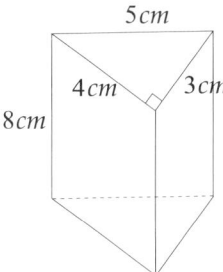

Solution

Lateral Surface Area, $L.A. = 4 \cdot 8 + 3 \cdot 8 + 5 \cdot 8 = 8(4+3+5) = 96\,cm^2$.

Surface Area, $A = L.A. + 2\text{ bases} = 96 + 2 \cdot \dfrac{1}{2} \cdot 3 \cdot 4 = 108\,cm^2$.

Volume, $V = \text{base} \times \text{height} = \left(\dfrac{1}{2} \cdot 3 \cdot 4\right) \cdot 8 = 48\,cm^3$.

➢ $L.A. = 96\,cm^2, A = 108\,cm^2, V = 48\,cm^3$.

2. Cylinders and Cones

1 Cylinder

Cylinder: A polyhedron that has two parallel bases (usually circular) connected by a curved surface.

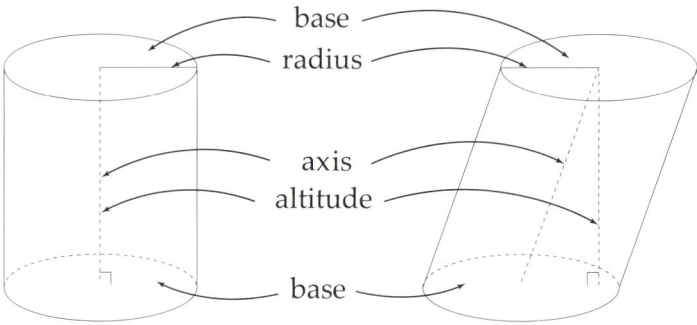

Right Cylinder   Oblique Cylinder

Surface Area and Volume of Cylinders

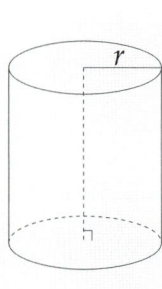 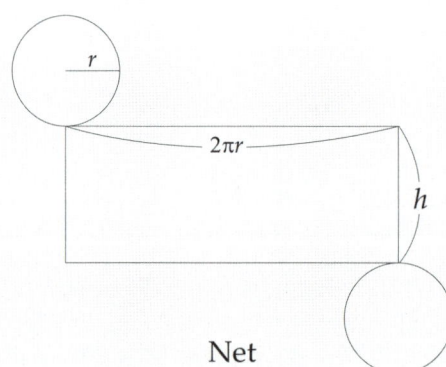

Net

Surface Area: $A = 2\pi r^2 + 2\pi rh$

Lateral Surface Area: $L.A. = 2\pi rh$

Volume: $V = \text{base} \times \text{height} = \pi r^2 h$

2 Cone

Cone: A polyhedron having a circular base and one vertex.

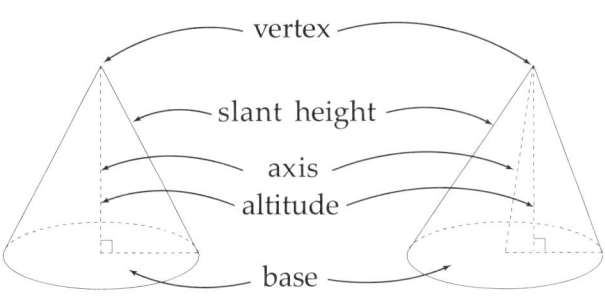

Right Cone   Oblique Cone

Surface Area and Volume of Cones

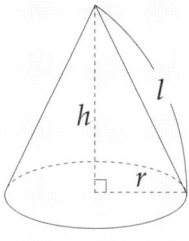 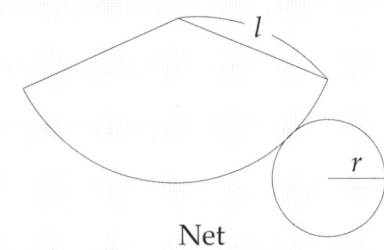

Net

Surface Area: $A = \pi r^2 + \pi r l$

Lateral Surface Area: $L.A. = \pi r l$

Volume: $V = \dfrac{1}{3} \times \text{base} \times \text{height} = \dfrac{1}{3}\pi r^2 h$

Examples

Find the surface area and volume of the cylinder.

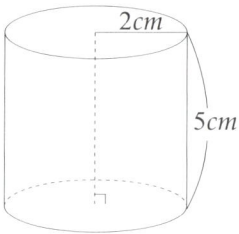

Solution

Surface Area, $A = 2\pi r^2 + 2\pi rh = 2\pi(2)^2 + 2\pi(2)(5) = 28\pi\, cm^2$.

Volume, $V = \pi r^2 h = \pi(2)^2(5) = 20\pi\, cm^3$.

➢ $A = 28\pi\, cm^2, V = 20\pi\, cm^3$.

Examples

Find the surface area and volume of the cone.

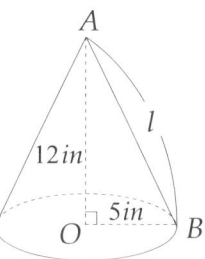

Solution

First, in $\triangle AOB$, $l = \sqrt{12^2 + 5^2} = 13\, in$.

Surface Area, $A = \pi r^2 + \pi rl = \pi(5)^2 + \pi \cdot 5 \cdot 13 = 90\pi\, in^2$.

Volume, $V = \frac{1}{3}\pi r^2 h = \frac{1}{3}\pi \cdot (5)^2 \cdot 12 = 100\pi\, in^3$.

➢ $A = 90\pi\, in^2, V = 100\pi\, in^3$.

3. Spheres

1 Sphere

Sphere: The set of points in space at a given distance from a fixed point.

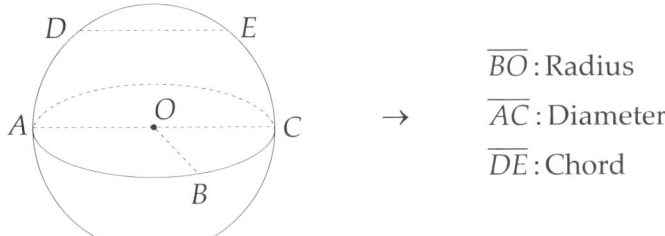

$\overline{BO}$: Radius
$\overline{AC}$: Diameter
$\overline{DE}$: Chord

A plane can intersect a sphere in a point or in a circle.

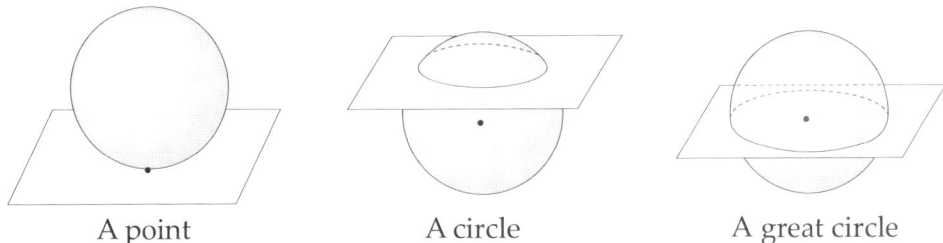

A point   A circle   A great circle

(1) **Great Circle**: The intersection of a sphere with any plane passing through the center of the sphere.

(2) **Hemisphere**: Half of a sphere bounded by a great circle.

Surface Area and Volume of Spheres

Surface Area: $A = 4\pi r^2$.

Volume: $V = \dfrac{4}{3}\pi r^3$

Examples

Find the surface area and volume of the sphere with radius 3 *cm*.

Solution

Surface Area, $A = 4\pi r^2 = 4\pi(3)^2 = 36\pi\, cm^2$.

Volume, $V = \dfrac{4}{3}\pi r^3 = \dfrac{4}{3}\pi \cdot (3)^3 = 36\pi\, cm^3$.

➢ $A = 36\pi\, cm^2, V = 36\pi\, cm^3$.

Review Exercise

1. Find the surface area and volume of each polyhedron.

(1)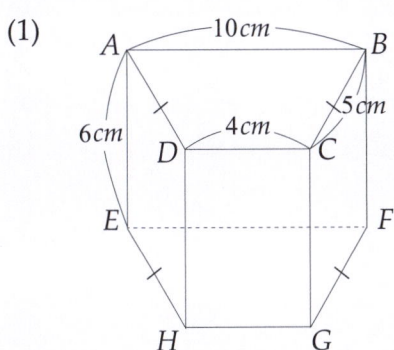

(2)

(3)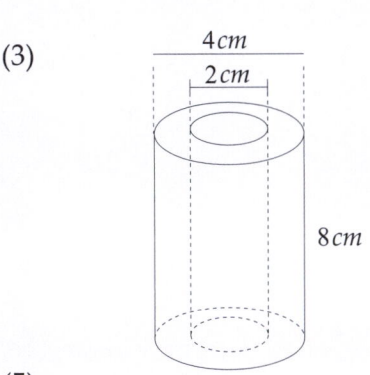

(4)

(5)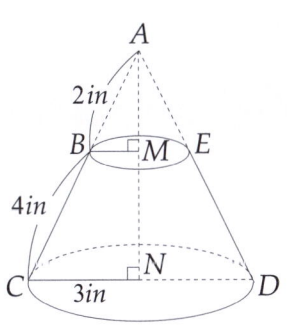

(6)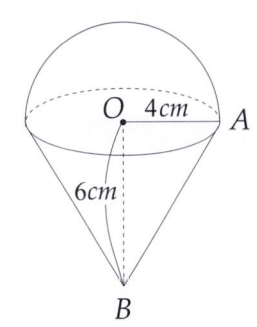

Solution

(1)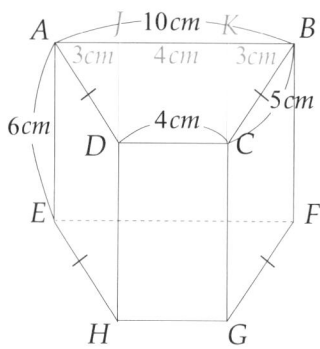

In $\triangle ADJ$, $\overline{DJ} = \sqrt{5^2 - 3^2} = 4$.

Base, $B = \dfrac{1}{2}(4+10) \cdot 4 = 28$.

Lateral Area, $L.A. = (4+5+10+5) \cdot 6 = 144$.

Surface Area, $A = 2B + L.A. = 2 \cdot 28 + 144 = 200$.

Volume, $V = B \times h = 28 \cdot 6 = 168$.

➤ $A = 200 \ cm^2, V = 168 \ cm^3$.

(2)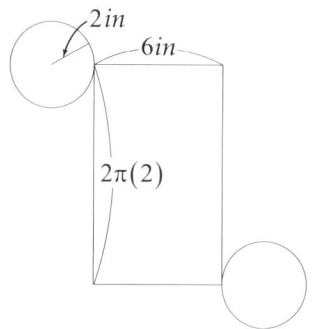

Base, $B = \pi(2)^2 = 4\pi$.

Lateral Area, $L.A. = 2\pi(2) \cdot 6 = 24\pi$.

Surface Area, $A = 2B + L.A. = 2 \cdot 4\pi + 24\pi = 32\pi$.

Volume, $V = B \times h = 4\pi \cdot 6 = 24\pi$.

➤ $A = 32\pi \ in^2, V = 24\pi \ in^3$.

(3)

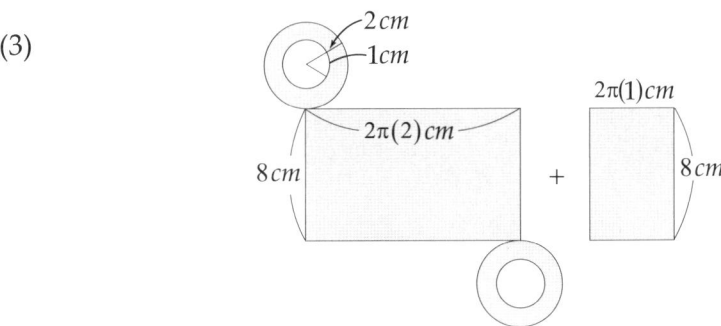

Base, $B = \pi(2)^2 - \pi(1)^2 = 3\pi$.

L.A. of small cylinder, $L.A._s = 2\pi(1) \cdot 8 = 16\pi$.

L.A. of larger cylinder, $L.A._l = 2\pi(2) \cdot 8 = 32\pi$.

Surface Area, $A = 2B + L.A._s + L.A._l$.

$= 2 \cdot 3\pi + 16\pi + 32\pi = 54\pi$.

Volume, $V = B \times h = 3\pi \cdot 8 = 24\pi$.

➢ $A = 54\pi \, cm^2, V = 24\pi \, cm^3$.

(4)

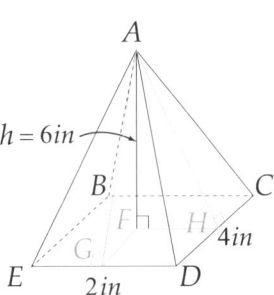

Base, $B = 2 \cdot 4 = 8$.

In $\triangle AFH$, $\overline{FH} = 1$ and $\overline{AH} = \sqrt{6^2 + 1^2} = \sqrt{37}$.

Area of $\triangle ABE$ and $\triangle ACD$ are each $\frac{1}{2} \cdot 4 \cdot \sqrt{37} = \frac{4\sqrt{37}}{2}$.

In $\triangle AFG$, $\overline{FG} = 2$ and $\overline{AG} = \sqrt{6^2 + 2^2} = 2\sqrt{10}$.

Area of $\triangle ABC$ and $\triangle AED$ are each $\frac{1}{2} \cdot 2 \cdot 2\sqrt{10} = 2\sqrt{10}$.

Surface Area, $A = B + 2 \cdot \triangle ABE + 2 \cdot \triangle ABC$

$= 8 + 2 \cdot \frac{4\sqrt{37}}{2} + 2 \cdot 2\sqrt{10} = 8 + 4\sqrt{37} + 4\sqrt{10}$.

Volume, $V = \frac{1}{3} \times B \times h = \frac{1}{3} \cdot 8 \cdot 6 = 16\pi$.

➢ $A = \left(8 + 4\sqrt{37} + 4\sqrt{10}\right) in^2, V = 16\pi \, in^3$.

(5) Since larger cone ACD is similar to smaller cone ABE,
$\dfrac{\overline{AB}}{\overline{AC}} = \dfrac{\overline{BM}}{\overline{CN}}$, $\dfrac{2}{2+4} = \dfrac{\overline{BM}}{3}$, $\overline{BM} = 1$.
In $\triangle ABM$, $\overline{AM} = \sqrt{2^2 - 1^2} = \sqrt{3}$ and in $\triangle ACN$, $\overline{AN} = \sqrt{6^2 - 3^2} = 3\sqrt{3}$.
Larger Base, $B_l = \pi(3)^2 = 9\pi$; Smaller Base, $B_s = \pi(1)^2 = \pi$.
Lateral Area, $L.A. = \pi \cdot 3 \cdot 6 - \pi \cdot 1 \cdot 2 = 16\pi$.
Surface Area, $A = B_l + B_s + L.A. = 9\pi + \pi + 16\pi = 26\pi$.
Volume, $V = \dfrac{1}{3} \times B_l \times \overline{AN} - \dfrac{1}{3} \times B_S \times \overline{AM} = \dfrac{1}{3} \cdot 9\pi \cdot 3\sqrt{3} - \dfrac{1}{3} \cdot \pi \cdot \sqrt{3} = \dfrac{26\sqrt{3}}{3}\pi$.

➤ $A = 26\pi \ in^2, V = \dfrac{26\sqrt{3}}{3}\pi \ in^3$.

(6) Surface area of the hemisphere, $A_H = \dfrac{1}{2} \cdot 4\pi(4)^2 = 32\pi$.
In $\triangle AOB$, $\overline{AB} = \sqrt{4^2 + 6^2} = 2\sqrt{13}$.
Lateral area of the cone, $L.A._C = \pi \cdot 4 \cdot 2\sqrt{13} = 8\sqrt{13}\pi$.
Surface Area, $A = A_H + L.A._C = 32\pi + 8\sqrt{13}\pi$.
Volume of the hemisphere, $V_H = \dfrac{1}{2} \cdot \dfrac{4}{3}\pi(4)^3 = \dfrac{128}{3}\pi$.
Volume of the cone, $V_C = \dfrac{1}{3} \cdot \pi(4)^2 \cdot 6 = 32\pi$.
Volume, $V = V_H + V_C = \dfrac{128}{3}\pi + 32\pi = \dfrac{224}{3}\pi$.

➤ $A = (32 + 8\sqrt{13})\pi \ cm^2, V = \dfrac{224}{3}\pi \ cm^3$.

2. Find the area of a quadrilateral ABGH in the figure below.

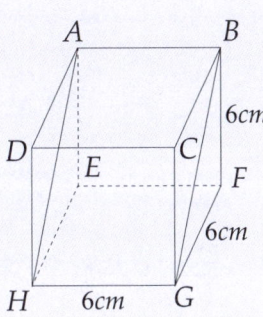

Solution

Since $\overline{AB}$ and $\overline{HG}$ are ⊥ to faces $ADHE$ and $BCGF$,
they are both ⊥ to $\overline{AH}$ and $\overline{BG}$. So, $ABGH$ is a rectangle.
Now, in $\triangle AEH$, $\overline{AH} = \sqrt{6^2 + 6^2} = 6\sqrt{2}$.
So, the area of $ABGH$, $A = \overline{AH} \cdot \overline{AB} = 6\sqrt{2} \cdot 6 = 36\sqrt{2}$.
➢ $A = 36\sqrt{2}\ cm^2$.

3. Given the rectangular prism below, find the volume of the pyramid BCDG.

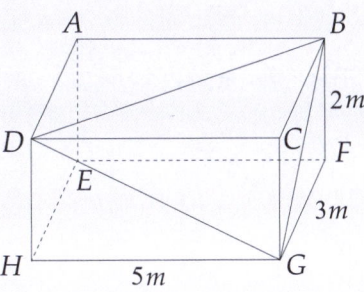

Solution

Base of the pyramid $BCGD$ is $\triangle BCG$.
Area of $\triangle BCG$, $B = \dfrac{1}{2} \cdot 3 \cdot 2 = 3$.
Volume of the pyramid $BCGD$,
$V = \dfrac{1}{3} \times B \times \overline{CD} = \dfrac{1}{3} \cdot 3 \cdot 5 = 5$.
➢ $V = 5\ m^3$.

4. A sector of a circle with radius 6 *in* is rolled so that it becomes the top of the cone. Find the volume of this cone.

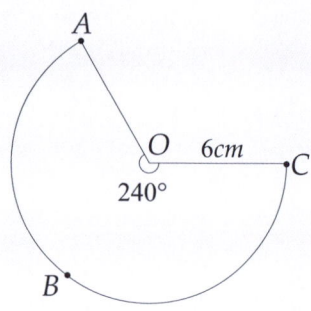

Solution

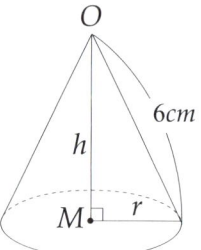

Notice that $\overset{\frown}{ABC} = 2\pi r$, $2\pi(6) \cdot \dfrac{240°}{360°} = 2\pi r$, $r = 4$.

In $\triangle OMA$, $h = \sqrt{6^2 - 4^2} = 2\sqrt{5}$. Base, $B = \pi(4)^2 = 16\pi$.

Volume, $V = \dfrac{1}{3} \times B \times h = \dfrac{1}{3} \cdot 16\pi \cdot 2\sqrt{5} = \dfrac{32\sqrt{5}}{3}\pi$.

➢ $V = \dfrac{32\sqrt{5}}{3}\pi \ cm^3$.

5. If an equilateral triangle with side $4\,cm$ is rotated $360°$ around one of its sides, what is the volume of this resulting solid?

☼ Solution

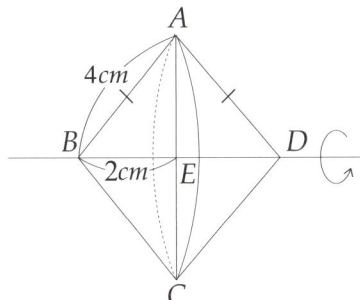

As shown in figure above, the resulting solid after rotation is two cones with common base. Also, since $\triangle ABD$ is equilateral, $h = 2$.

In $\triangle ABE$, $r = \sqrt{4^2 - 2^2} = 2\sqrt{3}$.

Vome of cone ABC, $V_L = \dfrac{1}{3}\pi r^2 h = \dfrac{1}{3}\pi \left(2\sqrt{3}\right)^2 \cdot 2 = 8\pi$.

Vome of solid, $V = 2V_L = 2 \cdot 8\pi = 16\pi$.

➢ $V = 16\pi\ cm^3$.

6. A right square pyramid is shown in figure below. Find each of the following.

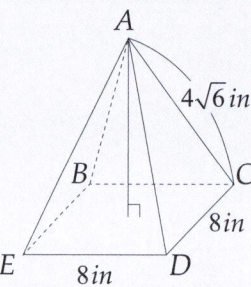

(1) Height (2) Slant height
(3) Surface area (4) Volume

Solution

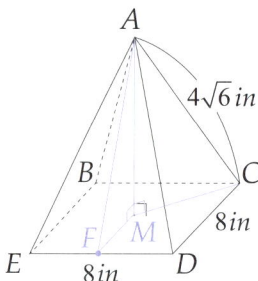

(1) In square $BCDE$, $\overline{CE} = 8\sqrt{2}$ and $\overline{CM} = \dfrac{\overline{CE}}{2} = 4\sqrt{2}$.

In $\triangle AMC$, $\overline{AM} = \sqrt{\left(4\sqrt{6}\right)^2 - \left(4\sqrt{2}\right)^2} = 8$.

➢ Height, $\overline{AM} = 8$.

(2) In square $BCDE$, $\overline{FM} = \dfrac{\overline{CD}}{2} = 4$.

In $\triangle AMF$, $\overline{AF} = \sqrt{8^2 + 4^2} = 4\sqrt{5}$.

➢ Slant height, $\overline{AF} = 4\sqrt{5}$.

(3) Base, $B = 8 \cdot 8 = 64$.

Surface Area, $A = B + 4 \cdot \triangle AED = 64 + 4\left(\dfrac{1}{2} \cdot 8 \cdot 4\sqrt{5}\right) = 64 + 64\sqrt{5}$.

➢ $A = 64 + 64\sqrt{5}$.

(4) Volume, $V = \dfrac{1}{3} \times B \times \overline{AM} = \dfrac{1}{3} \cdot 64 \cdot 8 = \dfrac{512}{3}$.

➢ $V = \dfrac{512}{3}$.

7. If a cube with side length $\sqrt{2}$ in is inscribed in a sphere, what is the volume of the sphere?

Solution

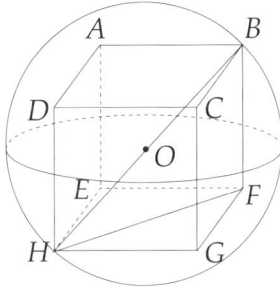

Notice that if a cube is inscribed in a sphere, space diagonal of the cube, $\overline{BH}$, passes through the center of the sphere.

In a square $EFGH$, $\overline{FH} = \sqrt{\left(\sqrt{2}\right)^2 + \left(\sqrt{2}\right)^2} = 2$.

In $\triangle BFH$, $\overline{BH} = \sqrt{2^2 + \left(\sqrt{2}\right)^2} = \sqrt{6}$. So, the radius of the sphere $\overline{BO} = \dfrac{\sqrt{6}}{2}$.

Volume of the sphere, $V = \dfrac{4}{3}\pi \cdot \left(\dfrac{\sqrt{6}}{2}\right)^3 = \sqrt{6}\pi$.

➤ $V = \sqrt{6}\pi \text{ in}^3$.

8. A regular hexagonal prism is shown in figure below. Find each of the following.

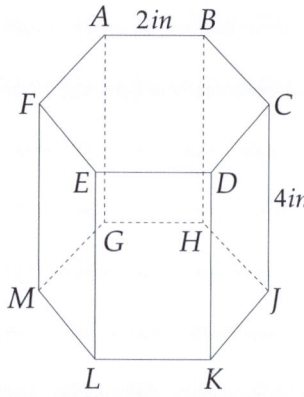

(1) Surface Area (2) Volume
(3) $\overline{CL}$ (4) Area of $\triangle FLJ$

Solution

(1) The area of the base $ABCDEF$ is sum of six little equilateral triangles as shown in figure below.

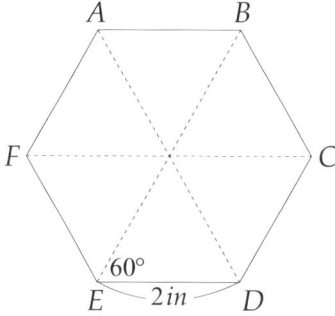

Area of the Base, $B = 6 \cdot \left(\dfrac{\sqrt{3}}{4} \cdot 2^2 \right) = 6\sqrt{3}$.

Lateral Area, $L.A. = 6 \times EDKL = 6 \cdot (2 \cdot 4) = 48$.

Surface Area, $A = 2B + L.A. = 2 \cdot 6\sqrt{3} + 48 = 12\sqrt{3} + 48$.

➤ $A = \left(12\sqrt{3} + 48 \right) \, in^2$.

(2) Volume, $V = B \times \overline{CJ} = 6\sqrt{3} \cdot 4 = 24\sqrt{3}$.

➤ $V = 24\sqrt{3} \, in^3$.

(3)

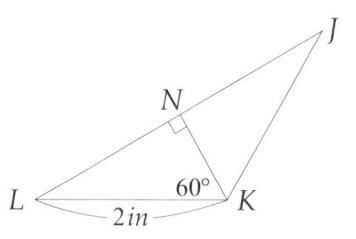 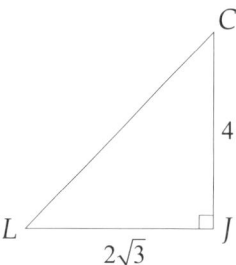

First, in △JKL, draw $\overline{KN} \perp$ to $\overline{LJ}$.
Since each interior angle of regular hexagon is 120°,
∠LKN = 60° and ∠NLK = 180° − 90° − 60° = 30°.
So, △LKN is 30° − 60° − 90° triangle and $\overline{LN} = \sqrt{3}$, $\overline{LJ} = 2\sqrt{3}$.
Now, in △CJL, note that $\overline{LJ} \perp \overline{CJ}$ because the base of prims is $\perp$ to $\overline{CJ}$.
Therefore, $\overline{CL} = \sqrt{4^2 + (2\sqrt{3})^2} = 2\sqrt{7}$.
➢ $\overline{CL} = 2\sqrt{7}$ in.

(4) Since the face FELM is $\perp$ to the base of the prism, $\overline{FL} \perp \overline{LJ}$.
In the face FELM, $\overline{FL} = \sqrt{2^2 + 4^2} = 2\sqrt{5}$.

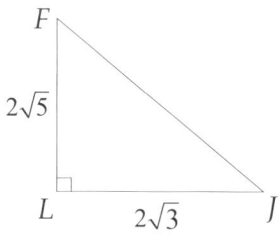

Now, the area of △FLJ, $A = \dfrac{1}{2} \cdot 2\sqrt{5} \cdot 2\sqrt{3} = 2\sqrt{15}$.
➢ $A = 2\sqrt{15}\ in^2$.

Chapter 9   SOLUTION: PAGE 380   *Practice Problems*

01 Find the surface area in the figure below.

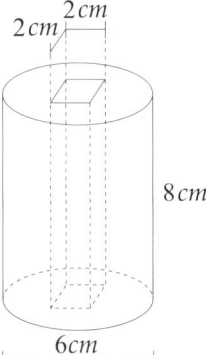

02 A pyramid has a 6cm by 6cm square base and an altitude of 4cm. What is the surface area of this pyramid?

03 If two concentric spheres have radii, 4 and 2, respectively, what is the volume of the space formed in between spheres?

04 A right circular cylinder has a height twice as long as the radius of its base. If the volume of cylinder is 54π cubic feet, what is the surface area of the cylinder?

Chapter 9   *Practice Problems*

05 If the volume of the figure below is $90\pi\,in^3$, what is the radius of the cylinder?

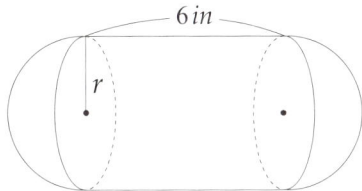

06 A right circular cylinder and a sphere have equal volume and radii. If the radius of each solid is 2 inches, what is the lateral surface area of the cylinder?

07 The volume of a right circular cylinder is 86 cubic inches. For a smaller cylinder, the radius is decreased by 30% and the height is decreases by 20%. What is the volume of the smaller cylinder?

08 A cube with side length $8cm$ is sliced into four rectangular prisms with equal volume, as shown in the figure below. What is the surface area of all four rectangular prims?

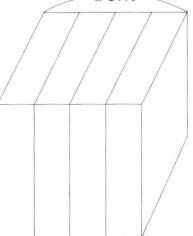

Chapter 9   *Practice Problems*

09 If the surface area of a cube is x^2, then what is the volume of this cube in terms of x?

10 A rectangle $ABCD$ is rotated 360° around through line k. Find the volume of this resulting solid.

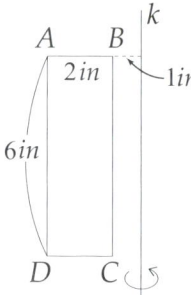

11 A right circular cylinder is inscribed in a cube with an edge of length 4. What is the volume of the cylinder?

12 If both of the bases in the figure below are equilateral triangles, what is the volume of this figure?

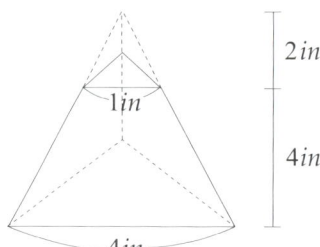

226

Chapter 9　　　　　　　　　　　　　　　　　　　　　　*Practice Problems*

13 Find the surface area of the figure below.

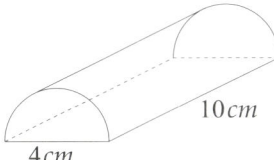

14 If the radius of sphere *A* is twice as long as the radius of sphere *B*, then what is the ratio of the volume of sphere *A* to the volume of sphere *B*?

15 A cone is cut by a plane through its vertex and center of the base, as shown in the figure below. Find the surface area of this figure.

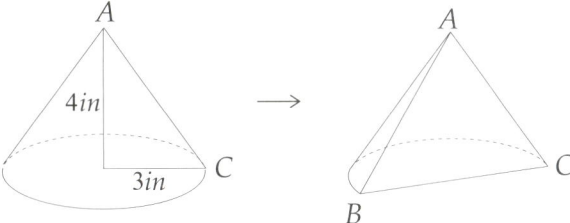

16 If the volume of a sphere is the same numerical value as its surface area, what is the radius of this sphere?

Three-Dimensional Geometry 227

Chapter 9 — Practice Problems

17 A cube ABCDEFGH with side length 4 cm is shown in the figure below. If J and K are midpoints of $\overline{HG}$ and $\overline{GF}$, respectively, find each of the following.

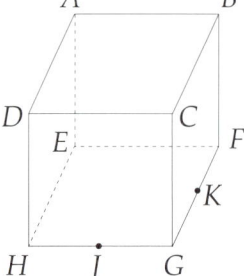

(1) $\overline{JK}$
(2) $\overline{AK}$
(3) Area of $\triangle AJK$
(4) Volume of $AJKE$

18 A right circular cone with the radius 4 in and height 6 in is sliced perpendicular to the height as shown in the figure below. If the volume of smaller cone is exactly 25% of the volume of the original cone, what is the height of the smaller cone?

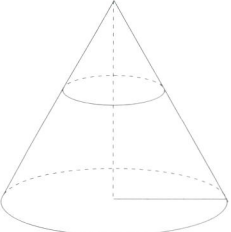

19 If the shaded region in a right triangle ABD below is rotated 360° around through $\overline{BD}$, what is the volume of this resulting solid?

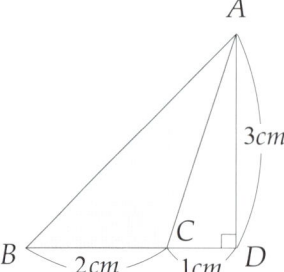

Chapter 9 *Practice Problems*

20 The radius of the base of a right circular cone is 12 and the radius of a parallel cross section is 4. If the distance between the base and the cross section is 6, what is the volume of the cone?

21 A right circular cone has a volume of 20. If the radius and height of this cone increases 10% and 25 %, respectively, what would be the volume of new cone?

# CHAPTER 10

Coordinate Geometry

1. Lines

We have learned about lines from Algebra 1. In this section, we will review how equations can be used to represent lines.

1 Slope

Slope: The measure of the steepness of a line.

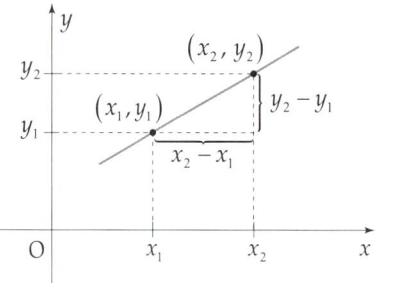
→ Slope, $m = \dfrac{rise}{run} = \dfrac{\Delta y}{\Delta x} = \dfrac{y_2 - y_1}{x_2 - x_1}$

2 Slope-Intercept Equation

Slope-Intercept Equation of a Line: If the equation of a line is written in the form $y = mx + b$, then m is the slope of the line and b is the y-intercept.

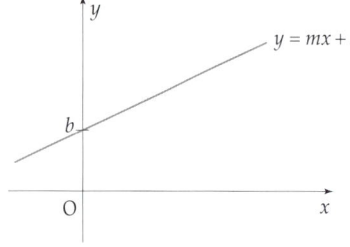
→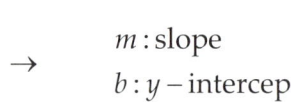
m : slope
b : y – intercept

3 Point-Slope Equation

Point-Slope Equation of a Line: If the equation of a line is written in the form $y - y_1 = m(x - x_1)$, then m is the slope of the line and (x_1, y_1) are the coordinates of the given point.

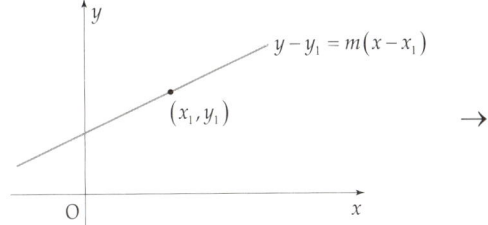

$\rightarrow$ m : slope

(x_1, y_1) : coordinate of the point

4 Parallel Lines

Parallel Lines: Two lines $y = m_1x + b$ and $y = m_2x + c$ are parallel if their slopes are the same.

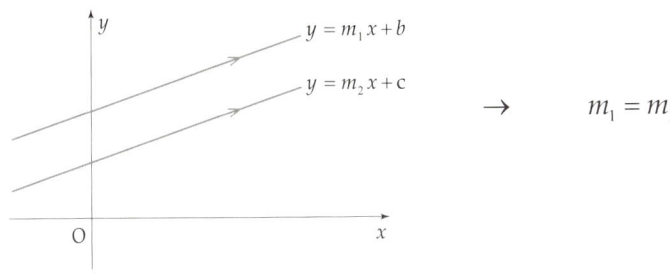

$\rightarrow$ $m_1 = m_2$

5 Perpendicular Lines

Perpendicular Lines: Two lines $y = m_1x + b$ and $y = m_2x + c$ are perpendicular if the product of their slopes is equal to -1.

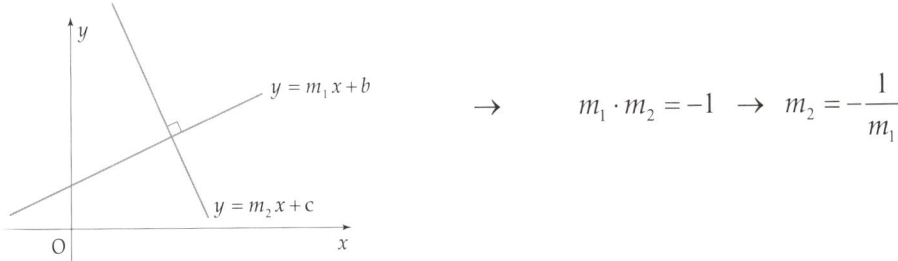

$\rightarrow$ $m_1 \cdot m_2 = -1$ $\rightarrow$ $m_2 = -\dfrac{1}{m_1}$

6 Distance Formula

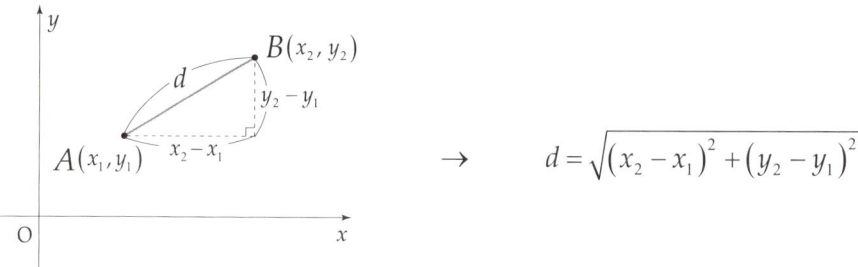

$$d = \sqrt{(x_2 - x_1)^2 + (y_2 - y_1)^2}$$

Proof:

By Pythagorean Theorem,
$$d^2 = (x_2 - x_1)^2 + (y_2 - y_1)^2$$
$$d = \pm\sqrt{(x_2 - x_1)^2 + (y_2 - y_1)^2}$$
Since the distance d is always positive,
$$d = \sqrt{(x_2 - x_1)^2 + (y_2 - y_1)^2}.$$

Similarly, the distance formula in three-dimensions is defined as:

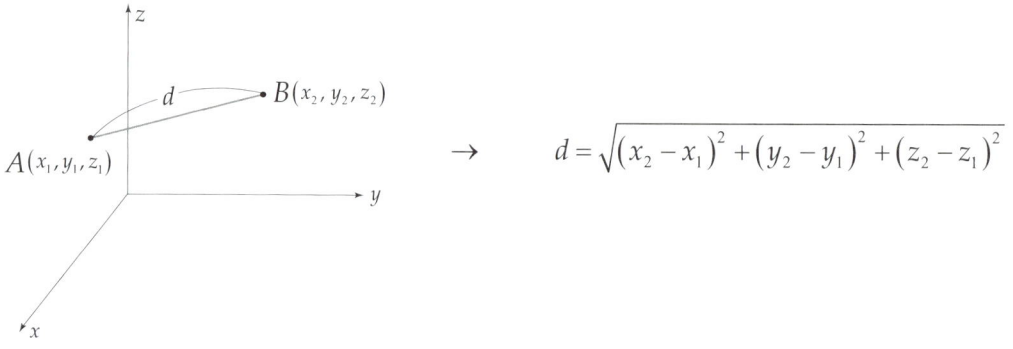

$$d = \sqrt{(x_2 - x_1)^2 + (y_2 - y_1)^2 + (z_2 - z_1)^2}$$

7 Mid-Point Formula

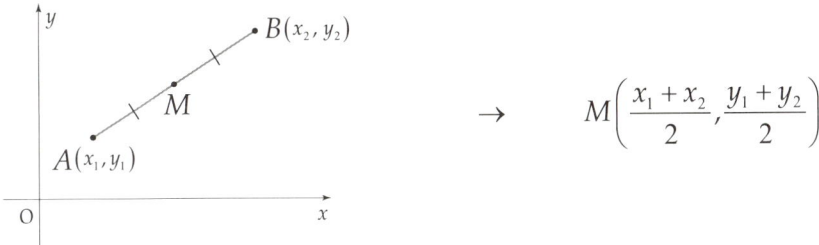

$$M\left(\frac{x_1 + x_2}{2}, \frac{y_1 + y_2}{2}\right)$$

Proof:

$$\overline{AM} = \sqrt{\left(\frac{x_1 + x_2}{2} - x_1\right)^2 + \left(\frac{y_1 + y_2}{2} - y_1\right)^2}$$

$$= \sqrt{\left(\frac{x_1 + x_2 - 2x_1}{2}\right)^2 + \left(\frac{y_1 + y_2 - 2y_1}{2}\right)^2} = \sqrt{\left(\frac{x_2 - x_1}{2}\right)^2 + \left(\frac{y_2 - y_1}{2}\right)^2}$$

$$\overline{BM} = \sqrt{\left(x_2 - \frac{x_1 + x_2}{2}\right)^2 + \left(y_2 - \frac{y_1 + y_2}{2}\right)^2}$$

$$= \sqrt{\left(\frac{2x_2 - x_1 + x_2}{2}\right)^2 + \left(\frac{2y_2 - y_1 + y_2}{2}\right)^2} = \sqrt{\left(\frac{x_2 - x_1}{2}\right)^2 + \left(\frac{y_2 - y_1}{2}\right)^2}$$

So, $\overline{AM} \cong \overline{BM}$.

Similarly, the midpoint formula in three-dimensions is defined as:

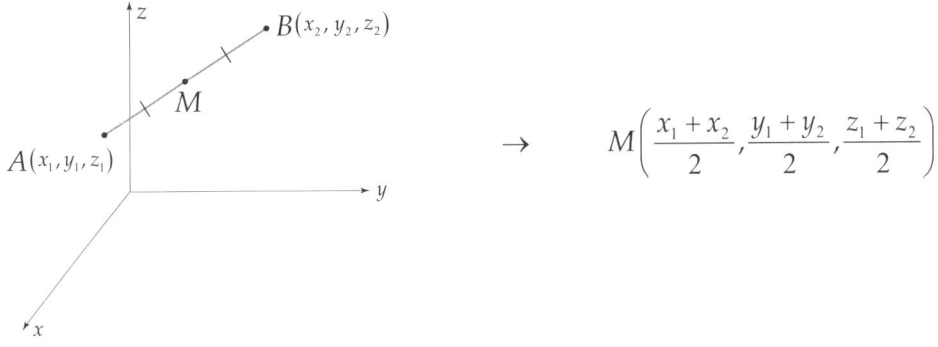

$$M\left(\frac{x_1 + x_2}{2}, \frac{y_1 + y_2}{2}, \frac{z_1 + z_2}{2}\right)$$

Examples

Find an equation of the line passing through the points $(-1,0)$ and $(2,6)$.

Solution

Slope, $m = \dfrac{6-0}{2-(-1)} = 2.$

Using the point-slope equation, $y - y_1 = m(x - x_1)$,
where $m = 2$ and $(x_1, y_1) = (-1, 0)$,
$y - 0 = 2(x+1) \to y = 2x + 2.$
➢ $y = 2x + 2.$

Examples

Find the distance between $A(3,6)$ and $B(-1,3)$.

Solution

$d = \sqrt{(-1-3)^2 + (3-6)^2} = \sqrt{4^2 + 3^2} = 5.$
➢ $d = 5.$

2. Equation of Circles and Spheres

1 Equation of a Circle

Equation of a Circle: The equation of a circle is derived from the distance formula.

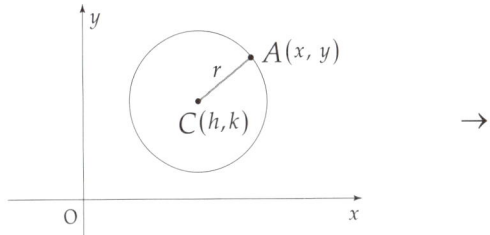

$x^2 + y^2 = r^2$

center: $(0,0)$, radius: r

$(x-h)^2 + (y-k)^2 = r^2$

center: (h,k), radius: r

Proof:

The distance r is, $r = \sqrt{(x-h)^2 + (y-k)^2}$

So, $(x-h)^2 + (y-k)^2 = r^2$.

2 Equation of a Sphere

Equation of a Sphere: The equation of a sphere is derived from the distance formula in three-dimensions.

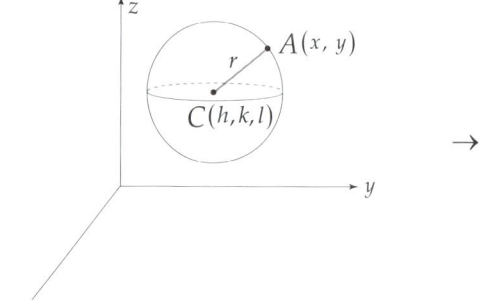

$$x^2 + y^2 + z^2 = r^2$$
center: $(0,0,0)$, radius: r

$$(x-h)^2 + (y-k)^2 + (z-l)^2 = r^2$$
center: (h,k,l), radius: r

Proof:

The distance r is, $r = \sqrt{(x-h)^2 + (y-k)^2 + (z-l)^2}$

So, $(x-h)^2 + (y-k)^2 + (z-l)^2 = r^2$.

Examples

Find the center and radius of the circle $x^2 + y^2 - 2y = 3$.

Solution

First, rewrite the quation of the circle in $(x-h)^2 + (y-k)^2 = r^2$ by completing the square.
$x^2 + y^2 - 2y = 3$
$x^2 + y^2 - 2y + 1 - 1 = 3$
$x^2 + (y-1)^2 = 4$
➢ Center: $(0,1)$, Radius: 2.

3. Coordinate Proof

In geometry, we can assign coordinates to figures and use the coordinates to prove theorem. Here are two important procedures for proving a theorem.

(1) If necessary, place each figure in a convenient position of coordinate plane.
(2) Apply the principles of coordinate geometry.

Examples

Prove that $A(3,4), B(5,2),$ and $C(0,1)$ is a right triangle.

Solution

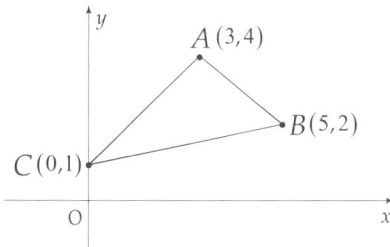

Method 1:

Using the distance formula,
$\overline{AB} = \sqrt{(5-3)^2 + (2-4)^2} = \sqrt{4+4} = 2\sqrt{2}.$
$\overline{AC} = \sqrt{(0-3)^2 + (1-4)^2} = \sqrt{9+9} = 3\sqrt{2}.$
$\overline{BC} = \sqrt{(0-5)^2 + (1-2)^2} = \sqrt{25+1} = \sqrt{26}.$
Now, we need to show $\overline{BC}^2 = \overline{AB}^2 + \overline{AC}^2$ is true.
$\overline{BC}^2 = (\sqrt{26})^2 = 26, \overline{AB}^2 = (2\sqrt{2})^2 = 8,$ and $\overline{AC}^2 = (3\sqrt{2})^2 = 18.$
Since $26 = 8 + 18,$ $\overline{BC}^2 = \overline{AB}^2 + \overline{AC}^2$ is true.
So, $\triangle ABC$ is a right triangle.

Method 2:

Using the slope of the line,

Slope of $\overline{AB}$, $m_{\overline{AB}} = \dfrac{2-4}{5-3} = -1$.

Slope of $\overline{AC}$, $m_{\overline{AC}} = \dfrac{1-4}{0-3} = 1$.

Since $\overline{AB} \cdot \overline{AC} = (-1)(1) = -1$, $\overline{AB} \perp \overline{AC}$.

So, $\triangle ABC$ is a right triangle.

Review Exercise

1. Given points $A(-2,3)$ and $B(1,-3)$, find each of the following.

   (1) Length of $\overline{AB}$.
   (2) Equation in slope-intercept form for line $\overrightarrow{AB}$.
   (3) Equation in point-slope form for the line that is parallel to $\overrightarrow{AB}$ and passes through $C(3,4)$.
   (4) Equation of the perpendicular bisector of $\overline{AB}$.

Solution

(1) Using the distance formula,
$$\overline{AB} = \sqrt{(-3-3)^2 + (1-(-2))^2} = 3\sqrt{5}.$$
➤ $\overline{AB} = 3\sqrt{5}.$

(2) Equation in slope-intercept form is $y = mx + b$.
Slope of $\overline{AB}$, $m_{\overline{AB}} = \dfrac{-3-3}{1-(-2)} = -2.$
Using the slope $m_{\overline{AB}} = -2$ and the point $B(1,-3)$,
$y = mx + b$, $y = -2x + b$, $-3 = -2(1) + b$, $b = -1$.
So, $y = -2x - 1$.
➤ $y = -2x - 1.$

(3) Equation in point-slope form is $y - y_1 = m(x - x_1)$.
Since the line is parallel to $\overline{AB}$ and passes through $C(3,4)$,
$y - y_1 = m(x - x_1)$, $y - 4 = -2(x - 3)$, $y = -2x + 10$.
So, $y = -2x + 10$.
➤ $y = -2x + 10.$

(4) The perpendicular bisector of $\overline{AB}$ has a slope $-\dfrac{1}{m_{\overline{AB}}}$ and passes through the midpoint of $\overline{AB}$, $M_{\overline{AB}}\left(\dfrac{-2+1}{2},\dfrac{3-3}{2}\right)=M_{\overline{AB}}\left(-\dfrac{1}{2},0\right)$.

Using the equation in point-slope form,

$y-y_1=m(x-x_1)$, $y-0=\dfrac{1}{2}\left(x-\left(-\dfrac{1}{2}\right)\right)$, $y=\dfrac{1}{2}x+\dfrac{1}{4}$.

➢ $y=\dfrac{1}{2}x+\dfrac{1}{4}$.

2. Prove that the triangle with coordinates $A(-2,0), B(3,12)$, and $C(-9,7)$ is an isosceles triangle.

Solution

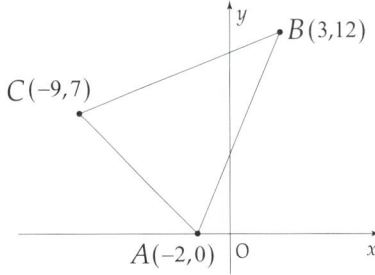

We need to show two of three sides of $\triangle ABC$ are congruent.

$\overline{AB}=\sqrt{(3+2)^2+(12-0)^2}=13$.

$\overline{AC}=\sqrt{(-9+2)^2+(7-0)^2}=7\sqrt{2}$.

$\overline{BC}=\sqrt{(-9-3)^2+(7-12)^2}=13$.

Since $\overline{AB}\cong\overline{BC}$, $\triangle ABC$ is an isosceles triangle.

3. Prove that the quadrilateral with the coordinates $A(2,5), B(-2,3), C(0,-1),$ and $D(4,1)$ is a parallelogram.

Solution

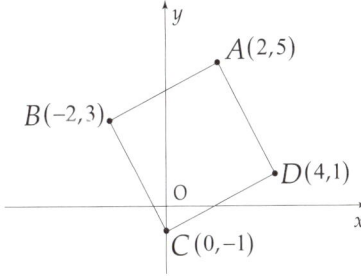

We need to show both pairs of opposite sides are parallel.

Slope of $\overline{AB}$, $m_{\overline{AB}} = \dfrac{3-5}{-2-2} = \dfrac{1}{2}$ and slope of $\overline{CD}$, $m_{\overline{CD}} = \dfrac{1-(-1)}{4-0} = \dfrac{1}{2}$.

Since $m_{\overline{AB}} = m_{\overline{CD}}$, $\overline{AB} // \overline{CD}$.

Slope of $\overline{BC}$, $m_{\overline{BC}} = \dfrac{-1-3}{0-(-2)} = -2$ and slope of $\overline{AD}$, $m_{\overline{AD}} = \dfrac{1-5}{4-2} = -2$.

Since $m_{\overline{BC}} = m_{\overline{AD}}$, $\overline{BC} // \overline{AD}$.

So, the quadrilateral $ABCD$ is a parallelogram.

4. A line with slope -2 passes through the point $(2,4)$. Find the area of the triangle in the first quadrant formed by this line, the x-axis, and the y-axis.

Solution

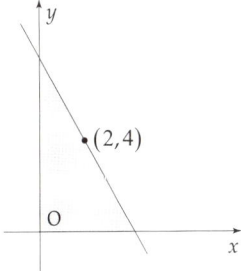

Since the slope $m = -2$ and the point is $(2,4)$,

$y = mx + b$, $y = -2x + b$, $4 = -2(2) + b$, $b = 8 \to y = -2x + 8$

So the y-intercept of the line is 8 and the x-intercept is $0 = -2x + 8$, $x = 4$.

Now, the area of the triangle, $A = \dfrac{1}{2} \cdot 4 \cdot 8 = 16$.

➢ $A = 16$.

5. Find the area of the region that lies outside the circle $x^2 + y^2 + 4y = 0$ but inside the circle $x^2 + y^2 - 4x + 4y = 8$.

Solution

By completing the square in both equations, we have
$$x^2 + y^2 + 4y = 0$$
$$x^2 + y^2 + 4y + 4 - 4 = 0$$
$$x^2 + (y+2)^2 = 4$$
A circle with center $(0,-2)$ and radius 2.
$$x^2 + y^2 - 4x + 4y = 8$$
$$x^2 - 4x + 4 - 4 + y^2 + 4y + 4 - 4 = 8$$
$$(x-2)^2 + (y+2)^2 = 16$$
A circle with center $(2,-2)$ and radius 4.

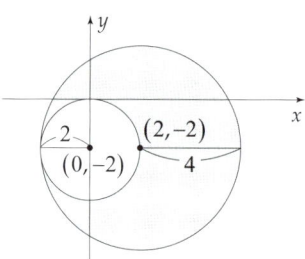

The area of shaded region, $A = \pi(4)^2 - \pi(2)^2 = 12\pi$.
➢ $A = 12\pi$.

6. Find the shortest possible distance between a point on the graph of $x^2 + y^2 - 4x = 5$ and a point on the graph of $x^2 + y^2 + 8x - 6y + 21 = 0$.

Solution

By completing the square in both equations, we have

$x^2 + y^2 - 4x = 5$

$x^2 - 4x + 4 - 4 + y^2 = 5$

$(x-2)^2 + y^2 = 9$

A circle with center $(2,0)$ and radius 3.

$x^2 + y^2 + 8x - 6y + 21 = 0$

$x^2 + 8x + 16 - 16 + y^2 - 6y + 9 - 9 + 21 = 0$

$(x+4)^2 + (y-3)^2 = 4$

A circle with center $(-4,3)$ and radius 2.

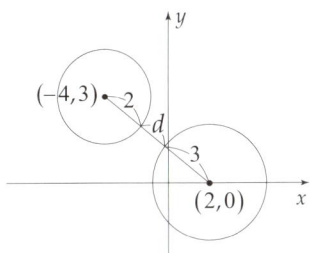

As shown in figure above, the shortest distance d is the distance between two centers minus two radii of the circle.

$d = \sqrt{(-4-2)^2 + (3-0)^2} - 3 - 2 = 3\sqrt{5} - 5$.

➢ $d = 3\sqrt{5} - 5$.

7. A trapezoid ABCD is shown in the figure below. Prove that the length of the median is the average of the lengths of the bases.

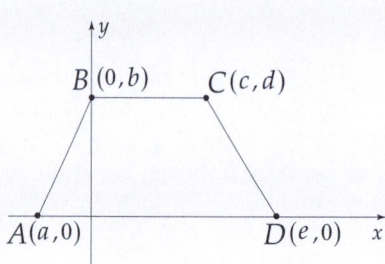

Solution

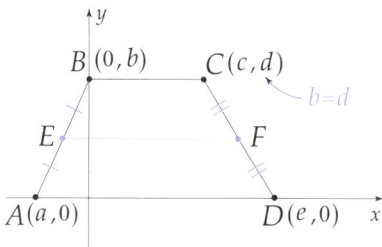

Since $ABCD$ is a trapezoid, $\overline{BC} \parallel \overline{AD}$ so that $b = d$.

The midpoint of $\overline{AB}$ is $E\left(\dfrac{a}{2}, \dfrac{b}{2}\right)$ and $\overline{CD}$ is $F\left(\dfrac{c+e}{2}, \dfrac{b}{2}\right)$.

Using the distance formula,

$\overline{BC} = \sqrt{(c-0)^2 + (b-b)^2} = c$, $\overline{AD} = \sqrt{(e-a)^2 + (0-0)^2} = e - a$,

and $\overline{EF} = \sqrt{\left(\dfrac{c+e}{2} - \dfrac{a}{2}\right)^2 + \left(\dfrac{b}{2} - \dfrac{b}{2}\right)^2} = \dfrac{c+e-a}{2}$.

Now, $\dfrac{\overline{BC} + \overline{AD}}{2} = \dfrac{c+e-a}{2} = \overline{EF}$.

Chapter 10

SOLUTION: PAGE 396

Practice Problems

01 Prove that the triangle with coordinates $A(-2,-2)$, $B(1,2)$, and $C(5,-1)$ is an isosceles right triangle.

02 Prove that the quadrilateral with the coordinates $A(-2,3)$, $B(-5,-4)$, $C(2,-1)$, and $D(5,6)$ is a rhombus but not a square.

03 Prove that the quadrilateral with the coordinates $A(-1,2)$, $B(3,0)$, $C(4,-3)$, and $D(-4,1)$ is an isosceles trapezoid.

04 Line l is perpendicular to the graph of $x + 3y = 4$ and passes through $(-1,1)$. Find the equation of the line l.

Chapter 10 *Practice Problems*

05 Let k be the line that passes through the points $(2,4)$ and $(a,0)$.

(1) For what value(s) of a is the slope of k not defined?

(2) Find an equation for line k in terms of a.

(3) If the line k forms a triangle with the coordinates axes in the first quadrant, find the value(s) of a such that the area of the triangle is 16.

06 Find all possible values for x if the triangle with vertices $A(4,-1)$, $B(5,6)$, and $C(1,x)$ is a right triangle.

07 In $\triangle ABC$, if $\overline{AB} = 4$, $\overline{AC} = 2$, and $\angle BAC = 30°$, what is the measure of $\overline{BC}$?

Chapter 10 *Practice Problems*

08 Find the slope of the line through (3,1) if the triangle formed by the line, the *x*-axis, and the *y*-axis has area 6.

09 A triangle in the first quadrant is formed by two lines passing through the origin and the line $x = 6$. The slope of one of the lines through the origin is twice the slope of the other line through the origin. Find the slopes of the two lines so that the area of the triangle is 36.

10 An equilateral triangle *ABC* has coordinates $A(-1,4)$ and $B(3,4)$. Find all possible coordinates of point *C*.

11 Find the shortest distance from $(-2,3)$ to the line $4x - 2y = 3$.

Chapter 10 — *Practice Problems*

12 Find the area of the region that is enclosed by the graph of the equation $x^2 + y^2 - 6x + 8y = 0$.

13 Given the points $A(-2,5)$ and $B(4,1)$, write an equation of a circle whose diameter is $\overline{AB}$.

14 Find the two points at which the graph of $x^2 + y^2 - 36 = 0$ and $x^2 + y^2 - 2x - 30 = 0$ intersect.

15 Find the values of k so that the radius of the circle $x^2 + y^2 + 2x - ky = 4$ has radius 3.

Chapter 10   Practice Problems

16 Find the equation of the line tangent to the circle $x^2 + y^2 - 4x + 8y + 15 = 0$ at the point $(3, -2)$.

17 Find the radius of each circle that passes through $(1, 2)$ and is tangent to both the x-axis and the y-axis.

18 Find all values of a such that the point of intersection of the lines $y = ax + 4$ and $y = -x + 7$ lie on the circle $x^2 + y^2 = 29$.

CHAPTER 11

Introduction to Trigonometry

1. Trigonometric Ratios

Trigonometry: Measurements of triangles.

1 Trigonometric Ratios

Trigonometric Ratios: A ratio of the length of two sides of a right triangle. The most common ratios are sine, cosine, and tangent. Their abbreviations are *sin*, *cos*, and *tan*, respectively.

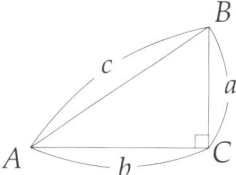

Sine ratio of angle A: $\sin A = \dfrac{a}{c} = \dfrac{\text{opposite leg}}{\text{hypotenuse}}$.

Cosine ratio of angle A: $\cos A = \dfrac{b}{c} = \dfrac{\text{adjacent leg}}{\text{hypotenuse}}$.

Tangent ratio of angle A: $\tan A = \dfrac{a}{b} = \dfrac{\text{opposite leg}}{\text{adjacent leg}}$.

(1) If we use a different angle, then the adjacent and opposite legs reverse. Also, remember that we never use the right angle for trigonometric ratios and the hypotenuse never changes position.

(2) The value of a trigonometric ratio depends *only* on the measure of the angle. It does not depend on the size of the triangle.

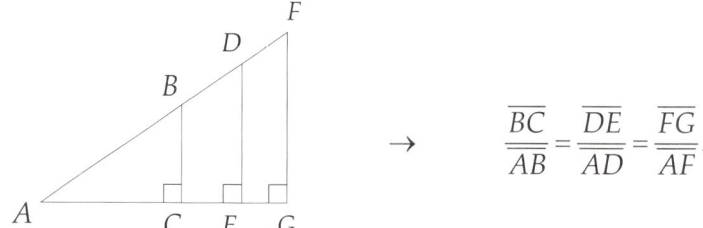

△ABC, △ADE, and △AFG are all right triangles that share a common angle, ∠A. So, the triangles are similar by AA Similarity. In △ABC, △ADE, and △AFG, $\sin A = \frac{\overline{BC}}{\overline{AB}}$, $\sin A = \frac{\overline{DE}}{\overline{AD}}$, and $\sin A = \frac{\overline{FG}}{\overline{AF}}$, respectively. Because the triangles are similar, the ratios are equal. That is $\frac{\overline{BC}}{\overline{AB}} = \frac{\overline{DE}}{\overline{AD}} = \frac{\overline{FG}}{\overline{AF}}$.

2 SOH-CAH-TOA

SOH-CAH-TOA: A way of remembering how to compute the sine, cosine, and tangent of an angle.

$$S = \frac{O}{H} \qquad C = \frac{A}{H} \qquad T = \frac{O}{A}$$

(1) SOH stands for Sine equals Opposite over Hypotenuse.
(2) CAH stands for Cosine equals Adjacent over Hypotenuse.
(3) TOA stands for Tangent equals Opposite over Adjacent.

Examples

Find the sine, cosine, and tangent of angle A.

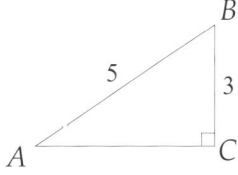

Solution

In △ABC, $\overline{AC} = \sqrt{5^2 - 3^2} = 4$.

$\sin A = \frac{\overline{BC}}{\overline{AB}} = \frac{3}{5}$, $\cos A = \frac{\overline{AC}}{\overline{AB}} = \frac{4}{5}$, $\tan A = \frac{\overline{BC}}{\overline{AC}} = \frac{3}{4}$.

➢ $\sin A = \frac{3}{5}$, $\cos A = \frac{4}{5}$, $\tan A = \frac{3}{4}$.

2. Trigonometric Ratios of Special Angles

1. 30° – 45° – 60° Angles

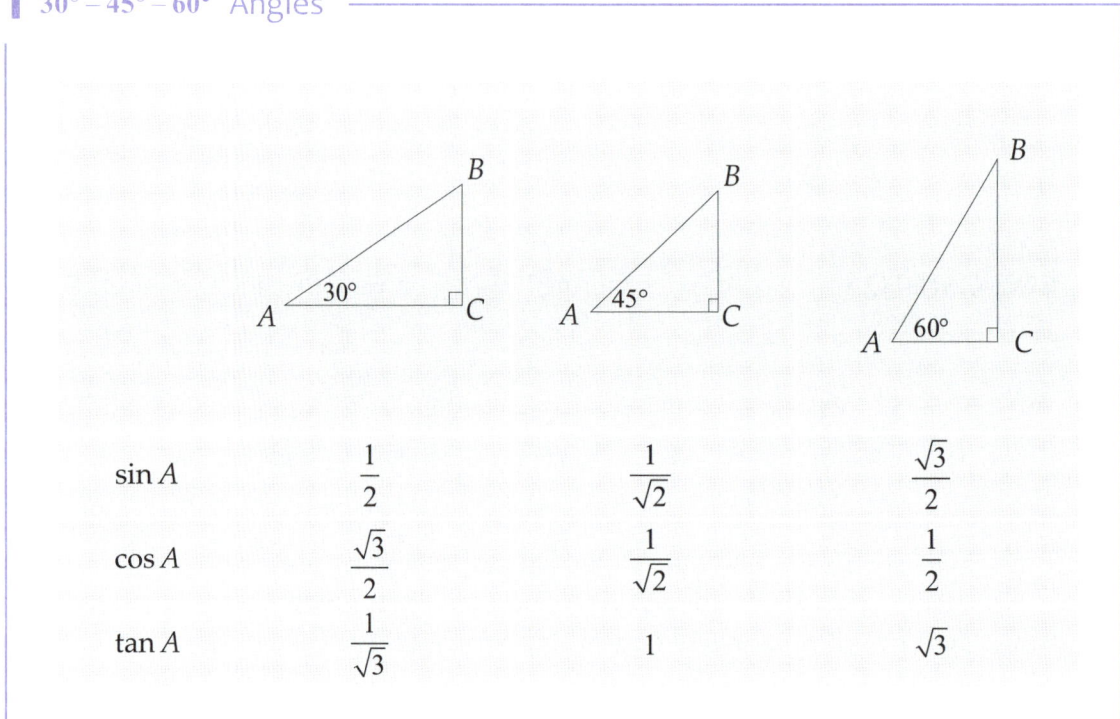

	30°	45°	60°
sin A	$\dfrac{1}{2}$	$\dfrac{1}{\sqrt{2}}$	$\dfrac{\sqrt{3}}{2}$
cos A	$\dfrac{\sqrt{3}}{2}$	$\dfrac{1}{\sqrt{2}}$	$\dfrac{1}{2}$
tan A	$\dfrac{1}{\sqrt{3}}$	1	$\sqrt{3}$

2. Angle between a line and the x-axis

Angle between a line and the x-axis: Given a line with slope m and an angle θ between a line and the x-axis, $m = \tan\theta$.

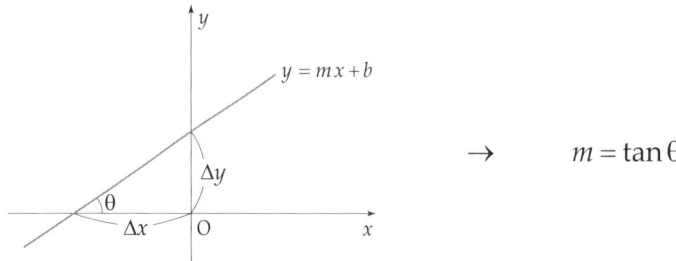

$\rightarrow \quad m = \tan\theta$

$$\text{Slope } m = \frac{\Delta y}{\Delta x} = \frac{\text{opposite leg}}{\text{adjacent leg}} = \tan\theta$$

Examples

Find x and y using trigonometric ratios.

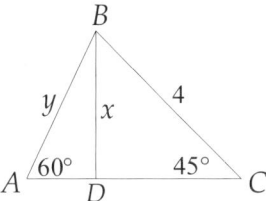

Solution

In $\triangle CBD$, $\sin C = \dfrac{\overline{BD}}{\overline{BC}}$.

$\sin 45° = \dfrac{x}{4}$, $x = 4\sin 45°$, $x = 4 \cdot \dfrac{\sqrt{2}}{2} = 2\sqrt{2}$.

In $\triangle ABD$, $\sin A = \dfrac{\overline{BD}}{\overline{AB}}$.

$\sin 60° = \dfrac{x}{y}$, $y = \dfrac{x}{\sin 60°}$, $y = \dfrac{2\sqrt{2}}{\dfrac{\sqrt{3}}{2}} = \dfrac{4\sqrt{2}}{\sqrt{3}} = \dfrac{4\sqrt{6}}{3}$.

➢ $x = 2\sqrt{2}, y = \dfrac{4\sqrt{6}}{3}$.

Examples

In the figure below, find the value of $\tan\theta$.

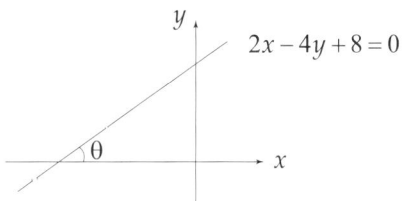

Solution

$2x - 4y + 8 = 0 \rightarrow y = \dfrac{1}{2}x + 2$

So, $\tan\theta = \dfrac{1}{2}$.

➢ $\tan\theta = \dfrac{1}{2}$.

3. Trigonometry and Area

1 Area of a Triangle

(1) ∠A is acute   (2) ∠A is obtuse

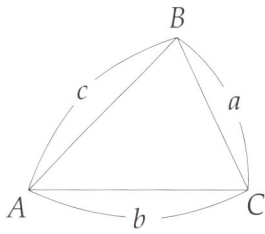 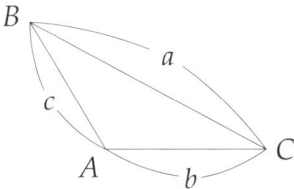

$$\text{Area} = \frac{1}{2}bc\sin A \qquad \text{Area} = \frac{1}{2}bc\sin(180° - A)$$

Proof:

(1) ∠A is acute

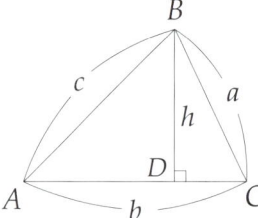

First, the area of the triangle, $\text{Area} = \frac{1}{2} \cdot b \cdot h$.

In △ABD, $\sin A = \dfrac{h}{c}$ and $h = c\sin A$. So, $\text{Area} = \frac{1}{2} \cdot b \cdot h = \frac{1}{2}bc\sin A$.

(2) ∠A is obtuse

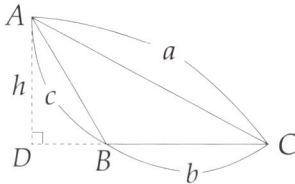

First, $\angle BAD = 180° - \angle A$ and the area of the triangle, $Area = \frac{1}{2} \cdot b \cdot h$.

In $\triangle ABD$, $\sin \angle BAD = \frac{h}{c}$, $\sin(180° - \angle A) = \frac{h}{c}$, $h = c\sin(180° - \angle A)$.

So, $Area = \frac{1}{2} \cdot b \cdot h = \frac{1}{2}bc\sin(180° - \angle A)$.

2 Area of a Parallelogram

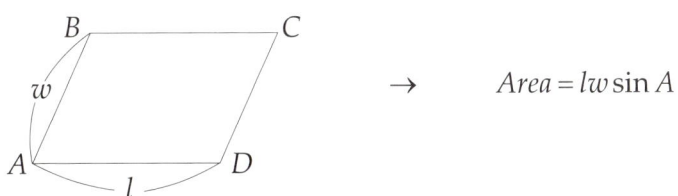

$$Area = lw \sin A$$

Proof:

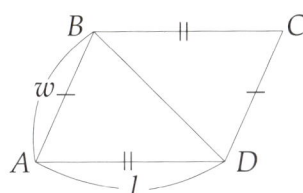

First, draw a diagonal $\overline{BD}$.

In a parallelogram $ABCD$, $\overline{AB} \cong \overline{DC}$ and $\overline{BC} \cong \overline{AD}$.

Also, $\triangle ABD$ and $\triangle CDB$ share a common side $\overline{BD}$. So, $\triangle ABD \cong \triangle CDB$ by SSS.

Since the area of $\triangle ABD$ is $\frac{1}{2}lw \sin A$, the area of parallelogram $ABCD$ is

$2 \cdot \frac{1}{2}lw \sin A = lw \sin A$.

Examples

Find the area of △ABC.

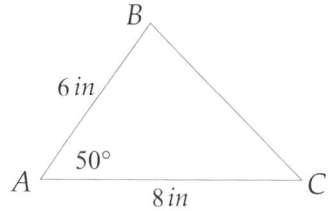

Solution

The area of △ABC is $Area = \frac{1}{2}bc\sin A = \frac{1}{2} \cdot 8 \cdot 6 \sin 50° = 18.39\ in^2$.

➤ $Area = 18.39\ in^2$.

Examples

Find the area of parallelogram ABCD below.

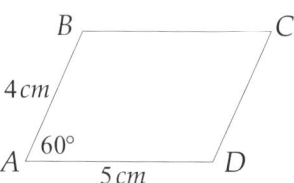

Solution

The area of parallelogram ABCD is

$Area = \overline{AB} \cdot \overline{AD} \sin A = 4 \cdot 5 \sin 60° = 4 \cdot 5 \cdot \frac{\sqrt{3}}{2} = 10\sqrt{3}\ cm^2$

➤ $Area = 10\sqrt{3}\ cm^2$.

4. Application of Trigonometry

1 Angle of Elevation

Angle of Elevation: The angle between the horizontal and the line of sight to an object above the horizontal.

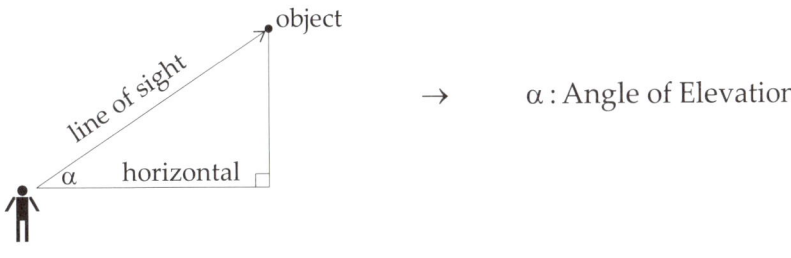

→ α : Angle of Elevation

2 Angle of Depression

Angle of Depression: The angle between the horizontal and the line of sight to an object beneath the horizontal.

→ β : Angle of Depression

 Examples

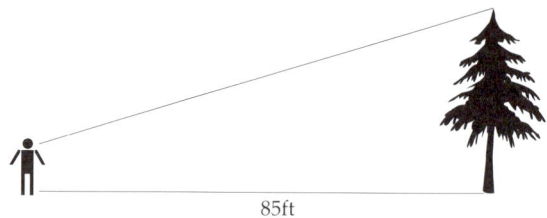

David is 6 ft tall and is looking at the top of a tree 85 ft away, as shown in the figure. If David measures the angle of elevation from his eye level to the top of the tree 10°, what is the height of the tree?

Solution

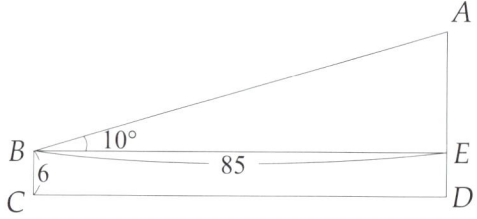

The height of the tree is $\overline{AD}$.

$\tan 10° = \dfrac{\overline{AE}}{85}$, $\overline{AE} = 85 \tan 10° = 14.99$.

Since $\overline{AD} = \overline{AE} + \overline{ED}$ and $\overline{ED} = \overline{BC} = 6$,

$\overline{AD} = 14.99 + 6 = 20.99$.

➢ $\overline{AD} = 20.99$ ft.

Review Exercise

1. Find the indicated trigonometric ratio.

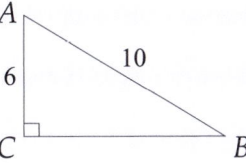

(1) $\sin A$ (2) $\cos A$ (3) $\tan A$
(4) $\sin B$ (5) $\cos B$ (6) $\tan B$

Solution

$\overline{BC} = \sqrt{10^2 - 6^2} = 8.$

(1) $\sin A = \dfrac{\overline{BC}}{\overline{AB}} = \dfrac{8}{10} = \dfrac{4}{5}$
➢ $\sin A = \dfrac{4}{5}.$

(2) $\cos A = \dfrac{\overline{AC}}{\overline{AB}} = \dfrac{6}{10} = \dfrac{3}{5}$
➢ $\cos A = \dfrac{3}{5}.$

(3) $\tan A = \dfrac{\overline{BC}}{\overline{AC}} = \dfrac{8}{6} = \dfrac{4}{3}$
➢ $\tan A = \dfrac{4}{3}.$

(4) $\sin B = \dfrac{\overline{AC}}{\overline{AB}} = \dfrac{6}{10} = \dfrac{3}{5}$
➢ $\sin B = \dfrac{3}{5}.$

(5) $\cos B = \dfrac{\overline{BC}}{\overline{AB}} = \dfrac{8}{10} = \dfrac{4}{5}$
➢ $\cos B = \dfrac{4}{5}.$

(6) $\tan B = \dfrac{\overline{AC}}{\overline{BC}} = \dfrac{6}{8} = \dfrac{3}{4}$
➢ $\tan B = \dfrac{3}{4}.$

2. Given that $\sin A = \dfrac{1}{3}$, find each of the following.

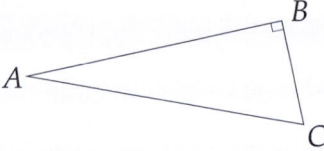

(1) $\cos A$ (2) $\tan C$

(3) $\dfrac{\sin C}{\cos C}$ (4) $\sin^2 A + \cos^2 A$

✓ Note: $\sin^2 A = (\sin A)^2$, $\cos^2 A = (\cos A)^2$, and $\tan^2 A = (\tan A)^2$.

Solution

$\sin A = \dfrac{1}{3} \rightarrow \overline{BC} = 1$ and $\overline{AC} = 3$

$\overline{AB} = \sqrt{3^2 - 1^2} = 2\sqrt{2}$.

(1) $\cos A = \dfrac{\overline{AB}}{\overline{AC}} = \dfrac{2\sqrt{2}}{3}$

➢ $\cos A = \dfrac{2\sqrt{2}}{3}$.

(2) $\tan C = \dfrac{\overline{AB}}{\overline{BC}} = \dfrac{2\sqrt{2}}{1} = 2\sqrt{2}$

➢ $\tan C = 2\sqrt{2}$.

(3) $\dfrac{\sin C}{\cos C} = \dfrac{\dfrac{\overline{AB}}{\overline{AC}}}{\dfrac{\overline{BC}}{\overline{AC}}} = \dfrac{\overline{AB}}{\overline{BC}} = \tan C = 2\sqrt{2}$

➢ $\dfrac{\sin C}{\cos C} = 2\sqrt{2}$.

(4) $\sin^2 A + \cos^2 A = \left(\dfrac{1}{3}\right)^2 + \left(\dfrac{2\sqrt{2}}{3}\right)^2$

$= \dfrac{1}{9} + \dfrac{8}{9} = 1$

➢ $\sin^2 A + \cos^2 A = 1$.

3. Find the indicated trigonometric ratio.

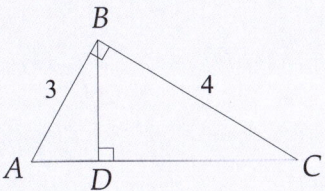

(1) $\sin \angle ABD$ (2) $\tan \angle ABD$
(3) $\cos \angle CBD$ (4) $\sin \angle CBD$

Solution

In $\triangle ACB$, $\overline{AC} = \sqrt{3^2 + 4^2} = 5$ and $\triangle ACB \sim \triangle ABD \sim \triangle BCD$ by AA Similarity.

(1) $\sin \angle ABD = \sin C = \dfrac{\overline{AB}}{\overline{AC}} = \dfrac{3}{5}$

➢ $\sin \angle ABD = \dfrac{3}{5}$.

(2) $\tan \angle ABD = \tan C = \dfrac{\overline{AB}}{\overline{BC}} = \dfrac{3}{4}$

➢ $\tan \angle ABD = \dfrac{3}{4}$.

(3) $\cos \angle CBD = \cos A = \dfrac{\overline{AB}}{\overline{AC}} = \dfrac{3}{5}$

➢ $\cos \angle CBD = \dfrac{3}{5}$.

(4) $\sin \angle CBD = \sin A = \dfrac{\overline{BC}}{\overline{AC}} = \dfrac{4}{5}$

➢ $\sin \angle CBD = \dfrac{4}{5}$.

4. Calculate each of the following.

(1) $\sin 30° + \cos 30° + \tan 60°$

(2) $\sin 45° \times \cos 60° - \cos 45°$

(3) $2\sin 30° + \sqrt{2}\cos 45° - \sqrt{3}\tan 60°$

(4) $\tan^2 45°\left(\sin^2 45° + \cos^2 45°\right)$

Solution

(1) $\sin 30° + \cos 30° + \tan 60° = \dfrac{1}{2} + \dfrac{\sqrt{3}}{2} + \sqrt{3} = \dfrac{1+3\sqrt{3}}{2}$

➢ $\sin 30° + \cos 30° + \tan 60° = \dfrac{1+3\sqrt{3}}{2}$.

(2) $\sin 45° \times \cos 60° - \cos 45° = \dfrac{1}{\sqrt{2}} \times \dfrac{1}{2} - \dfrac{1}{\sqrt{2}} = \dfrac{-1}{2\sqrt{2}} = -\dfrac{\sqrt{2}}{4}$

➢ $\sin 45° \times \cos 60° - \cos 45° = -\dfrac{\sqrt{2}}{4}$.

(3) $2\sin 30° + \sqrt{2}\cos 45° - \sqrt{3}\tan 60° = 2 \cdot \dfrac{1}{2} + \sqrt{2} \cdot \dfrac{1}{\sqrt{2}} - \sqrt{3} \cdot \sqrt{3} = -1$

➢ $2\sin 30° + \sqrt{2}\cos 45° - \sqrt{3}\tan 60° = -1$.

(4) $\tan^2 45°\left(\sin^2 45° + \cos^2 45°\right) = 1^2\left(\left(\dfrac{1}{\sqrt{2}}\right)^2 + \left(\dfrac{1}{\sqrt{2}}\right)^2\right) = \dfrac{1}{2} + \dfrac{1}{2} = 1$

➢ $\tan^2 45°\left(\sin^2 45° + \cos^2 45°\right) = 1$.

5. In the figure below, find the value of $x+y$.

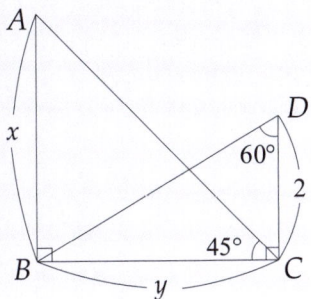

Solution

Since $\angle CBD = 30°$, $\triangle BDC$ is $30° - 60° - 90°$ triangle.

So, $\dfrac{\overline{BC}}{\overline{CD}} = \dfrac{\sqrt{3}}{1} = \dfrac{y}{2} =$, $y = 2\sqrt{3}$.

Since $\angle A = 45°$, $\triangle CAB$ is $45° - 45° - 45°$ triangle.

So, $\dfrac{\overline{AB}}{\overline{BC}} = \dfrac{1}{1} = \dfrac{x}{2\sqrt{3}}$, $x = 2\sqrt{3}$. Now, $x + y = 2\sqrt{3} + 2\sqrt{3} = 4\sqrt{3}$.

➢ $x + y = 4\sqrt{3}$.

6. Find the area of each figure below.

(1)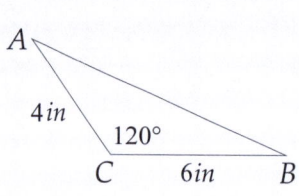

(2)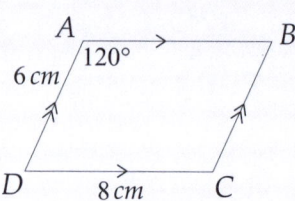

(3)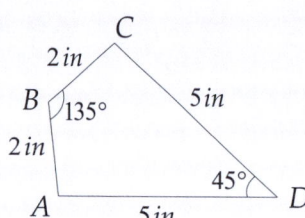

(4)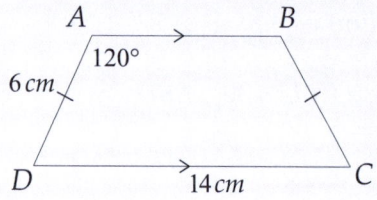

Solution

(1) $Area = \dfrac{1}{2} \cdot 4 \cdot 6 \cdot \sin(180° - 120°)$

$= 12 \cdot \sin 60° = 12 \cdot \dfrac{\sqrt{3}}{2} = 6\sqrt{3}.$

➢ $Area = 6\sqrt{3} \, in^2.$

(2) $\angle D = 180° - 120° = 60°.$

$Area = 6 \cdot 8 \cdot \sin 60° = 48 \cdot \dfrac{\sqrt{3}}{2}$

$= 24\sqrt{3}.$

➢ $Area = 24\sqrt{3} \, cm^2.$

(3)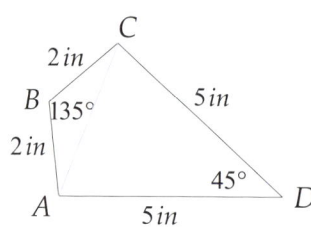

The area of $\triangle ABC = \dfrac{1}{2} \cdot 2 \cdot 2 \cdot \sin(180° - 135°)$

$= 2 \sin 45° = 2 \cdot \dfrac{1}{\sqrt{2}} = \dfrac{2}{\sqrt{2}} = \sqrt{2}.$

The area of △ACD = $\frac{1}{2} \cdot 5 \cdot 5 \cdot \sin 45° = \frac{25}{2} \cdot \frac{1}{\sqrt{2}} = \frac{25\sqrt{2}}{4}$.

So, the area of quadrilateral ABCD = $\sqrt{2} + \frac{25\sqrt{2}}{4} = \frac{29\sqrt{2}}{4}$.

➤ Area = $\frac{29\sqrt{2}}{4} in^2$.

(4) First, $\angle D = 180° - 120° = 60°$ and $\angle C \cong \angle D = 60°$.

Now, draw $\overline{BE}$ that is parallel to $\overline{AD}$ as shown in the figure below.

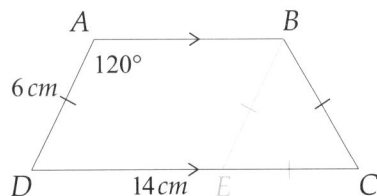

Then, $\angle BEC = 60°$ so that △BEC is equilateral.

So, $\overline{CE} = 6$ and $\overline{DE} = 14 - 6 = 8$.

The area of parallelogram ABED = $6 \cdot 8 \cdot \sin 60° = 48 \cdot \frac{\sqrt{3}}{2} = 24\sqrt{3}$.

The area of △BEC = $\frac{\sqrt{3}}{4} \cdot 6^2 = 9\sqrt{3}$.

So, the area of trapezoid ABCD = $24\sqrt{3} + 9\sqrt{3} = 33\sqrt{3}$.

➤ Area = $33\sqrt{3} \, cm^2$.

7. If $\sin A = \dfrac{3}{5}$ in the figure below, then what is the value of $\overline{AC}$?

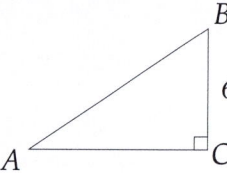

Solution

$$\sin A = \dfrac{\overline{BC}}{\overline{AB}} = \dfrac{3}{5}, \quad \dfrac{6}{\overline{AB}} = \dfrac{3}{5}, \quad \overline{AB} = 10.$$
$$\overline{AC} = \sqrt{10^2 - 6^2} = 8.$$
➢ $\overline{AC} = 8.$

8. If $\cos A = k$ in a right triangle ABC in the figure below, what is $\tan A$ in terms of k?

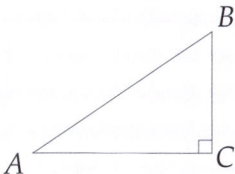

Solution

Since $\cos A = k$, one possible side length of $\overline{AB}$ and $\overline{AC}$ are 1 and k, respectively, as shown in the figure below.

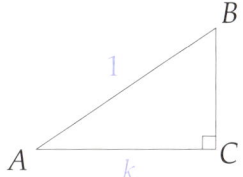

Then, $\overline{BC} = \sqrt{\overline{AB}^2 - \overline{AC}^2} = \sqrt{1-k^2}$.

$\tan A = \dfrac{\overline{BC}}{\overline{AC}} = \dfrac{\sqrt{1-k^2}}{k}$

➤ $\tan A = \dfrac{\sqrt{1-k^2}}{k}$.

9. Joe who is about 6 feet tall is standing 300 feet from the base of a building. If he measures the angle of elevation from the top of his head to the top of the building to be $30°$ how tall is the building?

Solution

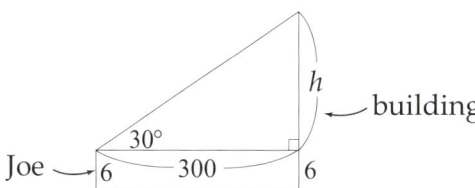

$\tan 30° = \dfrac{h}{300}$, $h = 300\tan 30° = 300 \cdot \dfrac{1}{\sqrt{3}} = 300 \cdot \dfrac{\sqrt{3}}{3} = 100\sqrt{3}$.

Since the height of the building is $h + 6$, the building is $\left(100\sqrt{3} + 6\right)$ ft tall.

➤ The building is $\left(100\sqrt{3} + 6\right)$ ft tall.

10. A bus is $62\,m$ from the base of a building $45\,m$ high, shown in the below. Find the angle of elevation from the bus to the top of the building.

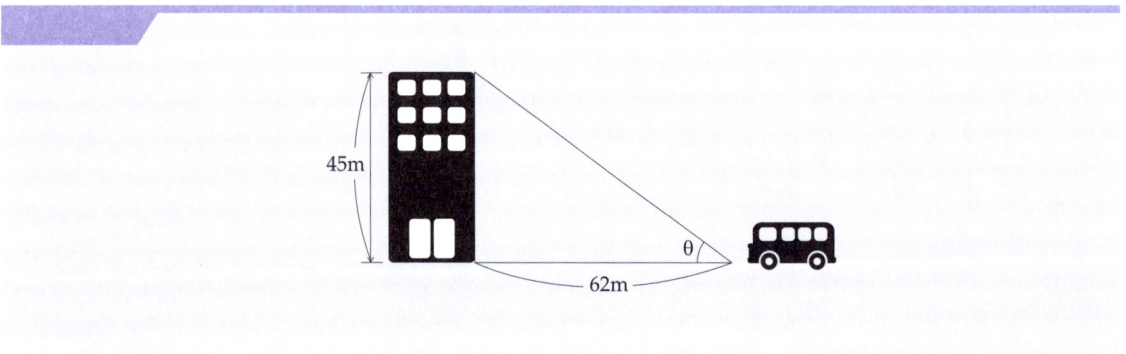

Solution

$\tan\theta = \dfrac{45}{62}$, $\theta = \tan^{-1}\left(\dfrac{45}{62}\right)$

Using the calculator, $\theta = \tan^{-1}\left(\dfrac{45}{62}\right) = 35.97°$.

➤ $\theta = 35.97°$.

Chapter 11   SOLUTION: PAGE 410   *Practice Problems*

01 In the figure below, find $\tan A$.

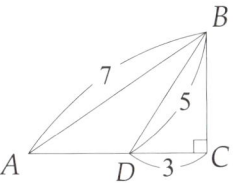

02 If $\overline{BC} \parallel \overline{DE}$ and $\tan A = \dfrac{3}{4}$ in the figure below, find each of the following.

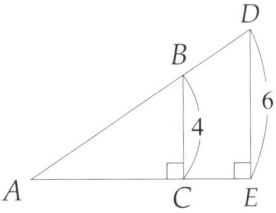

(1) $\overline{AB}$ (2) $\overline{CE}$

03 Find indicated trigonometric ratio for each of the following figure below.

(1) $\sin \angle CBD$ (2) $\cos \angle DCE$

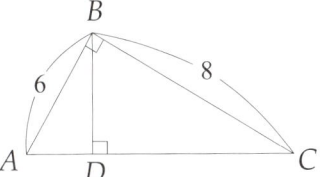   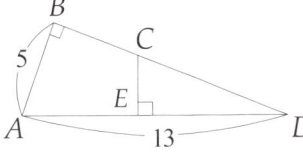

(3) $\sin D + \cos D$ (4) $\tan \angle ACB$

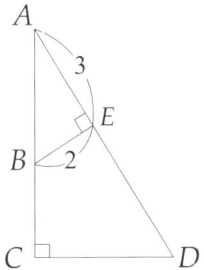   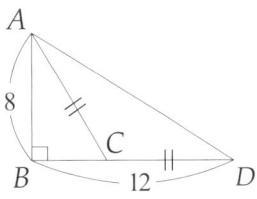

Introduction to Trigonometry 273

Chapter 11 *Practice Problems*

(5) $\sin \angle AGE$

(6) $\cos \angle CEF$

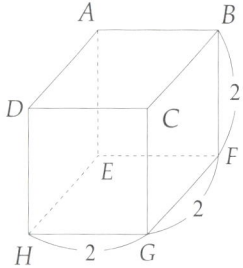

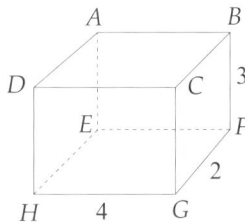

04 In the figure below, $\overline{AB}$ is a diameter of the circle and C is a point on the circle. If $\cos \alpha = \dfrac{1}{3}$, then what is the value of $\cos \beta$?

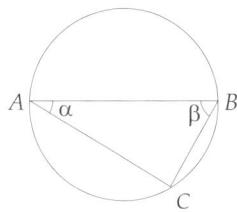

05 If $\overline{BD}$ is tangent to a circle O at point C as shown in the figure below, what is $\sin x$?

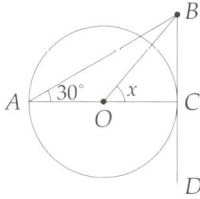

Chapter 11 — Practice Problems

06 Find indicated value for each of the following figure below.

(1) $\overline{AC} + \overline{BD}$

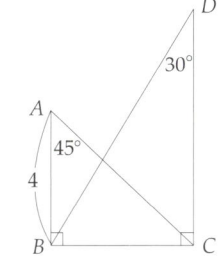

(2) $\overline{AC} + \overline{BD}$

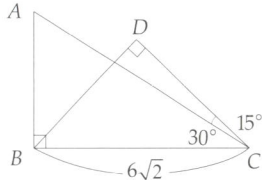

(3) $\tan \angle BAC$

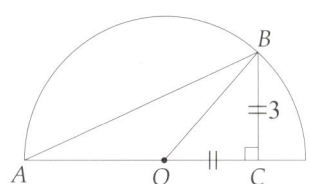

(4) $\overline{BD} + \overline{CE}$

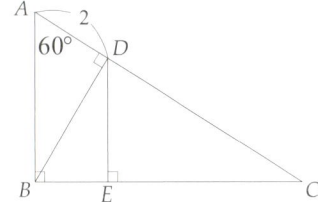

(5) $\tan \angle BAD$

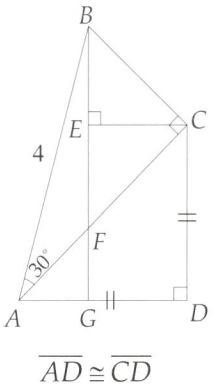

$\overline{AD} \cong \overline{CD}$

(6) $\sin \angle BAD + \sin D$

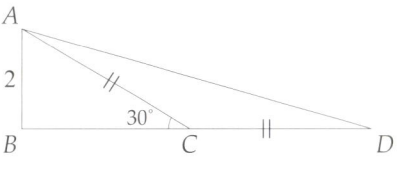

07 If $\sin \theta = m$ and $\cos \theta = n$, where $0 < \theta < 90°$, then what is the value of $\tan \theta$ in terms of m and n?

Chapter 11 — Practice Problems

08 If $0 < x < 90°$ and $\cos x = m$, then what is the value of $\tan x$ in terms of m?

09 In the figure below, find the area of shaded region.

(1) $\angle BAD \cong \angle CAD$ and area of $\triangle ACD = 20\,in^2$

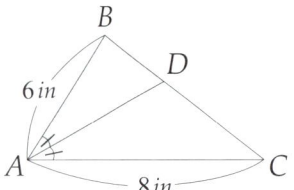

(2) $\overline{BE} \,/\!/\, \overline{CD}$ and $\overline{BC} \,/\!/\, \overline{ED}$

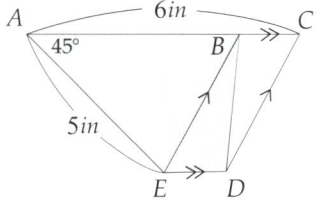

(3) $ABCE$ is a square

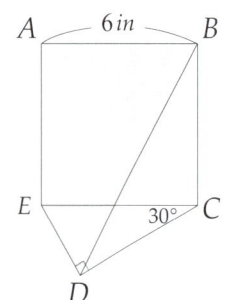

(4)

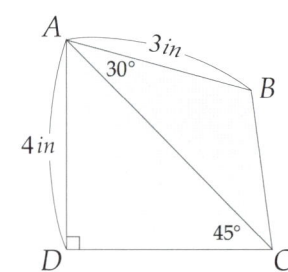

(5)

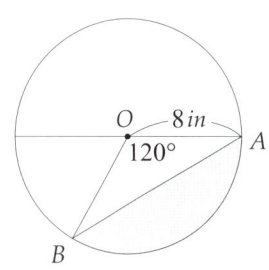

(6) $ABCDEF$ is a regular hexagon

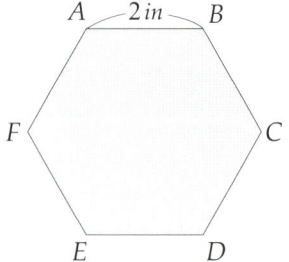

Chapter 11　　　　　　　　　　　　　　　　　　　*Practice Problems*

10 In the figure below, find each of the following.

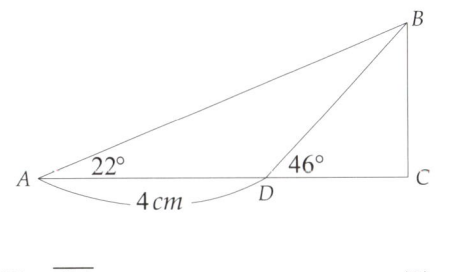

　　(1)　$\overline{CD}$　　　　　　　　　　　　(2)　$\overline{BC}$

11 If the slope of line k and h is $\dfrac{1}{3}$ and $\dfrac{2}{3}$, respectively, what is the measure of the angle formed at the intersection of k and h?

12 Without using a calculator, find the value of $\sin 15°$.

Chapter 11   *Practice Problems*

13 A 20 feet tall light house on a 40 feet tall cliff makes angles of depression 18° and 25° with two boats respectively, as shown in the figure below. Find the distance between the two boats.

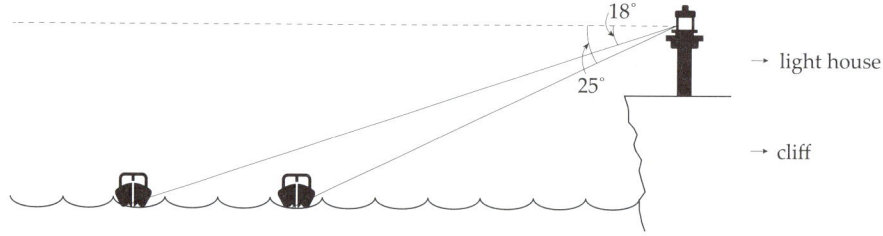

14 A 6 feet tall person starts to walk directly towards a vertical building that is 45 feet tall. What is the distance the person traveled if the angle of elevation from person's top of head to the top of the building changes from 15° to 20°?

15 A surveyor determines the angle of elevation of a building from level ground to be 45°. If the surveyor moves 20 feet towards the building, then the measure of the angle of elevation becomes 60°. What is the height of the building?

Practice Problems Solution

Chapter 2 *Practice Problems Solution*

01 Find the value of x.

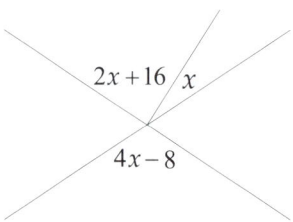

Solution

$(2x+16) + x = 4x - 8$
$3x + 16 = 4x - 8$
$x = 24$

➤ $x = 24$.

02 If $\angle EOC = 4\angle DOC$ and $\angle AOC = 2\angle BOC$ in the figure below, what is the measure of $\angle DOB$?

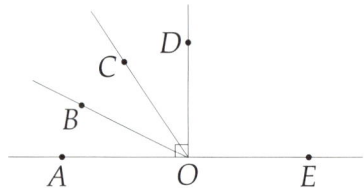

Solution

$\angle EOC = 4\angle DOC$ and $\angle AOC = 2\angle BOC$
$90° + \angle DOC = 4\angle DOC$ $\qquad$ $90° - \angle DOC = 2\angle BOC$
$90° = 3\angle DOC \rightarrow \angle DOC = 30°$ $\qquad$ $60° = 2\angle BOC \rightarrow \angle BOC = 30°$

So, $\angle DOB = \angle DOC + \angle BOC = 60°$

➤ $\angle DOB = 60°$.

Chapter 2　　　　　　　　　　　　　　　　*Practice Problems Solution*

03　Find the value of *a*.

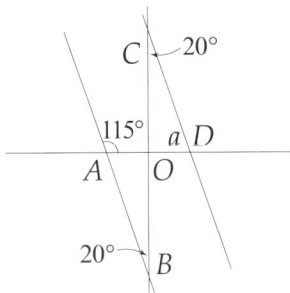

Solution

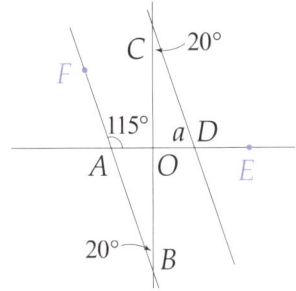

Since ∠DCO ≅ ∠ABO, $\overline{CD} \parallel \overline{AB}$.
So, ∠FAE ≅ ∠CDE = 115°
$a = 180° - ∠CDE = 65°$.

➢　$a = 65°$.

04　Let △ABC have interior angles in the ratio 1 : 2 : 3. What is the measure of its largest exterior angle?

Solution

The smallest interior angle of △ABC is
$180° \times \dfrac{1}{1+2+3} = 30°$.
So, the largest exterior angle is $180° - 30° = 150°$.

➢　The largest exterior angle is 150°.

Chapter 2

Practice Problems Solution

05 If *l // k* and *m // n* in the figure below, what is the value of *x*?

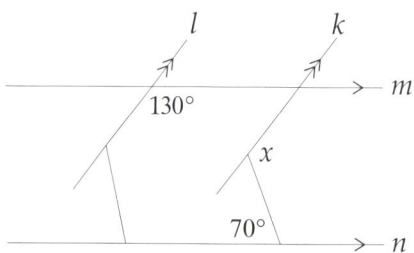

☼ Solution

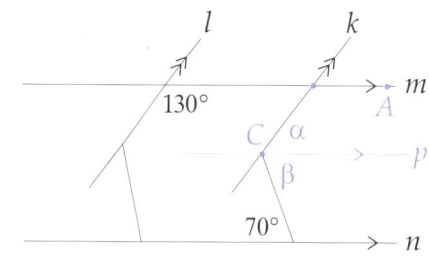

First, since *l // k*, $\angle ABC = 130°$.
Now, draw a line *p* that is parallel to *m* and *n*.
Then, since *m // p*, $\angle ABC + \alpha = 180° \to \alpha = 50°$
Also, since *n // p*, and $\beta = 70°$.
So, $x = \alpha + \beta = 120°$.

➤ $x = 120°$.

06 If *l // k* in the figure below, what is the value of *x*?

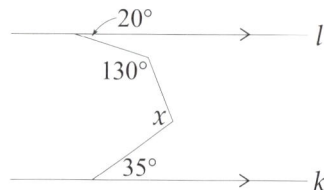

☼ Solution

Draw two lines *m* and *n* that is parallel to *l* and *k*.

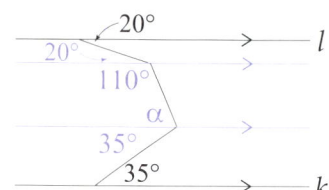

$110° + \alpha = 180° \to \alpha = 70°$
$x = \alpha + 35° = 105°$.

➤ $x = 105°$.

Chapter 2 — *Practice Problems Solution*

07 If $l /\!/ k$ in the figure below, what is the value of $x + y + z + m$?

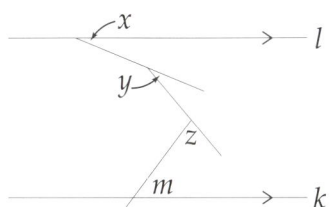

Solution

Draw two lines a and b that is parallel to l and k.

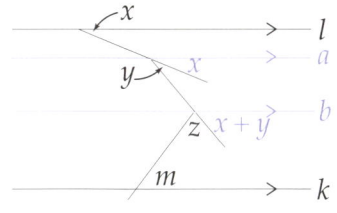

Since $b /\!/ k$,
$$m + \big(z + (x + y)\big) = x + y + z + m = 180°.$$

➤ $x + y + z + m = 180°.$

08 If $l /\!/ k$ in the figure below, what is the value of x?

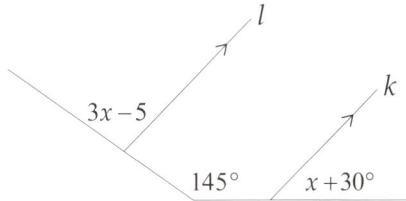

Solution

Draw a line m that is parallel to l and k.

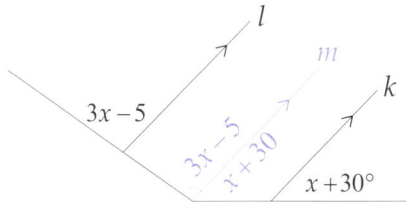

$(3x - 5) + (x + 30) = 145°$
$4x + 25° = 145°$
$4x = 120° \rightarrow x = 30°$

➤ $x = 30°.$

Chapter 2 — Practice Problems Solution

09 If $l // k$ and $m // n$ in the figure below, what is the value of $a + b$?

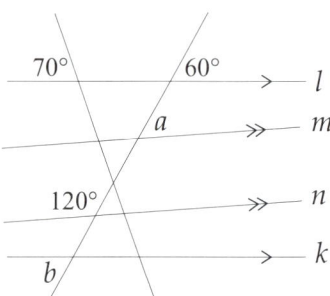

Solution

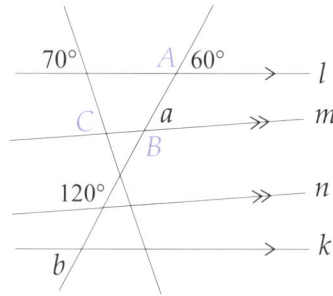

Since $m // n$, $\angle ABC = 120°$.
$\angle ABC + a = 180° \rightarrow a = 60°$
Since $l // k$, $b = 60°$.
So, $a + b = 120°$.

➤ $a + b = 120°$.

10 If $l // k$ in the figure below, what is the value of x?

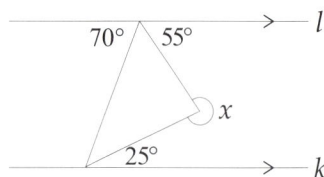

Solution

Draw a line p that is parallel to l and k.

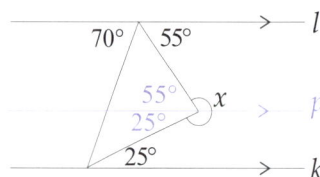

$x + 55° + 25° = 360°$
$x + 80° = 360° \rightarrow x = 280°$.

➤ $x = 280°$.

Chapter 2 *Practice Problems Solution*

11 If $l // k$, $\angle EAD \cong \angle BAD$, and $\angle FCD \cong \angle BCD$ in the figure below, what is the value of $\angle ADC$?

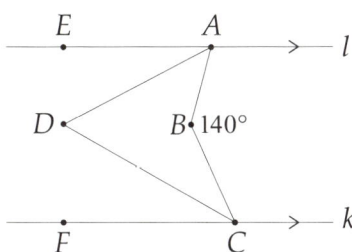

Solution

Draw two lines m and n that is parallel to l and k.
Also, let $\angle EAD \cong \angle BAD = a$ and $\angle FCD \cong \angle BCD = b$.

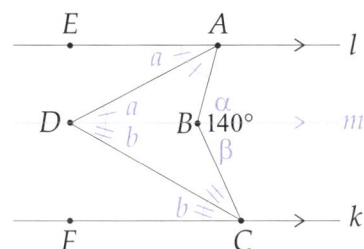

Since $l // m$ and $k // m$ respectively, $\alpha = 2a$ and $\beta = 2b$.
So, $\alpha + \beta = 2a + 2b = 140° \rightarrow 2(a+b) = 140° \rightarrow a+b = 70°$.
Therefore $\angle ADC = a + b = 70°$.

➢ $\angle ADC = 70°$.

Chapter 2　　　　　　　　　　　　　　*Practice Problem Solution*

12 A piece of folded rectangular paper is shown in the figure below. If ∠BED = 92°, what is the measure of ∠BFE?

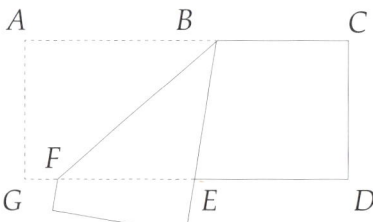

Solution

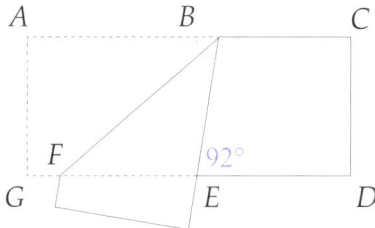

Since $\overline{AC} \parallel \overline{GD}$, ∠BED ≅ ∠EBA = 92° and
∠BEF = 180° − 92° = 88°.
Also, since the paper is folded, ∠ABF ≅ ∠EBF
and ∠EBF = $\dfrac{\angle EBA}{2}$ = 46°.
So, ∠BFE = 180° − ∠BEF − ∠EBF = 46°.

➢　∠BFE = 46°.

Chapter 2 — Practice Problems Solution

13 Find the acute angle formed by the minute and hour hands of a clock at

(1) 7:30 A.M.   (2) 4:35 P.M.

Solution

At 12:00 A.M. or 12:00 P.M., the angle between the two hands is 0.

(1) At 7:30 A.M., the hour hand moves by an angle $7 \times \dfrac{360°}{12} + \dfrac{30}{60} \times \dfrac{360°}{12} = 225°$ from the position at 12:00 A.M. At 7:30 A.M., the minute hand moves by an angle $\dfrac{30}{60} \times 360° = 180°$ from the position at 12:00 A.M. So, the angle between the two hands of the clock at 7:30 A.M. is $225° - 180° = 45°$.

➢ 45°.

(2) At 4:35 P.M., the hour hand moves by an angle $4 \times \dfrac{360°}{12} + \dfrac{35}{60} \times \dfrac{360°}{12} = 137.5°$ from the position at 12:00 P.M. At 4:35 P.M., the minute hand moves by an angle $\dfrac{35}{60} \times 360° = 210°$ from the position at 12:00 P.M. So, the angle between the two hands of the clock at 4:35 P.M. is $210° - 137.5° = 72.5°$.

➢ 72.5°.

Chapter 2 *Practice Problems Solution*

14 Suppose $\overline{AO} \perp \overline{CO}$ and $\overline{BO} \perp \overline{DO}$ in the figure below.
If $\angle AOB + \angle COD = 100°$, what is the measure of $\angle BOC$?

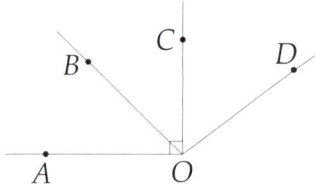

Solution

$\overline{AO} \perp \overline{CO} \to \angle AOB + \angle BOC = 90°$ (1)

$\overline{BO} \perp \overline{DO} \to \angle COD + \angle BOC = 90°$ (2)

$(1)+(2) \to \angle AOB + \angle COD + 2\angle BOC = 180°$

$100° + 2\angle BOC = 180° \to \angle BOC = 40°$

➤ $\angle BOC = 40°$.

15 If $l // k$ in the figure below and $\angle ABD = 4\angle CBD$, what is the measure of $\angle CBD$?

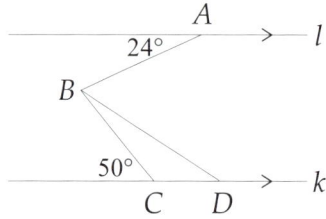

Solution

Draw a lines m that is parallel to l and k.

$\angle ABD = 4\angle CBD$

$\angle ABD + \angle CBD = 24° + 50°$

$4\angle CBD + \angle CBD = 74°$

$5\angle CBD = 74° \to \angle CBD = \dfrac{74°}{5} = 14.8°$

➤ $\angle CBD = 14.8°$.

Chapter 2   *Practice Problems Solution*

16 If ∠BAC ≅ ∠CAD in △ABD, what is the value of $a+b$?

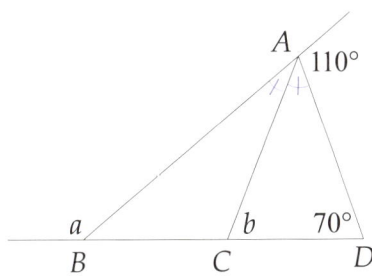

Solution

$\angle BAC + \angle CAD = 180° - 110° = 70°$

Since $\angle BAC \cong \angle CAD$, $\angle CAD = \dfrac{70°}{2} = 35°$.

In △ACD, $b = 180° - \angle CAD - 70° = 75°$.

$\angle ACB = 180° - b = 105°$

In △ABD, $a = \angle BAD + 70° = 140°$.

So, $a + b = 215°$

➢ $a + b = 215°$.

17 One angle of a triangle is equal to the sum of the other two angles. If one of the angles of the triangle is 30°, what is the measure of the other two angles?

Solution

Let the measure of three angles of a triangle be $a, b,$ and 30°, respectively, where $a > b$.

$a = b + 30°$

Since the sum of three angles of a triangle is 180°,

$a + b + 30° = 180°$

$(b + 30°) + b + 30° = 180°$

$2b + 60° = 180° \rightarrow b = 60°$

$a = b + 30° = 90°$

➢ Two angles are 90° and 60°.

Chapter 2 *Practice Problems Solution*

18 If ∠FBC ≅ ∠CBD ≅ ∠DBE and ∠BAC ≅ ∠CAD ≅ ∠DAE in the figure below, what is the value of ∠BCA + ∠BDA?

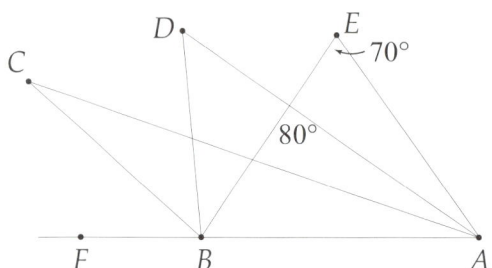

Solution

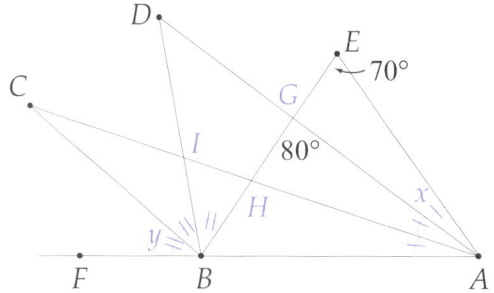

Let ∠BAC ≅ ∠CAD ≅ ∠DAE = x and
∠FBC ≅ ∠CBD ≅ ∠DBE = y, respectively.
In △AEG, $x + 70° = 80° \rightarrow x = 10°$.
In △ABE, ∠ABE = $180° - 3x - 70° = 80°$
and ∠FBE = $180° - ∠ABE \rightarrow 3y = 180° - 80° \rightarrow y = \dfrac{100°}{3}$.

In △ABD, ∠BDA = $180° - 2x - (∠ABE + y)$
$= 180° - 2(10°) - \left(80° + \dfrac{100°}{3}\right) = \dfrac{140°}{3}$.
In △ABC, ∠BCA = $180° - x - (2y + ∠ABE)$
$= 180° - 10° - \left(\dfrac{200°}{3} + 80°\right) = \dfrac{70°}{3}$.
So, ∠BCA + ∠BDA = 70°.

➢ ∠BCA + ∠BDA = 70°.

Chapter 3

Practice Problems Solution

01 If two angles of an equilateral triangle have measures $2a - 42°$ and $3b + 15°$, what is the value of $a + b$?

Solution

$2a - 42° = 60° \rightarrow a = 51°$
$3b + 15° = 60° \rightarrow b = 15°$
$a + b = 66°$.

➢ $a + b = 66°$.

02 If two triangles are congruent in the figure below, what is the measure of $\overline{DE}$?

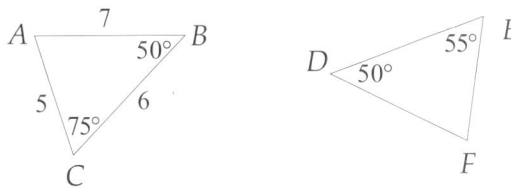

Solution

First, $\angle A = 180° - 50° - 75° = 55°$ and
$\angle F = 180° - 50° - 55° = 75°$. So, $\triangle ABC \cong \triangle EDF$.
By CPCTC, $\overline{DE} \cong \overline{AB} = 7$.

➢ $\overline{DE} = 7$.

Chapter 3 *Practice Problems Solution*

03 Given that $\overline{AB} \cong \overline{CD}$ and $\overline{BC} \cong \overline{AD}$, prove that $\angle BAC \cong \angle DCA$.

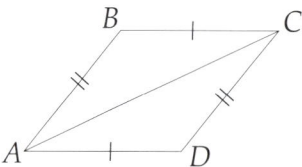

Solution

Statements	Reasons
1. $\overline{AB} \cong \overline{CD}, \overline{BC} \cong \overline{AD}$	1. Given
2. $\overline{AC} \cong \overline{AC}$	2. Reflexive property
3. $\triangle ABC \cong \triangle CDA$	3. SSS Congruence
4. $\angle BAC \cong \angle DCA$	4. CPCTC

04 If O is the midpoint of $\overline{AC}$ and $\overline{BD}$ in the figure below, what is the value of x and y?

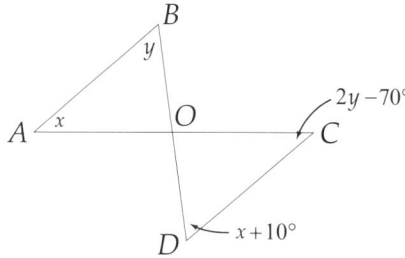

Solution

Since $\overline{BO} \cong \overline{DO}$, $\overline{AO} \cong \overline{CO}$, and $\angle AOB \cong \angle COD$,
$\triangle AOB \cong \triangle COD$ by SAS Congruence.
So, $x = 2y - 70°$ and $y = x + 10°$ by CPCTC.
$x = 2(x + 10°) - 70°$
$x = 2x - 50° \rightarrow x = 50°$
$y = x + 10° = 60°$

➤ $x = 50°$, $y = 60°$.

Chapter 3 — Practice Problems Solution

05 If $\overline{AB} \cong \overline{BE} \cong \overline{CE} \cong \overline{CD}$, what is the measure of $\angle ABE$?

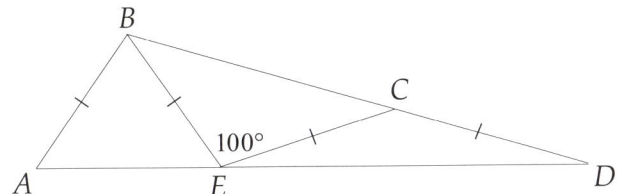

Solution

$\overline{BE} \cong \overline{CE} \rightarrow \angle EBC \cong \angle ECB = \dfrac{180° - 100°}{2} = 40°$

$\angle ECD = 180° - \angle ECB = 140°$

$\overline{CE} \cong \overline{CD} \rightarrow \angle CED \cong \angle CDE = \dfrac{180° - 140°}{2} = 20°$

$\angle AEB = 180° - 100° - \angle CED = 60°$

$\overline{AB} \cong \overline{BE} \rightarrow \angle AEB \cong \angle EAB = 60°$

$\angle ABE = 180° - \angle AEB - \angle EAB = 60°$

➢ $\angle ABE = 60°$.

06 Given $\overline{AD} \perp \overline{DC}$, $\overline{BC} \perp \overline{CD}$, and E is the midpoint of $\overline{AB}$, prove that $\overline{AD} \cong \overline{BC}$.

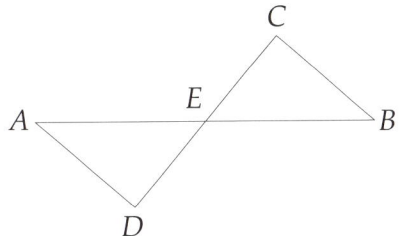

Solution

Statements	Reasons
1. $\overline{AD} \perp \overline{DC}$	1. Given
2. $\angle ADE = 90°$	2. Def. of $\perp$
3. $\overline{BC} \perp \overline{CD}$	3. Given
4. $\angle BCE = 90°$	4. Def. of $\perp$
5. $\angle ADE \cong \angle BCE$	5. Substitution property
6. $\overline{AE} \cong \overline{BE}$	6. Def. of midpoint
7. $\angle AED \cong \angle BEC$	7. Vertical $\angle$s
8. $\triangle AED \cong \triangle BEC$	8. AAS Congruence
9. $\overline{AD} \cong \overline{BC}$	9. CPCTC

Chapter 3 — *Practice Problems Solution*

07 Given that △ABC is equilateral and $\overline{AD} \cong \overline{BE} \cong \overline{CF}$, prove that △DEF is equilateral.

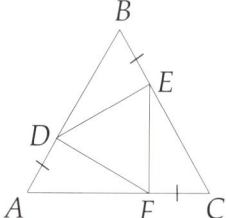

Solution

Statements	Reasons
1. △ABC is equilateral	1. Given
2. $\overline{AB} \cong \overline{BC} \cong \overline{AC}$	2. Def. of equilateral △
3. $\angle A \cong \angle B \cong \angle C = 60°$	3. Def. of equilateral △
4. $\overline{AD} \cong \overline{BE} \cong \overline{CF}$	4. Given
5. $\overline{AB} - \overline{AD} \cong \overline{BC} - \overline{BE} \cong \overline{AC} - \overline{CF}$	5. Subtraction property
6. $\overline{BD} \cong \overline{CE} \cong \overline{AF}$	6. Substitution property
7. △AFD ≅ △CEF ≅ △BDE	7. SAS Congruence
8. $\overline{FD} \cong \overline{EF} \cong \overline{DE}$	8. CPCTC
9. △DEF is equilateral	9. Because $\overline{FD} \cong \overline{EF} \cong \overline{DE}$.

Chapter 3 — Practice Problems Solution

08 If $\overline{AC} \cong \overline{AB}$ and $\overline{BC} \cong \overline{BD} \cong \overline{AD}$ in the figure below, what is the measure of $\angle ABD$?

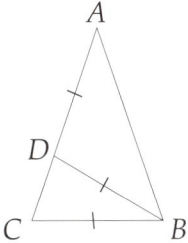

Solution

Let $\angle C = x$.
$\overline{AC} \cong \overline{AB} \to \angle C \cong \angle CBA = x$, $\overline{BC} \cong \overline{BD} \to \angle C \cong \angle BDC = x$,
and $\overline{BD} \cong \overline{AD} \to \angle A \cong \angle ABD$.
In $\triangle ABD$, $\angle BDC = \angle A + \angle ABD$.
$x = 2\angle A \to \angle A = \dfrac{x}{2}$ and $\angle ABD = \dfrac{x}{2}$.
In $\triangle ABC$, $\angle C + \angle CBA + \angle A = x + x + \dfrac{x}{2} = 180° \to \dfrac{5}{2}x = 180° \to x = 72°$
$\angle ABD = \dfrac{x}{2} = 36°$.

➤ $\angle ABD = 36°$.

Chapter 3   *Practice Problems Solution*

09 Given that $\overline{AB} \cong \overline{BC}$ and $\overline{AE} \cong \overline{ED} \cong \overline{DC}$, prove that $\angle BED \cong \angle BDE$.

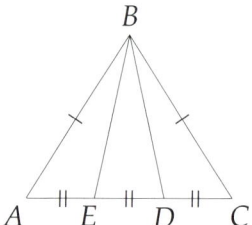

Solution

Statements	Reasons
1. $\overline{AB} \cong \overline{BC}$	1. Given
2. $\triangle ABC$ is isosceles $\triangle$.	2. Because $\overline{AB} \cong \overline{BC}$.
3. $\angle BAE \cong \angle BCD$	3. Def. isosceles $\triangle$
4. $\overline{AE} \cong \overline{DC}$	4. Given
5. $\triangle ABE \cong \triangle CBD$	5. SAS Congruence
6. $\angle BEA \cong \angle BDC$	6. CPCTC
7. $\angle BED = 180° - \angle BEA$ $\angle BDE = 180° - \angle BDC$	7. Subtraction property
8. $\angle BED \cong \angle BDE$	8. Substitution property

10 If $\angle BDC = 100°$ in the figure from question 9, what is the measure of $\angle EBD$?

Solution

First, $\angle BDE = 180° - \angle BDC = 80°$.
Since $\triangle ABE \cong \triangle CBD$, $\overline{BD} \cong \overline{BE}$ by CPCTC and this tells us that $\angle BDE \cong \angle BED = 80°$.
So, $\angle EBD = 180° - \angle BDE - \angle BED = 20°$.

➢ $\angle EBD = 20°$.

Chapter 3 — Practice Problems Solution

11 If triangle ABC is equilateral and $\overline{AD} \cong \overline{BE}$ in the figure below, what is the measure of $\angle BOC$?

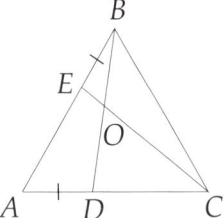

Solution

Since $\triangle ABE$ is equilateral, $\overline{AB} \cong \overline{BC}$ and $\angle A \cong \angle CBE = 60°$.
Also, $\overline{AD} \cong \overline{BE}$. Therefore, $\triangle ABD \cong \triangle BCE$ by SAS Congruence.
and $\angle BCE \cong \angle ABD$ by CPCTC.
Now, $\angle BOC = 180° - (\angle BCE + \angle OBC)$
$= 180° - (\angle ABD + \angle OBC) = 180° - 60° = 120°$.

➢ $\angle BOC = 120°$.

Chapter 3 — *Practice Problems Solution*

12 If B and F is the midpoint of $\overline{AC}$ and $\overline{AE}$ respectively, and $\angle ABF \cong \angle AFB$, prove that $\triangle BFC \cong \triangle FBE$.

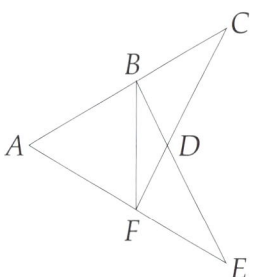

Solution

Statements	Reasons
1. $\angle ABF \cong \angle AFB$	1. Given
2. $\triangle ABF$ is isosceles $\triangle$.	2. Because $\angle ABF \cong \angle AFB$.
3. $\overline{AB} \cong \overline{AF}$	3. Def. of isosceles $\triangle$
4. B and F is the midpoint of $\overline{AC}$ and $\overline{AE}$	4. Given
5. $\overline{AB} \cong \overline{BC}, \overline{AF} \cong \overline{FE}$	5. Def. of midpoint
6. $\overline{BC} \cong \overline{FE}$	6. Substitution property
7. $\overline{BF} \cong \overline{BF}$	7. Reflexive property
8. $\angle CBF = 180° - \angle ABF$ $\angle EFB = 180° - \angle AFB$	8. Def. of straight $\angle$s
9. $\angle CBF = \angle EFB$	9. Substitution property
10. $\triangle BFC \cong \triangle FBE$	10. SAS Congruence

Chapter 3 — Practice Problems Solution

13 Given triangle ABC is equilateral and $\overline{AD} \cong \overline{BE} \cong \overline{CF}$, prove each of the following.

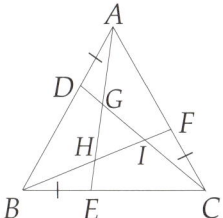

(1) $\triangle ABE \cong \triangle BCF \cong \triangle CAD$

(2) $\triangle ADG \cong \triangle BEH \cong \triangle CFI$

(3) $\triangle GHI$ is equilateral.

Solution

(1) $\triangle ABE \cong \triangle BCF \cong \triangle CAD$

Statements	Reasons
1. $\triangle ABC$ is equilateral	1. Given
2. $\overline{AB} \cong \overline{BC} \cong \overline{AC}$	2. Def. of equilateral $\triangle$
3. $\angle ABC \cong \angle BCA \cong \angle CAB = 60°$	3. Def. of equilateral $\triangle$
4. $\overline{AD} \cong \overline{BE} \cong \overline{CF}$	4. Given
5. $\triangle ABE \cong \triangle BCF \cong \triangle CAD$	5. SAS Congruence

(2) $\triangle ADG \cong \triangle BEH \cong \triangle CFI$

Statements	Reasons
1. $\overline{AD} \cong \overline{BE} \cong \overline{CF}$	1. Given
2. $\triangle ABE \cong \triangle BCF \cong \triangle CAD$	2. Proved from (1)
3. $\angle BAE \cong \angle CBF \cong \angle ACD$	3. CPCTC
4. $\angle BEA \cong \angle CFB \cong \angle ADC$	4. CPCTC
5. $\triangle ADG \cong \triangle BEH \cong \triangle CFI$	5. ASA Congruence

Chapter 3   *Practice Problems Solution*

(3) △GHI is equilateral.

Statements	Reasons
1. △ABE ≅ △BCF ≅ △CAD	1. Proved from (1)
2. $\overline{AE} \cong \overline{BF} \cong \overline{CD}$	2. CPCTC
3. △ADG ≅ △BEH ≅ △CFI	3. Proved from (2)
4. $\overline{DG} \cong \overline{EH} \cong \overline{FI}$	4. CPCTC
5. $\overline{AG} \cong \overline{BH} \cong \overline{CI}$	5. CPCTC
6. $\overline{HG} = \overline{AE} - \overline{AG} - \overline{EH}$ $\overline{IH} = \overline{BF} - \overline{BH} - \overline{FI}$ $\overline{GI} = \overline{CD} - \overline{CI} - \overline{DG}$	6. Segment subtraction postulate
7. $\overline{HG} \cong \overline{IH} \cong \overline{GI}$	7. Substitution property
8. △GHI is equilateral.	8. Because $\overline{HG} \cong \overline{IH} \cong \overline{GI}$.

14 If $\overline{AE} \perp \overline{EC}$, $\overline{AC} \perp \overline{DB}$, and $\overline{AE} \cong \overline{AB}$ in the figure below, what is the measure of ∠ADE?

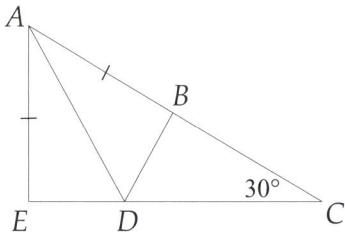

Solution

First, △AED and △ABD are right △s because
$\overline{AE} \perp \overline{EC} \to \angle AED = 90°$, $\overline{AC} \perp \overline{DB} \to \angle ABD = 90°$.
Since $\overline{AD} \cong \overline{AD}$ and $\overline{AE} \cong \overline{AB}$, △AED ≅ △ABD by HL Congruence.
So, ∠ADE ≅ ∠ADB by CPCTC.
Now, in △BCD, ∠BDC = 180° − ∠DBC − 30° = 180° − 90° − 30° = 60°.
Finally, ∠ADE + ∠ADB + ∠BDC = 180° → 2∠ADE = 120° → ∠ADE = 60°.

➤ ∠ADE = 60°.

Chapter 3   *Practice Problems Solution*

15 Given $\overline{AF} \cong \overline{AB}, \overline{FE} \cong \overline{BC}, \overline{ED} \cong \overline{CD}$, and $\angle FAD \cong \angle BAD$, prove that $\angle FED \cong \angle BCD$.

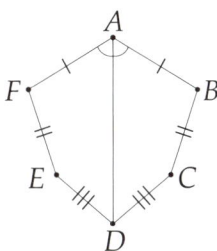

☼ **Solution**

Statements	Reasons
1. Draw $\overline{FD}$ and $\overline{BD}$.	1. A segment can be drawn between 2 points.
2. $\overline{AF} \cong \overline{AB}, \angle FAD \cong \angle BAD$	2. Given
3. $\overline{AD} \cong \overline{AD}$	3. Reflexive property
4. $\triangle AFD \cong \triangle ABD$	4. SAS Congruence
5. $\overline{FD} \cong \overline{BD}$	5. CPCTC
6. $\overline{FE} \cong \overline{BC}, \overline{ED} \cong \overline{CD}$	6. Given
7. $\triangle FED \cong \triangle BCD$	7. SSS Congruence
8. $\angle FED \cong \angle BCD$	8. CPCTC

Chapter 3 — *Practice Problems Solution*

16 Given triangles *ABE* and *BCD* are equilateral, prove that $\triangle BDA \cong \triangle BCE$.

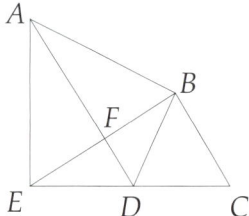

☼ Solution

Since $\triangle ABE$ and $\triangle BCD$ are equilateral,
$\overline{AB} \cong \overline{EB}$ and $\overline{BD} \cong \overline{BC}$ respectively. Also, $\angle ABE \cong \angle BCD$.
$\angle ABD = \angle ABE + \angle EBD = \angle CBD + \angle EBD = \angle EBC$
Therefore, $\triangle BDA \cong \triangle BCE$ by SAS Congruence.

17 If $\overline{AB} \perp \overline{BD}$, $\overline{BE} \perp \overline{AD}$, and $\angle EAF \cong \angle BAF$, what is the measure of $\overline{BF}$?

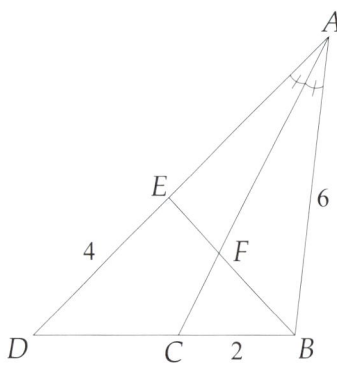

☼ Solution

$\overline{AB} \perp \overline{BD} \rightarrow \angle ABD = 90°$ and $\overline{BE} \perp \overline{AD} \rightarrow \angle AEF = 90°$.
Let $\angle EAF \cong \angle BAF = x$. In $\triangle AFE$, $\angle AFE = 90° - x$.
Also, $\angle AFE \cong \angle BFC = 90° - x$. In $\triangle ABC$, $\angle BCA = 90° - x$.
Since $\angle BFC \cong \angle BCA$, $\triangle BCF$ is an isosceles $\triangle$ and $\overline{BC} \cong \overline{BF} = 2$.

➢ $\overline{BF} = 2$.

302

Chapter 4 — Practice Problems Solution

01 Find the value of x in each of the following.

(1)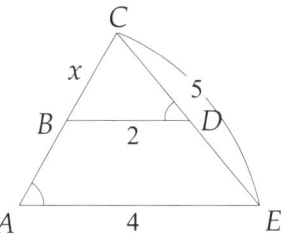

(2)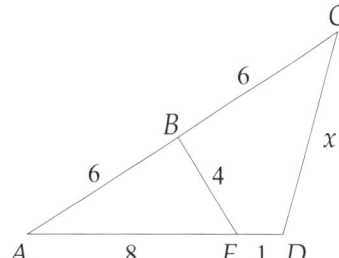

(3)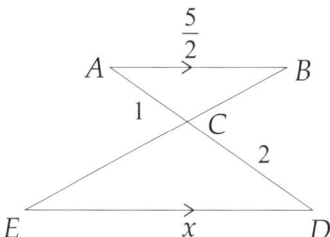

(4)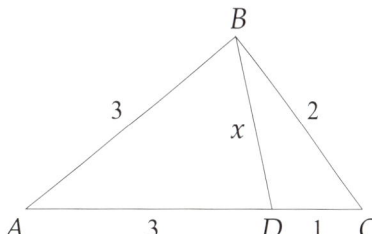

(5)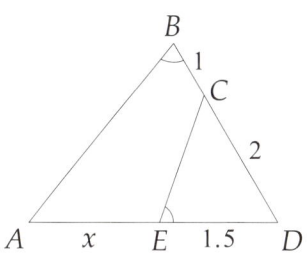

(6) 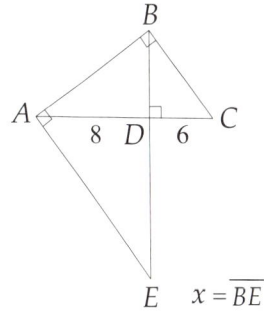 $x = \overline{BE}$

(7)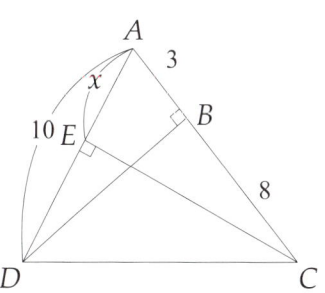

(8)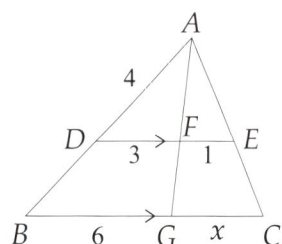

Chapter 4

Practice Problems Solution

Solution

(1) $\angle C \cong \angle C$ and $\angle CDB \cong \angle CAE$
$\rightarrow \triangle CDB \sim \triangle CAE$ by AA Similarity
$\dfrac{x}{\overline{CE}} = \dfrac{\overline{BD}}{\overline{EA}} \rightarrow \dfrac{x}{5} = \dfrac{2}{4} \rightarrow x = \dfrac{5}{2}$

➤ $x = \dfrac{5}{2}$.

(2) $\angle A \cong \angle A$ and $\dfrac{\overline{AB}}{\overline{AD}} = \dfrac{\overline{AE}}{\overline{AC}} = \dfrac{2}{3}$
$\rightarrow \triangle ABE \sim \triangle ADC$ by SAS Similarity
$\dfrac{\overline{AB}}{\overline{AD}} = \dfrac{\overline{BE}}{x} \rightarrow \dfrac{6}{8+1} = \dfrac{4}{x} \rightarrow x = 6$

➤ $x = 6$.

(3) $\overline{AB} \parallel \overline{ED} \rightarrow \angle ABE \cong \angle DEB$
and $\angle ACE \cong \angle DCE$
$\rightarrow \triangle ABC \sim \triangle DEC$ by AA Similarity
$\dfrac{\overline{AC}}{\overline{DC}} = \dfrac{\overline{AB}}{x} \rightarrow \dfrac{1}{2} = \dfrac{\frac{5}{2}}{x} \rightarrow x = 5$

➤ $x = 5$.

(4) $\angle C \cong \angle C$ and $\dfrac{\overline{CD}}{\overline{CB}} = \dfrac{\overline{BC}}{\overline{AC}} = \dfrac{1}{2}$
$\rightarrow \triangle CBD \sim \triangle CAB$ by SAS Similarity
$\dfrac{\overline{CD}}{\overline{CB}} = \dfrac{x}{\overline{AB}} \rightarrow \dfrac{1}{2} = \dfrac{x}{3} \rightarrow x = \dfrac{3}{2}$

➤ $x = \dfrac{3}{2}$.

(5) $\angle D \cong \angle D$ and $\angle B \cong \angle E$
$\rightarrow \triangle BDA \sim \triangle EDC$ by AA Similarity
$\dfrac{\overline{BD}}{\overline{ED}} = \dfrac{x + \overline{ED}}{\overline{CD}} \rightarrow \dfrac{1+2}{1.5} = \dfrac{x+1.5}{2} \rightarrow x = \dfrac{5}{2}$

➤ $x = \dfrac{5}{2}$.

(6) $\overline{BD}^2 = \overline{AD} \cdot \overline{CD} = 48 \rightarrow \overline{BD} = 4\sqrt{3}$
$\overline{AD}^2 = \overline{BD} \cdot \overline{ED}$
$8^2 = 4\sqrt{3} \cdot \overline{ED} \rightarrow \overline{ED} = \dfrac{16\sqrt{3}}{3}$
$x = \overline{BD} + \overline{ED} = 4\sqrt{3} + \dfrac{16\sqrt{3}}{3} = \dfrac{28\sqrt{3}}{3}$

➤ $x = \dfrac{28\sqrt{3}}{3}$.

(7) $\angle A \cong \angle A$ and $\angle AEC \cong \angle ABD$
$\rightarrow \triangle AEC \sim \triangle ABD$ by AA Similarity
$\dfrac{\overline{AC}}{\overline{AD}} = \dfrac{x}{\overline{AB}} \rightarrow \dfrac{3+8}{10} = \dfrac{x}{3} \rightarrow x = \dfrac{33}{10}$

➤ $x = \dfrac{33}{10}$.

(8) $\overline{DF} \parallel \overline{BG} \rightarrow \angle ADF \cong \angle ABG$
and $\angle DAF \cong \angle BAG$
$\rightarrow \triangle ADF \sim \triangle ABG$ by AA Similarity
$\dfrac{\overline{DF}}{\overline{BG}} = \dfrac{\overline{AD}}{\overline{AB}} \rightarrow \dfrac{3}{6} = \dfrac{4}{\overline{AB}} \rightarrow \overline{AB} = 8$
Also, $\angle DAE \cong \angle BAC$
$\rightarrow \triangle ADE \sim \triangle ABC$ by AA Similarity
$\dfrac{\overline{AD}}{\overline{AB}} = \dfrac{\overline{DE}}{\overline{BG}+x} \rightarrow \dfrac{4}{8} = \dfrac{3+1}{6+x} \rightarrow x = 2$

➤ $x = 2$.

Chapter 4   *Practice Problems Solution*

02 If $\overline{AB}//\overline{EF}//\overline{CD}$ and $\dfrac{\overline{AE}}{\overline{EC}}=\dfrac{4}{3}$, what is the measure of $\overline{CD}$?

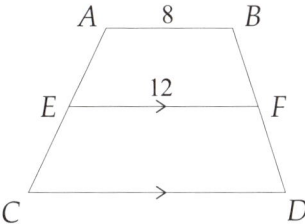

Solution

Draw $\overline{BH}$ that is parallel to $\overline{AC}$.

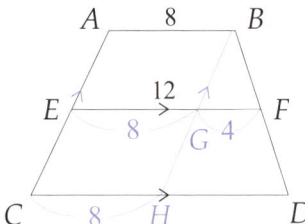

$\triangle BGF \sim \triangle BHD$ by AA Similarity.

$\dfrac{\overline{AE}}{\overline{EC}}=\dfrac{\overline{BG}}{\overline{GH}}=\dfrac{4}{3}$ and $\dfrac{\overline{BH}}{\overline{BG}}=\dfrac{\overline{HD}}{\overline{GF}} \rightarrow \dfrac{4+3}{4}=\dfrac{\overline{HD}}{4} \rightarrow \overline{HD}=7$

$\overline{CD}=\overline{CH}+\overline{HD}=8+7=15$

➤ $\overline{CD}=15$.

Chapter 4 — Practice Problems Solution

03 The triangle has side lengths of 3 inches, 4 inches, and 6 inches. If one of the side lengths of a similar triangle is 12 inches, what is the minimum number of inches possible in the perimeter of this similar triangle?

☀ **Solution**

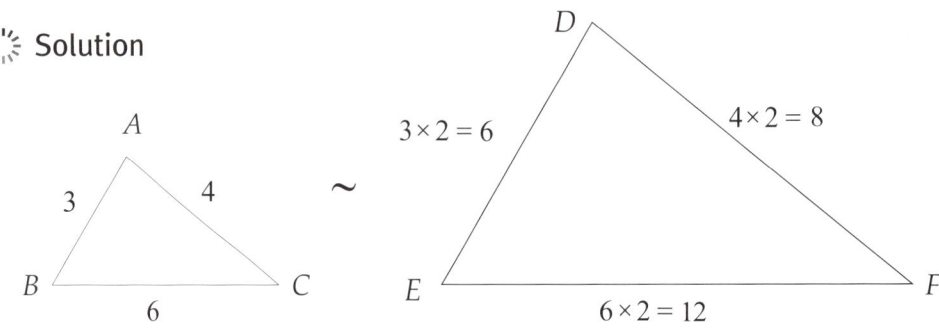

The perimeter of $\triangle DEF$ is minimum if $\dfrac{\overline{AC}}{\overline{DF}} = \dfrac{6}{12} = \dfrac{1}{2}$.

So, the minimum perimeter p of $\triangle DEF$ is $6+8+12=26$.

➤ $p = 26$.

04 Points C and F are midpoints of $\overline{GD}$ and $\overline{AE}$, respectively, such that $\overline{AG}\,//\,\overline{CF}\,//\,\overline{DE}$. What is the measure of $\overline{DE}$?

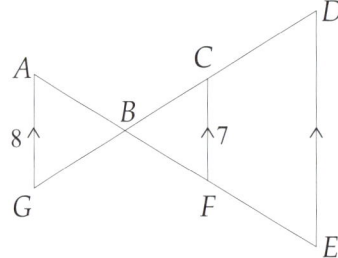

☀ **Solution**

$\triangle GAB \sim \triangle CFB$ by AA Similarity.

$\dfrac{\overline{AG}}{\overline{FC}} = \dfrac{\overline{BG}}{\overline{BC}} = \dfrac{8}{7}$ and $\overline{CD} = \overline{BG} + \overline{BC} = 15$.

$\triangle BFC \sim \triangle BED$ by AA Similarity.

$\dfrac{\overline{BD}}{\overline{BC}} = \dfrac{\overline{BC}+\overline{CD}}{\overline{BC}} = \dfrac{\overline{DE}}{\overline{CF}} \rightarrow \dfrac{7+15}{7} = \dfrac{\overline{DE}}{7} \rightarrow \overline{DE} = 22$

➤ $\overline{DE} = 22$.

Chapter 4 — Practice Problems Solution

05 If $\overline{AC} \perp \overline{BD}$ and $\overline{AB} \perp \overline{BC}$, what is the measure of $\overline{BD}$?

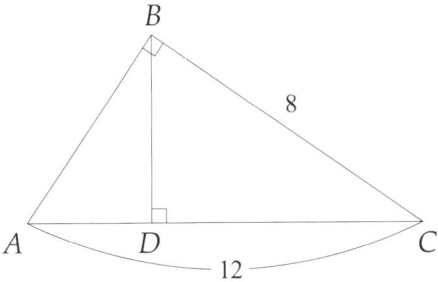

Solution

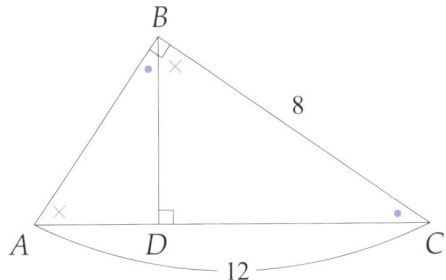

$\triangle ABC \sim \triangle BDC$ by AA Similarity.

$$\dfrac{\overline{AC}}{\overline{BC}} = \dfrac{\overline{BC}}{\overline{CD}} \rightarrow \dfrac{12}{8} = \dfrac{8}{\overline{CD}} \rightarrow \overline{CD} = \dfrac{16}{3}$$

$$\overline{AD} = \overline{AC} - \overline{CD} = 12 - \dfrac{16}{3} = \dfrac{20}{3}$$

$$\overline{BD}^2 = \overline{AD} \cdot \overline{CD} = \dfrac{20}{3} \cdot \dfrac{16}{3} \rightarrow \overline{BD} = \dfrac{8\sqrt{5}}{3}$$

➢ $\overline{BD} = \dfrac{8\sqrt{5}}{3}$.

Chapter 4 — *Practice Problems Solution*

06 In the figure below, what is the measure of $\overline{CF}$?

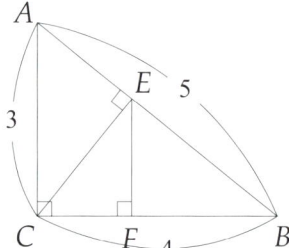

☀ **Solution**

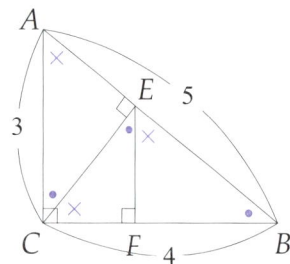

$\triangle ABC \sim \triangle CBE$ by AA Similarity.

$$\dfrac{\overline{AB}}{\overline{CB}} = \dfrac{\overline{AC}}{\overline{CE}} \rightarrow \dfrac{5}{4} = \dfrac{3}{\overline{CE}} \rightarrow \overline{CE} = \dfrac{12}{5}$$

$\triangle ABC \sim \triangle CEF$ by AA Similarity.

$$\dfrac{\overline{AB}}{\overline{CE}} = \dfrac{\overline{AC}}{\overline{CF}} \rightarrow \dfrac{5}{\tfrac{12}{5}} = \dfrac{3}{\overline{CF}} \rightarrow \overline{CF} = \dfrac{36}{25}$$

➢ $\overline{CF} = \dfrac{36}{25}$.

Chapter 4 — *Practice Problems Solution*

07
Given $\overline{AE} \perp \overline{CF}$ and $\overline{AC} \perp \overline{EB}$, prove that $\triangle CBD \sim \triangle EFD \sim \triangle CFA \sim \triangle EBA$.

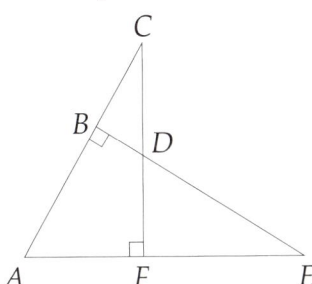

Solution

Let $\angle C = a$ and $\angle CDB = b$, respectively.
Note that $a + b = 90° \to a = 90° - b \to b = 90° - a$.
$\angle EDF = \angle CDB = b$ and $\angle E = 90° - \angle CDB = 90° - b = a$.
$\angle A = 90° - \angle C = 90° - a = b$.
Therefore, $\triangle CBD \sim \triangle EFD \sim \triangle CFA \sim \triangle EBA$ by AA Similarity.

08
If $\overline{AB} // \overline{EF} // \overline{CD}$, what is the measure of $\overline{EF}$?

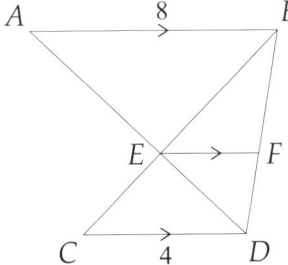

Solution

$\triangle ABE \sim \triangle DCE$ by AA Similarity.
$$\frac{\overline{BE}}{\overline{CE}} = \frac{\overline{AD}}{\overline{DC}} = \frac{8}{4} = \frac{2}{1}$$
$\triangle BEF \sim \triangle BCD$ by AA Similarity.
$$\frac{\overline{BE}}{\overline{BC}} = \frac{\overline{EF}}{\overline{CD}} \to \frac{2}{2+1} = \frac{\overline{EF}}{4} \to \overline{EF} = \frac{8}{3}$$

➤ $\overline{EF} = \dfrac{8}{3}$.

Chapter 4 *Practice Problems Solution*

09 If a piece of rectangular paper is folded as shown in the figure below, what is the measure of $\overline{FC}$?

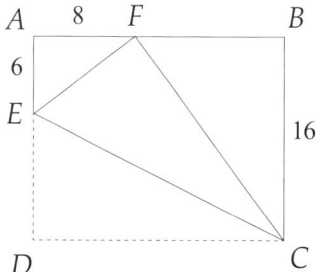

Solution

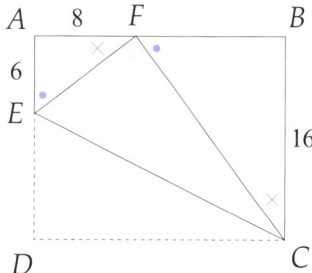

In $\triangle AFE$ and $\triangle BCF$, $\angle AFE + \angle BFC = 90°$
and $\angle BFC + \angle BCF = 90° \rightarrow \angle AFE \cong \angle BCF$.
Also, $\angle A \cong \angle B$. So, $\triangle AFE \sim \triangle BCF$ by AA Similarity.
$\overline{DE} = \overline{BC} - \overline{AE} = 16 - 6 = 10$ and $\overline{DE} \cong \overline{FE} = 10$.
$\dfrac{\overline{AF}}{\overline{BC}} = \dfrac{\overline{EF}}{\overline{FC}} \rightarrow \dfrac{8}{16} = \dfrac{10}{\overline{FC}} \rightarrow \overline{FC} = 20$

➢ $\overline{FC} = 20$.

Chapter 4   *Practice Problems Solution*

10 If $\overline{AD}$ and $\overline{BE}$ are angle bisectors of $\angle BAC$ and $\angle ABC$, respectively, what is the measure of $\overline{BD}$?

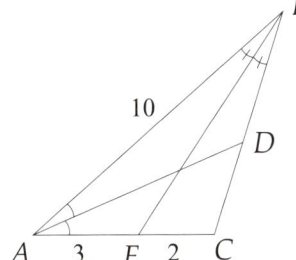

Solution

Since $\overline{BE}$ is a angle bisector of $\angle ABC$,

$$\frac{\overline{AB}}{\overline{BC}} = \frac{\overline{AE}}{\overline{EC}} \rightarrow \frac{10}{\overline{BC}} = \frac{3}{2} \rightarrow \overline{BC} = \frac{20}{3}$$

Since $\overline{AD}$ is a angle bisector of $\angle BAC$,

$$\frac{\overline{AB}}{\overline{AC}} = \frac{\overline{BD}}{\overline{DC}} \rightarrow \frac{10}{3+2} = \frac{\overline{BD}}{\frac{20}{3} - \overline{BD}}$$

$$\rightarrow 10\left(\frac{20}{3} - \overline{BD}\right) = 5\overline{BD} \rightarrow \overline{BD} = \frac{40}{9}$$

➤ $\overline{BD} = \frac{40}{9}$.

11 Given $\overline{AB} // \overline{DE}$ and $\overline{BC} // \overline{EF}$, prove that $\triangle ABC \sim \triangle DEF$.

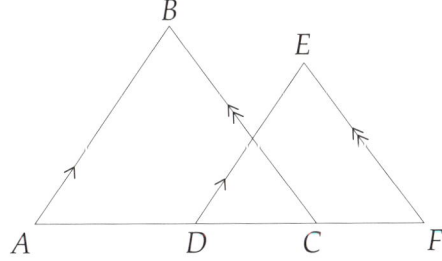

Solution

$\overline{AB} // \overline{DE} \rightarrow \angle BAC \cong \angle EDF$

$\overline{BC} // \overline{EF} \rightarrow \angle BCA \cong \angle EFD$

So, $\triangle ABC \sim \triangle DEF$ by AA Similarity.

Chapter 4 — *Practice Problems Solution*

12 Given $\overline{AE} \perp \overline{AC}, \overline{AD} \perp \overline{DE},$ and $\overline{EB}$ is an angle bisector of $\angle AED$, prove that $\angle ABF \cong \angle AFB$.

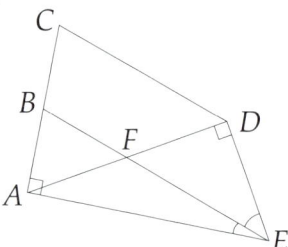

Solution

$\angle ABF = \angle ABE = 90° - \angle AEF$
$= 90° - \angle DEF = \angle DFE = \angle AFB.$
So, $\angle ABF \cong \angle AFB.$

13 If $\triangle ABC \sim \triangle CDE$, what is the measure of $\overline{BF}$?

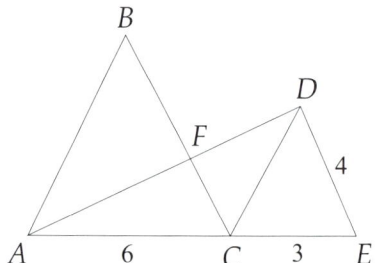

Solution

Since $\triangle ABC \sim \triangle CDE$,

$\dfrac{\overline{BC}}{\overline{DE}} = \dfrac{\overline{AC}}{\overline{CE}} \rightarrow \dfrac{\overline{BC}}{4} = \dfrac{6}{3} \rightarrow \overline{BC} = 8.$

Also, since $\angle FCA \cong \angle DEA$ and $\angle FAC \cong \angle DAE$,

$\triangle FAC \sim \triangle DAE$ by AA Similarity.

$\dfrac{\overline{AC}}{\overline{AE}} = \dfrac{\overline{FC}}{\overline{DE}} \rightarrow \dfrac{6}{6+3} = \dfrac{\overline{FC}}{4} \rightarrow \overline{FC} = \dfrac{8}{3}$

$\overline{BF} = \overline{BC} - \overline{FC} = 8 - \dfrac{8}{3} = \dfrac{16}{3}$

➤ $\overline{BF} = \dfrac{16}{3}.$

Chapter 4 — Practice Problems Solution

14 In the figure below, a triangle *ACE* is equilateral and $\triangle AFB \cong \triangle DFB$.

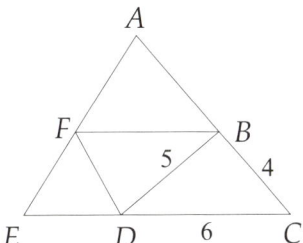

(1) Prove that $\triangle EDF \sim \triangle CBD$.   (2) Find the measure of $\overline{DF}$.

Solution

(1) First, $\angle E \cong \angle C \cong \angle A \cong \angle FDB = 60°$.
In $\triangle EFD$, $\angle EDF + \angle EFD = 180° - 60° = 120°$.
Also, $\angle EDF + \angle CDB = 180° - 60° = 120°$.
So, $\angle EDF + \angle EFD = \angle EDF + \angle CDB \rightarrow \angle EFD \cong \angle CDB$.
This tells us that $\triangle EDF \sim \triangle CBD$ by AA Similarity.

(2) $\overline{DB} \cong \overline{AB} = 5$ and $\overline{AC} \cong \overline{CE}$
$\rightarrow \overline{AB} + \overline{BC} = \overline{CD} + \overline{DE} \rightarrow 5 + 4 = 6 + \overline{DE} \rightarrow \overline{DE} = 3$.
Since $\triangle EDF \sim \triangle CBD$,
$\dfrac{\overline{DF}}{\overline{BD}} = \dfrac{\overline{DE}}{\overline{BC}} \rightarrow \dfrac{\overline{DF}}{5} = \dfrac{3}{4} \rightarrow \overline{DF} = \dfrac{15}{4}$.

➤ $\overline{DF} = \dfrac{15}{4}$.

Chapter 4 *Practice Problems Solution*

15 If ∠BAE ≅ ∠CBF ≅ ∠ACD, what is the ratio of $\overline{DE}$ to $\overline{EF}$?

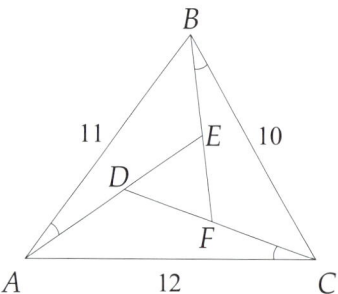

Solution

In △ACD,
∠EDF = ∠CAD + ∠ACD = ∠CAD + ∠BAE = ∠BAC.
In △BCF,
∠DFE = ∠BCF + ∠CBF = ∠BCF + ∠ACD = ∠ACB
Therefore, △DEF ~ △ABC by AA Similarity.

So, $\dfrac{\overline{DE}}{\overline{EF}} = \dfrac{\overline{AB}}{\overline{BC}} = \dfrac{11}{10}$.

➤ $\dfrac{\overline{AB}}{\overline{BC}} = \dfrac{11}{10}$.

Chapter 5 — Practice Problems Solution

01 In each of the following below, if point M is the circumcenter of $\triangle ABC$, what is the value of x?

(1)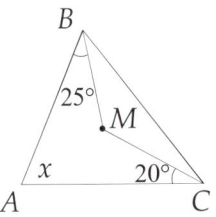

(2)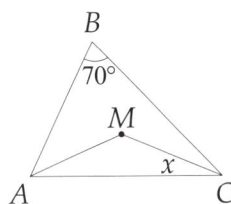

(3)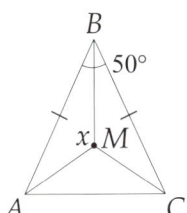

(4)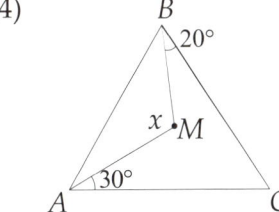

Solution

(1)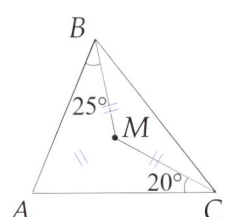

Since $\overline{AM} \cong \overline{BM} \cong \overline{CM}$,
$\angle CAM \cong \angle ACM = 20°$ and $\angle BAM \cong \angle ABM = 25°$.
So, $x = \angle CAM + \angle BAM = 45°$.

➤ $x = 45°$.

Chapter 5   *Practice Problems Solution*

(2)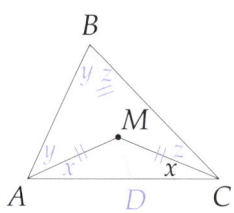

In △ABM, ∠AMD = 2y and in △CBM, ∠CMD = 2z.
So, ∠AMC = ∠AMD + ∠CMD = 2y + 2z = 2(y + z) = 2∠ABC.
→ ∠AMC = 2 · 70° = 140°
In △AMC, 2x + ∠AMC = 180° → 2x + 140° = 180° → x = 20°.

➤ x = 20°.

(3) Since $\overline{BA} \cong \overline{BC}$, ∠ACB = $\frac{1}{2}$(180° − 50°) = 65°.
So, x = 2∠ACB = 2 · 65° = 130°.

➤ x = 130°.

(4)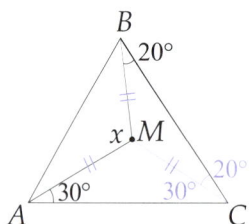

Since $\overline{AM} \cong \overline{BM} \cong \overline{CM}$,
∠CAM ≅ ∠ACM = 30° and ∠CBM ≅ ∠BCM = 20°.
So, ∠ACB = ∠ACM + ∠BCM = 50°.
x = 2∠ACB = 2 · 50° = 100°.

➤ x = 100°.

Chapter 5 — Practice Problems Solution

02 In each of the following below, if point M is the <u>incenter</u> of $\triangle ABC$, what is the value of x?

(1)
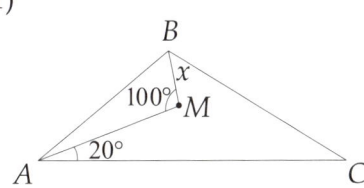

(2)
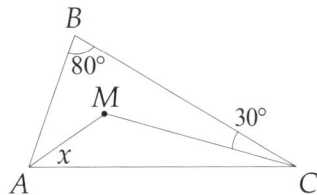

(3)
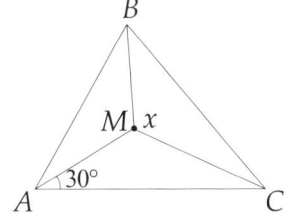

(4)
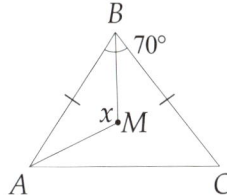

Solution

(1)
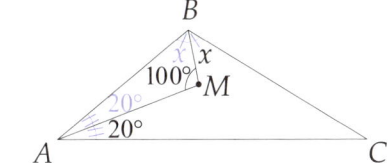

Since $\overline{AM}$ and $\overline{BM}$ are angle bisectors of $\angle BAC$ and $\angle ABC$ respectively, $\angle BAM = 20°$ and $\angle ABM = x$.
In $\triangle ABM$, $x = 180° - \angle BAM - \angle AMB = 180° - 20° - 100° = 60°$.

➤ $x = 60°$.

Chapter 5 *Practice Problems Solution*

(2)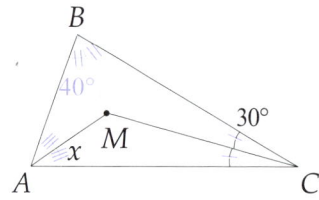

Since $\overline{AM}$, $\overline{BM}$, and $\overline{CM}$ are angle bisectors,

$\angle ABM + \angle BCM + \angle CAM = \dfrac{180°}{2} = 90°$.

$40° + 30° + x = 90° \rightarrow x = 20°$.

➤ $x = 20°$.

(3)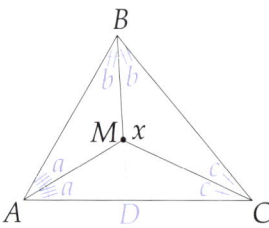

First, $a + b + c = 90°$.

In $\triangle ABM$, $\angle AMD = a + b$ and in $\triangle CBM$, $\angle CMD = b + c$.

$\angle AMC = \angle AMD + \angle CMD = a + b + b + c = 90° + b = 90° + \dfrac{1}{2}\angle ABC$.

In the same manner, $\angle BMC = 90° + \dfrac{1}{2}\angle BAC \rightarrow x = 90° + \dfrac{1}{2}(2 \cdot 30°) = 120°$.

➤ $x = 120°$.

(4) Since $\overline{BA} \cong \overline{BC}$, $\angle C = \dfrac{1}{2}(180° - 70°) = 55°$.

So, $x = 90° + \dfrac{1}{2}\angle C = 90° + \dfrac{55°}{2} = 117.5°$.

➤ $x = 117.5°$.

Chapter 5　　　　　　　　　　　　　　　　　　Practice Problems Solution

03 In each of the following below, if point M is the centroid of $\triangle ABC$, what is the value of x?

(1) 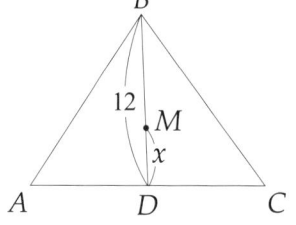　　　　(2)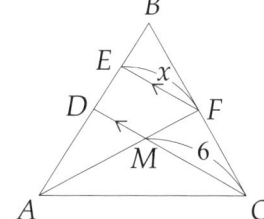

☀ Solution

(1) $\overline{DM} = \dfrac{1}{3}\overline{BD} \to x = \dfrac{1}{3} \cdot 12 = 4.$

➤ $x = 4.$

(2) $\dfrac{\overline{CM}}{\overline{DM}} = \dfrac{6}{\overline{DM}} = \dfrac{2}{1} \to \overline{DM} = 3$

$\overline{EF} \parallel \overline{DC} \to \triangle BEF \sim \triangle BDC$ by AA Similarity.

Since F is a midpoint of $\overline{BC}$, $\dfrac{\overline{BF}}{\overline{BC}} = \dfrac{\overline{EF}}{\overline{CD}} \to \dfrac{1}{2} = \dfrac{x}{3+6} \to x = \dfrac{9}{2}.$

➤ $x = \dfrac{9}{2}.$

Chapter 5 — *Practice Problems Solution*

04 The area of △DME is $6\,in^2$. If point M is centroid of △ABC, what is the area of △BCM?

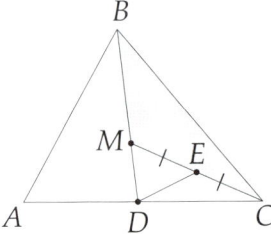

Solution

Since $\overline{ME} \cong \overline{CE}$, △CED = △DME = 6.
So, △DMC = △CED + △DME = 12.
Also, since M is centroid of △ABC, △BCM = 2 · △DMC = 2 · 12 = 24.

➤ △BCM = 24 in^2.

05 The area of △ABC is $72\,in^2$. If points M and N are centroids of △ABC and △AMC, respectively, what is the area of △AMN?

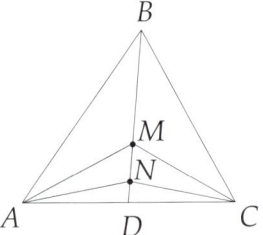

Solution

Since M is centroid of △ABC, $\triangle AMD = \dfrac{1}{6} \cdot \triangle ABC = \dfrac{1}{6} \cdot 72 = 12$.

Also, since N is centroid of △AMC,

$\overline{MN} = \dfrac{2}{3} \cdot \overline{MD}$ and $\triangle AMN = \dfrac{2}{3} \cdot \triangle AMD = \dfrac{2}{3} \cdot 12 = 8$.

➤ △AMN = 8 in^2.

Chapter 5 *Practice Problems Solution*

06 If points M and N are circumcenter and incenter of △ABC, respectively, what is the value of x?

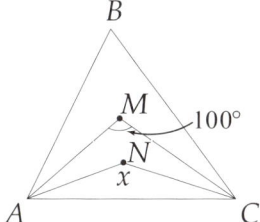

Solution

Since M is circumcenter of △ABC,

$\angle AMC = \dfrac{1}{2} \cdot \angle B \rightarrow 100° = \dfrac{1}{2} \cdot \angle B \rightarrow \angle B = 50°$.

Also, since N is incenter of △ABC,

$x = \angle ANC = 90° + \dfrac{1}{2} \cdot \angle B = 90° + \dfrac{1}{2} \cdot 50° = 115°$.

➢ $x = 115°$.

Chapter 5 — Practice Problems Solution

07 Given an isosceles triangle ABC in the figure below, find its circumradius and the inradius.

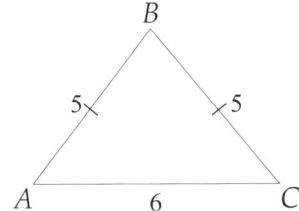

Solution

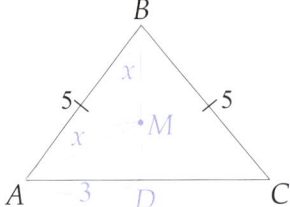

If we let M be the circumcenter of $\triangle ABC$, x = circumradius.
$\overline{AD} = \sqrt{5^2 - 3^2} = 4$ and $\overline{MD} = 4 - x$.
In $\triangle BMD$, $3^2 + (4-x)^2 = x^2$
$9 + 16 - 8x + x^2 = x^2 \rightarrow x = \dfrac{25}{8}$

Now, let the inradius and semiperimeter of $\triangle ABC$ be r and s.
Since $\triangle ABC = rs$, $\dfrac{1}{2} \cdot 6 \cdot 4 = r\left(\dfrac{5+5+6}{2}\right)$
$\rightarrow 12 = 8r \rightarrow r = \dfrac{3}{2}$.

➤ Circumradius = $\dfrac{25}{8}$, Inradius = $\dfrac{3}{2}$.

Chapter 5 — Practice Problems Solution

08 Find the value of x.

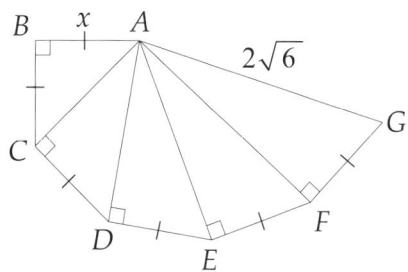

Solution

$\overline{AC} = \sqrt{\overline{AB}^2 + \overline{BC}^2} = \sqrt{x^2 + x^2} = \sqrt{2}x.$

$\overline{AD} = \sqrt{\overline{AC}^2 + \overline{CD}^2} = \sqrt{(\sqrt{2}x)^2 + x^2} = \sqrt{3}x.$

$\overline{AE} = \sqrt{\overline{AD}^2 + \overline{DE}^2} = \sqrt{(\sqrt{3}x)^2 + x^2} = 2x.$

$\overline{AF} = \sqrt{\overline{AE}^2 + \overline{EF}^2} = \sqrt{(2x)^2 + x^2} = \sqrt{5}x.$

$\overline{AG} = \sqrt{\overline{AF}^2 + \overline{FG}^2} = \sqrt{(\sqrt{5}x)^2 + x^2} = \sqrt{6}x$

$\sqrt{6}x = 2\sqrt{6} \rightarrow x = 2.$

➤ $x = 2.$

09 Find all positive integers a for which it is possible for $2a+4$, $a+7$, and $4a+7$ to be the side lengths of a triangle.

Solution

Since $4a + 7$ is greater than both $2a + 4$ and $a + 7$ for all positive integers a,

$(2a + 4) + (a + 7) > 4a + 7$

$3a + 11 > 4a + 7$

$4 > a \rightarrow a = 1, 2, 3$

➤ $a = 1, 2, 3.$

 **Chapter 5** *Practice Problems Solution*

10 Given the point M is circumcenter of $\triangle ABC$, prove that $\angle AMC = 2\angle B$.

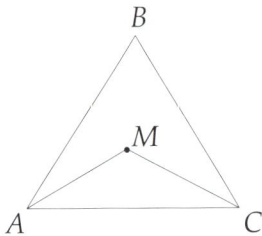

☼ **Solution**

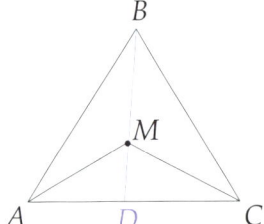

Draw $\overline{BD}$ that passes through the point M.
Since M is circumcenter of $\triangle ABC$, $\overline{AM} \cong \overline{BM} \cong \overline{CM}$
and $\angle BAM \cong \angle ABM$ and $\angle BCM \cong \angle CBM$.
In $\triangle ABM$, $\angle AMD = \angle BAM + \angle ABM$ and in $\triangle CBM$, $\angle CMD = \angle CBM + \angle BCM$.
So, $\angle AMC = \angle AMD + \angle CMD = \angle BAM + \angle ABM + \angle CBM + \angle BCM$
$= 2\angle ABM + 2\angle CBM = 2(\angle ABM + \angle CBM) = 2\angle ABC = 2\angle B$.

Chapter 5 — Practice Problems Solution

11 Given the point M is incenter of $\triangle ABC$, prove that $\angle AMC = 90° + \dfrac{1}{2}\angle B$.

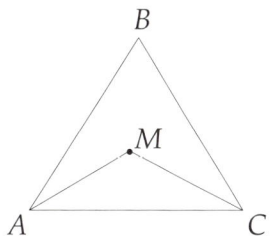

Solution

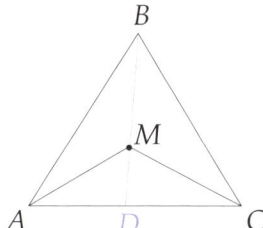

Draw $\overline{BD}$ that passes through the point M.

Since M is incenter of $\triangle ABC$, $\overline{AM}$, $\overline{BM}$, and $\overline{CM}$ are alngle bisectors of $\angle BCA$, $\angle ABC$ and $\angle ACB$.

So, $\angle BAM \cong \angle CAM$, $\angle ABM \cong \angle CBM$, and $\angle ACM \cong \angle BCM$.

Also, $\angle BAM + \angle CBM + \angle ACM = \dfrac{1}{2}\cdot 180° = 90°$.

In $\triangle ABM$, $\angle AMD = \angle BAM + \angle ABM$ and in $\triangle CBM$, $\angle CMD = \angle CBM + \angle BCM$.

So, $\angle AMC = \angle AMD + \angle CMD = \angle BAM + \angle ABM + \angle CBM + \angle BCM$

$= (\angle BAM + \angle CBM + \angle ACM) + \angle ABM = 90° + \dfrac{1}{2}\angle ABC = 90° + \dfrac{1}{2}\angle B.$

Chapter 5 — Practice Problems Solution

12 Given $\overline{BD}$ is a median of $\triangle ABC$, prove that $\overline{BD} > \dfrac{\overline{BA} + \overline{BC} - \overline{AC}}{2}$.

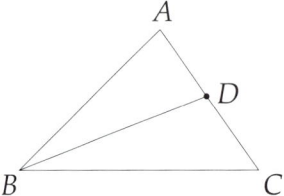

Solution

By the Triangle Inequality to both $\triangle BAD$ and $\triangle BCD$,
$\overline{BD} + \overline{AD} > \overline{BA} \rightarrow (1)$ and $\overline{BD} + \overline{CD} > \overline{BC} \rightarrow (2)$.
Since $\overline{AC} = \overline{AD} + \overline{CD}$, $(1)+(2)$ gives us
$2\overline{BD} + \overline{AD} + \overline{CD} > \overline{BA} + \overline{BC}$
$2\overline{BD} + \overline{AC} > \overline{BA} + \overline{BC}$
$2\overline{BD} > \overline{BA} + \overline{BC} - \overline{AC}$
$\overline{BD} > \dfrac{\overline{BA} + \overline{BC} - \overline{AC}}{2}$.

Chapter 5 — Practice Problems Solution

13 In each of the following figure below, prove that $c^2 = a^2 + b^2$.

(1)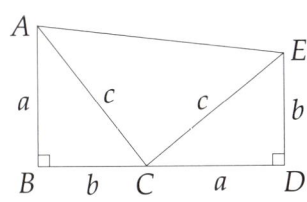

(2)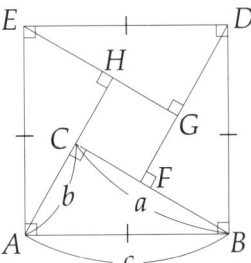

Solution

(1) $\triangle ABC \cong \triangle CDE$ by SSS Congruence and $\angle BAC \cong \angle DCE$ by CPCTC.
Since, $\angle BAC + \angle BCA = 90°$,
$\angle ACE = 180° - (\angle DCE + \angle BCA) = 180° - 90° = 90°$.
Now, since the area of trapezoid $ABED$ is equal to sum of the area of $\triangle ABC + \triangle ACE + \triangle CDE$,

$$\frac{1}{2}(a+b)(a+b) = \frac{1}{2}ab + \frac{1}{2}ab + \frac{1}{2}c^2$$

$$a^2 + 2ab + b^2 = 2ab + c^2$$

$$a^2 + b^2 = c^2.$$

*We will discuss more about the area of trapezoid in chapter 6.

(2) In $\triangle ABC$, $\angle ABC + \angle BAC = 90°$.
Since $\angle BAC + \angle EAH = 90°$,
$\angle ABC + \angle BAC = \angle BAC + \angle EAH \rightarrow \angle ABC \cong \angle EAH$
and $\angle ABC + \angle BAC = \angle AEH + \angle EAH \rightarrow \angle BAC \cong \angle AEH$
So, $\triangle ABC \cong \triangle EAH$ by ASA Congruence.
In the same manner, $\triangle ABC \cong \triangle EAH \cong \triangle DEG \cong \triangle BDF$.
Now, since $CFGH$ is a square with each side length $a - b$,
the area of a square $ABDE$ is equal to the sum of area of $\triangle ABC, \triangle EAH, \triangle DEG, \triangle BDF$ and a square $CFGH$.
$ABDE = 4 \cdot \triangle ABC + CFGH$

$$c^2 = 4\left(\frac{1}{2} \cdot a \cdot b\right) + (a-b)^2$$

$$c^2 = 2ab + a^2 - 2ab + b^2$$

$$c^2 = a^2 + b^2.$$

Chapter 5 *Practice Problems Solution*

14 Given $\angle A > 90°$, prove that $\overline{BC}^2 > \overline{AB}^2 + \overline{AC}^2$.

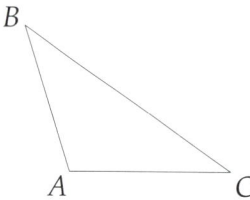

Solution

Draw $\overline{BD}$ and $\overline{AD}$ such that $\overline{BD} \perp \overline{AD}$.

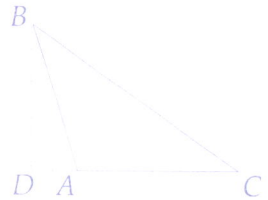

$\overline{BC}^2 = \overline{BD}^2 + \overline{CD}^2 = \overline{AB}^2 - \overline{AD}^2 + \left(\overline{AC} + \overline{AD}\right)^2$

$\overline{BC}^2 = \overline{AB}^2 - \overline{AD}^2 + \overline{AC}^2 + 2\overline{AC} \cdot \overline{AD} + \overline{AD}^2$

$\overline{BC}^2 = \overline{AB}^2 + \overline{AC}^2 + 2\overline{AC} \cdot \overline{AD}$

Since $2\overline{AC} \cdot \overline{AD} > 0$, $\overline{BC}^2 > \overline{AB}^2 + \overline{AC}^2$.

Chapter 6 — Practice Problems Solution

01 Prove that sum of any two consecutive angles in the parallelogram is 180°.

Solution

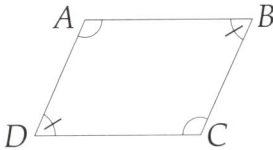

Statements	Reasons
1. ABCD is a parallelogram	1. Given
2. $\angle A + \angle B + \angle C + \angle D = 360°$	2. Def. of quadrilateral
3. $\angle A \cong \angle C, \angle B \cong \angle D$	3. Property of parallelogram
4. $\angle A + \angle B + \angle A + \angle B = 360°$	4. Substitution property
5. $2\angle A + 2\angle B = 360°$	5. Simplify
6. $\angle A + \angle B = 180°$	6. Division property

02 Given one pair of opposite sides of a quadrilateral is both parallel and congruent, prove that the quadrilateral is a parallelogram.

Solution

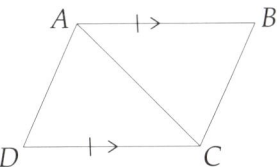

Statements	Reasons
1. ABCD is a parallelogram and $\overline{AB} \cong \overline{CD}, \overline{AB} \parallel \overline{CD}$	1. Given
2. $\angle BAC \cong \angle DCA$	2. Alterate interior $\angle$s
3. $\overline{AC} \cong \overline{CA}$	3. Reflexive property
4. $\triangle BAC \cong \triangle DCA$	4. SAS Congruence
5. $\angle DAC \cong \angle BCA$	5. CPCTC
6. $\overline{AD} \parallel \overline{BC}$	6. $\angle DAC \& \angle BCA$ are alt. int. $\angle$s and $\angle DAC \cong \angle BCA$
7. ABCD is a parallelogram	7. Def. of parallelogram

Chapter 6

Practice Problems Solution

03 A parallelogram *ABCD* is given below. For each of the following, find the value of *x*

(1)
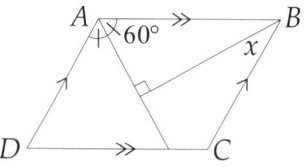

(2)
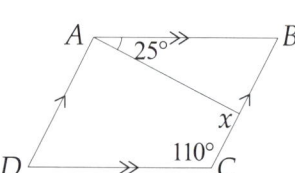

(3)
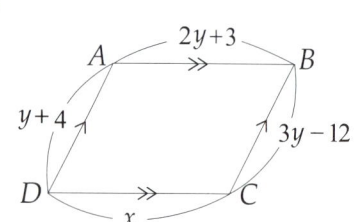

(4)
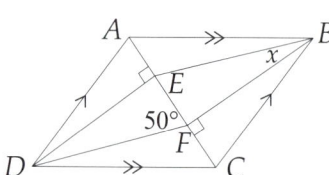

(5)
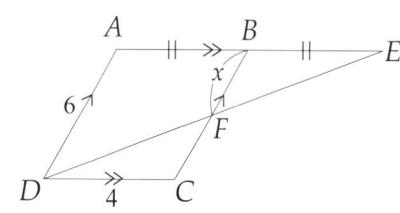

(6)
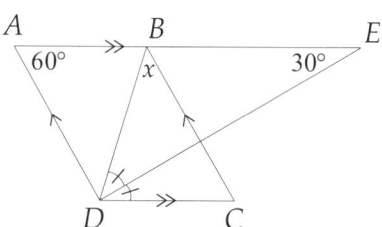

Solution

(1)
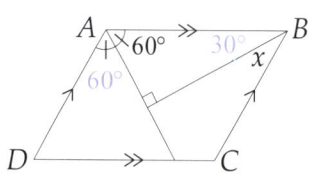

(2)
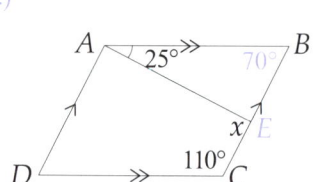

Chapter 6 *Practice Problems Solution*

Since $\angle DAB + \angle ABC = 180°$,
$60° + 60° + 30° + x = 180°$
$x = 30°$.

In $\triangle BCE$, $x = \angle EAB + \angle EBA$
$x = 25° + 70° = 95°$.

➤ $x = 30°$.

➤ $x = 95°$.

(3) Since $\overline{AD} \cong \overline{BC}$, $y + 4 = 3y - 12 \rightarrow y = 8$
Since $\overline{DC} \cong \overline{AB}$, $x = 2y + 3 = 2 \cdot 8 + 3 = 19$

➤ $x = 19$.

(4) Since $\angle DEA \cong \angle BFC = 90°$, $\overline{DE} \parallel \overline{BF}$. So, $\angle ADE \cong \angle CBF$.
This proves that $\triangle ADE \cong \triangle CBF$ by AAS Congruence and $\overline{DE} \cong \overline{BF}$ by CPCTC.
Since $\overline{DE} \parallel \overline{BF}$ and $\overline{DE} \cong \overline{BF}$, $DEBF$ is a parallelogram
and $\angle DFB + \angle FBE = 180° \rightarrow (50° + 90°) + x = 180° \rightarrow x = 40°$.

➤ $x = 40°$.

(5) $\overline{AB} \cong \overline{BE} \cong \overline{DC}$. Since $\overline{BE} \cong \overline{DC}$, $\angle EBF \cong \angle DCF$ and $\angle BEF \cong \angle CDF$
So, $\triangle BEF \cong \triangle CDF$ by ASA Congruence and $\overline{BF} \cong \overline{CF}$ by CPCTC.
$\overline{AD} = 2\overline{BF} \rightarrow 6 = 2x \rightarrow x = 3$.

➤ $x = 3$.

(6) $\angle A \cong \angle C = 60°$ and $\angle ADC = 180° - 60° = 120°$.
In $\triangle ADE$, $\angle ADE = 180° - 60° - 30° = 90°$.
So, $\angle EDC = \angle ADC - \angle ADE = 120° - 90° = 30°$
and $\angle BDC = 2\angle EDC = 2 \cdot 30° = 60°$.
In $\triangle BDC$, $x = 180° - \angle BDC - \angle C = 180° - 60° - 60° = 60°$.

➤ $x = 60°$.

Chapter 6 *Practice Problems Solution*

04 A trapezoid *ABCD* is given below. If $\overline{AB} \cong \overline{BC} \cong \overline{CD}$, what is the measure of $\overline{AD}$?

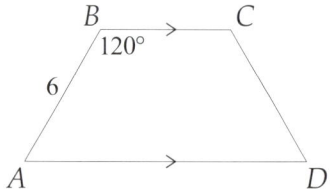

Solution

Draw $\overline{EC}$ parallel to $\overline{AB}$.

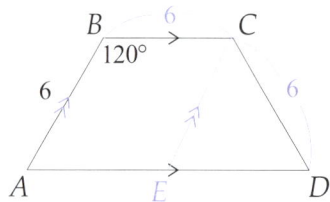

Since $\overline{AB} \cong \overline{CD}$, *ABCD* is an isosceles trapezoid and $\angle A \cong \angle D = 180° - 120° = 60°$.
Since $\overline{AB} \parallel \overline{EC}$, $\angle A \cong \angle CED = 60°$. So, $\triangle CDE$ is equilateral.
Therefore, $\overline{AD} = \overline{AE} + \overline{ED} = \overline{BC} + \overline{CD} = 6 + 6 = 12$.

➢ $\overline{AD} = 12$.

Chapter 6 — Practice Problems Solution

05 A trapezoid $ABCD$ is given below. If $\overline{AB} \cong \overline{BC} \cong \overline{CD}$, what is the measure of $\angle ADC$?

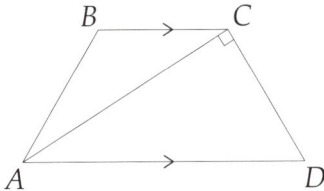

Solution

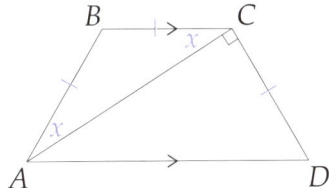

Since $\overline{AB} \cong \overline{CD}$, $ABCD$ is an isosceles trapezoid and $\angle BCD = 90° + x$.
In $\triangle ABC$, $\angle B = 180° - 2x$.
Since $\angle B \cong \angle BCD$, $180° - 2x = 90° + x \rightarrow x = 30°$.
Now, $\angle BCD = 180° - 2 \cdot 30° = 120°$ and $\angle ADC = 180° - 120° = 60°$.

➤ $\angle ADC = 60°$.

Chapter 6 — Practice Problems Solution

06 Prove that the median of a trapezoid is parallel to the bases.

Solution

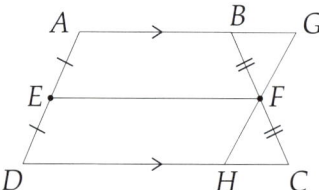

Statements	Reasons
1. ABCD is a trapezoid and $\overline{EF}$ is median.	1. Given
2. $\overline{AB} \parallel \overline{DC}$	2. Def. of parallelogram
3. $\overline{AD} \parallel \overline{GH}$	3. Draw $\overline{GH}$ parallel to $\overline{AD}$
4. $\angle GBF \cong \angle HCF$	4. Alternate interior $\angle$s
5. $\angle BFG \cong \angle CFH$	5. Vertical $\angle$s
6. $\overline{BF} \cong \overline{CF}$	6. Because F is midpoint of $\overline{BC}$.
7. $\triangle BFG \cong \triangle CFH$	7. ASA Congruence
8. $\overline{GF} \cong \overline{HF}, \overline{BG} \cong \overline{CH}$	8. CPCTC
9. AGHD is a parallelogram	9. Because $\overline{AB} \parallel \overline{DC}$ and $\overline{AD} \parallel \overline{GH}$.
10. $\overline{AD} \cong \overline{GH}$	10. Property of parallelogram
11. $\overline{AE} = \dfrac{\overline{AD}}{2}$ and $\overline{GF} = \dfrac{\overline{GH}}{2}$	11. Def. of midpoint
12. $\overline{AE} \cong \overline{GF}$	12. Substitution property
13. AGFE is a parallelogram	13. $\overline{AE}$ & $\overline{GF}$ are both $\parallel$ and $\cong$
14. $\overline{AG} \parallel \overline{EF}$	14. Def. of parallelogram

Chapter 6

Practice Problems Solution

07 Prove that the median of a trapezoid is one half the sum of the measures of the bases.

Solution

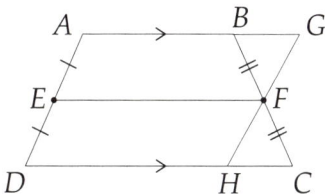

Statements	Reasons
1. $ABCD$ is a trapezoid and $\overline{EF}$ is median.	1. Given
2. $\overline{AB} \parallel \overline{DC}$	2. Def. of parallelogram
3. $\overline{AB} \parallel \overline{EF}$	3. Proved from practice problem 6.
4. $\overline{EF} \parallel \overline{DC}$	4. Transitive property
5. $\overline{AG} \cong \overline{EF} \cong \overline{DH}$	5. Equal opposite sides
6. $2\overline{EF} = \overline{AG} + \overline{DH}$	6. Addition property
7. $\overline{AG} = \overline{AB} + \overline{BG}$	7. Segment addition property
8. $\overline{DH} = \overline{DC} - \overline{HC}$	8. Segment subtraction property
9. $2\overline{EF} = \overline{AB} + \overline{BG} + \overline{DC} - \overline{HC}$	9. Substitution property
10. $2\overline{EF} = \overline{AB} + \overline{DC}$	10. Because $\overline{BG} \cong \overline{HC}$ from practice problem 6.

Chapter 6 *Practice Problems Solution*

08 If $ABCD$ is a trapezoid with $\overline{EG} = 3$ and $\overline{GF} = 5$, what is the measure of $\overline{AB} + \overline{CD}$?

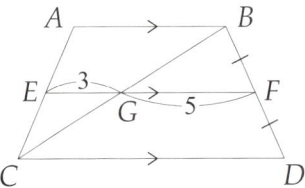

Solution

Since F is midpoint of $\overline{BD}$ and $\overline{AB} \parallel \overline{EF} \parallel \overline{CD}$, EF is median of trapezoid $ABDC$.

$$\overline{EF} = \frac{1}{2}\left(\overline{AB} + \overline{CD}\right)$$

$$3 + 5 = \frac{1}{2}\overline{AB} + \overline{CD} \rightarrow \overline{AB} + \overline{CD} = 16$$

➤ $\overline{AB} + \overline{CD} = 16.$

Chapter 6   *Practice Problems Solution*

09 A rectangle *ABCD* is given below. If $\overline{AE}$ is an angle bisector of $\angle DAC$ and $\overline{AE} \cong \overline{CE}$, what is the measure of $\angle AED$?

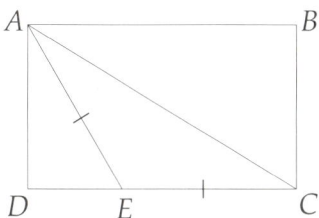

☼ **Solution**

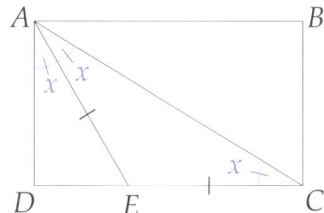

In $\triangle AEC$, $\angle AED = \angle EAC + \angle ECA = x + x = 2x$
In $\triangle ADE$, $x + 2x + 90° = 180 \rightarrow x = 30°$
$\angle AED = 2x = 60°$.

➤ $\angle AED = 60°$.

Practice Problems 337

Chapter 6 — Practice Problems Solution

10 A rhombus *ABCD* is given below. If *CDE* is an equilateral triangle, what is the measure of $\angle BEC$?

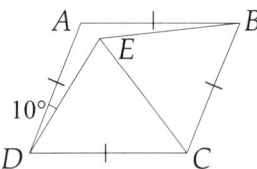

Solution

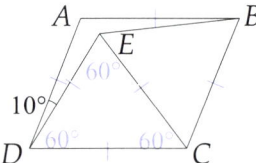

$\angle ADC = 60° + 10° = 70°$, $\angle DCB = 180° - 70° = 110°$

$\angle BCE = 110° - 60° = 50°$

Since $\triangle BCE$ is an isosceles triangle, $\angle BEC = \dfrac{180° - \angle BCE}{2} = \dfrac{180° - 50°}{2} = 65°$.

➤ $\angle BEC = 65°$.

Chapter 6 — Practice Problems Solution

11 A square $ABCD$ is given below. If $\overline{DE} \cong \overline{DF}$, what is the measure of $\angle DFE$?

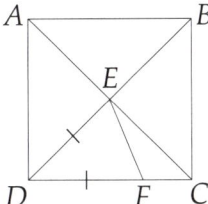

✦ Solution

Since $\triangle BAD \cong \triangle BCD$ by SAS Congruence, $\angle ADB \cong \angle CDB$.

$\angle CDB \cong \angle FDE = \dfrac{90°}{2} = 45°$.

Since $\triangle DEF$ is an isosceles triangle, $\angle DFE = \dfrac{180° - 45°}{2} = 67.5°$.

➤ $\angle DFE = 67.5°$.

Chapter 6 *Practice Problems Solution*

12 A square ABCD is given below. If $\overline{AE} \cong \overline{BG}$, what is the measure of $\angle DFG$?

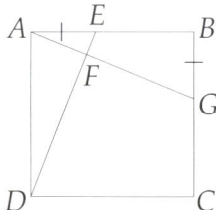

Solution

Since $\triangle ABG \cong \triangle DAE$ by SAS Congruence, $\angle BAG \cong \angle ADE$.
$\angle BAG + \angle DAG = 90°$, $\angle ADE + \angle DAG = 90°$
In $\triangle ADF$, $\angle DFG = \angle ADE + \angle DAG = 90°$.

➤ $\angle DFG = 90°$.

13 In quadrilateral ABCD, E, F, G, and H are midpoints of $\overline{AB}, \overline{BC}, \overline{CD}$, and $\overline{DA}$, respectively. Prove that EFGH is a parallelogram.

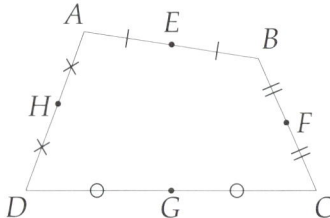

Solution

Since E and H are the midpoints of $\overline{AB}$ and $\overline{AD}$, $\overline{EH} \parallel \overline{BD}$.
Similarly, since F and G are the midpoints of $\overline{BC}$ and $\overline{CD}$, $\overline{FG} \parallel \overline{BD}$.
So, $\overline{EH} \parallel \overline{FG}$. In the same manner, $\overline{EF} \parallel \overline{HG}$.
Therefore, since $\overline{EH} \parallel \overline{FG}$ and $\overline{EF} \parallel \overline{HG}$, EFGH is a parallelogram.

Chapter 6

Practice Problems Solution

14

A square *ABCD* and an isosceles triangle *AEF* with $\overline{AE} \cong \overline{AF}$ is given below. What is the measure of $\angle CEF$?

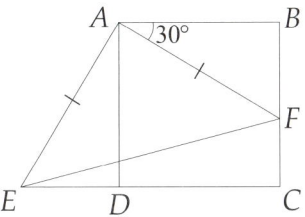

Solution

In $\triangle ADE$, $\angle ADE = 90°$ and in $\triangle ABF$, $\angle B = 90°$.
Also, $\overline{AB} \cong \overline{AD}$ and $\overline{AE} \cong \overline{AF}$, $\triangle ADE \cong \triangle ABF$ by HL Congruence.
$\angle AED \cong \angle AFB = 90° - 30° = 60°$.
So, $\angle EAD = 30°$ and $\angle EAF = \angle EAD + \angle DAF = 30° + (90° - 30°) = 90°$.
Since $\overline{AE} \cong \overline{AF}$, $\angle AEF = \dfrac{180° - 90°}{2} = 45°$.
Therefore, $\angle CEF = \angle AED - \angle AEF = 60° - 45° = 15°$.

➤ $\angle CEF = 15°$.

Chapter 6 — *Practice Problems Solution*

15 Given the diagonals of a quadrilateral bisect each other, prove that the quadrilateral is a parallelogram.

Solution

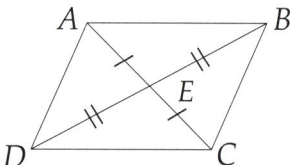

Statements	Reasons
1. $ABCD$ is a quadrilateral and $\overline{AE} \cong \overline{CE}, \overline{BE} \cong \overline{DE}$.	1. Given
2. $\angle AEB \cong \angle CED$	2. Vertical $\angle$s
3. $\triangle AEB \cong \triangle CED$	3. SAS Congruence
4. $\overline{AB} \cong \overline{CD}$	4. CPCTC
5. $\angle ABE \cong \angle CDE$	5. CPCTC
6. $\overline{AB} \parallel \overline{CD}$	6. Because $\angle ABE \cong \angle CDE$ and they are alternate interior $\angle$s.
7. $ABCD$ is a parallelogram.	7. Because $\overline{AB} \parallel \overline{CD}$ and $\overline{AB} \cong \overline{CD}$.

Chapter 6 — Practice Problems Solution

16 A rhombus $ABCD$ is given below. If $\overline{CE} \cong \overline{DE}$, what is the measure of $\angle BCE$?

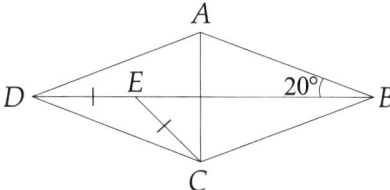

Solution

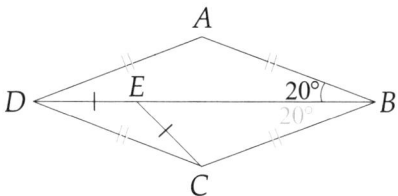

Since $\overline{CB} \cong \overline{CD}$, $\angle CBD \cong \angle CDB = 20°$.

Also, since $\overline{ED} \cong \overline{EC}$, $\angle EDC \cong \angle ECD = 20°$.

In $\triangle BCD$, $\angle CBD + \angle CDB + \angle ECD + \angle BCE$
$= 20° + 20° + 20° + \angle BCE = 180° \rightarrow \angle BCE = 120°$.

▸ $\angle BCE = 120°$.

Chapter 7 *Practice Problems Solution*

01 In each of the following below, find the value of *x*.

(1)
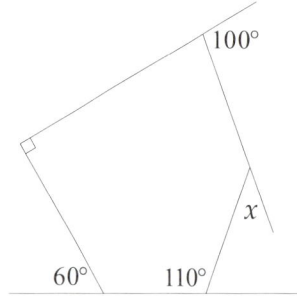

(2)
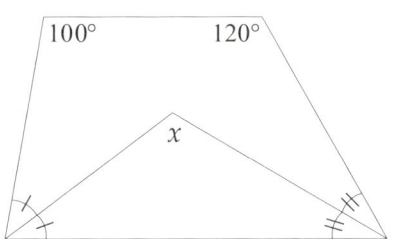

(3)
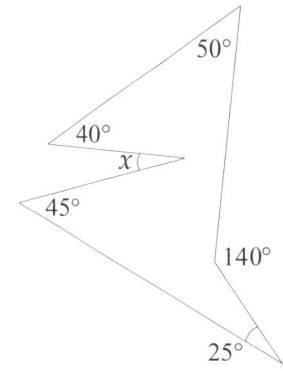

(4)
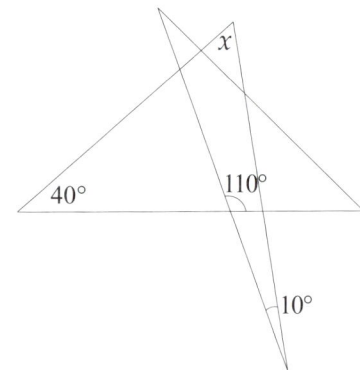

☀ Solution

(1)
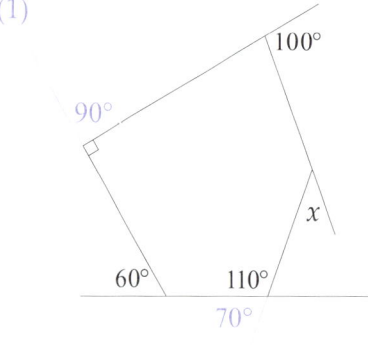

$x + 70° + 60° + 90° + 100° = 360°$
$x = 40°$

➤ $x = 40°$.

Chapter 7 — *Practice Problems Solution*

(2)

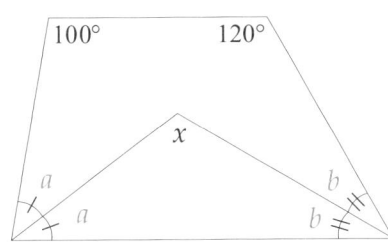

$100° + 120° + 2a + 2b = 360°$

$2a + 2b = 140° \rightarrow a + b = 70°$

$x = 180° - (a+b) = 180° - 110°$

➢ $x = 110°$.

(3)

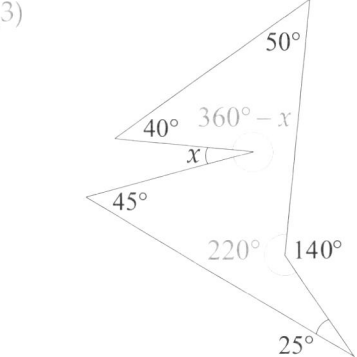

Sum of interior angles: $180 \cdot (6-2) = 720°$.

$40° + 50° + 220° + 25° + 45° + (360° - x) = 720°$

$740° - x = 720° \rightarrow x = 20°$

➢ $x = 20°$.

(4)

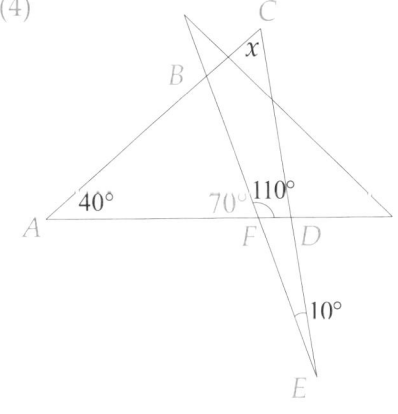

In $\triangle ABF$, $\angle CBE = 40° + 70° = 110°$.
In $\triangle BCE$, $x = 180° - \angle CBE + \angle E$
$= 180° - 110° - 10° = 60°$.

➢ $x = 60°$.

Chapter 7　　　　　　　　　　　　*Practice Problems Solution*

02　In the figure below, find the value of ∠1 + ∠2 + ∠3 + ∠4 + ∠5 + ∠6.

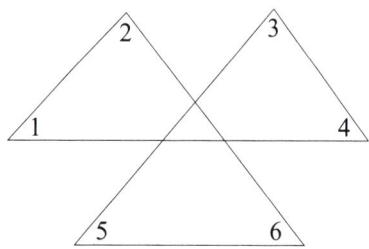

☀ **Solution**

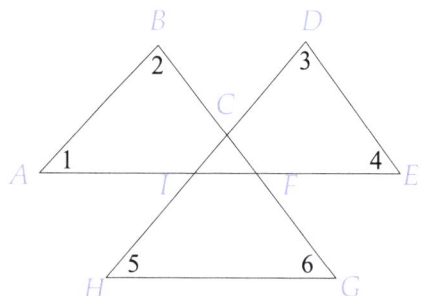

In △CHG, ∠BCH = ∠5 + ∠6 and in △DIE, ∠DIA = ∠3 + ∠4.
In a quadrilateral ABCI, ∠A + ∠B + ∠DIA + ∠BCH
= ∠1 + ∠2 + ∠3 + ∠4 + ∠5 + ∠6 = 360°.

➤　∠1 + ∠2 + ∠3 + ∠4 + ∠5 + ∠6 = 360°.

Chapter 7　　　　　　　　　　*Practice Problems Solution*

03　In the figure below, find the value of $\angle 1 + \angle 2 + \angle 3 + \angle 4$.

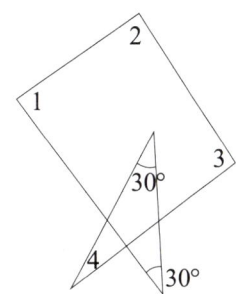

Solution

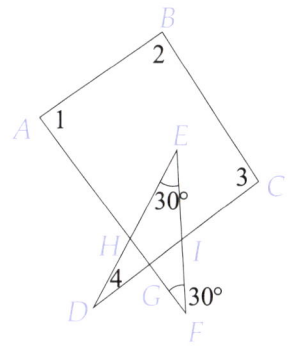

In $\triangle EFH$, $\angle DHF = 30° + 30° = 60°$ and in $\triangle DIE$, $\angle DIA = \angle 3 + \angle 4$.
In $\triangle DHG$, $\angle DGF = \angle 4 + \angle DHF = \angle 4 + 60° = \angle AGC$.
In a quadrilateral $ABCG$, $\angle A + \angle B + \angle C + \angle AGC$
$= \angle 1 + \angle 2 + \angle 3 + \angle 4 + 60° = 360° \rightarrow \angle 1 + \angle 2 + \angle 3 + \angle 4 = 300°$.

➤　$\angle 1 + \angle 2 + \angle 3 + \angle 4 = 300°$.

Chapter 7 — *Practice Problems Solution*

04 A regular hexagon *ABCDEF* is given below. What is the measure of ∠BGE?

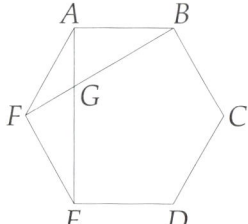

☀ **Solution**

Each angle of a regular hexagon *ABCDEF* : $\dfrac{180°\cdot(6-2)}{6}=120°$.

Since $\overline{AB}\cong\overline{AF}$ in $\triangle ABF$, $\angle AFB = \dfrac{180°-120°}{2}=30°$ and

Since $\overline{FE}\cong\overline{FA}$ in $\triangle FAE$, $\angle FAE = \dfrac{180°-120°}{2}=30°$.

$\angle BGE \cong \angle AGF = 180°-30°-30°=120°$.

➤ ∠BGE = 120°.

05 If the ratio of one interior angle to one exterior angle in a regular polygon is 3 to 1, then what is the measure of sum of interior angles?

☀ **Solution**

Let the interior and exterior angle be 3*a* and *a*, respectively.
So, the measure of one interior angle of the polygon is $3\cdot 45°=135°$.
Now, the number of sides, *n*, of the polygon is
$\dfrac{180°\cdot(n-2)}{n}=135° \to 180n-360=135n \to n=8$.
Finally, the measure of sum of interior angles is $135°\cdot 8=1080°$.

➤ The measure of sum of interior angles is 1080°.

Chapter 7 — *Practice Problems Solution*

06 Two rectangles *ABCD* and *EFBD* are given below. If the area of rectangle *ABCD* is $12\,m^2$, what is the area of rectangle *EFBD*?

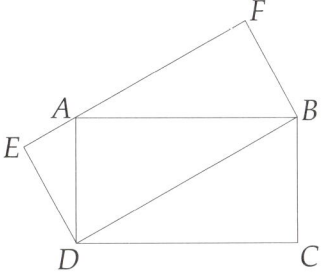

Solution

△*ADB* and rectangle *EFBD* share the same altitude from *A* to $\overline{BD}$. So, the area of $EFBD = 2 \cdot \triangle ADB$.

Since △*ADB* is half of rectangle *ABCD*, the area of $ABCD = 2 \cdot \triangle ADB$.

So, the area of *EFBD* is equal to the area of *ABCD*.

➤ The area of *EFBD* is $12\,in^2$.

Chapter 7

Practice Problems Solution

07 Find the area of trapezoid *ABCD* given below.

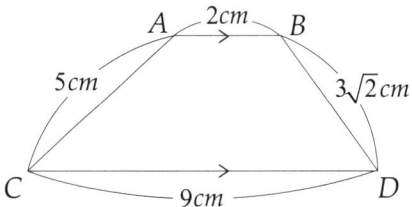

Solution

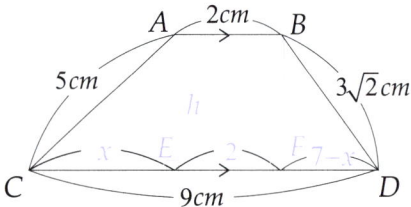

In order to find the area, all we need to find is h.
Using pythagorean theorem in $\triangle ADE$ and $\triangle BCF$,
$h^2 + x^2 = 5^2 \rightarrow h^2 = 25 - x^2 \rightarrow (1)$
$h^2 + (7-x)^2 = (3\sqrt{2})^2 \rightarrow (2)$
By substituting (1) into (2), we have
$(25 - x^2) + (7 - x)^2 = 18$
$25 - x^2 + 49 - 14x + x^2 = 18$
$-14x = -56 \rightarrow x = 4$ and $h = \sqrt{25 - 4^2} = 3$.
So, the area of parallelogram $ABCD$ is $\dfrac{1}{2} \cdot (2+9) \cdot 3 = \dfrac{33}{2}$.

Chapter 7   *Practice Problems Solution*

08 A parallelogram *ABCD* is given below. If the area of △*AEF* and △*DEG* are $4in^2$ and $8in^2$, what is the area of parallelogram *ABCD*?

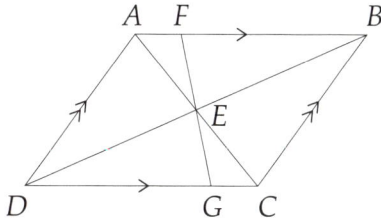

☼ Solution

Since *ABCD* is a parallelogram, $\overline{AE} \cong \overline{CE}$ and ∠*FAE* ≅ ∠*GCE*.
Also, ∠*AEF* ≅ ∠*CEG* (Vertical ∠s). So, △*AEF* ≅ △*CEG* by ASA Congruence.
Now, the area of △*CEG* = $4in^2$ and △*DEC* = $4in^2 + 8in^2 = 12in^2$.
Since △*DEC* = $\frac{1}{4}$ × area of *ABCD*,
the area of parallelogram *ABCD* is $4 \times 12 in = 48 in$.

➤ The area of parallelogram *ABCD* is $48in$.

Chapter 7 — Practice Problems Solution

09 A rhombus $ABCD$ is given below. If $\overline{AD} = 2x+5$, $\overline{CE} = 3x$, and $\overline{BE} = x+1$, what is the area of rhombus $ABCD$?

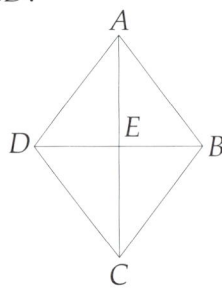

Solution

Since $ABCD$ is a rhombus, $\overline{AD} \cong \overline{BC}$. In $\triangle BEC$,
$(x+1)^2 + (3x)^2 = (2x+5)^2$
$x^2 + 2x + 1 + 9x^2 = 4x^2 + 20x + 25$
$6x^2 - 18x - 24 = 0 \to x^2 - 3x - 4 = 0$
$(x-4)(x+1) = 0 \to x = 4$.
The area of rhombus $ABCD$ is
$\dfrac{1}{2} \cdot \overline{AC} \cdot \overline{BD} = \dfrac{1}{2} \cdot 2\overline{CE} \cdot 2\overline{BE} = 2 \cdot (3 \cdot 4) \cdot (4+1) = 120$

➢ The area of rhombus $ABCD$ is 120.

Chapter 7 — Practice Problems Solution

10 Two squares *ABCD* and *EFGH* are given below. Find the area of shaded region.

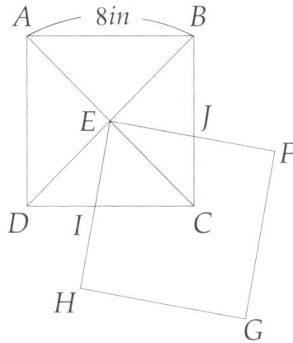

Solution

In $\triangle DEI$ and $\triangle CEJ$, $\overline{DE} \cong \overline{CE}$, $\angle EDI \cong \angle ECJ$, and $\angle DEI = 90° - \angle CEI = \angle CEJ$. So, $\triangle DEI \cong \triangle CEJ$ by ASA Congruence. Now, the area of quadrilateral $EJCI = \triangle CEJ + \triangle CEI = \triangle DEI + \triangle CEI$
$= \triangle DEC = \dfrac{1}{4} \cdot 8 \cdot 8 = 16$.

➢ The area of shaded region *EJCI* is 16.

Chapter 7 *Practice Problems Solution*

11 If the length of $\widehat{AB}$ is twice long as the length of $\widehat{BC}$, what is the measure of ∠ABO?

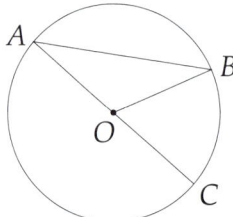

☼ **Solution**

Since $\dfrac{\widehat{AB}}{\widehat{BC}} = \dfrac{2}{1}$, $\angle AOB = 180° \times \dfrac{2}{2+1} = 120°$.

In $\triangle AOB$, $\overline{AO} \cong \overline{BO}$ so that $\angle ABO = \dfrac{180° - 120°}{2} = 30°$.

▸ ∠ABO = 30°.

12 If ∠AOB : ∠BOC : ∠COA is 2 : 3 : 4, what is the area of sector BOC?

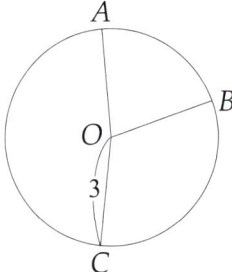

☼ **Solution**

The area of circle O is $\pi(3)^2 = 9\pi$.

Since ∠AOB : ∠BOC : ∠COA = 2 : 3 : 4, $\angle BOC = \dfrac{360°}{2+3+4} \times 3 = 120°$.

So, the area of sector BOC is $9\pi \times \dfrac{120°}{360°} = 3\pi$.

▸ The area of sector BOC is 3π.

Chapter 7 — Practice Problems Solution

13 If $\overline{AB} // \overline{OC}$ and $\widehat{CD} = 4\,in$ in the figure below, what is the measure of $\widehat{AB}$?

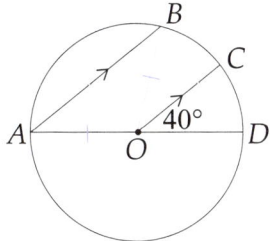

Solution

Since $\overline{AB} // \overline{OC}$, $\angle COD \cong \angle BAO = 40°$.
Also, since $\overline{OA} // \overline{OB}$, $\angle BAO \cong \angle ABO = 40°$.
In $\triangle ABO$, $\angle AOB = 180° - 2 \cdot 40° = 100°$.

Now, $\dfrac{\widehat{AB}}{\widehat{CD}} = \dfrac{100°}{40°} \rightarrow \dfrac{\widehat{AB}}{4} = \dfrac{5}{2} \rightarrow \widehat{AB} = 10$.

➤ $\widehat{AB} = 10\,in.$

Chapter 7　　　　　　　　　　　　　　*Practice Problems Solution*

14 In each of the following, find the area of shaded region.

(1)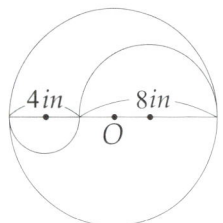

(2)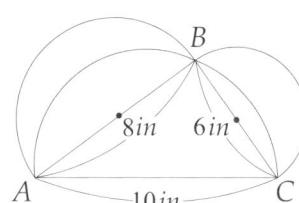

(3)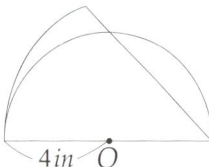

(4)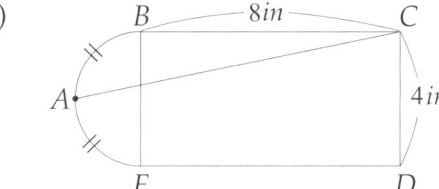

☼ Solution

(1)

$$\text{Area of shaded region} = \frac{\pi(6)^2}{2} - \frac{\pi(4)^2}{2} + \frac{\pi(2)^2}{2} = 12\pi.$$

➤ Area of shaded region $= 12\pi\, in^2$.

(2)

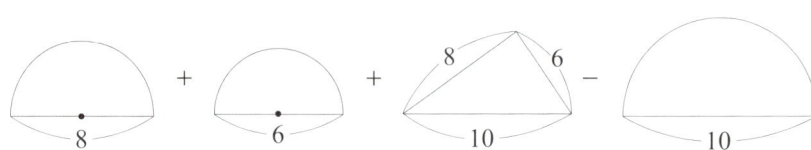

Chapter 7   *Practice Problems Solution*

In $\triangle ABC$, since $6^2 + 8^2 = 10^2$, $\triangle ABC$ is a right triangle.

Area of shaded region $= \dfrac{\pi(4)^2}{2} + \dfrac{\pi(3)^2}{2} + \dfrac{8 \cdot 6}{2} - \dfrac{\pi(5)^2}{2} = 24$.

➢ Area of shaded region $= 24\, in^2$.

(3)

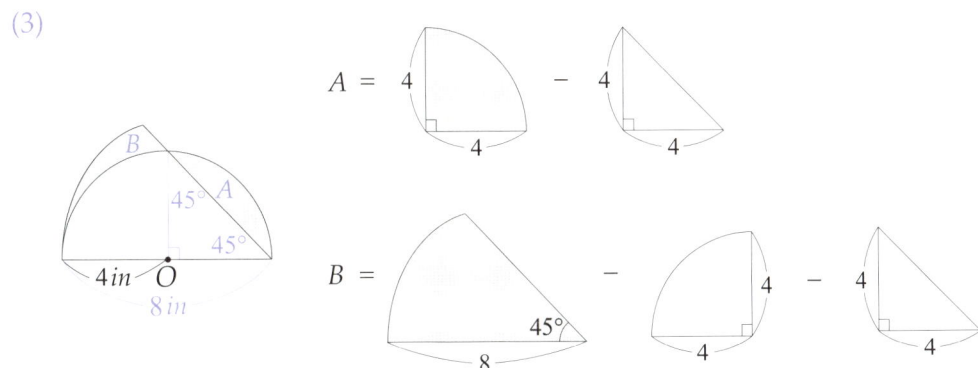

$A = \dfrac{\pi(4)^2}{4} - \dfrac{4 \cdot 4}{2} = 4\pi - 8$.

$B = \pi(8)^2 \cdot \dfrac{45°}{360°} - \dfrac{\pi(4)^2}{4} - \dfrac{4 \cdot 4}{2} = 4\pi - 8$.

So, $A + B = (4\pi - 8) + (4\pi - 8) = 8\pi - 16$.

➢ Area of shaded region $= (8\pi - 16)\, in^2$.

(4)

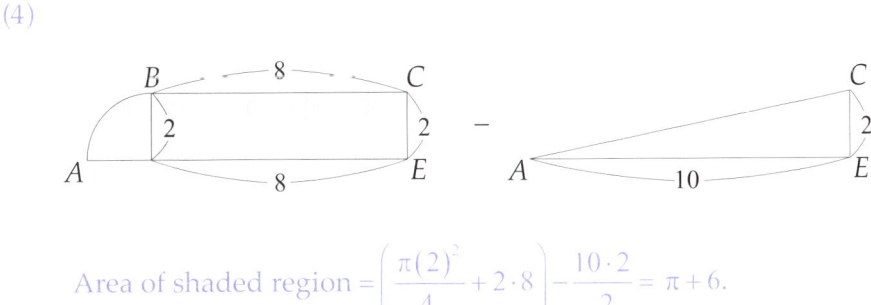

Area of shaded region $= \left(\dfrac{\pi(2)^2}{4} + 2 \cdot 8 \right) - \dfrac{10 \cdot 2}{2} = \pi + 6$.

➢ Area of shaded region $= (\pi + 6)\, in^2$.

Practice Problems 357

Chapter 7 — Practice Problems Solution

15 A regular octagon $ABCDEFGH$ with side length 2 is given below. Find each of the following area.

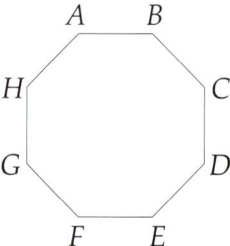

(1) $ABCDEFGH$ (2) $ABDG$

Solution

(1)

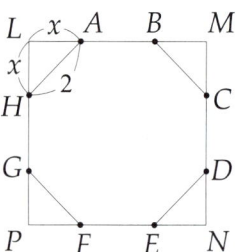

First, let's form a square $LMNP$ as shown in figure above.

Each angle of a regular octagon is $\dfrac{180° \cdot (8-2)}{8} = 135°$.

So, each corner triangles are $45° - 45° - 90°$ triangles.

In $\triangle ALH$, $x^2 + x^2 = 2^2 \rightarrow x = \sqrt{2}$.

Now, the area of $ABCDEFGH = LMNP - 4 \cdot \triangle AHL$

$\left(2\sqrt{2}+2\right)^2 - 4\left(\dfrac{1}{2} \cdot \sqrt{2} \cdot \sqrt{2}\right) = 8 + 8\sqrt{2} + 4 - 4 = 8 + 8\sqrt{2}.$

➤ The area of $ABCDEFGH = 8 + 8\sqrt{2}$.

Chapter 7 — Practice Problems Solution

(2)

From previous problem, we found out $x = \sqrt{2}$.

The area of $ABDG = ABNM + 2 \cdot \triangle AGM$

$$= 2 \cdot (\sqrt{2} + 2) + 2 \cdot \frac{\sqrt{2} \cdot (\sqrt{2} + 2)}{2}$$

$$= 2\sqrt{2} + 4 + 2 + 2\sqrt{2} = 6 + 4\sqrt{2}.$$

➢ The area of $ABDG = 6 + 4\sqrt{2}$.

Chapter 7 — *Practice Problems Solution*

16 Find the probability that a point chosen at random in each figure is in the shaded region.

(1)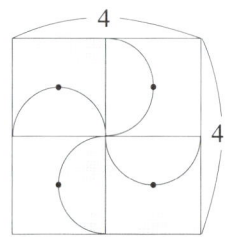

(2)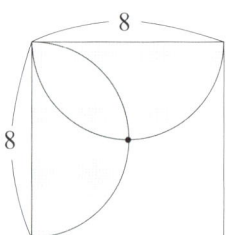

Solution

(1)

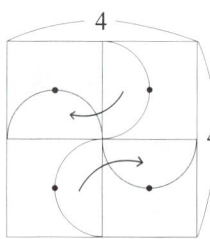

$$P = \frac{2(2\cdot 2)}{4\cdot 4} = \frac{1}{2}.$$

➤ $P = \dfrac{1}{2}.$

(2)

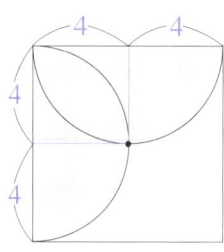

The area of shaded region

$$= 4\cdot 4 + 2\cdot \frac{\pi(4)^2}{4} = 16 + 8\pi.$$

$$P = \frac{16 + 8\pi}{8\cdot 8} = \frac{2+\pi}{8}.$$

➤ $P = \dfrac{2+\pi}{8}.$

Chapter 8 — *Practice Problems Solution*

01 Given two arcs are congruent in a circle, prove that their corresponding chords are congruent.

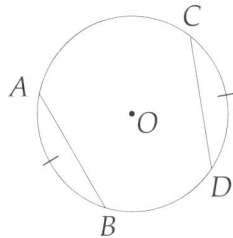

* Solution

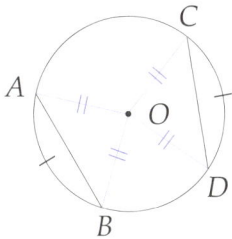

Statements	Reasons
1. $\overset{\frown}{AB} \cong \overset{\frown}{CD}$	1. Given
2. $\angle AOB \cong \angle COD$	2. Because $\overset{\frown}{AB} \cong \overset{\frown}{CD}$
3. $\overline{AO} \cong \overline{BO} \cong \overline{CO} \cong \overline{DO}$	3. Radii of a circle are $\cong$
4. $\triangle AOB \cong \triangle COD$	4. SAS Congruence
5. $\overline{AB} \cong \overline{CD}$	5. CPCTC

Chapter 8 — Practice Problems Solution

02 Find x in each of the following.

(1)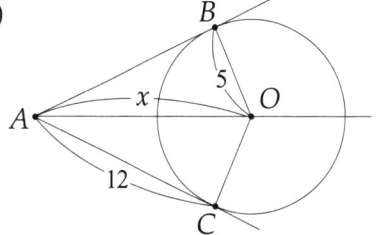

(2)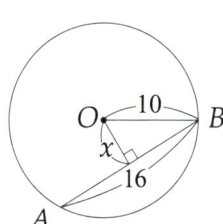

(3)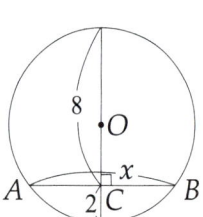

(4)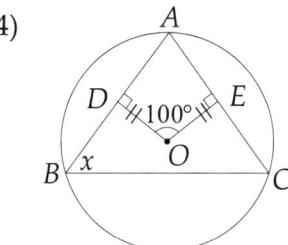

Solution

(1)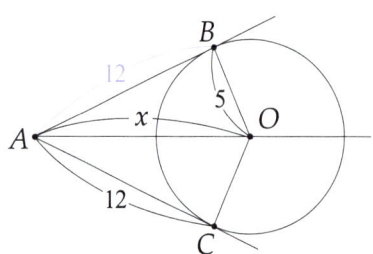

$x = \sqrt{12^2 + 5^2} = 13$.

➤ $x = 13$.

(2)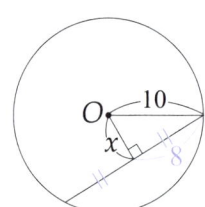

$x = \sqrt{10^2 - 8^2} = 6$.

➤ $x = 6$.

Chapter 8 *Practice Problems Solution*

(3)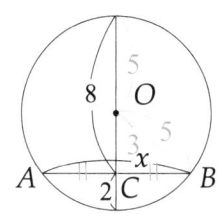

$\overline{BC} = \sqrt{5^2 - 3^2} = 4.$
$x = 2 \cdot \overline{BC} = 2 \cdot 4 = 8.$
➤ $x = 8.$

(4) In $\triangle DOE$,
$\angle A = 360° - 100° - 2(90°) = 80°.$
Since $\overline{OD} \cong \overline{OE},\ \overline{AB} \cong \overline{AC}$ and
$\angle B \cong \angle C = x.$
In $\triangle ABC,\ 80° + 2x = 180°$
$\to x = 50°.$
➤ $x = 50°.$

Chapter 8

Practice Problems Solution

03 If $\overline{AB}$ and $\overline{AC}$ are tangent to the circle O, what is the area of shaded region?

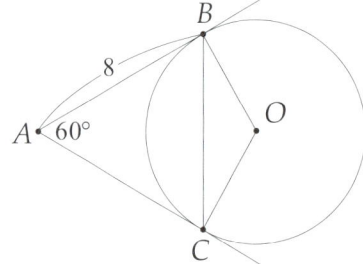

Solution

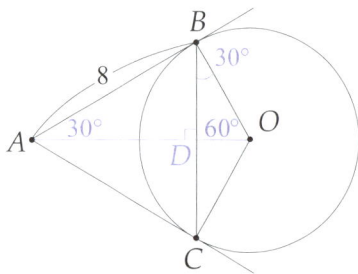

Since $\triangle ABO$ is $30° - 60° - 90°$ triangle,

$$\frac{\overline{BO}}{\overline{AB}} = \frac{\overline{BO}}{8} = \frac{1}{\sqrt{3}} \to \overline{BO} = \frac{8}{\sqrt{3}}.$$

Also, since $\triangle BOD$ is $30° - 60° - 90°$ triangle,

$$\frac{\overline{DO}}{\overline{BO}} = \frac{\overline{DO}}{\frac{8}{\sqrt{3}}} = \frac{1}{2} \to \overline{DO} = \frac{4}{\sqrt{3}} \text{ and } \frac{\overline{BD}}{\overline{BO}} = \frac{\overline{BD}}{\frac{8}{\sqrt{3}}} = \frac{\sqrt{3}}{2} \to \overline{BD} = 4.$$

The area of $\triangle BOC = 2 \cdot \triangle BOD = 2 \left(\dfrac{\frac{4}{\sqrt{3}} \cdot 4}{2} \right) = \dfrac{16}{\sqrt{3}} = \dfrac{16\sqrt{3}}{3}$.

➢ The area of shaded region is $\dfrac{16\sqrt{3}}{3}$.

Chapter 8 — Practice Problems Solution

04
A portion of a circle O with radius $4\,cm$ is folded through $\overline{AB}$ as shown in the figure below. If $\overline{CD} \cong \overline{DE}$, what is the area of $\triangle BDE$?

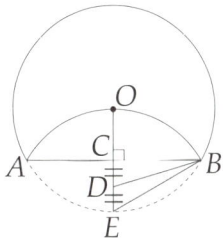

Solution

Since $\overline{OE} = 4$, $\overline{CO} \cong \overline{CE} = 2$, $\overline{DE} = \dfrac{\overline{CE}}{2} = 1$, and $\overline{OE} \cong \overline{OB} = 4$.

In $\triangle OBC$, $\overline{BC} = \sqrt{4^2 - 2^2} = 2\sqrt{3}$.

So, the area of $\triangle BDE = \dfrac{1}{2} \cdot \overline{DE} \cdot \overline{BC} = \dfrac{1}{2} \cdot 1 \cdot 2\sqrt{3} = \sqrt{3}$.

➤ The area of $\triangle BDE$ is $\sqrt{3}$.

Chapter 8 *Practice Problems Solution*

05 Find x in each of the following.

(1)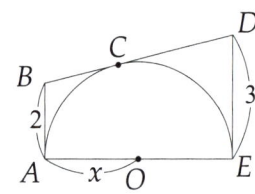

(2)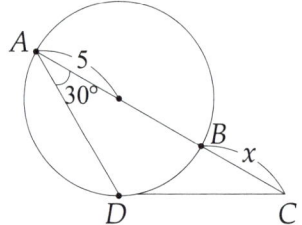

Solution

(1) Draw $\overline{BF}$ that is parallel to $\overline{AE}$ as shown in figure below.

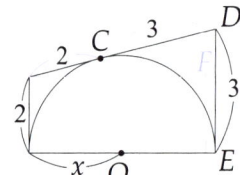

In $\triangle BDF$, $\overline{BF} = \sqrt{(2+3)^2 - 1^2} = 2\sqrt{6}$.

Since $\overline{AO} = \dfrac{\overline{BF}}{2}$, $x = \dfrac{2\sqrt{6}}{2} = \sqrt{6}$.

➤ $x = \sqrt{6}$.

(2)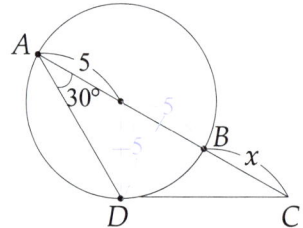

Since $\overline{AO} \cong \overline{AD}$, $\angle OAD \cong \angle ODA = 30°$.

In $\triangle OAD$, $\angle COD = \angle OAD + \angle ODA = 60°$ and in $\triangle OCD$, $\angle C = 30°$.

So, $\triangle COD$ is $30° - 60° - 90°$ triangle.

Therefore, $\dfrac{\overline{OD}}{\overline{OC}} = \dfrac{5}{5+x} = \dfrac{1}{2} \to x = 5$.

➤ $x = 5$.

Chapter 8 — Practice Problems Solution

06 Find the perimeter of $\triangle BCD$ in the figure below.

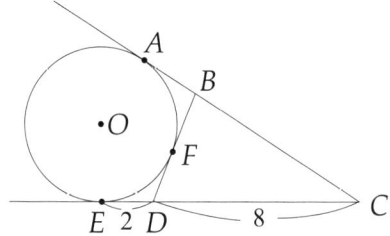

☼ Solution

First, $\overline{CA} \cong \overline{CE} = 10$.

Since $\overline{BA} \cong \overline{BF}$ and $\overline{DE} \cong \overline{DF}$, the perimeter of $\triangle BCD$ is

$\overline{CB} + \overline{CD} + \overline{BD} = \overline{CB} + \overline{CD} + \overline{BF} + \overline{DF}$
$= \overline{CB} + \overline{CD} + \overline{BA} + \overline{DE} = \overline{CA} + \overline{CE} = 10 + 10 = 20$.

➤ The perimeter of $\triangle BCD = 20$.

Chapter 8 — *Practice Problems Solution*

07 In the figure below, prove that $\angle CAD = \dfrac{\widehat{CD} - \widehat{BD}}{2}$.

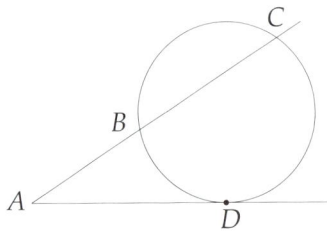

Solution

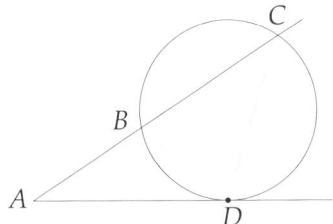

In $\triangle ABD$, $\angle CBD = \angle CAD + \angle BDA$.

Since $\angle CBD = \dfrac{\widehat{CD}}{2}$ and $\angle BDA = \dfrac{\widehat{BD}}{2}$,

$\dfrac{\widehat{CD}}{2} = \angle CAD + \dfrac{\widehat{BD}}{2}$

$\angle CAD = \dfrac{\widehat{CD}}{2} - \dfrac{\widehat{BD}}{2} = \dfrac{\widehat{CD} - \widehat{BD}}{2}.$

Chapter 8

Practice Problems Solution

08 In the figure below, prove that $\angle BAC = \dfrac{\widehat{BDC} - \widehat{BC}}{2}$.

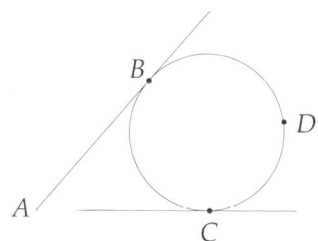

☼ Solution

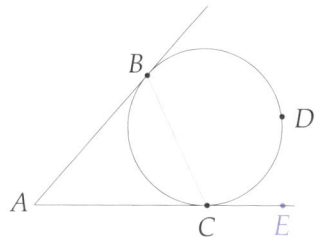

In $\triangle ABC$, $\angle BCE = \angle BAC + \angle ABC$.

Since $\angle BCE = \dfrac{\widehat{BDC}}{2}$ and $\angle ABC = \dfrac{\widehat{BC}}{2}$,

$\dfrac{\widehat{BDC}}{2} = \angle BAC + \dfrac{\widehat{BC}}{2}$

$\angle BAC = \dfrac{\widehat{BDC}}{2} - \dfrac{\widehat{BC}}{2} = \dfrac{\widehat{BDC} - \widehat{BC}}{2}$.

Chapter 8 — Practice Problems Solution

09 Find x in each of the following.

(1)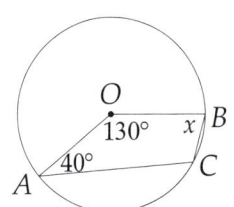

(2)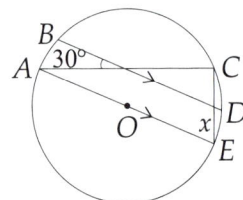

(3)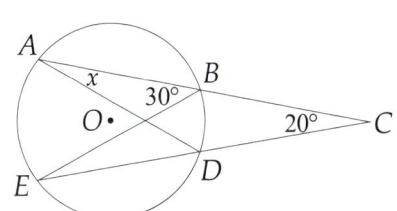

(4)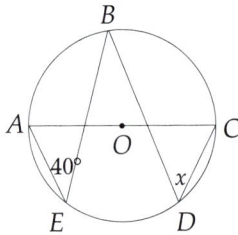

(5)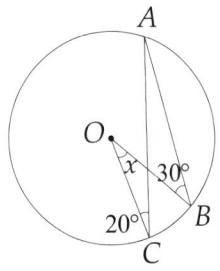

(6)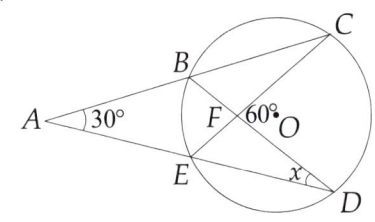

☼ Solution

(1) Since $\overparen{ACB} = \angle AOB = 130°$, $\overparen{AB} = 360° - 130° = 230°$
and $\angle ACB = \dfrac{\overparen{AB}}{2} = \dfrac{230°}{2} = 115°$.
In quadrilateral $AOBC$, $x = 360° - 115° - 130° - 40° = 75°$.
➤ $x = 75°$.

(2) Since $\overline{BD} \parallel \overline{AE}$, $\angle CAE = 30°$ (alternate interior $\angle$s)
Also, since $\overline{AE}$ is a diameter of circle O, $\angle ACE = 90°$.
So, in $\triangle ACE$, $x = 180° - 90° - 30° = 60°$.
➤ $x = 60°$.

Chapter 8 *Practice Problems Solution*

(3) In $\triangle BCE$, $\angle BEC + 20° = 30° \rightarrow \angle BEC = 10°$.
Since both $\angle BAD$ and $\angle BED$ intercept $\overset{\frown}{BD}$,
$\angle BAD \cong \angle BED \rightarrow x = 10°$.
➤ $x = 10°$.

(4) First, draw $\overline{CE}$.
Since $\overline{AC}$ is a diameter of circle O, $\angle AEC = 90°$.
So, $\angle BEC = 90° - 40° = 50°$.
Since both $\angle BEC$ and $\angle BDC$ intercept $\overset{\frown}{BC}$,
$\angle BDC \cong \angle BEC \rightarrow x = 50°$.
➤ $x = 50°$.

(5) First, draw two diameters $\overline{BD}$ and $\overline{CE}$ as shown in figure below.

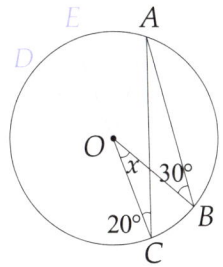

Since $\angle DBA$ and $\angle ECA$ intercepts $\overset{\frown}{DEA}$ and $\overset{\frown}{EA}$ respectively,
$\angle DOA = 2 \cdot 30° = 60°$ and $\angle EOA = 2 \cdot 20° = 40°$.
So, $\angle DOE = x = \angle DOA - \angle EOA = 60° - 40° = 20°$.
$\rightarrow x = 20°$.

➤ $x = 20°$.

(6) Since both $\angle BDE$ and $\angle BCE$ intercept $\overset{\frown}{BE}$, $\angle BDE \cong \angle BCE = x$.
In $\triangle ABD$, $\angle DBC = 30° + x$.
Also, in $\triangle BCF$, $\angle CFD = (30° + x) + x \rightarrow 60° = 2x + 30° \rightarrow x = 15°$.
$\rightarrow x = 15°$.
➤ $x = 15°$.

Chapter 8 *Practice Problems Solution*

10 If $\widehat{AB}:\widehat{BC}:\widehat{CA} = 1:2:3$, what is the measure of $\angle CAD$?

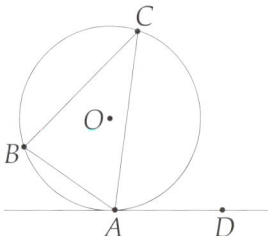

☀ **Solution**

Since $\widehat{AB}:\widehat{BC}:\widehat{CA} = 1:2:3$, $\widehat{CA} = \dfrac{3}{1+2+3} \times 360° = 180°$.

So, $\angle CAD = \dfrac{\widehat{CA}}{2} = \dfrac{180°}{2} = 90°$.

➢ $\angle CAD = 90°$.

11 In the figure below, prove that $\angle EBD = \dfrac{\widehat{BD} + \widehat{BC}}{2}$.

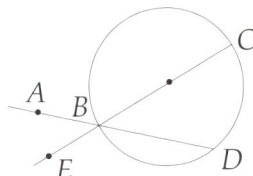

☀ **Solution**

Since $\angle CBD = \dfrac{\widehat{CD}}{2}$, $\angle EBD = 180° - \angle CBD = 180° - \dfrac{\widehat{CD}}{2}$.

Also, since $\widehat{BC} + \widehat{CD} + \widehat{BD} = 360°$, $\widehat{CD} = 360° - \widehat{BC} - \widehat{BD}$

and $\dfrac{\widehat{CD}}{2} = 180° - \dfrac{\widehat{BC}}{2} - \dfrac{\widehat{BD}}{2}$.

So, $\angle EBD = 180° - \dfrac{\widehat{CD}}{2} = 180° - \left(180° - \dfrac{\widehat{BC}}{2} - \dfrac{\widehat{BD}}{2}\right) = \dfrac{\widehat{BD} + \widehat{BC}}{2}$.

Chapter 8  *Practice Problems Solution*

12 Find x in each of the following.

(1) 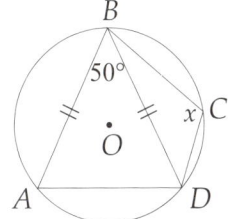 (2)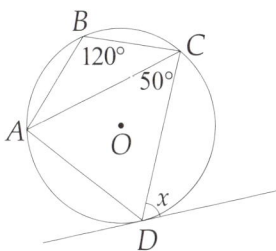

(3) 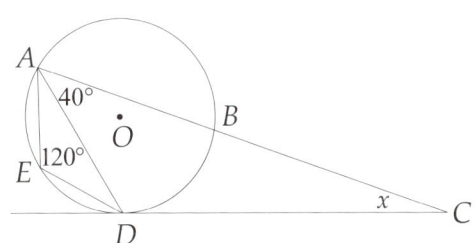 (4)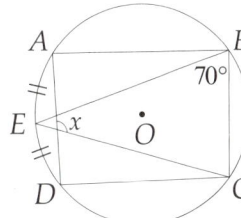

(5) 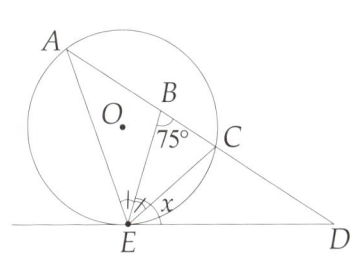 (6)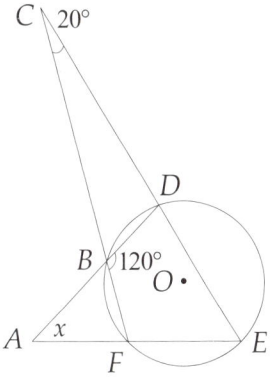

☀ Solution

(1) In $\triangle ABD$, $\angle A = \dfrac{180° - 50°}{2} = 65°$.

In cyclic quadrilateral $ABCD$, $\angle A + \angle C = 180°$

$65° + x = 180° \rightarrow x = 115°$.

➢ $x = 115°$.

Chapter 8   *Practice Problems Solution*

(2) In cyclic quadrilateral $ABCD$, $\angle ADC = 180° - 120° = 60°$.
In $\triangle ACD$, $\angle A = 180° - 50° - 60° = 70°$.
So, $x = \dfrac{\widehat{CD}}{2} = \angle A = 70°$.
➤ $x = 70°$.

(3)

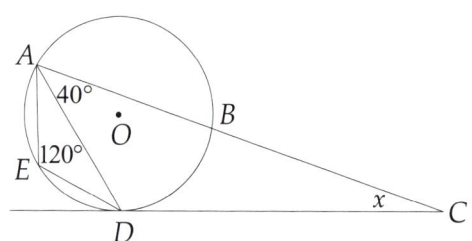

In cyclic quadrilateral $ABDE$, $\angle ABD = 180° - 120° = 60°$.
So, $\angle CBD = 180° - 60° = 120°$.
Also, $\angle BAD = \dfrac{\widehat{BD}}{2} = \angle BDC = 40°$.
In $\triangle BCD$, $x = 180° - 120° - 40° = 20°$.
➤ $x = 20°$.

(4) Since $\widehat{AE} \cong \widehat{DE}$, $\angle ABE \cong \angle ECD$.
In cyclic quadrilateral $ABCD$, $\angle B + \angle D = 180°$
$\angle ABE + 70° + \angle D = 180° \rightarrow \angle D = 110° - \angle ABE$.
Since $x = \angle ECD + \angle D$, $x = \angle ECD + 110° - \angle ABE = 110°$.
➤ $x = 110°$.

(5) $\angle BEA = \angle BEC$ and $\angle CED = \dfrac{\widehat{CE}}{2} = \angle CAE$.
In $\triangle ABE$, $\angle EBD = 75° = \angle BAE + \angle BEA$.
$x = \angle BEC + \angle CED = \angle BEA + \angle BAE = \angle EBD = 75°$.
➤ $x = 75°$.

Chapter 8   *Practice Problems Solution*

(6) First, $\angle CBD = 180° - 120° = 60°$.
In cyclic quadrilateral $BDEF$, $\angle E = 180° - 120° = 60°$.
In $\triangle ADE$, $\angle CDB = \angle E + \angle A = 60° + x$.
So, in $\triangle CBD$, $\angle C + \angle CBD + \angle CDB = 180°$,
$20° + 60° + 60° + x = 180° \rightarrow x = 40°$.
➢ $x = 40°$.

13   In the figure below, prove that $\overline{AB} \cdot \overline{AC} = \overline{AD} \cdot \overline{AE}$.

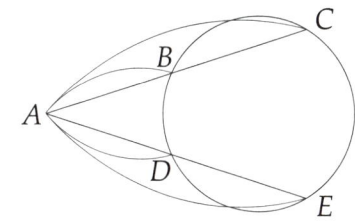

☼ Solution

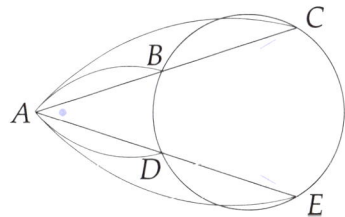

$\angle CAD \cong \angle EAB$ and $\dfrac{\overset{\frown}{BD}}{2} = \angle BCD \cong \angle BED$.

This tells us that $\triangle CAD \sim \triangle EAB$ by AA Similarity.

So, $\dfrac{\overline{AD}}{\overline{AB}} = \dfrac{\overline{AC}}{\overline{AE}} \rightarrow \overline{AB} \cdot \overline{AC} = \overline{AD} \cdot \overline{AE}$

Chapter 8 *Practice Problems Solution*

14 In the figure below, prove that $\overline{AB} \cdot \overline{AC} = \overline{AD}^2$.

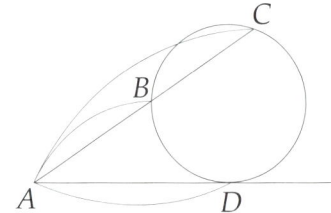

Solution

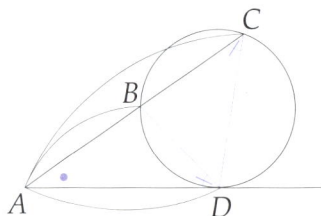

$\angle CAD \cong \angle DAB$ and $\dfrac{\overarc{BD}}{2} = \angle ACD \cong \angle ADB$.

This tells us that $\triangle ACD \sim \triangle ADB$ by AA Similarity.

So, $\dfrac{\overline{AC}}{\overline{AD}} = \dfrac{\overline{AD}}{\overline{AB}} \rightarrow \overline{AB} \cdot \overline{AC} = \overline{AD}^2$

Chapter 8 — *Practice Problems Solution*

15 Find x in each of the following.

(1)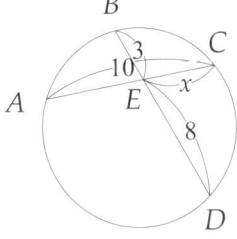

$\overline{CE} < \overline{AE}$

(2)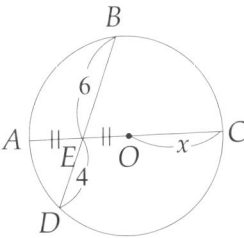

(3)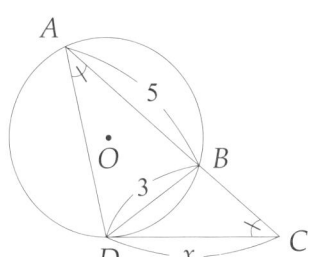

(4)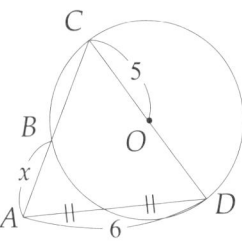

$\overline{AC} \cong \overline{CD}$

(5)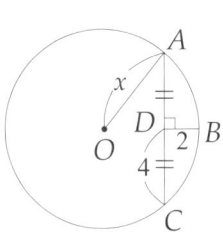

(6)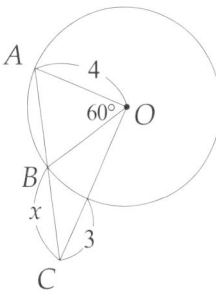

(7)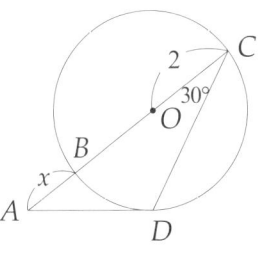

(8)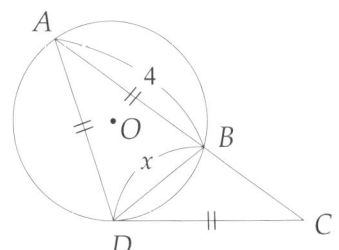

Chapter 8 — Practice Problems Solution

Solution

(1) $\overline{BE} \cdot \overline{DE} = \overline{AE} \cdot \overline{CE}$
$(10-x) \cdot x = 3 \cdot 8$
$x^2 - 10x + 24 = 0$
$(x-6)(x-4) = 0, \; x = 6 \text{ or } x = 4.$
Since $\overline{CE} < \overline{AE}, \; x = 4.$
➤ $x = 4.$

(2) $\overline{AE} \cong \overline{EO} = \dfrac{x}{2}$
$\overline{BE} \cdot \overline{CE} = \overline{BE} \cdot \overline{DE}$
$\dfrac{x}{2} \cdot \left(x + \dfrac{x}{2}\right) = 6 \cdot 4$
$\dfrac{3x^2}{4} = 24$
$x^2 = 32, \; x = 4\sqrt{2}$
➤ $x = 4\sqrt{2}.$

(3) Since $\angle BCD \cong \angle BAD \cong \angle BDA,$
$\overline{BC} = 3.$
$\overline{CB} \cdot \overline{CA} = \overline{CD}^2$
$3 \cdot (3 + 5) = x^2$
$x^2 = 24, \; x = 2\sqrt{6}$
➤ $x = 2\sqrt{6}.$

(4)

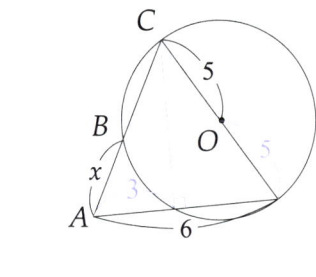

$\overline{CD} \cong \overline{AC} = 10.$
$\overline{AB} \cdot \overline{AC} = \overline{AE} \cdot \overline{AD}$
$x \cdot 10 = 3 \cdot 6, \; x = 1.8$
➤ $x = 1.8.$

Chapter 8 *Practice Problems Solution*

(5)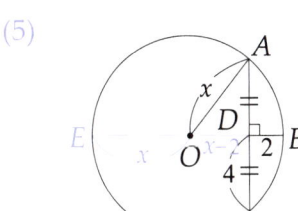

$$\overline{ED}\cdot\overline{BD}=\overline{AD}\cdot\overline{CD}$$
$$(x+x-2)\cdot 2 = 4\cdot 4$$
$$4x-4=16,\ x=5$$
➤ $x=5$.

(6)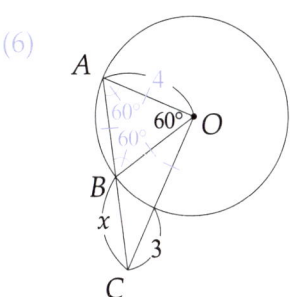

$$\overline{CD}\cdot\overline{CO}=\overline{CB}\cdot\overline{CA}$$
$$3\cdot(3+4)=x\cdot(x+4)$$
$$x^2+4x-21=0$$
$$(x+7)(x-3)=0,\ x=-7\ \text{or}\ x=3$$
Since $x>0,\ x=3$.
➤ $x=3$.

(7)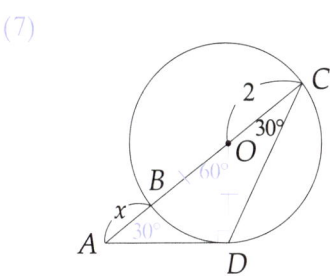

$\overline{OC}\cong\overline{OB}\cong\overline{OD}=2$.
Since $\triangle AOD$ is $30°-60°-90°$,
$\overline{AD}=\sqrt{3}\cdot\overline{OD}=2\sqrt{3}$
and $\overline{AO}=2\cdot\overline{OD}=4$.
$x=\overline{AO}-\overline{OB}=4-2=2$.
➤ $x=2$.

(8) $\overline{AB}\cong\overline{AD}\cong\overline{CD}=4$.
Since $\overline{AD}\cong\overline{CD}$, $\angle DAB\cong\angle DCB$.
Since $\angle DAB\cong\angle CDB$,
$\angle DAB\cong\angle DCB\cong\angle CDB$.
So, $\overline{BD}\cong\overline{CB}=x$.
$$\overline{CB}\cdot\overline{CA}=\overline{CD}^2$$
$$x\cdot(x+4)=4^2$$
$$x^2+4x-16=0$$
Using quadratic formula,
$x=-2+2\sqrt{5}$.
➤ $x=-2+2\sqrt{5}$

Chapter 9 — *Practice Problems Solution*

01 Find the surface area in the figure below.

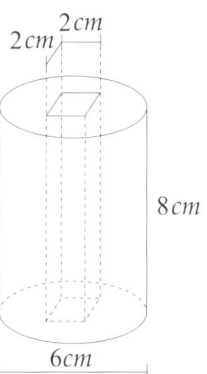

Solution

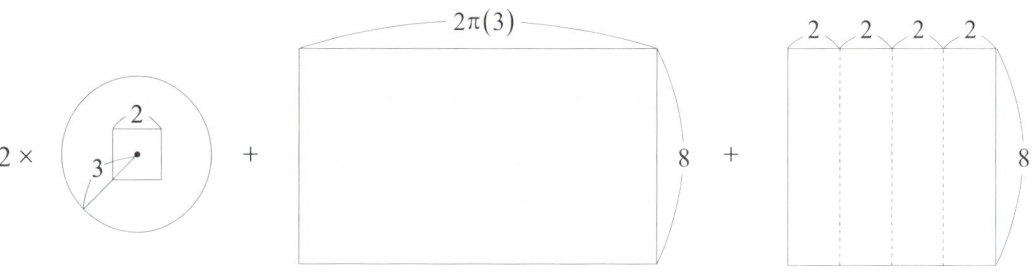

Surface Area, $A = 2 \times \left(\pi(3)^2 - 2 \cdot 2 \right) + 2\pi(3) \cdot 8 + 8 \cdot 8 = 66\pi + 56$.

➤ $A = (66\pi + 56)\, cm^2$.

02 A pyramid has a 6cm by 6cm square base and an altitude of 4cm. What is the surface area of this pyramid?

Solution

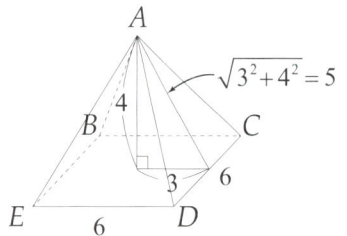

Surface Area, $A = 4 \times \triangle ADC + BCDE$

$= 4 \times \left(\dfrac{6 \cdot 5}{2} \right) + 6^2 = 96$.

➤ $A = 96\, cm^2$.

Chapter 9 — Practice Problems Solution

03 If two concentric spheres have radii, 4 and 2, respectively, what is the volume of the space formed in between spheres?

Solution

Vome of the space between 2 spheres,

$$V = V_{r=4} - V_{r=2} = \frac{4}{3}\pi(4)^3 - \frac{4}{3}\pi(2)^3 = \frac{224\pi}{3}.$$

➤ $V = \dfrac{224\pi}{3}.$

04 A right circular cylinder has a height twice as long as the radius of its base. If the volume of cylinder is 54π cubic feet, what is the surface area of the cylinder?

Solution

Since the height h is equal to twice of radius r, $h = 2r$.
The volume, $V = \pi r^2 h$
$54\pi = \pi r^2 (2r) \rightarrow r = 3$ and $h = 6$.
Surface Area, $A = 2\cdot\pi(3)^2 + 2\pi(3)\cdot 6 = 54\pi.$

➤ $A = 54\pi\ ft^2.$

Chapter 9 — Practice Problems Solution

05 If the volume of the figure below is $90\pi \, in^3$, what is the radius of the cylinder?

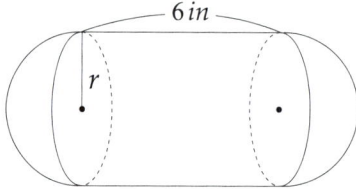

Solution

The volume, $V = 2 \times \text{hemisphere} + \text{cylinder}$.

$$V = 2 \times \left(\frac{1}{2} \cdot \frac{4}{3}\pi r^3\right) + \pi r^2 \cdot 6 = 90\pi.$$

$$\frac{4}{3}\pi r^3 + 6\pi r^2 = 90\pi$$

$$2r^3 + 9r^2 = 135, \quad r = 3$$

➤ $r = 3 \, in.$

Chapter 9 — Practice Problems Solution

06
A right circular cylinder and a sphere have equal volume and radii. If the radius of each solid is 2 inches, what is the lateral surface area of the cylinder?

Solution

The volume of cylinder, $V_{cylinder}$, is equal to the voluem of sphere, V_{sphere}.
$V_{cylinder} = V_{sphere}$ and $r = 2$.

$$\pi r^2 h = \frac{4}{3}\pi r^3$$

$$\pi (2)^2 h = \frac{4}{3}\pi (2)^3 \to h = \frac{8}{3}$$

Lateral Surface Area, $L.A. = 2\pi r h = 2\pi \cdot 2 \cdot \frac{8}{3} = \frac{32\pi}{3}$.

➤ $L.A. = \dfrac{32\pi}{3} in^2$.

07
The volume of a right circular cylinder is 86 cubic inches. For a smaller cylinder, the radius is decreased by 30% and the height is decreases by 20%. What is the volume of the smaller cylinder?

Solution

The voluem of cylinder, $V = \pi r^2 h = 86$.
For a smaller cylinder, $r \to 0.7r$ and $h \to 0.8h$.
The voluem of small cylinder,
$V_{small} = \pi(0.7r)^2 (0.8h) = 0.392\pi r^2 h = 0.392 \times 86 = 33.71$.

➤ $V_{small} = 33.71 in^3$.

Chapter 9 — Practice Problems Solution

08 A cube with side length $8\,cm$ is sliced into four rectangular prisms with equal volume, as shown in the figure below. What is the surface area of all four rectangular prims?

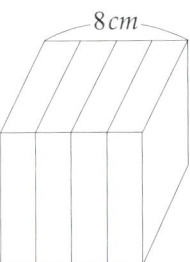

Solution

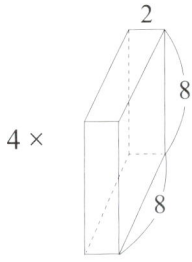

Base of each prism, $B = 2(8 \cdot 8) = 128$.
Lateral area of each prism, $L.A. = 4 \cdot (2 \cdot 8) = 64$.
Surface area of all four prims, $A = 4 \cdot (128 + 64) = 768$.

➤ $A = 768\,cm^3$.

Chapter 9 — *Practice Problems Solution*

09 If the surface area of a cube is x^2, then what is the volume of this cube in terms of x?

Solution

Let each side of the cube be s.

Surface Area, $A = 6s^2 = x^2 \rightarrow s = \dfrac{x}{\sqrt{6}}$

Volume, $V = s^3 = \left(\dfrac{x}{\sqrt{6}}\right)^3 = \dfrac{\sqrt{6}x^3}{36}$.

➤ $V = \dfrac{\sqrt{6}x^3}{36}$.

Chapter 9 *Practice Problems Solution*

10 A rectangle ABCD is rotated 360° around through line k. Find the volume of this resulting solid.

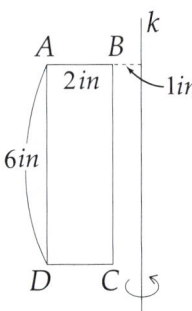

☼ **Solution**

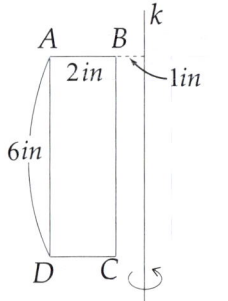

The volume of resulting solid V is equal to the volume of cylinder with radius $\overline{AO}$ minus the volume of cylinder with radius $\overline{BO}$.
$\overline{AO} = 3$ and $\overline{BO} = 2$.
$V = \pi(3)^2(6) - \pi(1)^2(6) = 48\pi$.

➤ $V = 48\pi \, in^3$.

Chapter 9 *Practice Problems Solution*

11 A right circular cylinder is inscribed in a cube with an edge of length 4. What is the volume of the cylinder?

 **Solution**

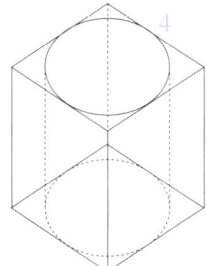

Since the diameter of cylinder is 4, its radius r is 2.

The volume of cylinder, $V = \pi r^2 h = \pi(2)^2 \cdot 4 = 16\pi$.

➤ $V = 16\pi$.

Chapter 9 — *Practice Problems Solution*

12 If both of the bases in the figure below are equilateral triangles, what is the volume of this figure?

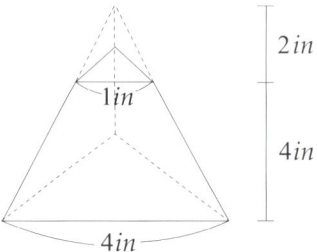

Solution

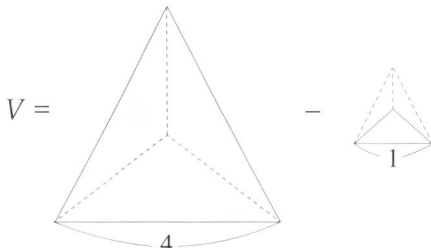

The volume of solid, $V = \dfrac{1}{3} \cdot \dfrac{\sqrt{3}}{4} \cdot 4^2 \cdot 6 - \dfrac{1}{3} \cdot \dfrac{\sqrt{3}}{4} \cdot 1^2 \cdot 2 = \dfrac{47\sqrt{3}}{6}$.

➤ $V = \dfrac{47\sqrt{3}}{6} in^3$.

Chapter 9 — *Practice Problems Solution*

13. Find the surface area of the figure below.

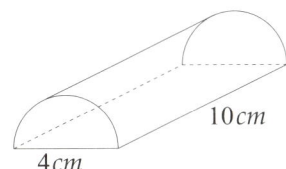

Solution

$$\text{Surface Area}, A = 2 \times \frac{\pi(2)^2}{2} + \frac{2\pi(2)}{2} \cdot 10 + 10 \cdot 4 = 24\pi + 40.$$

➤ $A = (24\pi + 40)\,cm^2.$

14. If the radius of sphere A is twice as long as the radius of sphere B, then what is the ratio of the volume of sphere A to the volume of sphere B?

Solution

The radius of sphere A, r_A, is equal to twice the radius of sphere B, r_B. So, $r_A = 2r_B$.

$$\frac{\text{The volume of sphere } A}{\text{The volume of sphere } B} = \frac{V_A}{V_B} = \frac{\frac{4}{3}\pi r_A^3}{\frac{4}{3}\pi r_B^3} = \frac{r_A^3}{r_B^3} = \left(\frac{2r_B}{r_B}\right)^3 = 8.$$

➤ The ratio is 8.

Chapter 9 *Practice Problems Solution*

15 A cone is cut by a plane through its vertex and center of the base, as shown in the figure below. Find the surface area of this figure.

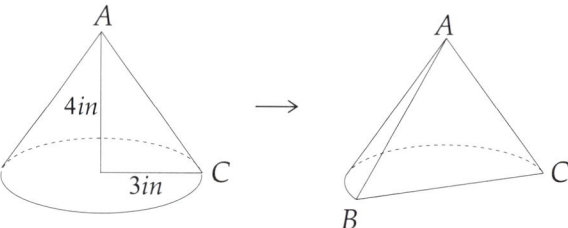

Solution

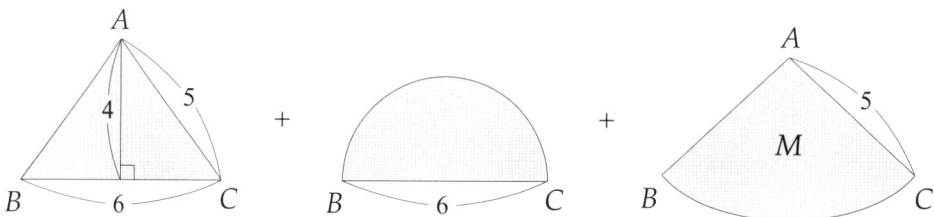

First, $\overline{AC} = \sqrt{3^2 + 4^2} = 5$

Also, the area of figure M is a half of the lateral surface area of original cone.

So, the surface area, $A = \frac{1}{2} \cdot 6 \cdot 4 + \frac{1}{2} \cdot \pi (3)^2 + \frac{1}{2} \cdot \pi \cdot 3 \cdot 5 = 12 + 12\pi$

➤ $A = (12 + 12\pi) in^2.$

Chapter 9   *Practice Problems Solution*

16   If the volume of a sphere is the same numerical value as its surface area, what is the radius of this sphere?

Solution

The volume, V is equal to the surface area, A.

$$V = A \rightarrow \frac{4}{3}\pi r^3 = 4\pi r^2 \rightarrow r = 3.$$

$r = 3.$

17   A cube $ABCDEFGH$ with side length $4\,cm$ is shown in the figure below. If J and K are midpoints of $\overline{HG}$ and $\overline{GF}$, respectively, find each of the following.

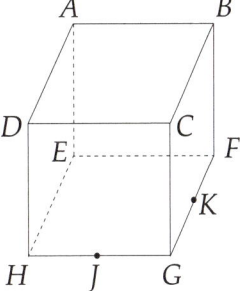

(1) $\overline{JK}$ (2) $\overline{AK}$
(3)   Area of $\triangle AJK$ (4)   Volume of $AJKE$

Solution

(1)

$\overline{JK} = \sqrt{2^2 + 2^2} = 2\sqrt{2}.$

$\overline{JK} = 2\sqrt{2}\,cm.$

Chapter 9 *Practice Problems Solution*

(2)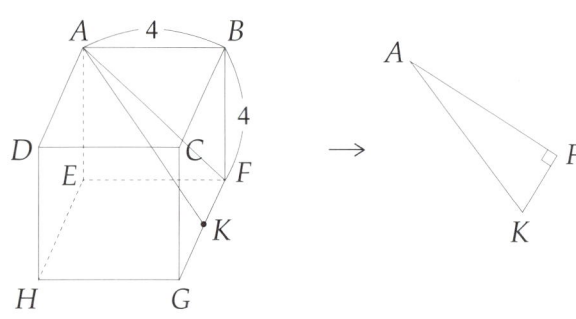

$\overline{KF} = \dfrac{\overline{FG}}{2} = 2$ and $\overline{AF} = \sqrt{4^2 + 4^2} = 4\sqrt{2}$.

In $\triangle AFK$, $\overline{AK} = \sqrt{\left(4\sqrt{2}\right)^2 + 2^2} = 6$.   ➤ $\overline{AK} = 6\,cm$.

(3)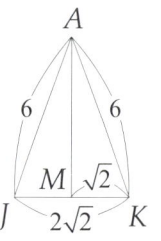

Just like $\overline{AK} = 6$ from $\triangle AFK$, $\overline{AJ} = 6$ from $\triangle AHJ$.

In $\triangle AMK$, $\overline{AM} = \sqrt{6^2 - \left(\sqrt{2}\right)^2} = \sqrt{34}$.

So, the area of $\triangle AJK$ is $\dfrac{1}{2} \cdot 2\sqrt{2} \cdot \sqrt{34} = 2\sqrt{17}$.

➤ The area of $\triangle AJK = 2\sqrt{17}\,cm^2$.

(4)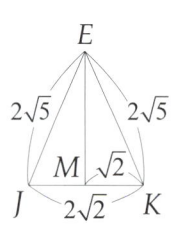

In $\triangle EHJ$ and $\triangle EFK$, $\overline{EJ} = \sqrt{4^2 + 2^2} = 2\sqrt{5}$ and $\overline{EK} = \sqrt{4^2 + 2^2} = 2\sqrt{5}$, respectively.

Also, in $\triangle ENK$, $\overline{EM} = \sqrt{\left(2\sqrt{5}\right)^2 - \left(\sqrt{2}\right)^2} = 3\sqrt{2}$

So, the area of $\triangle EJK = \dfrac{1}{2} \cdot 2\sqrt{2} \cdot 3\sqrt{2} = 6$.

Now, the volume of $AJKE$, $V = \dfrac{1}{3} \cdot 6 \cdot 4 = 8$.

➤ $V = 8\,cm^3$.

Chapter 9 — Practice Problems Solution

18 A right circular cone with the radius $4\,in$ and height $6\,in$ is sliced perpendicular to the height as shown in the figure below. If the volume of smaller cone is exactly 25% of the volume of the original cone, what is the height of the smaller cone?

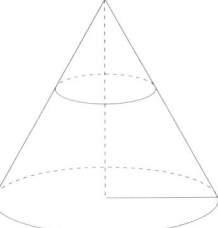

Solution

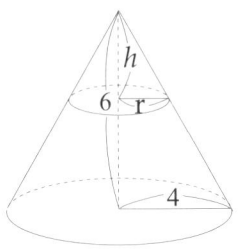

$V_{smaller} = \dfrac{1}{3}\pi r^2 h$ and $V_{larger} = \dfrac{1}{3}\pi(4)^2 \cdot 6$.

Since two cones are similar, $\dfrac{h}{6} = \dfrac{r}{4} \rightarrow r = \dfrac{2h}{3}$.

Since $V_{smaller} = 0.25 V_{larger}$, $\dfrac{1}{3}\pi r^2 h = 0.25\left(\dfrac{1}{3}\pi(4)^2 \cdot 6\right)$.

$r^2 h = 24$, $\left(\dfrac{2h}{3}\right)^2 h = 24$

$h^3 = 54 \rightarrow h = 3\sqrt[3]{2}$

➢ The height of smaller cone, $h = 3\sqrt[3]{2}\,in.$

Chapter 9 — Practice Problems Solution

19 If the shaded region in a right triangle ABD below is rotated 360° aroun through $\overline{BD}$, what is the volume of this resulting solid?

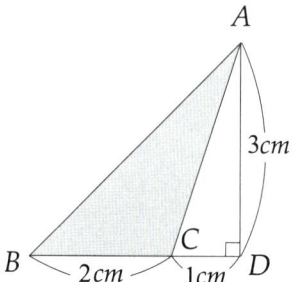

☼ Solution

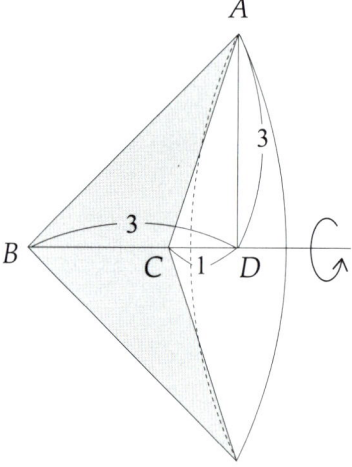

The volume of this resulting solid V is the volume V_L with radius $\overline{AD}$ and height $\overline{BD}$ minus the volume V_S with radius $\overline{AD}$ and height $\overline{CD}$.

$$V = V_L - V_S = \frac{1}{3}\pi(3)^2 \cdot 3 - \frac{1}{3}\pi(3)^2 \cdot 1 = 6\pi.$$

➤ $V = 6\pi \, cm^3$.

Chapter 9 — Practice Problems Solution

20 The radius of the base of a right circular cone is 12 and the radius of a parallel cross section is 4. If the distance between the base and the cross section is 6, what is the volume of the cone?

Solution

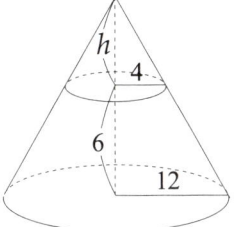

Since two cones are similar, $\dfrac{h+6}{h} = \dfrac{12}{4}$

$4h + 24 = 12h \rightarrow h = 3$.

The volume of the cone, $V = \dfrac{1}{3}\pi(12)^2(3+6) = 432\pi$.

▸ $V = 432\pi$.

21 A right circular cone has a volume of 20. If the radius and height of this cone increases 10% and 25%, respectively, what would be the volume of new cone?

Solution

$V = \dfrac{1}{3}\pi r^2 h = 20$. $r \rightarrow 1.1r$ and $h \rightarrow 1.25h$.

The volume of new cone, $V_{new} = \dfrac{1}{3}\pi(1.1r)^2(1.25h)$

$= \dfrac{1}{3}\pi r^2 h (1.1)^2(1.25) = 20 \cdot (1.1)^2(1.25) = 30.25$.

▸ $V_{new} = 30.25$.

Chapter 10 *Practice Problems Solution*

01 Prove that the triangle with coordinates $A(-2,-2)$, $B(1,2)$, and $C(5,-1)$ is an isosceles right triangle.

Solution

$\overline{AB} = \sqrt{(1+2)^2 + (2+2)^2} = 5$, $\overline{AC} = \sqrt{(5+2)^2 + (-1+2)^2} = 5\sqrt{2}$,
and $\overline{BC} = \sqrt{(5-1)^2 + (-1-2)^2} = 5$.
$\overline{AB}^2 + \overline{BC}^2 = \overline{AC}^2 \rightarrow 5^2 + 5^2 = (5\sqrt{2})^2 \rightarrow 25 + 25 = 50$
Since $\overline{AB} \cong \overline{BC}$ and $\overline{AB}^2 + \overline{BC}^2 = \overline{AC}^2$, $\triangle ABC$ is an isosceles right triangle.

02 Prove that the quadrilateral with the coordinates $A(-2,3)$, $B(-5,-4)$, $C(2,-1)$, and $D(5,6)$ is a rhombus but not a square.

Solution

$\overline{AB} = \sqrt{(-5+2)^2 + (-4-3)^2} = \sqrt{58}$, $\overline{BC} = \sqrt{(2+5)^2 + (-1+4)^2} = \sqrt{58}$,
$\overline{CD} = \sqrt{(5-2)^2 + (6+1)^2} = \sqrt{58}$, and $\overline{AD} = \sqrt{(5+2)^2 + (6-3)^2} = \sqrt{58}$.
Slope of $\overline{AB}$, $m_{\overline{AB}} = \dfrac{-4-3}{-5+2} = \dfrac{7}{3}$ and slope of $\overline{BC}$, $m_{\overline{BC}} = \dfrac{-1+4}{2+5} = \dfrac{3}{7}$.
Since $\overline{AB} \cong \overline{BC} \cong \overline{CD} \cong \overline{AD}$ and $m_{\overline{AB}} \cdot m_{\overline{BC}} = 1 \neq -1$,
ABCD is a rhombus but not a square.

Chapter 10 — Practice Problems Solution

03 Prove that the quadrilateral with the coordinates $A(-1,2)$, $B(3,0)$, $C(4,-3)$, and $D(-4,1)$ is an isosceles trapezoid.

Solution

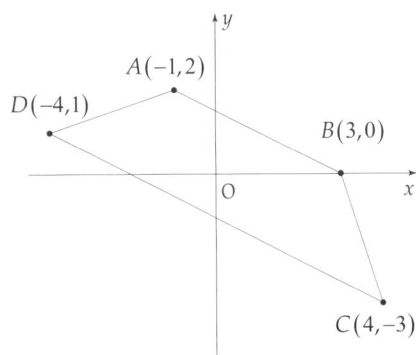

$\overline{AD} = \sqrt{(-4+1)^2 + (1-2)^2} = \sqrt{10}$ and $\overline{BC} = \sqrt{(4-3)^2 + (-3-0)^2} = \sqrt{10}$.

Slope of $\overline{AB}$, $m_{AB} = \dfrac{0-2}{3+1} = -\dfrac{1}{2}$ and slope of $\overline{DC}$, $m_{DC} = \dfrac{-3-1}{4+4} = -\dfrac{1}{2}$.

Since $\overline{AD} \cong \overline{BC}$ and $m_{AB} = m_{DC}$, $ABCD$ is an isosceles trapezoid.

04 Line l is perpendicular to the graph of $x + 3y = 4$ and passes through $(-1,1)$. Find the equation of the line l.

Solution

Line $l: y = mx + b$

$x + 3y = 4 \rightarrow y = -\dfrac{1}{3}x + \dfrac{4}{3}$

Since $m \cdot \left(-\dfrac{1}{3}\right) = -1$, $m = 3$ and $y = 3x + b \rightarrow 1 = 3(-1) + b \rightarrow b = 4$.

So, the equation of the line l is $y = 3x + 4$.

▸ The equation of the line l is $y = 3x + 4$.

Chapter 10   Practice Problems Solution

05   Let k be the line that passes through the points $(2,4)$ and $(a,0)$.

(1) For what value(s) of a is the slope of k not defined?

(2) Find an equation for line k in terms of a.

(3) If the line k forms a triangle with the coordinates axes in the first quadrant, find the value(s) of a such that the area of the triangle is 16.

Solution

(1) Slope of k, $m_k = \dfrac{4-0}{2-a} \to 2-a=0$, $a=2$.

➤ $a=2$.

(2) Slope $m = \dfrac{4-0}{2-a} = \dfrac{4}{2-a}$.

$y = mx + b \to y = \dfrac{4}{2-a}x + b$

Since the line k passes through $(2,4)$,

$4 = \dfrac{4}{2-a}(2) + b \to b = 4 - \dfrac{8}{2-a}$

So, $y = \dfrac{4}{2-a}x + \left(4 - \dfrac{8}{2-a}\right)$.

➤ $y = \dfrac{4}{2-a}x + \left(4 - \dfrac{8}{2-a}\right)$.

(3) The area of the triangle, $A = \dfrac{1}{2} \cdot a \cdot \left(4 - \dfrac{8}{2-a}\right) = 16$.

$a \cdot \left(\dfrac{4(2-a)-8}{2-a}\right) = 32$

$a(-4a) = 32(2-a)$

$4a^2 - 32a + 64 = 0$

$a^2 - 8a + 16 = 0$

$(a-4)^2 = 0 \to a = 4$.

➤ $a = 4$.

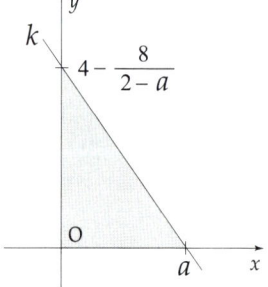

398

Chapter 10   *Practice Problems Solution*

06 Find all possible values for x if the triangle with vertices $A(4,-1)$, $B(5,6)$, and $C(1,x)$ is a right triangle.

Solution

Slope of $\overline{AB}$, $m_{\overline{AB}} = \dfrac{6+1}{5-4} = 7$, slope of $\overline{AC}$, $m_{\overline{AC}} = \dfrac{x+1}{1-4} = -\dfrac{x+1}{3}$,

and slope of $\overline{BC}$, $m_{\overline{BC}} = \dfrac{x-6}{1-5} = -\dfrac{x-6}{4}$.

(1) If $\angle A = 90°$, $m_{\overline{AB}} \cdot m_{\overline{AC}} = -1$

$7 \cdot \left(-\dfrac{x+1}{3}\right) = -1 \to x+1 = \dfrac{3}{7} \to x = -\dfrac{4}{7}$.

(2) If $\angle B = 90°$, $m_{\overline{AB}} \cdot m_{\overline{BC}} = -1$

$7 \cdot \left(-\dfrac{x-6}{4}\right) = -1 \to x-6 = \dfrac{4}{7} \to x = \dfrac{46}{7}$.

(3) If $\angle C = 90°$, $m_{\overline{AC}} \cdot m_{\overline{BC}} = -1$

$\left(-\dfrac{x+1}{3}\right) \cdot \left(-\dfrac{x-6}{4}\right) = -1 \to (x+1)(x-6) = -12$

$x^2 - 5x + 6 = 0$

$(x-2)(x-3) = 0 \to x = 2$ or $x = 3$.

> Possible values for x are $-\dfrac{4}{7}, \dfrac{46}{7}, 2$, and 3.

Chapter 10 *Practice Problems Solution*

07 In △ABC, if $\overline{AB} = 4$, $\overline{AC} = 2$, and $\angle BAC = 30°$, what is the measure of $\overline{BC}$?

Solution

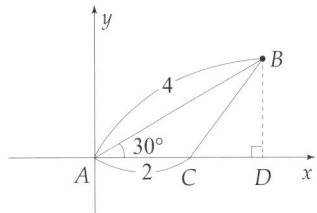

Since △ABD is a 30° – 60° – 90° triangle,

$\overline{BD} = \dfrac{\overline{AB}}{2} = 2$ and $\overline{AD} = \overline{BD} \cdot \sqrt{3} = 2\sqrt{3}$.

So, since the coordinate for B and C is $(2\sqrt{3}, 2)$ and $(2, 0)$ respectively,

$\overline{BC} = \sqrt{(2 - 2\sqrt{3})^2 + (0 - 2)^2} = \sqrt{20 - 8\sqrt{3}}$.

➢ $\overline{BC} = \sqrt{20 - 8\sqrt{3}}$.

Chapter 10 — Practice Problems Solution

08 Find the slope of the line through (3,1) if the triangle formed by the line, the x-axis, and the y-axis has area 6.

Solution

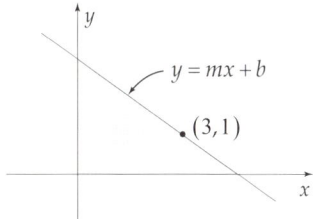

$y = mx + b$

Since the line passes through the point $(3,1)$, $1 = m \cdot 3 + b$.

$b = 1 - 3m$ and $y = mx + (1 - 3m)$.

So, the y intercept is $1 - 3m$ and x intercept is

$0 = mx + (1 - 3m) \to x = \dfrac{3m - 1}{m}$.

The area triangle, $A = \dfrac{1}{2} \cdot \dfrac{3m - 1}{m} \cdot (1 - 3m) = 6$

$(3m - 1)(1 - 3m) = 12m$

$9m^2 + 6m + 1 = 0$

$(3m + 1)^2 = 0 \to m = -\dfrac{1}{3}$.

> The slope $m = -\dfrac{1}{3}$.

Chapter 10 *Practice Problems Solution*

09 A triangle in the first quadrant is formed by two lines passing through the origin and the line $x = 6$. The slope of one of the lines through the origin is twice the slope of the other line through the origin. Find the slopes of the two lines so that the area of the triangle is 36.

Solution

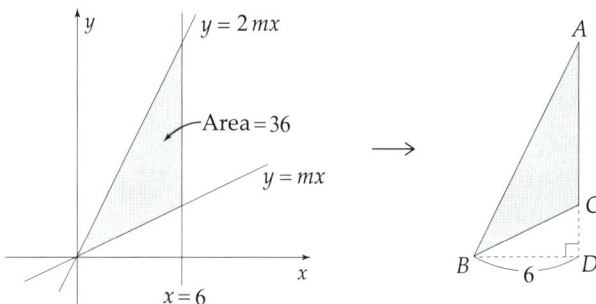

Since both lines pass through the origin, we can say that the equation of lines are $y = mx$ and $y = 2mx$ respectively.
$\overline{AC} = 2m(6) - m(6) = 6m$.
So, the area of $\triangle ABC = \dfrac{1}{2} \cdot \overline{AC} \cdot \overline{BD} = \dfrac{1}{2} \cdot 6m \cdot 6 = 36 \rightarrow m = 2$ and $2m = 4$.

➤ The slope of two lines are 2 and 4.

Chapter 10   *Practice Problems Solution*

10 An equilateral triangle ABC has coordinates $A(-1,4)$ and $B(3,4)$. Find all possible coordinates of point C.

☀ Solution

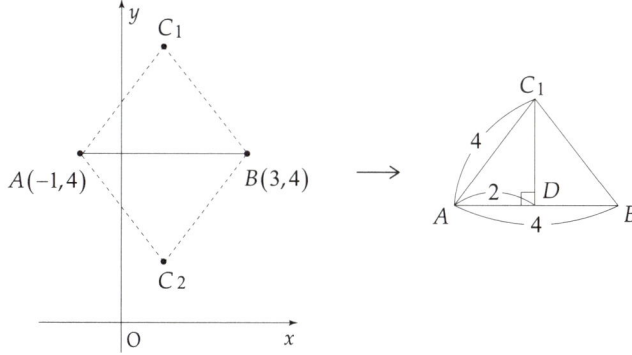

The coordinates of point C is either C_1 or C_2.

In $\triangle AC_1 D$, $\overline{C_1 D} = \sqrt{4^2 - 2^2} = 2\sqrt{3}$.

So, $C_1 = (-1+2, 4+2\sqrt{3}) = (1, 4+2\sqrt{3})$

Also, $C_1 = (-1+2, 4-2\sqrt{3}) = (1, 4-2\sqrt{3})$

➤ The coordinates of point C is $(1, 4+2\sqrt{3})$ or $(1, 4-2\sqrt{3})$.

Chapter 10 — *Practice Problems Solution*

11 Find the shortest distance from $(-2,3)$ to the line $4x - 2y = 3$.

Solution

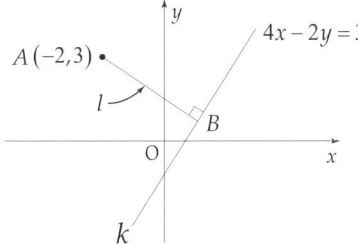

$k: 4x - 2y = 3 \rightarrow y = 2x - \dfrac{3}{2}$.

Since $l \parallel k$, the slope of the line l, $m = -\dfrac{1}{2}$.

$l: y = -\dfrac{1}{2}x + b$ and $3 = -\dfrac{1}{2}(-2) + b \rightarrow b = 2$.

So, the equation of line l is $y = -\dfrac{1}{2}x + 2$.

Now, since l and k intersect at B, $-\dfrac{1}{2}x + 2 = 2x - \dfrac{3}{2}$.

$\dfrac{5}{2}x = \dfrac{7}{2} \rightarrow x = \dfrac{7}{5}$ and $y = 2\left(\dfrac{7}{5}\right) - \dfrac{3}{2} = \dfrac{13}{10}$. So, $B = \left(\dfrac{7}{5}, \dfrac{13}{10}\right)$.

Finally, the shortest distance $\overline{AB} = \sqrt{\left(\dfrac{7}{5}+2\right)^2 + \left(\dfrac{13}{10}-3\right)^2} = \dfrac{17\sqrt{5}}{10}$.

➢ The shortest distance $\overline{AB} = \dfrac{17\sqrt{5}}{10}$.

Chapter 10 — *Practice Problems Solution*

12 Find the area of the region that is enclosed by the graph of the equation $x^2 + y^2 - 6x + 8y = 0$.

Solution

$x^2 + y^2 - 6x + 8y = 0$

$x^2 - 6x + 9 - 9 + y^2 + 8y + 16 - 16 = 0$

$(x-3)^2 + (y+4)^2 = 25 \to$ A circle with center $(3,-4)$ and radius 5.

So, the area is $\pi(5)^2 = 25\pi$.

➤ The area is 25π.

13 Given the points $A(-2,5)$ and $B(4,1)$, write an equation of a circle whose diameter is $\overline{AB}$.

Solution

The center is the midpoint, M, of $\overline{AB}$ is $M = \left(\dfrac{-2+4}{2}, \dfrac{5+1}{2}\right) = (1,3)$.

The radius, r, is $r = \dfrac{\overline{AB}}{2} = \dfrac{\sqrt{(4+2)^2 + (1-5)^2}}{2} = \dfrac{2\sqrt{13}}{2} = \sqrt{13}$.

So, the equation of this circle is $(x-1)^2 + (y-3)^2 = 13$.

➤ The equation is $(x-1)^2 + (y-3)^2 = 13$.

Chapter 10 — *Practice Problems Solution*

14 Find the two points at which the graph of $x^2 + y^2 - 36 = 0$ and $x^2 + y^2 - 2x - 30 = 0$ intersect.

Solution

$x^2 + y^2 - 36 = 0 \rightarrow y^2 = 36 - x^2 \rightarrow (1)$
$x^2 + y^2 - 2x - 30 = 0 \rightarrow (2)$
By plugging (1) into (2), we have
$x^2 + (36 - x^2) - 2x - 30 = 0$
$6 - 2x = 0 \rightarrow x = 3.$
Now, plug $x = 3$ into the equation (1).
$y^2 = 36 - 3^2 = 27 \rightarrow y = \pm 3\sqrt{3}.$
So, the two intersecting points are $(3, 3\sqrt{3})$ and $(3, -3\sqrt{3})$.

➤ The two points are $(3, 3\sqrt{3})$ and $(3, -3\sqrt{3})$.

15 Find the values of k so that the radius of the circle $x^2 + y^2 + 2x - ky = 4$ has radius 3.

Solution

$x^2 + y^2 + 2x - ky = 4$
$x^2 + 2x + 1 - 1 + y^2 - ky + \left(\dfrac{k}{2}\right)^2 - \left(\dfrac{k}{2}\right)^2 = 4$
$(x+1)^2 + \left(y - \dfrac{k}{2}\right)^2 = 5 + \dfrac{k^2}{4}$
Since the radius of the circle is 3,
$5 + \dfrac{k^2}{4} = 3^2 \rightarrow \dfrac{k^2}{4} = 4$
$k^2 = 16 \rightarrow k = \pm 4$

➤ $k = \pm 4.$

Chapter 10 — Practice Problems Solution

16. Find the equation of the line tangent to the circle $x^2 + y^2 - 4x + 8y + 15 = 0$ at the point $(3, -2)$.

Solution

$x^2 + y^2 - 4x + 8y + 15 = 0$

$x^2 - 4x + 4 - 4 + y^2 + 8y + 16 - 16 + 15 = 0$

$(x-2)^2 + (y+4)^2 = 5 \rightarrow$ center is $(2, -4)$ and radius is $\sqrt{5}$.

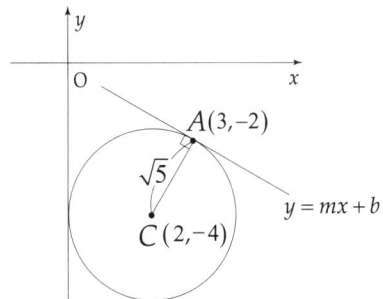

The slope of $\overline{AC}$, $m_{AC} = \dfrac{-4+2}{2-3} = 2$ so $m = -\dfrac{1}{2}$.

Now, $y = -\dfrac{1}{2}x + b \rightarrow -2 = -\dfrac{1}{2}(3) + b \rightarrow b = -\dfrac{1}{2}$.

So, the equation of the line $y = -\dfrac{1}{2}x - \dfrac{1}{2}$.

➤ The equation of the line $y = -\dfrac{1}{2}x - \dfrac{1}{2}$.

Chapter 10 — *Practice Problems Solution*

17 Find the radius of each circle that passes through $(1,2)$ and is tangent to both the x-axis and the y-axis.

Solution

Since the circle is tangent to both axes, the x and y coordinates are equal. So, let the center be (r, r) and the radius be r.

$(x - r)^2 + (y - r)^2 = r^2$

$(1 - r)^2 + (2 - r)^2 = r^2$

$1 - 2r + r^2 + 4 - 4r + r^2 = r^2$

$r^2 - 6r + 5 = 0$

$(r - 1)(r - 5) = 0 \rightarrow r = 1$ or $r = 5$.

➤ The two possible radii are 1 and 5.

Chapter 10 *Practice Problems Solution*

18 Find all values of a such that the point of intersection of the lines $y = ax + 4$ and $y = -x + 7$ lie on the circle $x^2 + y^2 = 29$.

Solution

The point of intersection of two line $y = ax + 4$ and $y = -x + 7$ is
$$ax + 4 = -x + 7$$
$$x(a+1) = 3$$
$$x = \frac{3}{a+1} \text{ and } y = -\frac{3}{a+1} + 7.$$
By plugging these value into $x^2 + y^2 = 29$, we have
$$\left(\frac{3}{a+1}\right)^2 + \left(-\frac{3}{a+1} + 7\right)^2 = 29$$
$$\frac{9}{(a+1)^2} + \frac{9}{(a+1)^2} - \frac{42}{a+1} + 49 = 29$$
$$\frac{18 - 42(a+1)}{(a+1)^2} = -20$$
$$42a + 24 = 20(a+1)^2$$
$$10a^2 - a - 2 = 0$$
$$(5a+2)(2a-1) = 0 \rightarrow a = -\frac{2}{5} \text{ or } a = \frac{1}{2}.$$

➢ The values of a are $a = -\frac{2}{5}$ and $a = \frac{1}{2}$.

Chapter 11 — Practice Problems Solution

01 In the figure below, find $\tan A$.

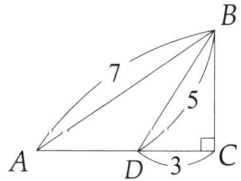

☼ Solution

In $\triangle BCD$, $\overline{BC} = \sqrt{5^2 - 3^2} = 4$.

In $\triangle ABC$, $\overline{AC} = \sqrt{7^2 - 4^2} = \sqrt{33}$.

$\tan A = \dfrac{\overline{BC}}{\overline{AC}} = \dfrac{4}{\sqrt{33}}$.

➤ $\tan A = \dfrac{4}{\sqrt{33}}$.

Chapter 11 — Practice Problems Solution

02 If $\overline{BC} \parallel \overline{DE}$ and $\tan A = \dfrac{3}{4}$ in the figure below, find each of the following.

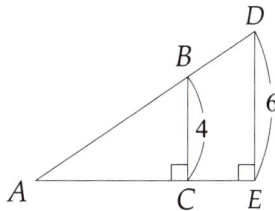

(1) $\overline{AB}$ (2) $\overline{CE}$

Solution

(1) In $\triangle ABC$, $\tan A = \dfrac{4}{\overline{AC}} = \dfrac{3}{4} \rightarrow \overline{AC} = \dfrac{16}{3}$.

$\overline{AB} = \sqrt{4^2 + \left(\dfrac{16}{3}\right)^2} = \dfrac{20}{3}$.

▸ $\overline{AB} = \dfrac{20}{3}$.

(2) In $\triangle ADE$, $\tan A = \dfrac{6}{\overline{AE}} = \dfrac{3}{4} \rightarrow \overline{AE} = 8$.

$\overline{CE} = \overline{AE} - \overline{AC} = 8 - \dfrac{16}{3} = \dfrac{8}{3}$.

▸ $\overline{CE} = \dfrac{8}{3}$.

Chapter 11 — *Practice Problems Solution*

03 Find indicated trigonometric ratio for each of the following figure below.

(1) sin ∠CBD

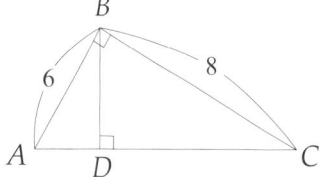

(2) cos ∠DCE

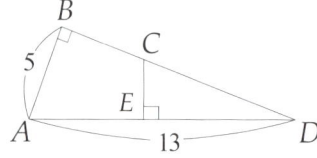

(3) sin D + cos D

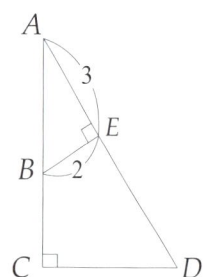

(4) tan ∠ACB

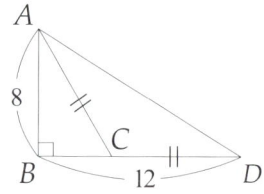

(5) sin ∠AGE

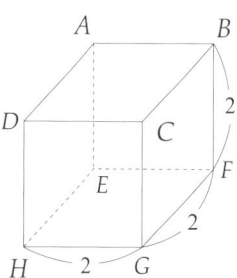

(6) cos ∠CEF

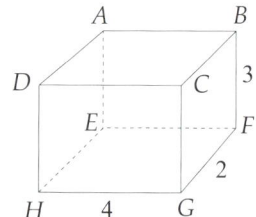

Chapter 11 — Practice Problems Solution

Solution

(1) In $\triangle ABC$, $\overline{AC} = \sqrt{6^2 + 8^2} = 10$.
Since $\triangle BCD \sim \triangle ACB$ by AA Similarity,
$$\sin \angle CBD = \sin \angle BAC = \frac{\overline{BC}}{\overline{AC}} = \frac{8}{10} = \frac{4}{5}.$$
➤ $\sin \angle CBD = \dfrac{4}{5}$.

(2) Since $\triangle ABD \sim \triangle CED$ by AA Similarity,
$$\cos \angle DCE = \cos \angle BAD = \frac{\overline{AB}}{\overline{AD}} = \frac{5}{13}.$$
➤ $\cos \angle DCE = \dfrac{5}{13}$.

(3) In $\triangle ABE$, $\overline{AB} = \sqrt{2^2 + 3^2} = \sqrt{13}$.
Since $\triangle ACD \sim \triangle AEB$ by AA Similarity,
$$\sin \angle D = \sin \angle ABE = \frac{\overline{AE}}{\overline{AB}} = \frac{3}{\sqrt{13}} \text{ and } \cos \angle D = \cos \angle ABE = \frac{\overline{BE}}{\overline{AB}} = \frac{2}{\sqrt{13}}$$
So, $\sin \angle D + \cos \angle D = \dfrac{3}{\sqrt{13}} + \dfrac{2}{\sqrt{13}} = \dfrac{5}{\sqrt{13}} = \dfrac{5\sqrt{13}}{13}$.
➤ $\sin \angle D + \cos \angle D = \dfrac{5\sqrt{13}}{13}$.

(4) First, $\overline{BC} = 12 - \overline{CD} = 12 - \overline{AC}$
In $\triangle ABC$, $\overline{AC}^2 = (12 - \overline{AC})^2 + 8^2$
$\overline{AC}^2 = 144 - 24\overline{AC} + \overline{AC}^2 + 64$
$24\overline{AC} = 208 \rightarrow \overline{AC} = \dfrac{26}{3}$ and $\overline{BC} = 12 - \dfrac{26}{3} = \dfrac{10}{3}$.
$\tan \angle ACB = \dfrac{\overline{AB}}{\overline{BC}} = \dfrac{8}{\frac{10}{3}} = \dfrac{12}{5}$.
➤ $\tan \angle ACB = \dfrac{12}{5}$.

Chapter 11 — *Practice Problems Solution*

(5)

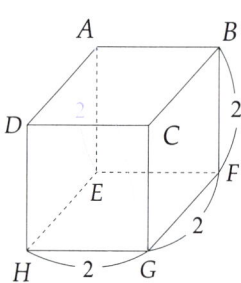

In $\triangle EHG$, $\overline{EG} = \sqrt{2^2 + 2^2} = 2\sqrt{2}$.

In $\triangle AEG$, $\overline{AG} = \sqrt{2^2 + \left(2\sqrt{2}\right)^2} = 2\sqrt{3}$.

$\sin \angle AGE = \dfrac{\overline{AE}}{\overline{AG}} = \dfrac{2}{2\sqrt{3}} = \dfrac{\sqrt{3}}{3}$.

➤ $\sin \angle AGE = \dfrac{\sqrt{3}}{3}$.

(6)

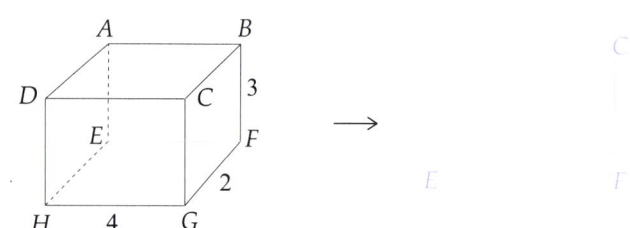

In $\triangle EFG$, $\overline{EG} = \sqrt{4^2 + 2^2} = 2\sqrt{5}$ and $\overline{CE} = \sqrt{3^2 + \left(2\sqrt{5}\right)^2} = \sqrt{29}$.

$\cos \angle CEF = \dfrac{\overline{EF}}{\overline{CE}} = \dfrac{4}{\sqrt{29}} = \dfrac{4\sqrt{29}}{29}$.

➤ $\cos \angle CEF = \dfrac{4\sqrt{29}}{29}$.

Chapter 11 — Practice Problems Solution

04 In the figure below, $\overline{AB}$ is a diameter of the circle and C is a point on the circle. If $\cos\alpha = \dfrac{1}{3}$, then what is the value of $\cos\beta$?

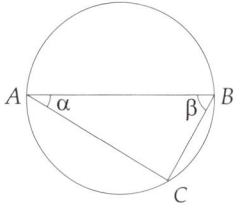

Solution

Since $\overline{AB}$ is a diameter of the circle, $\angle C = 90°$.

$\cos\alpha = \dfrac{1}{3} \to \overline{AB} = 3$ and $\overline{AC} = 1$.

In $\triangle ABC$, $\overline{BC} = \sqrt{3^2 - 1^2} = 2\sqrt{2}$.

$\cos\beta = \dfrac{\overline{BC}}{\overline{AB}} = \dfrac{2\sqrt{2}}{3}$.

➢ $\cos\beta = \dfrac{2\sqrt{2}}{3}$.

Chapter 11   *Practice Problems Solution*

05   If $\overline{BD}$ is tangent to a circle O at point C as shown in the figure below, what is $\sin x$?

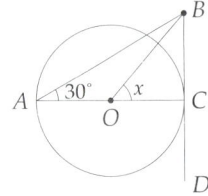

Solution

Since $\triangle ABC$ is $30° - 60° - 90°$ triangle, $\overline{AC} = \sqrt{3} \cdot \overline{BC}$.

So, $\overline{OC} = \dfrac{\overline{AC}}{2} = \dfrac{\sqrt{3} \cdot \overline{BC}}{2}$.

In $\triangle BOC$, $\overline{BO} = \sqrt{\overline{BC}^2 + \left(\dfrac{\sqrt{3} \cdot \overline{BC}}{2}\right)^2} = \dfrac{\sqrt{7} \cdot \overline{BC}}{2}$.

$\sin x = \dfrac{\overline{BC}}{\overline{BO}} = \dfrac{\overline{BC}}{\dfrac{\sqrt{7} \cdot \overline{BC}}{2}} = \dfrac{2}{\sqrt{7}} = \dfrac{2\sqrt{7}}{7}$.

➤ $\sin x = \dfrac{2\sqrt{7}}{7}$.

Chapter 11 *Practice Problems Solution*

06 Find indicated value for each of the following figure below.

(1) $\overline{AC} + \overline{BD}$

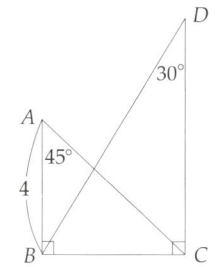

(2) $\overline{AC} + \overline{BD}$

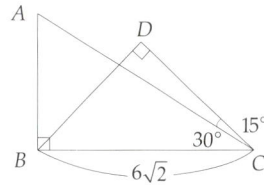

(3) $\tan \angle BAC$

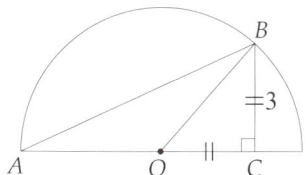

(4) $\overline{BD} + \overline{CE}$

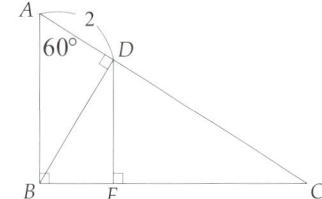

(5) $\tan \angle BAD$

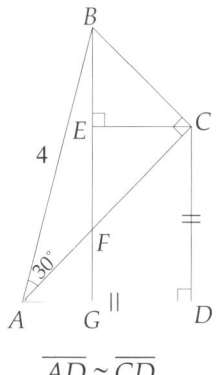

$\overline{AD} \cong \overline{CD}$

(6) $\sin \angle BAD + \sin D$

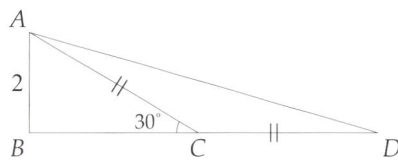

Chapter 11 *Practice Problems Solution*

Solution

(1) Since $\triangle ABC$ is $45°-45°-90°$ triangle, $BC = 4$ and $AC = 4\sqrt{2}$.
Also, since $\triangle BCD$ is $30°-60°-90°$ triangle, $\overline{BD} = 2 \cdot 4 = 8$.
So, $\overline{AC} + \overline{BD} = 4\sqrt{2} + 8$.
➤ $\overline{AC} + \overline{BD} = 4\sqrt{2} + 8$.

(2) Since $\triangle CBD$ is $45°-45°-90°$ triangle, $\overline{BD} = \dfrac{\overline{BC}}{\sqrt{2}} = \dfrac{6\sqrt{2}}{\sqrt{2}} = 6$.
Also, since $\triangle ABC$ is $30°-60°-90°$ triangle,
$\overline{AC} = \dfrac{2}{\sqrt{3}} \cdot \overline{BC} = \dfrac{2}{\sqrt{3}} \cdot 6\sqrt{2} = \dfrac{12\sqrt{2}}{\sqrt{3}} = 4\sqrt{6}$.
➤ So, $\overline{AC} + \overline{BD} = 4\sqrt{6} + 6$.

(3) In $\triangle OBC$, $\overline{OB} = \sqrt{3^2 + 3^2} = 3\sqrt{2}$ and $\overline{OA} \cong \overline{OB} = 3\sqrt{2}$.
So, $\tan \angle BAC = \dfrac{\overline{BC}}{\overline{AC}} = \dfrac{3}{3\sqrt{2} + 3}$.
➤ $\tan \angle BAC = \dfrac{3}{3\sqrt{2} + 3}$.

(4)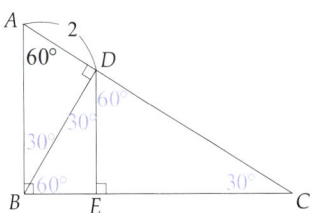

In $\triangle ABD$, $\overline{BD} = \sqrt{3} \cdot \overline{AD} = 2\sqrt{3}$.
In $\triangle BDE$, $\overline{DE} = \dfrac{\sqrt{3}}{2} \cdot \overline{BD} = \dfrac{\sqrt{3}}{2} \cdot 2\sqrt{3} = 3$.
In $\triangle CDE$, $\overline{CE} = \sqrt{3} \cdot \overline{DE} = 3\sqrt{3}$.
So, $\overline{BD} + \overline{CE} = 2\sqrt{3} + 3\sqrt{3} = 5\sqrt{3}$.
➤ $\overline{BD} + \overline{CE} = 5\sqrt{3}$.

Chapter 11 — Practice Problems Solution

(5)

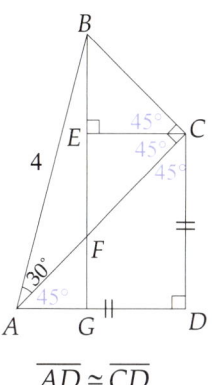

$\overline{AD} \cong \overline{CD}$

Since $\triangle ABC$ is $30° - 60° - 90°$ triangle,

$\overline{BC} = \dfrac{\overline{AB}}{2} = \dfrac{4}{2} = 2$ and $\overline{AC} = \sqrt{3} \cdot \overline{BC} = 2\sqrt{3}$.

Since $\triangle BCE$ is $45° - 45° - 90°$ triangle,

$\overline{BE} \cong \overline{CE} = \dfrac{\overline{BC}}{\sqrt{2}} = \dfrac{2}{\sqrt{2}} = \sqrt{2}$. Also, $\overline{CE} \cong \overline{DG} = \sqrt{2}$.

Since $\triangle ACD$ is $45° - 45° - 90°$ triangle,

$\overline{CD} \cong \overline{AD} = \dfrac{\overline{AC}}{\sqrt{2}} = \dfrac{2\sqrt{3}}{\sqrt{2}} = \sqrt{6}$ and $\overline{CD} \cong \overline{EG} = \sqrt{6}$.

Now, $\tan \angle BAD = \tan \angle BAG = \dfrac{\overline{BG}}{\overline{AG}} = \dfrac{\overline{BE} + \overline{EG}}{\overline{AD} - \overline{DG}} = \dfrac{\sqrt{2} + \sqrt{6}}{\sqrt{6} - \sqrt{2}} = 2 + \sqrt{3}$.

➤ $\tan \angle BAD = 2 + \sqrt{3}$.

(6) Since $\triangle ABC$ is $30° - 60° - 90°$ triangle,

$\overline{BC} = \sqrt{3} \cdot \overline{AB} = 2\sqrt{3}$ and $\overline{AC} = 2 \cdot \overline{AB} = 4$.

Also, since $\overline{CA} \cong \overline{CD} = 4$, $\overline{BD} = 2\sqrt{3} + 4$

and in $\triangle ABD$, $\overline{AD} = \sqrt{2^2 + \left(2\sqrt{3} + 4\right)^2} = \sqrt{32 + 16\sqrt{3}}$.

Now, $\sin \angle BAD + \sin D = \dfrac{\overline{BD}}{\overline{AD}} + \dfrac{\overline{AB}}{\overline{AD}} = \dfrac{2\sqrt{3} + 4}{\sqrt{32 + 16\sqrt{3}}} + \dfrac{2}{\sqrt{32 + 16\sqrt{3}}} = \dfrac{\sqrt{3} + 3}{2\sqrt{2 + \sqrt{3}}}$.

➤ $\sin \angle BAD + \sin D = \dfrac{\sqrt{3} + 3}{2\sqrt{2 + \sqrt{3}}}$.

Chapter 11 — *Practice Problems Solution*

07 If $\sin\theta = m$ and $\cos\theta = n$, where $0 < \theta < 90°$, then what is the value of $\tan\theta$ in terms of m and n?

☼ **Solution**

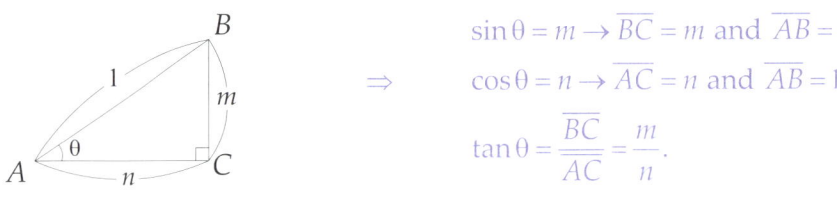

$$\begin{aligned} \sin\theta = m &\to \overline{BC} = m \text{ and } \overline{AB} = 1 \\ \cos\theta = n &\to \overline{AC} = n \text{ and } \overline{AB} = 1 \\ \tan\theta &= \frac{\overline{BC}}{\overline{AC}} = \frac{m}{n}. \end{aligned}$$

➤ $\tan\theta = \dfrac{m}{n}.$

08 If $0 < x < 90°$ and $\cos x = m$, then what is the value of $\tan x$ in terms of m?

☼ **Solution**

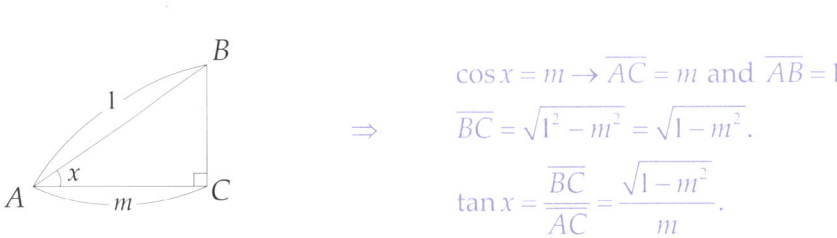

$$\begin{aligned} \cos x = m &\to \overline{AC} = m \text{ and } \overline{AB} = 1 \\ \overline{BC} &= \sqrt{1^2 - m^2} = \sqrt{1 - m^2}. \\ \tan x &= \frac{\overline{BC}}{\overline{AC}} = \frac{\sqrt{1 - m^2}}{m}. \end{aligned}$$

➤ $\tan x = \dfrac{\sqrt{1 - m^2}}{m}.$

Chapter 11 *Practice Problems Solution*

09 In the figure below, find the area of shaded region.

(1) ∠BAD ≅ ∠CAD and area of △ACD = 20 in²

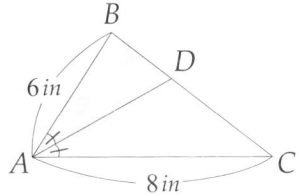

(2) $\overline{BE} \parallel \overline{CD}$ and $\overline{BC} \parallel \overline{ED}$

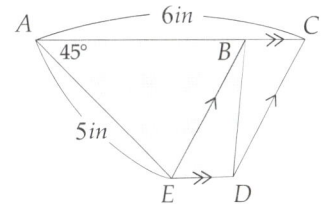

(3) ABCE is a square

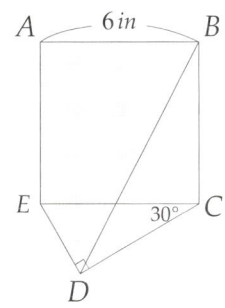

(4)

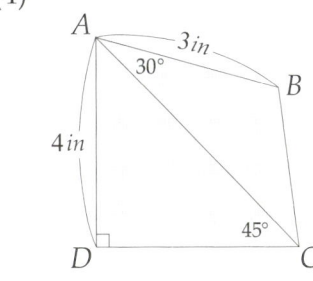

(5)

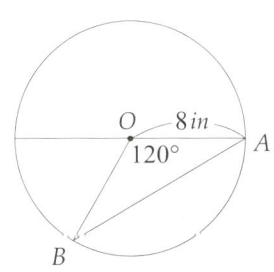

(6) ABCDEF is a regular hexagon

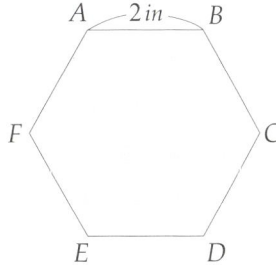

Chapter 11 *Practice Problems Solution*

Solution

(1) The area of $\triangle ACD = \dfrac{1}{2} \cdot 8 \cdot \overline{AD} \cdot \sin \angle CAD = 20 \to \overline{AD} \sin \angle CAD = 5$.

The area of shaded region,

$\triangle BAD = \dfrac{1}{2} \cdot 6 \cdot \overline{AD} \cdot \sin \angle BAD = 3 \cdot \overline{AD} \sin \angle CAD = 3 \cdot 5 = 15$.

➢ The area of shaded region is $15\, in^2$.

(2)

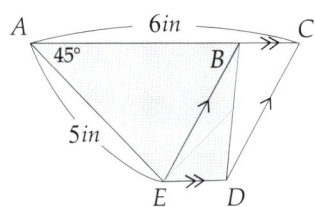

Since $BCDE$ is parallelogram, $\triangle BCE \cong \triangle EDB$.
So, the area of shaded region $ABDE$ is
$\triangle ABE + \triangle EDB = \triangle ABE + \triangle BCE = \triangle ACE$

$= \dfrac{1}{2} \cdot 6 \cdot 5 \cdot \sin 45° = 15 \cdot \dfrac{1}{\sqrt{2}} = \dfrac{15\sqrt{2}}{2}$.

➢ The area of shaded region is $\dfrac{15\sqrt{2}}{2}\, in^2$.

(3) Since $\overline{AB} \cong \overline{EC} = 6$ and $\triangle CDE$ is $30° - 60° - 90°$ triangle,

$\overline{DE} = \dfrac{\overline{EC}}{2} = 3$ and $\overline{DE} = \dfrac{\overline{EC}}{\sqrt{3}} = 3\sqrt{3}$.

Also, $\angle BCD = 90° + 30° = 120°$.
So, the area of shaded region $ABDE$ is
$ABCE + \triangle CDE - \triangle BCD$

$= 6^2 + \dfrac{1}{2} \cdot 3 \cdot 3\sqrt{3} - \dfrac{1}{2} \cdot 6 \cdot 3\sqrt{3} \cdot \sin(180° - 120°)$

$= 36 + \dfrac{9\sqrt{3}}{2} - 9\sqrt{3} \cdot \dfrac{\sqrt{3}}{2} = 36 - \dfrac{27}{2} + \dfrac{9\sqrt{3}}{2} = \dfrac{45 + 9\sqrt{3}}{2}$.

➢ The area of shaded region is $\dfrac{45 + 9\sqrt{3}}{2}\, in^2$.

Chapter 11 *Practice Problems Solution*

(4) Since $\triangle ACD$ is $45° - 45° - 90°$ triangle,
$\overline{AD} \cong \overline{CD} = 4$ and $\overline{AC} = \sqrt{2} \cdot \overline{AD} = 4\sqrt{2}$.
Also, $\angle BCD = 90° + 30° = 120°$.
So, the area of shaded region $ABCD$ is $\triangle ACD + \triangle ABC$
$= \frac{1}{2} \cdot 4 \cdot 4 + \frac{1}{2} \cdot 3 \cdot 4\sqrt{2} \cdot \sin 30° = 8 + 3\sqrt{2}$.

➤ The area of shaded region is $(8 + 3\sqrt{2}) in^2$.

(5) $\overline{OA} \cong \overline{OB} = 8$ and the area of shaded region is sector $AOB - \triangle AOB$.

Sector $AOB - \triangle AOB = \pi(8)^2 \cdot \frac{120°}{360°} - \frac{1}{2} \cdot 8 \cdot 8 \cdot \sin(180° - 120°)$

$= \frac{64\pi}{3} - 32 \cdot \frac{\sqrt{3}}{2} = \frac{64\pi}{3} - 16\sqrt{3}$.

➤ The area of shaded region is $\left(\frac{64\pi}{3} - 16\sqrt{3}\right) in^2$.

(6)

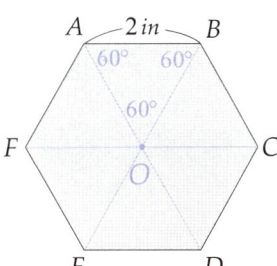

The area of shaded region $ABCDEF$ is $6 \times$ equilateral triangle AOB.

$6 \times \triangle AOB = 6 \times \frac{\sqrt{3}}{4} \cdot 2^2 = 6\sqrt{3}$.

➤ The area of shaded region is $6\sqrt{3} \, in^2$.

Chapter 11 *Practice Problems Solution*

10 In the figure below, find each of the following.

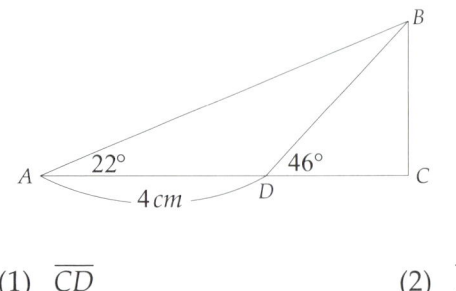

(1) $\overline{CD}$ (2) $\overline{BC}$

Solution

(1) In $\triangle ABC$, $\tan 22° = \dfrac{\overline{BC}}{\overline{AC}} = \dfrac{\overline{BC}}{4+\overline{CD}} \to (1)$

In $\triangle BDC$, $\tan 46° = \dfrac{\overline{BC}}{\overline{CD}} \to \overline{BC} = \tan 46° \cdot \overline{CD} \to (2)$

By plugging (2) into (1), we have $\tan 22° = \dfrac{\tan 46° \cdot \overline{CD}}{4+\overline{CD}}$

$\tan 22°(4+\overline{CD}) = \tan 46° \cdot \overline{CD}$

$\tan 46° \cdot \overline{CD} - \tan 22° \cdot \overline{CD} = 4\tan 22°$

$\overline{CD}(\tan 46° - \tan 22°) = 4\tan 22° \to \overline{CD} = \dfrac{4\tan 22°}{\tan 46° - \tan 22°}$.

Using calculator, $\overline{CD} = 2.559$.

➤ $\overline{CD} = 2.559$.

(2) In $\triangle BDC$, $\tan 46° = \dfrac{\overline{BC}}{\overline{CD}} = \dfrac{\overline{BC}}{2.559}$.

$\overline{BC} = 2.559 \cdot \tan 46° = 2.650$.

➤ $\overline{BC} = 2.650$.

Chapter 11 — Practice Problems Solution

11 If the slope of line k and h is $\frac{1}{3}$ and $\frac{2}{3}$, respectively, what is the measure of the angle formed at the intersection of k and h?

Solution

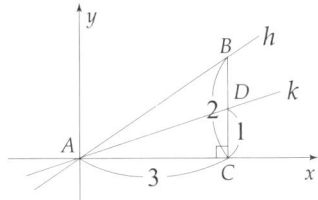

The angle formed at the intersection of k and h is $\angle BAD$.

In $\triangle ABC$, $\tan \angle BAC = \frac{2}{3} \rightarrow \angle BAC = \tan^{-1}\left(\frac{2}{3}\right)$.

In $\triangle ADC$, $\tan \angle DAC = \frac{1}{3} \rightarrow \angle DAC = \tan^{-1}\left(\frac{1}{3}\right)$.

So, $\angle BAD = \angle BAC - \angle DAC = \tan^{-1}\left(\frac{2}{3}\right) - \tan^{-1}\left(\frac{1}{3}\right) = 15.255°$.

➢ $\angle BAD = 15.255°$.

Chapter 11 *Practice Problems Solution*

12 Without using a calculator, find the value of sin15°.

Solution

First, draw $\triangle ABC$ with $\angle A = 15°$ and also draw $\overline{BD}$ such that $\overline{AD} \cong \overline{BD}$, as shown in figure below.

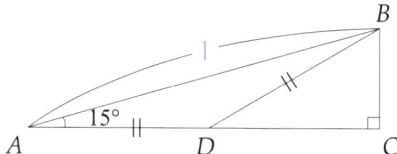

Since $\overline{AD} \cong \overline{BD}$, $\angle DBA = 15°$ and $\angle BDC = 30°$.
So, $\triangle BDC$ is $30°-60°-90°$ triangle.
In $\triangle BDC$, $\overline{CD} = \sqrt{3} \cdot \overline{BC}$ and $\overline{BD} = 2 \cdot \overline{BC}$. Also, $\overline{BD} \cong \overline{AD} = 2 \cdot \overline{BC}$.
Now, in $\triangle ABC$, $1^2 = \overline{BC}^2 + (\overline{AD} + \overline{CD})^2$.

$\overline{BC}^2 + (2 \cdot \overline{BC} + \sqrt{3} \cdot \overline{BC})^2 = 1 \rightarrow$ Let $\overline{BC} = x$.

$x^2 + 4x^2 + 4\sqrt{3}x^2 + 3x^2 = 1$

$8x^2 + 4\sqrt{3}x^2 = 1 \rightarrow x^2(8 + 4\sqrt{3}) = 1$

$x^2 = \dfrac{1}{8 + 4\sqrt{3}} \rightarrow x = \dfrac{1}{\sqrt{8 + 4\sqrt{3}}}$

Finally, $\sin 15° = \dfrac{\overline{BC}}{\overline{AB}} = \dfrac{x}{1} = \dfrac{1}{\sqrt{8 + 4\sqrt{3}}}$.

➢ $\sin 15° = \dfrac{1}{\sqrt{8 + 4\sqrt{3}}}$.

Chapter 11 *Practice Problems Solution*

13 A 20 feet tall light house on a 40 feet tall cliff makes angles of depression 18° and 25° with two boats respectively, as shown in the figure below. Find the distance between the two boats.

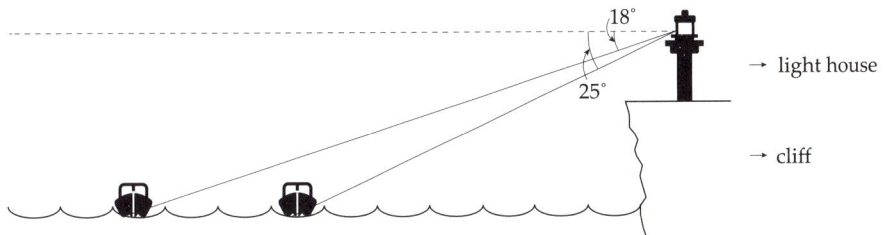

Solution

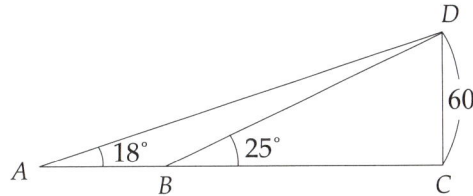

$\tan 18° = \dfrac{60}{AC} \rightarrow \overline{AC} = \dfrac{60}{\tan 18°} = 184.66$

$\tan 25° = \dfrac{60}{BC} \rightarrow \overline{BC} = \dfrac{60}{\tan 25°} = 128.67$

$\overline{AB} = \overline{AC} - \overline{BC} = 184.66 - 128.67 = 55.99$

So, the distance between the two boats is approximately 55.99 m.

➤ The distance between the two boats 55.99 m.

Chapter 11 — *Practice Problems Solution*

14 A 6 feet tall person starts to walk directly towards a vertical building that is 45 feet tall. What is the distance the person traveled if the angle of elevation from person's top of head to the top of the building changes from 15° to 20°?

Solution

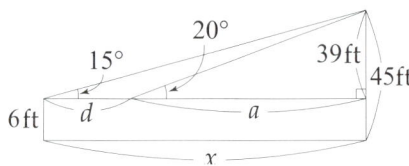

d is the distance the person traveled.

$$\tan 15° = \frac{39}{x}, \rightarrow x = \frac{39}{\tan 15°} = 145.55$$

$$\tan 20° = \frac{39}{a}, \rightarrow a = \frac{39}{\tan 20°} = 107.15$$

$$d = x - a = 145.55 - 107.15 = 38.4$$

So, the distance the person traveled is approximately 38.4 ft.

➤ The distance the person traveled is 38.4 ft.

Chapter 11

Practice Problems Solution

15 A surveyor determines the angle of elevation of a building from level ground to be 45°. If the surveyor moves 20 feet towards the building, then the measure of the angle of elevation becomes 60°. What is the height of the building?

Solution

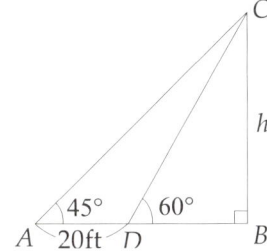

h is the height of the building.

Since $\triangle BCD$ is $30° - 60° - 90°$ triangle, $\overline{BD} = \dfrac{h}{\sqrt{3}}$.

Also, since $\triangle ABC$ is $45° - 45° - 90°$ triangle, $\overline{AB} \cong \overline{BC} = h$.

So, $20 + \dfrac{h}{\sqrt{3}} = h \rightarrow h\left(1 - \dfrac{1}{\sqrt{3}}\right) = 20$.

$h = \dfrac{20}{1 - \dfrac{1}{\sqrt{3}}} = 47.32$.

Therefore, the height of the building is approximately 47.32 ft.

➢ The height of the building is 47.32 ft.